D0076160

WHERE GOD AND SCIENCE MEET

WHERE GOD AND SCIENCE MEET

How Brain and Evolutionary Studies
Alter Our Understanding of Religion

VOLUME 2
The Neurology of Religious Experience

Edited by Patrick McNamara

PRAEGER PERSPECTIVES

Psychology, Religion, and Spirituality

J. Harold Ellens, Series Editor

Westport, Connecticut
London

BL
53
W 511
2006
vol. 2

Library of Congress Cataloging-in-Publication Data

Where God and science meet : how brain and evolutionary studies alter our understanding of religion / edited by Patrick McNamara.

  p. cm. — (Psychology, religion, and spirituality, ISSN 1546–8070)
  Includes index.
  ISBN 0–275–98788–4 (set) — ISBN 0–275–98789–2 (v. 1) — ISBN 0–275–98790–6 (v. 2) — ISBN 0–275–98791–4 (v. 3)
  1. Psychology, Religious. 2. Genetic psychology. 3. Evolutionary psychology. 4. Experience (Religion) 5. Neurology. I. McNamara, Patrick H.
  BL53.W511 2006
  200.1'9—dc22   2006021770

British Library Cataloguing in Publication Data is available.

Copyright © 2006 by Patrick McNamara

All rights reserved. No portion of this book may be reproduced, by any process or technique, without the express written consent of the publisher.

Library of Congress Catalog Card Number: 2006021770
ISBN: 0–275–98788–4 (set)
      0–275–98789–2 (vol. 1)
      0–275–98790–6 (vol. 2)
      0–275–98791–4 (vol. 3)
ISSN: 1546–8070

First published in 2006

Praeger Publishers, 88 Post Road West, Westport, CT 06881
An imprint of Greenwood Publishing Group, Inc.
www.praeger.com

Printed in the United States of America

The paper used in this book complies with the Permanent Paper Standard issued by the National Information Standards Organization (Z39.48–1984).

10 9 8 7 6 5 4 3 2 1

JKM Library
1100 East 55th Street
Chicago, IL 60615

CONTENTS

VOLUME 2
THE NEUROLOGY OF RELIGIOUS EXPERIENCE

Series Foreword

The interface between psychology, religion, and spirituality has been of great interest to scholars for a century. In the last three decades a broad popular appetite has developed for books which make practical sense out of the sophisticated research on these three subjects. Freud expressed an essentially deconstructive perspective on this matter and indicated that he saw the relationship between human psychology and religion to be a destructive interaction. Jung, on the other hand, was quite sure that these three aspects of the human spirit, psychology, religion, and spirituality, were constructively and inextricably linked.

Anton Boisen and Seward Hiltner derived much insight from both Freud and Jung, as well as from Adler and Reik, while pressing the matter forward with ingenious skill and illumination. Boisen and Hiltner fashioned a framework within which the quest for a sound and sensible definition of the interface between psychology, religion, and spirituality might best be described or expressed.[1] We are in their debt.

This series of General Interest Books, so wisely urged by Greenwood Press, and particularly by its editors, Deborah Carvalko and Suzanne I. Staszak-Silva, intends to define the terms and explore the interface of psychology, religion, and spirituality at the operational level of daily human experience. Each volume of the series identifies, analyzes, describes, and evaluates the full range of issues, of both popular and professional interest, that deal with the psychological factors at play (1) in the way religion takes shape and is expressed, (2) in the way spirituality functions within human persons and shapes both religious formation and expression, and (3) in the ways that spirituality is shaped and expressed by religion. The interest is psycho-spiritual. In terms of the rubrics of the disciplines and the science of psychology and spirituality this series of volumes investigates the *operational dynamics* of religion and spirituality.

The verbs "shape" and "express" in the above paragraph refer to the forces which prompt and form religion in persons and communities, as well as to the manifestations of religious behavior (1) in personal forms of spirituality, (2) in acts of spiritually motivated care for society, and (3) in ritual behaviors such as liturgies of worship. In these various aspects of human function the psychological and/or spiritual drivers are identified, isolated, and described in terms of the way in which they unconsciously and consciously operate in religion, thought, and behavior.

The books in this series are written for the general reader, the local library, and the undergraduate university student. They are also of significant interest to the informed professional, particularly in fields corollary to his or her primary interest. The volumes in this series have great value for clinical settings and treatment models, as well.

This series editor has spent an entire professional lifetime focused specifically upon research into the interface of psychology in religion and spirituality. These matters are of the highest urgency in human affairs today when religious motivation seems to be playing an increasing role, constructively and destructively, in the arena of social ethics, national politics, and world affairs. It is imperative that we find out immediately what the psychopathological factors are which shape a religion that can launch deadly assaults upon the World Trade Center in New York and murder 3,500 people, or a religion that motivates suicide bombers to kill themselves and murder dozens of their neighbors weekly, and a religion which prompts such unjust national policies as pre-emptive defense; all of which are wreaking havoc upon the social fabric, the democratic processes, the domestic tranquility, the economic stability and productivity, and the legitimate right to freedom from fear, in every nation in the world today.

This present set of three volumes, the project on religion and the brain, is an urgently needed and timely work, the motivation for which is surely endorsed enthusiastically by the entire world today, as the international community searches for strategies that will afford us better and deeper religious self-understanding as individuals and communities. This project addresses the deep genetic and biological sources of human nature which shape and drive our psychology and spirituality. Careful strategies of empirical, heuristic, and phenomenological research have been employed to give this work a solid scientific foundation and formation. Never before has so much wisdom and intelligence been brought to bear upon the dynamic linkage between human physiology, psychology, and spirituality. Each of these three aspects has been examined from every imaginable direction through the illumining lenses of the other two.

For fifty years such organizations as the Christian Association for Psychological Studies and such Graduate Departments of Psychology as those at Boston University, Fuller, Rosemead, Harvard, George Fox, Princeton, and the like, have been publishing significant building blocks of empirical, heuristic, and phenomenological research on issues dealing with religious behavior and psycho-spirituality. In this present project the insights generated by such patient and careful research are synthesized and integrated into a holistic psycho-spiritual world view, which takes the phenomenology of religion seriously.

Some of the influences of religion upon persons and society, now and throughout history, have been negative. However, most of the impact of the great religions upon human life and culture has been profoundly redemptive and generative of great good. It is urgent, therefore, that we discover and understand better what the psychological and spiritual forces are which empower people of faith and genuine spirituality to give themselves to all the creative and constructive enterprises that, throughout the centuries, have made of human life the humane, ordered, prosperous, and aesthetic experience it can be at its best. Surely the forces for good in both psychology and spirituality far exceed the powers and proclivities toward the evil that we see so prominently perpetrated in the name of religion in our world today.

This series of Greenwood Press volumes is dedicated to the greater understanding of *Psychology, Religion and Spirituality*, and thus to the profound understanding and empowerment of those psycho-spiritual drivers which can help us transcend the malignancy of our earthly pilgrimage and enormously enhance the humaneness and majesty of the human spirit, indeed, the potential for magnificence in human life.

J. Harold Ellens

NOTE

1. Aden, L., & Ellens, J. H. (1990). *Turning points in pastoral care: The legacy of Anton Boisen and Seward Hiltner.* Grand Rapids, MI: Baker.

ACKNOWLEDGMENTS

I would like to thank Debbie Carvalko from Greenwood Press for her advocacy of this project, for her help at every step of the way, and for her advice and encouragement at critical junctures of the project. I would also like to thank J. Harold Ellens for his belief in the importance of this project and for his sage advice throughout. Our advisory board members—Ray Paloutzian, Kenneth Pargament, Harold Koenig, Andrew Newberg, Scott Atran, and Donald Capps—in addition to their help in identifying topics to be covered also helped us to find the best authors to cover them! Advisors also kept the editor from making mistakes that could have cost the project dearly. In short, these advisors have immeasurably increased the quality of these volumes. I would also like to thank Lena Giang, Pattie Johnson, Anna Kookoolis, Jocelyn Sarmiento, and Sarah Varghese for their help with editing and formatting the references for all the chapters in the series—a thankless task at best, but these assistants did it both conscientiously and carefully. Finally, I would like to thank Ms. Erica Harris, my head research assistant, who helped out on all aspects of this project. Her organizational help has meant all the difference throughout. She did yeoman's work on the project Web site, kept track of correspondence with authors, and generally kept the project running smoothly and on schedule.

PREFACE

In recent years, several lines of evidence have converged on the conclusion that religiousness is associated with a specific and consistent set of biological processes. Religion appears to be a cultural universal. There may be a critical period (adolescence) during the life cycle of normally developing persons when religiousness is best transmitted from an older to a younger generation (see volume II, chapter 4). Individual differences in religiosity are associated with consistent health benefits (see volume I, chapter 7; volume III, chapter 2) as well as unique health risks (see volume III, chapters 4 and 8). Twin studies have shown that religiousness is moderately to highly heritable (see volume I, chapter 3). Genetic studies have implicated specific genes in religiousness (mostly genes that code for regulatory products of monoamine transmission in limbic-prefrontal networks; for reviews, see Comings, Gonzales, Saucier, Johnson, & MacMurray, 2000; D'Onofrio, Eaves, Murrelle, Maes, & Spilka, 1999; Hamer, 2004; see also volume I, chapter 3). Consistent with these preliminary genetic studies, neurochemical and neuropharmacologic studies have implicated limbic-prefrontal serotoninergic and dopaminergic mechanisms in mediation of religious experiences (see volume II, chapters 1 and 2; volume III, chapters 1 and 10). Neuroimaging and neuropsychologic studies have implicated a consistent set of neurocognitive systems and brain activation patterns in religious activity (mostly limbic-prefrontal networks (see volume II, chapters 2, 3, 8, and 9; volume III, chapter 7). A cognitive psychology of religious belief has revealed both the unique aspects of religious cognition as well as its commonalities with other basic cognitive processing routines (see volume I, chapters 6, 9, and 10; volume II, chapter 10). Finally, changes in self-reported religious experience by individuals suffering from obsessive-compulsive disorder; schizophrenia, Parkinson's disease, and temporal lobe epilepsy are in the expected direction if the previously mentioned neurocognitive networks (limbic-prefrontal) do in fact mediate core aspects of religiousness (see volume II, chapters 1 and 8; volume III, chapter 1).

Although the array of previously mentioned findings suggests to some investigators that it is reasonable to speak about potential neurocognitive specializations around religiosity, caution is in order when attempting to interpret the findings (see volume II, chapters 3, 5, 6, and 8; and all three commentaries). As in every other scientific enterprise, what is investigated in any given study is not the whole phenomenon of interest but rather only a small constituent part of the whole. The previously cited studies could not investigate "religion" per se. That is too vast a phenomenon to be studied in a single project. Instead, they tried to operationalize religiousness in various ways—with everything from a score on an inventory about religious practices to measurements on those practices themselves. Thus, we are reduced to making inferences about the nature of religiousness from data we collect via these questionnaire and observational/experimental methods. Making inferences about the nature of religion as a whole from neurobiologic correlations of one aspect of religiosity is, of course, fraught with danger (as all three commentators and several of our authors point out), but there is simply no other way to proceed. Inference and extrapolation from observations you collect on operationalized measures of the phenomenon you are interested in is necessary if you want to make progress. What is all-important, however, is to extrapolate, infer, and proceed with caution and humility. Constraints on incautious claims and inferences can often be obtained if you have a good theoretical framework from which to generate inferences about data meanings and from which you can develop falsifiable hypotheses. When it comes to biologic correlates of religiousness, the best available theory is evolution. Thus, several of the essays in these volumes discuss potential evolutionary and adaptive functions of religion.

Claims, however, about potential adaptive functions of religiousness also need to be treated with great caution and tested against the evidence. Several authors in these volumes address the question of whether religiousness can be considered an evolutionary adaptation (see volume I, chapters 1, 4, 5, 7, 8, and 10; volume II, chapter 4; volume III, chapter 6; and all three commentaries). For those scientists who think the evidence supports some variant of an adaptationist position (see volume I, chapters 4, 5, 7, and 10; volume II, chapter 4; volume III, chapter 6), the questions shift to what part of religiousness is actually adaptive and what functions might religiousness enact? Some theorists suggest that it is reasonable to speak about a "common core" religious experience fundamental to all forms of religiosity (see volume I, chapter 7; volume III, chapters 5 and 6). Some investigators suggest that the aspect of religiousness that was "selected" over evolutionary history was the capacity for trance, placebo responding, or altered states of consciousness, or ASC (see volume I, chapters 5 and 7; volume III, chapter 6). The capacity for trance, placebo responding, and ASC, of course, would yield both health benefits and arational or even irrational belief states over time. Other theorists (see volume I, chapters 4 and 5; volume II, chapter 4) suggest that the aspect of religiousness that was selected over evolutionary history was its ability, primarily via ritual displays and other "costly signals" (see volume I, chapters 2, 4, and 5; volume II, chapter 10), to solve the free-rider problem (where unscrupulous individuals exploit the benefits of group cooperation without paying any of the costs of that cooperation) and thereby promote cooperation among individuals within early human groups. Other theorists who tilt toward some kind of adaptationist position emphasize both costly signaling theory as well as gene–culture interactions to explain particular associations of religiosity, such as its ability to promote character strengths (volume I, chapter 2), its ability to protect against death-related fears (volume I, chapter 9; volume III, chapter 8), its ability to generate life meanings (volume III, chapter 3), its ability to address attachment needs (volume I, chapter 8; volume II, chapter 6), its links with the sources and phenomenology of dreams (volume III, chapter 9), and its similarities with special perceptual capacities of the aesthetic sense (volume II, chapter 7).

Although it has to be admitted that all these investigators have marshaled an impressive array of evidence to support their claims concerning religion's potential adaptive functions, all the authors of these theories realize that it is nearly impossible to demonstrate conclusively that some biopsychologic process is an adaptation, in the classical sense of that term. Several authors in these volumes have pointed out just how easy it is to get muddled when attempting to think through evolutionary approaches to a phenomenon as complex as religiousness (see volume I, chapters 1, 8 and 10; volume II, chapter 6; and all three commentaries). It is all too easy to overlook the harmful (and presumably nonadaptive) aspects of religiousness (see volume I, chapters 1 and 6; volume III, chapters 4 and 8). Ignorance of the complexity of religious phenomena, an underappreciation of the pervasive effects of social learning and cultural transmission on cognitive functions, and confusion around technical terms in evolutionary biology (such as adaptation, exaptation, and so forth) all militate against progress in this new science of the biology of religion.

To help think through problems of evolutionary change and adaptations in animals, the evolutionary biologist has often utilized the principles and methods of cladistics and phylogenetic analysis. Debates on potential adaptive functions of religion may benefit by taking a look at these methods. Cladistic methodology is used to analyze phylogenetic relationships in lineages that are recognized by the presence of shared and derived (advanced) characteristics. When cladistic methodology is supplemented with the advanced statistical tools of "phylogenetic analysis," you get precise and powerful techniques for reconstructing evolutionary history. These techniques have now been successfully used in the cultural arena, as in analyzing biocultural changes (e.g., language evolution). Scholars of ritual and religious practices have now amassed a huge amount of data on the historical development of ritual practices and on ritual practices in premodern human groups. There may therefore be enough data to reconstruct the evolutionary history of ritual practices in certain human lineages. If there is also enough data available on the history of various forms of healing practices of cooperative enterprises (e.g., farming or herding), it may be possible to assess change in ritual practices against change in these other forms of human activity. By superimposing phenotypic features (e.g., ritual practices) over accepted language phylogenies, one can reconstruct the history of evolutionary change in ritual practices as well as potential correlated change in health or in cooperative practices. Thus, hypotheses about potential adaptive functions of key aspects of religiousness may be tested quantitatively using these sorts of methods. With these sorts of methods, one could also potentially assess whether some aspect of religiousness (e.g., ritual practices) fit criteria for an adaptation or an exaptation. An adaptation involves the modification of a phenotypic feature (e.g., a particular ritual practice) that accompanies or parallels an evolutionary acquisition of a function (new healing practices or new forms of cooperation). However, in exaptation, the feature originates first rather than in parallel and only later is co-opted for the function in question. In short, because phylogenetic analysis involves quantitative reconstruction and analysis of histories of shared and derived traits, it provides powerful methods for identification of potential adaptive functions of religion. I draw attention to these techniques only to point out their potential. They have significant limitations, and they have not yet been applied to many problems in biocultural evolution. In particular, phylogenetic techniques have not yet been brought to bear on questions of the evolutionary history of religious practices. Nevertheless, they may be one way to shed some light on the problem of potential adaptive functions of religion.

The fact that reasonable speculations about potential adaptive functions of religion can be advanced at all is partly due to the startling consistency of the evidence summarized in these volumes on the neurobiologic correlates of religiousness. While tremendous progress has been made in identifying neurobiologic correlates of religiousness, it will be a challenge to place these findings in new theoretical frameworks that can do justice to the richness and complexity of the religious spirit. The essays in these volumes provide the necessary first tools to do just that.

Patrick McNamara

REFERENCES

Comings, D. E., Gonzales, N., Saucier, G., Johnson, J. P., & MacMurray J. P. (2000). The DRD4 gene and the spiritual transcendence scale of the character temperament index. *Psychiatric Genetics, 10,* 185–189.

D'Onofrio, B. M., Eaves, L. J., Murrelle, L., Maes, H. H., & Spilka, B. (1999). Understanding biological and social influences on religious attitudes and behaviors: A behavior genetic perspective. *Journal of Personality, 67,* 953–984.

Hamer, D. (2004). *The God gene: How faith is hardwired into our genes.* New York: Doubleday.

CHAPTER 1

The Chemistry of Religiosity: Evidence from Patients with Parkinson's Disease

Patrick McNamara, Raymon Durso, Ariel Brown, and Erica Harris

INTRODUCTION

While the scientific study of religion has gained momentum in recent years (see reviews Albright & Ashbrook, 2001; Andresen, 2001; Boyer, 2001; d'Aquilli & Newberg, 1999; Newberg, d'Aquilli, et al., 2001; Wilson, 2002), experimental neuropsychologic studies of religiosity have remained exceedingly rare. The time is ripe for development of an experimental approach to the study of the neurology of religion as a fairly large amount of preliminary and theoretical work on neurobiologic correlates of religious experience has been published (Albright & Ashbrook, 2001; d'Aquilli & Newberg, 1999; Newberg, Alavi, et al., 2001; Schroeder, 2001). d'Aquilli and Newberg's (1999) and Newberg et al.'s models of the neurobiology of religious experience are discussed below. Albright and Ashbrook (2001) and Ashbrook and Albright (1997) provide a reconceptualization of brain functions as shaped by religious impulses, emphasizing links of the frontal lobes with functions basic to religiosity such as the human capacity for empathy, agency, intentionality and purpose (Albright & Ashbrook, 2001; Ashbrook & Albright, 1997). We focus in this chapter on the potential role that both the mesocortical dopaminergic system and the frontal lobes play in support of religious cognition and behavior. The mesocortical dopaminergic system is simply a set of nerve fibers that specialize in use of dopamine as their neurotransmitter and that project from lower sites in the mid-brain to higher sites in the frontal cortex. They are important because they activate or turn on functions of the frontal lobes. The frontal lobes, in turn, handle very high-level executive functions of the brain such as activating other brain areas and orchestrating complex mental and motor functions. Because the meso-cortical dopaminergic systems project to the frontal lobes, we can expect correlated effects of dopamine and frontal system dysfunction on religiosity.

Investigation of potential dopaminergic contributions to religious behavior is vitally important because it might help to explain two religion-related phenomena of enormous significance to public health: (a) religion's association with improved health outcomes for some individuals and (b) religion's association with the adoption of a dangerous fanaticism and intolerance in other individuals. Dopaminergic circuits are known to exert a regulatory influence on hypothalamic, autonomic and neuro-hormonal systems that impact the ability to respond to stress (Buijs & Van Eden, 2000) and thus might indirectly contribute to health. Similarly, negative effects of religious belief might be at least partially clarified by comparison to neuropsychiatric symptoms typically associated with dysfunction in striatal-frontal dopaminergic circuits (Fiske & Haslam, 1997). For example, such dysfunction may give rise to symptoms of obsessive-compulsive spectrum disorder or a rigid adherence to maladaptive beliefs and behavioral routines (Fiske & Haslam, 1997; Jenike, Baeri, & Minichiello, 1998), as well as threats of violence when those routines are threatened (Pincus, 1999).

Evidence is accumulating from both neuroimaging and clinical work that points to a significant link between dopamine, frontal function and religiosity.

RELIGION AND THE FRONTAL LOBES

Religiosity has traditionally been linked to the temporal lobes (e.g., Bear & Fedio, 1977; d'Aquilli & Newberg, 1993; Persinger, 1987; Ramachandran, Hirstein, Armel, Tecome, & Iragul, 1997). But most of the evidence for a role of the temporal lobes in religious experience was based on observations of the behaviors of a small subset of temporal lobe epileptics who exhibited the inter-ictal behavioral syndrome (Dewhurst & Beard, 1970; Geschwind, 1983; Ramachandran et al., 1997). The "syndrome" included hyper-religiosity as one of its signs. d'Aquilli and Newberg (1993) very sensibly assume that all the major areas of the brain generate some aspect of the total religious experience. In their models of religion and brain, the job of the temporal lobes is to attach meaning and significance to events while posterior parietal sites participate in construction of both the sense of self and the accompanying sense of the dissolution of the self during mystical states. With respect to the frontal lobes, d'Aquilli and Newberg (1993) reviewed a number of studies that apparently established a link between sustained attention associated with the practice of meditation and EEG theta waves above the pre-frontal cortex. The EEG data therefore suggests that sustained meditation results in activation of prefrontal networks. Newberg, Alavi, Baime, Mozley, and d'Aquilli (1997) later confirmed these EEG data using SPECT imaging techniques. Regional cerebral blood flow changes were studied in six highly experienced meditators while they meditated. Results demonstrated significantly increased blood flow to the inferior frontal and dorsolateral prefrontal cortical regions while subjects engaged in intense meditation. More recently, Azari et al., (2001) reported greater dorsolateral frontal, dorsomedial frontal and medial parietal cortex activation during religious recitation in self-described religious subjects.

THE FRONTAL LOBES AND DOPAMINE

The frontal lobes comprise the large expanse of cortex in the anterior portions of the brain and increase in size and connectivity with both phylogenetic (evolutionary) and ontogenetic (individual) development (Banyas, 1999; Fuster, 1989; Goldman-Rakic, 1987; Passingham, 1995). They are not fully myelineated (functional) until the adolescent or adult years. They receive projections from the mediodorsal nucleus and give rise to primary motor cortex, as well as premotor, supplementary motor, and prefrontal areas. All of these areas send inhibitory efferents onto their sites of termination. The motor-premotor areas comprise Brodmann areas 4, 6, parts of Area 44 (Broca's area) and the frontal eye fields. The prefrontal areas are further subdivided into two large functional regions. The first prefrontal region includes paralimbic cortex of the anterior cingulate region and orbitofrontal cortex. The second prefrontal region is generally referred to as the dorsolateral prefrontal region and includes Brodmann areas 9, 10, 11, 12, 45, 46 and 47. Both frontal regions are densely innervated by dopaminergic (DA) fibers originating in the Ventral Tegmental Area (VTA) and the substantia Nigra (SN) (Arnsten, Matthew, Ubriani, Taylor, & Li, 1999; Golman-Rakic, 1987; Randolph-Scwartz, 1999). Most addicting substances (e.g., drugs, alcohol, food, etc.) exert their rewarding effects via stimulation of these meso-limbic, dopaminergic fibers projecting to the frontal lobes (Schultz et al., 1995). If dopaminergic tracts innervate frontal sites, then dopaminergic drugs might influence frontal functions. We will see below that this is in fact the case.

DOPAMINE AND RELIGIOSITY

Evidence is accumulating for a significant role of dopamine in supporting high levels of religiosity:

1. A polymorphism on the dopamine receptor gene, DRD4, has been found to be significantly associated with measures of spirituality and

self-transcendence on a personality scale (Comings, Gonzales, Saucier, Johnson, & MacMurray, 2000).

2. Disorders of excessive dopaminergic functioning, such as schizophrenia and obsessive compulsive disorder, are often associated with increases in religiosity (Abramowitz, Huppert, Cohen, Tolin, & Cahill, 2002; Brewerton, 1994; Saver & Rabin, 1997; Siddle, Haddock, Tarrier, & Faragher, 2002; Tek & Ulug, 2001; Wilson, 1998). Anti-psychotic agents that block dopaminergic actions at the level of the limbic system result in changes (typically diminishment) in religious behaviors and religious delusions in these patients.

3. Hallucinatory agents that purportedly enhance religious or mystical experiences may also enhance dopamine transmission. LSD and DMT, for example, block serotonin (5-HT) receptors (Cooper, Bloom, & Roth, 2003), and thus 5-HT activity cannot be the etiologic agent in these religious experiences. 5-HT, however, is known to exert tonic inhibitory effects on dopaminergic neurons (Cools, Stefanova, Barker, Robbins, & Owens, 2002; Daw, Kakade, & Dayan, 2002; Giacomelli, Palmery, Romanelli, Cheng, & Silvestrini, 1998; Millan, Lejeune, & Gobert, 2000; Vollenweider, 1998), particularly in the limbic system, and thus removal of the inhibitory 5-HT influence enhances DA activity resulting in religious and hallucinatory experiences (Carlsson, Waters, & Carlsson, 1999; Giacomelli et al., 1998; Iqbal & van Praag, 1995; Tomic & Joksimovic, 2000; Vollenweider, 1998).

4. Many religious behaviors and basic religious cognitive processes depend on the prefrontal lobes (see McNamara, 2002 for review), and prefrontal system functioning, in turn, is strongly influenced by dopaminergic activity (Goldman-Rakic, 1987).

5. Dopaminergic activity, particularly limbic-prefrontal activity, functions to signal significant or salient stimuli (Schultz et al., 1995), thus if DA activity is increased due to pharmacologic treatment, incoming information will more likely be tagged as overly significant and a greater number of experiences will be experienced as highly significant.

6. Changes in prefrontal function can be associated with changes in religious behaviors (McNamara, 2002).

RELIGION AND HEALTH

One of the reasons to study dopaminergic effects on religiosity is because religiosity has significant effects on health. Religion's effects on health may partially involve dopaminergic modulation of the hormonal and autonomic nervous systems. Measures of religiosity such as frequent prayer, frequent attendance at religious services, and intrinsic forms of religiosity appear to have beneficial effects on some aspects of physical and mental health (Beit-Hallahmi & Argyle, 1997; Comstock & Partridge, 1972; Ellison, Gay, & Glass, 1989; Idler, 1987; Koenig et al., 1998; Kune, Kune, & Watson, 1993; Levin & Vanderpool, 1989), particularly in the elderly (Koenig, 2001; Musick, Traphagan, Koenig, & Larson, 2000), yet this beneficial effect of religiosity remains unexplained. These positive effects range from improved subjective reports of enhanced well-being to objective reductions in somatic complaints and rates of hypertension, pain, cancer, and mortality. In their review of effects of religiosity on mental health, Levin and colleagues have summarized possible mediators of religions' effects on health. Levin, Taylor, and Chatters (1995) found that religiosity is usually associated with better mental health. Levin and Vanderpool (1989) in a meta-analysis of 28 studies of the relation between religiosity and subjective well-being and health found that religiosity correlates positively with subjective sense of well-being and other measures of health. Koenig et al. (1998) recently reported that respondents who both attended religious services and frequently prayed or studied the bible had 40 percent lower odds of having high blood pressure than controls who engaged in those religious activities less frequently. Similarly, a number of research teams (e.g., Koenig, 2001; Musick et al., 2000; Strawbridge, Cohen, Shema, & Kaplan, 1997) have replicated Comstock and Partridge's (1972) original findings of lower mortality rates for frequent religious attenders as compared with infrequent attenders.

Since Allport and Ross' pioneering work in the 1960s on intrinsic religiosity, a number of investigators (reviewed in Beit-Hallahmi & Argyle, 1997) have more recently reported strong associations between intrinsic religiosity and measures of mental and physical health. This link between intrinsic religiosity and the practice of private religious acts such as prayer and meditation suggests that adoption of a particular neuropsychologic mental state is an important mediator of religion's effects on mental and physical health. The intrinsic religious person practices a more interior form of religious observance than the extrinsic type. He or she frequently engages in private devotional practices and sees religion as an ultimate value rather than as a mere means to obtain other more utilitarian ends (such as social contacts). Persons with an extrinsic form of religiosity, on the other hand, tend to use religion instrumentally and opportunistically for their own ends. They are more comfortable with congregational forms of worship than are the intrinsics and find religion useful for various utilitarian reasons such as to provide social connections and opportunities. Batson, Shoenrade, and Ventis (1993) found that persons who scored high on measures of intrinsic as opposed to extrinsic religiosity tended to score better on measures of overall mental health than their nonreligious counterparts. Watson, Hood, Morris, and Hall (1984) found significant and positive correlations between measures of intrinsic religiosity and empathy. In their review of effects of religiosity on individuals who rate themselves as religious or who engage in private religious practices, Beit-Hallahmi and Argyle (1997) found that religiosity (particularly intrinsic religiosity) was associated with increases in subjective happiness, health, mental health, and altruism and decreases in some forms of sexual behaviors as well as rates of suicide, relative to nonreligious controls. Worthington, Kurusu, McCullough, and Sandage (1996) summarized a number of studies relevant to the issue of effects of private religious practices on mental function. Use of prayer, for example, was correlated with indices of hope and with subjective well-being, at least in religiously committed subjects. Prayer appeared to be a very common coping method for persons in distress whether they described themselves as religious or not. We (McNamara, Andresen, & Gellard 2003) recently found that optimal self-report health outcomes were associated with high prayer AND high frontal lobe scores. Neither, high prayer alone or high frontal scores were enough to yield optimal self-reported health, thus indicating a possible role for frontal function in mediating religion's effects on health.

RELIGIOSITY IN PARKINSON'S DISEASE: A LOW DOPAMINE DISORDER

If, as our review above seems to indicate, high levels of dopamine promote high levels of religiosity, then low levels of dopamine should be associated with lower than average levels of religiosity. We can test this idea by studying religiosity in patients with Parkinson's Disease (PD). Religiosity-related symptomology is relatively common in disorders that are associated with neo-striatal and limbic-prefrontal alterations such as schizophrenia (Cooper, Bloom, & Roth, 2003), obsessive-compulsive disorder (Vollenweider, 1998), and certain forms of temporal lobe epilepsy (Giacomelli et al., 1998; Millan, Lejeune, & Gobert, 2000). To our knowledge, however, there are no published reports of similar religiosity-related symptomology in PD—another prominent disorder of neo-striatal and prefrontal dysfunction (Daw, Kakade, & Dayan, 2002; Cools, Stefanova, Barker, Robbins, & Owens, 2002).

PARKINSON'S DISEASE

Parkinson's Disease is characterized by rigidity, bradykinesia, gait disorders, and sometimes tremors. The primary pathology involves loss of dopaminergic cells in the substantia nigra (SN) and in the ventral tegmental area (VTA) (Agid, Javoy-Agid, & Ruberg, 1987). As mentioned above, these two subcortical dopaminergic sites give rise to two projection systems important for motor, affective, and cognitive functioning. The nigrostriatal system, primarily implicated in motor functions, originates in the pars compacta of the SN and terminates in the striatum. The meso-limbic-cortical system contributes to cognitive and affective functioning. It originates in the VTA and terminates in the ventral striatum, amygdala, frontal lobes, and some other basal forebrain areas. In PD dopamine levels in the ventral striatum, frontal lobes, and hippocampus are approximately 40 percent of normal (Agid et al., 1987; Javoy-Agid & Agid, 1980; Scatton, Javoy-Agid, Rouquier, Dubois, & Agid, 1983; Shinotoh & Calne, 1995), but as mentioned above, chronic stimulation with levodopa results in transient above normal increases during the on-state in dopamine activity in limbic and prefrontal sites (Brooks, 2000; Carlsson, Waters, & Carolsson, 1999; Haslinger et al., 2001; Mattay et al., 2002; Piccini et al., 1997; Rascol et al., 1998; Sabatini, Boulanouar, & Fabre, 2000; Samuel et al., 1997). The degree of nigro-striatal impairment correlates with degree of motor impairment while VTA-mesocortical dopaminergic impairment correlates positively with the degree of affective and intellectual impairment (German, Manaye, Smith, Woodward, & Saper, 1989; Rinne, Rummukainen, Palijarvi, & Rinne, 1989; Torack & Morris, 1988) in affected individuals. As many as 40 percent to 60 percent of the cells in the SN are lost before clinical signs of disease become evident. Remaining neurons of the SN may also evidence the hallmark pathologic feature of Lewy bodies (cytoplasmic eosinophilic insolvent protein inclusions).

To study religiosity in patients with PD, we asked 22 male patients with moderately severe PD; and 20 healthy age-matched control subjects to complete a series of religiosity questionnaires, neuropsychologic tests, and mood function tests.

A wide range of religious preferences were represented by patients and controls who participated in these pilot studies. While Roman Catholics made up the bulk of the Parkinsonian sample (45%), several other faiths were represented in both the PD and control samples.

We used the Brief Multidimensional Measure of Religiousness/Spirituality (BMMRS, Fetzer Foundation) to measure religious attitudes and practices. The BMMRS contains 38 statements with Likert scale formats that cover 11 religious domains. These are: daily spiritual experiences, values/beliefs, forgiveness, private religious practices, religious and spiritual coping, religious support, religious/spiritual history, commitment, organizational religiousness, religious preference, and overall self-ranking (e.g., "To what extent do you consider yourself a religious person?"). The BMMRS was developed by a panel of experts on religion and health convened by the Fetzer Institute and the National Institutes of Health and Aging. It has excellent psychometric properties as well as publicly available norms for healthy older individuals.

We used the Rivermead Life Goals inventory (Schultz et al., 1995) to measure participants' subjective estimations of their major life goals. These included nine areas of personal concern from residential domestic arrangements and ability to personally care for oneself to financial status and work-related goals. Participants were asked to rate each life goal domain in importance from 0 (no importance) to 3 (extreme importance). After subjects rated the importance of these life goals, we then asked them to go back and rate each domain as to whether they felt it was on track or off track (0 = totally off track to 3 = totally on track). We used the question "My religion or life philosophy is . . ." to assess the subjective importance of religion to PD patients.

Our cognitive test battery was chosen with an emphasis on examining prefrontal neuropsychological function. The tests included the Stroop color-word interference procedure, the Tower of London mental planning task; and the Raven's test of visual intelligence. All of these tests have previously been shown to be altered in patients with PD (McNamara, 2002).

We assessed depression, stress, and anxiety with the Depression Anxiety and Stress Scale (DASS) developed by Lovibond and Lovibond (1995). The test includes 21 questions, seven in each of the depression, anxiety, and stress subscales.

We found that both controls and patients with PD reported that their residential domestic arrangements, personal care, work, relationship with primary partner, family life, contact with friends and financial affairs were on track and important to them. Patients with PD, however, rated their leisure activities/hobbies and their religion as less important than their age-matched counterparts–despite rating these same activities as being on track.

Patients with PD were significantly less religious than controls (Overall Index mean PDs = 7.1 (0.9); controls = 5.3 (1.4); $p < .04$), higher scores indicate less religiosity). Although patients with PD reported less religiosity on every scale compared to age-matched controls, the difference was significant only for the overall index and for the scale on private practices (i.e., prayer and meditation, private devotional reading; PD mean = 33.3 (7.2); controls 26.3 (7.9), $p = .050$).

As expected, the two groups differed significantly on Mini Mental State (MMSE), logical memory recall, mood tests, and Stroop interference/switching score. They did not differ significantly on the Tower of London and the Ravens Progressive Matrices Task.

Within the PD group, overall religiousness correlated with the Stroop interference/switching score (indicating the greater the frontal dysfunction the *lesser* the religiosity). Overall religiousness correlated negatively with the Ravens score, indicating that the better the performance on the Raven visual intelligence test, the *more* the religiousness. Within the healthy control group, religiosity was correlated with a measure of stress and inversely correlated with logical memory recall scores.

In summary, we found that patients with PD reported significantly lower levels of religiousness than did age-matched controls, and that this low level of religiosity was related primarily to a measure of prefrontal neuropsychological function rather than to age, education, mood, or to medication-related factors.

Why should patients with PD report less religiousness than age-matched healthy controls? We found that they were more depressed than age-matched controls, but religiousness scores were not significantly related to depression scores. One argument that has been presented is that religiousness may be inversely related to intelligence or education levels, in that people with higher intelligence or more education would be less likely to be religious. Our sample of patients with PD performed marginally better than controls on a measure of visual intelligence (Raven, 1965), and this measure was in turn significantly and inversely correlated with religiousness scores in patients with PD but not with controls. The latter finding suggests that in our sample the higher the visual intelligence, the greater the religiousness, indicating a possible relationship between intelligence and religiosity in this sample.

We did not find a significant correlation between the overall religiousness index and years of education in either the patients or the controls. The relationship between educational level and religiosity in healthy samples is, in any case, complex: high educational levels generally are positively correlated with frequent church attendance but negatively correlated with the occurrence of mystical or religious experiences (Comings, Gonzales, Saucier, Johnson, & MacMurray, 2000, p. 40). The correlation of religiosity with Stroop interference/switching scores (a measure of orbitofrontal inhibitory capacities), furthermore, argues against the "too intelligent" explanation for the lack of religiosity in patients with PD. It therefore appears that intelligence level is not a likely explanation of religiosity in these patients.

An alternative explanation for our major finding follows from the findings of our review of the relation between dopamine levels, the frontal lobes, and religiosity presented above. It may be that long-term forms of religiosity require participation of the motivational support normally supplied by the dopaminergic drive centers housed in neo-striatal and limbic-prefrontal circuits. The previously cited neuroimaging and neuropsychologic studies linking religious practices with prefrontal network activation is consistent with this hypothesis. Recent reports (Brown, 2002; Goberman & Coelho, 2002) linking scores on religiosity and measures of self-transcendence with genetic markers for the dopamine transport molecule and the DRD4 dopaminergic receptor gene (which is densely represented in prefrontal cortex) supports this hypothesis as well. Patients with PD experience relatively global reduction in central and forebrain dopamine activity as the disease progresses. If dopaminergic activity supports key aspects of religiosity, then it would not be surprising to find patients with PD lacking in overt signs of religiosity.

In summary, we found that patients with PD reported less religiosity than age-matched controls and that their scores on a battery of religiosity scales were consistently related to their performance on tests that measure frontal dysfunction. In short, patients with PD express less interest in religion and report consistently lower scores on measures of religiosity than age-matched controls. Given the correlation between prefrontal performance and religiosity scores, the profile of low interest and relatively low levels of religiosity among patients with PD may be related to dopaminergic and frontal dysfunction. Given these new findings, as well as our literature review above, we conclude that dopaminergic activity in the frontal lobes very likely significantly influences levels of religiousness.

REFERENCES

Abramowitz, J. S., Huppert, J. D., Cohen, A. B., Tolin, D. F., & Cahill, S. P. (2002). Religious obsessions and compulsions in a non-clinical sample: The Penn Inventory of Scrupulosity (PIOS). *Behaviour Research and Therapy, 40*(7), 825–838.

Agid, Y., Javoy-Agid, M., & Ruberg, M. (1987). Biochemistry of neurotransmitters in Parkinson's disease. In C. D. M. S. Fahn (Ed.), *Movement disorders 2* (pp. 166–230). New York: Butterworths and Co.

Albright, C., & Ashbrook, J. (2001). *Where God lives in the human brain.* Naperville: Sourcebooks, Inc.

Andresen, J. (2001). *Religion in mind: Cognitive perspectives on religious belief, ritual, and experience.* Cambridge: Cambridge University Press.

Arnsten, A., Matthew, R., Ubriani, R., Taylor, R.J., & Li, B. M. (1999). Alpha-1 noradrenergic receptor stimulation impairs prefrontal cortical cognitive function. *Biological Psychiatry, 45,* 26–31.

Ashbrook, J., & Albright, C. (1997). *The humanizing brain: Where religion and neuroscience meet.* Cleveland: Pilgrim Press.

Azari, N. P., Nickel, J., Wunderlich, G., Niedeggen, M., Hefter, H., Tellmann, L., et al. (2001). Neural correlates of religious experience. *European Journal of Neuroscience, 13*(8), 1649–1652.

Banyas, C.A. (1999). Evolution and phylogenetic history of the frontal lobes. In B. Miller & J. Cummings (Eds.), *The human frontal lobes: Functions and disorders* (pp. 83–106). New York: The Guilford Press.

Batson, C.D., Shoenrade, P., & Ventis, W.L. (1993). *Religion and the individual: A social-psychological perspective.* New York: Oxford University Press.

Bear, D. M., & Fedio, P. (1977). Quantitative analysis of interictal behavior in temporal lobe epilepsy. *Archives of Neurology, 34,* 454–467.

Beit-Hallahmi, B., & Argyle, M. (1997). *The psychology of religious behavior, belief, and experience.* New York: Rutledge.

Boyer, P. (2001). *Religion explained: The evolutionary origins of religious thought.* New York: Basic Books.

Brewerton, T. (1994). Hyperreligiosity in psychotic disorders. *Journal of Nervous and Mental Disease, 182*(5), 302–304.

Brooks, D. (2000). PET studies and motor complications in Parkinson's disease. *Trends in Neurosciences, 23*(Suppl. 1), S101–S108.

Brown, D. (2002). Sleep in Parkinson's disease and the parkinsonian syndromes. In T. Lee-Chiong, M. Sateia, & M. Carskadon (Eds.), *Sleep medicine* (pp. 509–520). London: Lippincott, Williams & Wilkins.

Buijs, R. M., & Van Eden, C.G. (2000). The integration of stress by the hypothalamus, amygdala and prefrontal cortex: Balance between the autonomic nervous system and the neuroendocrine system. *Progress in Brain Research, 126*, 117–132.

Carlsson, A., Waters, N., & Carlsson, M. L. (1999). Neurotransmitter interactions in schizophrenia-therapeutic implications. *European Archives of Psychiatry and Clinical Neuroscience, 249*(Suppl 4), 37–43.

Comings, D. E., Gonzales, N., Saucier, G., Johnson, J. P., MacMurray, J. P. (2000). The DRD4 gene and the spiritual transcendence scale of the character temperament index. *Psychiatric Genetics, 10*(4), 185–189.

Comstock, G. W., & Partridge, K. B. (1972). Church attendance and health. *Journal of Chronic Disease, 25*(12), 665–672.

Cools, R., Stefanova, E., Barker, R. A., Robbins, T. W., & Owen, A. M. (2002) Dopaminergic modulation of high-level cognition in Parkinson's disease: The role of the prefrontal cortex revealed by PET. *Brain, 125*(Pt 3), 584–594.

Cooper, J., Bloom, F., & Roth, R. (2003). *The biochemical basis of neuropharmacology* (8th ed.). Oxford: Oxford University Press.

d'Aquilli, E., & Newberg, A. B. (1993). Religious and mystical states: A neuropsychological model. *Zygon, 28*(2), 177–200.

d'Aquilli, E., & Newberg, A. (1999). *The mystical mind: Probing the biology of religious experience.* Minneapolis: Fortress Press.

Daw, N., Kakade, S., & Dayan, P. (2002). Opponent interactions between serotonin and dopamine. *Neural Network, 15*(4–6), 603–616.

Dewhurst, K., & Beard, A. W. (1970). Sudden religious conversions in temporal lobe epilepsy. *British Journal of Psychiatry, 117*, 497–507.

Ellison, C. G., Gay, D. A., & Glass T. A. (1989). Does religious commitment contribute to individual life satisfaction? *Social Forces, 68*, 100–123.

Fetzer Foundation. (1999). Multidimensional measurement of religiousness/ spirituality for use in heath research (pp. 1–95). Bethesda, MD: Fetzer Institute/ National Institute on Aging Working Group.

Fiske, A. P., & Haslam, N. (1997). Is obsessive-compulsive disorder a pathology of the human disposition to perform socially meaningful rituals? Evidence of similar content. *Journal of Nervous and Mental Disease, 185*(4), 211–222.

Fuster, J. M. (1989). *The prefrontal cortex.* Anatomy, physiology and neuropsychology of the frontal lobe (2nd ed.). New York: Raven Press.

German, D., Manaye, K., Smith, W., Woodward, D., & Saper, C. (1989). Mid-Brain dopaminergic cell loss in Parkinson's disease: Computer visualization. *Annals of Neurology, 26*, 507–514.

Geschwind, N. (1983). Interictal behavioral changes in epilepsy. *Epilepsia, 24*(Suppl 1), 523–530.

Giacomelli, S., Palmery, M., Romanelli, L., Cheng, C. Y., & Silvestrini, B. (1998). Lysergic acid diethylamide (LSD) is a partial agonist of D2 dopaminergic receptors and it potentiates dopamine-mediated prolactin secretion in lactotrophs in vitro. *Life Sciences, 63*(3), 215–222.

Goberman, A., & Coelho, C. (2002). Acoustic analysis of Parkinsonian speech I: Speech characteristics and L-Dopa therapy. *Neurorehabilitation, 17,* 237–246.

Goldman-Rakic, P. (1987). Circuitry of primate prefrontal cortex and regulation of behavior by representational memory. In V. Plum (Ed.), *Higher cortical function, Handbook of Physiology* (pp. 373–417). New York: American Physiological Society.

Haslinger, B., Erhard, P., Kampfe, N., Boecker, H., Rummeny, E., & Schwaiger, M. (2001). Event-related functional magnetic resonance imaging in Parkinson's disease before and after levodopa. *Brain, 124,* 558–570.

Idler, E. L. (1987). Religious involvement and the health of the elderly: Some hypotheses and an initial test. *Social Forces, 66,* 226–238.

Iqbal, N., & van Praag, H. (1995). The role of serotonin in schizophrenia. *European Neuropsychopharmacology, 5*(Suppl 1), 11–23.

Javoy-Agid, F., & Agid, Y. (1980). Is the mesocortical dopaminergic system involved in Parkinson's disease? *Neurology, 30,* 1326–1330.

Jenike, M. A., Baer, L., & Minichiello. (1998). *WE: Obsessive-compulsive disorders: Practical management* (3rd ed.). St. Louis: Mosby.

Koenig, H. G. (2001). *The healing power of faith: How belief and prayer can help you triumph over disease.* New York: Simon and Schuster.

Koenig, H. G., George, L. K., Hays, J. C., Larson, D. B., Cohen, H. J., & Blazer, D. G. (1998). The relationship between religious activities and blood pressure in older adults. *International Journal of Psychiatry in Medicine, 28,* 189–213.

Kune, G. A., Kune, S., & Watson, L. F. (1993). Perceived religiousness is protective for colorectal cancer: Data from the Melbourne colorectal cancer study. *Journal of the Royal Society of Medicine, 86,* 645–647.

Levin, J. S., Taylor, R. J., & Chatters, L. M. (1995). A multidimensional measure of religious involvement for African Americans. *Sociology Quarterly, 36,* 157–173.

Levin, J. S., & Vanderpool, H. Y. (1989). Is religion therapeutically significant for hypertension? *Social Science and Medicine, 29*(1), 69–78.

Lovibond, S., & Lovibond, P. (1995). Manual for the Depression Anxiety Stress Scales. Sydney: The Psychology Foundation of Australia, Inc.

Mattay, V. S., Tessitore, A., Callicott, J. H., Bertolino, A., Goldberg, T. E., Chase, T. N., et al. (2002). Dopaminergic modulation of cortical function in patients with Parkinson's disease. *Annals of Neurology, 51,* 156–164.

McNamara, P. (2002). The motivational origins of religious practices. *Zygon, 37*(1), 143–160.

McNamara, P., Andresen, J., & Gellard, J. (2003). Relation of religiosity and scores on verbal and non-verbal fluency to subjective reports of health in the elderly. *International Journal for the Psychology of Religion, 13*(4), 259–271.

Millan, M. J., Lejeune, F., & Gobert, A. (2000). Reciprocal autoreceptor and heteroreceptor control of serotonergic, dopaminergic and noradrenergic transmission in the frontal cortex: Relevance to the actions of antidepressant agents. *Journal of Psychopharmacology, 14*(2), 114–138.

Musick, M. A., Traphagan, J. W., Koenig, H. G., & Larson, D. B. (2000). Spirituality in physical health and aging. *Journal of Adult Development, 7*(2), 73–86.

Newberg, A., Alavi, A., Baime, M., Mozley, P. D., & d'Aquilli, E. (1997). The measurement of cerebral blood flow during the complex cognitive task of meditation using HMPAO-SPECT imaging. *Journal of Nuclear Medicine, 38,* 95.

Newberg, A., Alavi, A., Baime, M., Pourdehnad, M., Santanna, J., & d'Aquilli, E. (2001). The measurement of regional cerebral blood flow during the complex cognitive task of meditation: A preliminary SPECT study. *Psychiatry Research, 106*(2), 113–122.

Newberg, A., d'Aquilli, E., & Rause V. (2001). *Why God won't go away.* New York: Ballantine.

Passingham, R. E. (1995). *The frontal lobes and voluntary action.* New York: Oxford University Press.

Persinger, M. A. (1987). *Neuropsychological bases of God beliefs.* New York: Praeger.

Piccini, P., Morrish, P. K., Turjanski, N., Sawle, G. V., Burn, D. J., Weeks, R. A., et al. (1997). Dopaminergic function in familial Parkinson's disease: A clinical and 18F-dopa positron emission tomography study. *Annals of Neurology, 41*(2), 222–229.

Pincus, J. H. (1999). Aggression, criminality and the frontal lobes. In B. Miller & J. Cummings (Eds.), *The human frontal lobes: Functions and disorders* (pp. 547–556). New York: The Guilford Press.

Ramachandran, V. S., Hirstein, W. S., Armel, K. C., Tecoma, E., & Iragul, V. (1997). *The Neural Basis of Religious Experience.* Poster session presented at the 27th Annual Meeting for Society for Neuroscience, New Orleans, LA, October.

Randolph-Schwartz, J. (1999), Dopamine projections and frontal systems function. In B. Miller & J. Cummings (Eds.), *The human frontal lobes: Functions and disorders* (pp. 159–173). New York: The Guilford Press.

Rascol, O., Sabatini, U., Brefel, C., Fabre, N., Rai, S., Senard, J. M., et al. (1998). Cortical motor overactivation in parkinsonian patients with L-dopa-induced peak-dose dyskinesia. *Brain, 121*(3), 527–533.

Raven, J. C. (1965). *Guide to using the colored progressive matrices.* London: H.K. Lewis.

Rinne, J. O., Rummukainen, J., Paljarvi, L., & Rinne U. K. (1989). Dementia in Parkinson's disease is related to neuronal loss in the medial substantia nigra. *Annals of Neurology, 26*(1), 47–50.

Sabatini, U., Boulanouar, K., & Fabre, N. (2000). Cortical motor reorganization in akinetic patients with Parkinson's disease: A functional MRI study. *Brain, 123,* 394–403.

Samuel, M., Ceballos-Baumann, A. O., Turjanski, N., Boecker, H., Gorospe, A., & Linazasoro, G. (1997). Pallidotomy in Parkinson's disease increases supplementary motor area and prefrontal activation during performance of volitional movements an H2(15)O PET study. *Brain, 120,* 1301–1313.

Saver, J. L., & Rabin, J. (1997). The neural substrates of religious experience. *Journal of Neuropsychiatry and Clinical Neurosciences, 9*(3), 498–510.

Scatton, B., Javoy-Agid, F., Rouquier, L., Dubois, B., & Agid, Y. (1983). Reduction of cortical dopamine, neuroadrenaline, seratonin, and their metabolites in Parkinson's disease. *Brain Research, 275,* 321–328.

Schroeder, G. L. (2001). *The hidden face of God: How science reveals the ultimate truth.* New York: The Free Press.

Schultz, W., Romo, R., Ljungberg, J., Mirenowicz, J., Hollerman, J., & Dickinson, A. (1995). Reward-related signals carried by dopamine neurons. In J. Houk, J. Davis, & D. Beiser (Eds.), *Models of information processing in the basal ganglia* (pp. 233–248). Cambridge: MIT Press.

Shinotoh, H., & Calne, D. (1995). The use of PET in Parkinson's disease. *Brain and Cognition, 28,* 297–310.

Siddle, R., Haddock, G., Tarrier, N., & Faragher, E. B. (2002). Religious delusions in patients admitted to hospital with schizophrenia. *Social Psychiatry and Psychiatric Epidemiology, 37(3),* 130–138.

Strawbridge, W. J., Cohen, R. D., Shema, S. J., & Kaplan, G. A. (1997). Frequent attendance at religious services and mortality over 28 years. *American Journal of Public Health, 87,* 957–961.

Tek, C., & Ulug, B. (2001). Religiosity and religious obsessions in obsessive-compulsive disorder. *Psychiatry Research, 104(2),* 99–108.

Tomic, M., & Joksimovic, J. (2000). Psychomimetics moderately affect dopamine receptor binding in the rat brain. *Neurochemistry International, 36(2),* 137–142.

Torack, R. M., & Morris, J. C. (1988). The association of ventral tegmental area histopathology with adult dementia. *Archives of Neurology, 45(5),* 497–501.

Vollenweider, F. X. (1998). Advances and pathophysiological models of hallucinogenic drug actions in humans: A preamble to schizophrenia research. *Pharmacopsychiatry, 31(Suppl 2),* 92–103.

Watson, P. J., Hood, R. W., Morris, R. J., & Hall, J. R. (1984). Empathy, religious orientation, and social desirability. *Journal of Psychology, 117,* 211–216.

Wilson, D. S. (2002). *Darwin's cathedral: Evolution, religion and the nature of society.* Chicago: University of Chicago Press.

Wilson, W. P. (1998). Religion and psychoses. In H. Koenig (Ed.), *Handbook of religion and mental health* (pp. 161–174). San Diego: Academic Press.

Worthington, E. L., Kurusu, T. A., McCullough, M. E., & Sandage, S. J. (1996). Empirical research on religion and psychotherapeutic processes and outcomes: A 10-year review and research prospectus. *Psychological Bulletin, 119(3),* 448–487.

CHAPTER 2

RELIGIOUS AND SPIRITUAL PRACTICES: A NEUROCHEMICAL PERSPECTIVE

Andrew B. Newberg

INTRODUCTION

Spiritual practices such as meditation are complex neurocognitive tasks that have been utilized in almost every culture and tradition over the past several millennia. In the past 30 years, science has been able to explore the biological effects and mechanism of such practices in great detail. Initial studies focused more specifically on meditation practices. These studies measured changes in autonomic activity such as heart rate and blood pressure as well as electroencephalographic changes. More recent studies have explored changes in hormonal and immunological function associated with meditation. Studies have also explored the clinical effects of spiritual practices in relation to both physical and psychological disorders. Functional neuroimaging has opened a new window into the investigation of spiritual states with the ability to find neurological correlates of these experiences. In previous works, we have outlined a basic neurophysiological model for the mechanism underlying such practices. As this basic model has evolved, and as the results of more studies have been added, a more detailed synthesis of the neurochemical basis of such states can be elaborated. Such a model not only helps to further elucidate the mechanism underlying spiritual practices and experiences, but provides important information regarding the effects of these experiences on body physiology and creates a springboard for future research, particularly with regard to functional brain imaging.

CURRENT NEUROIMAGING TECHNIQUES

Functional and anatomical neuroimaging techniques have contributed dramatically to our understanding of the causes of various neurological disorders and in their diagnosis and management. Anatomical imaging techniques such as magnetic resonance imaging (MRI) and x-ray computed tomography (CT) are useful for determining structural changes in the brain. Functional imaging methods such as single photon emission computed tomography (SPECT) and positron emission tomography (PET) have been useful for measuring changes in blood flow, metabolism, and neurotransmitter activity in neuropsychiatric processes as well as activation states of the brain (see tables 2.1 and 2.2).

Brain activation studies have utilized neuroimaging techniques to explore cerebral function during various behavioral, motor, and cognitive tasks. These studies, usually utilizing SPECT, PET, and functional MRI, have helped to determine which parts of the brain are responsible for a variety of neurocognitive processes. Functional MRI, which has been extensively developed in the past several years, has been shown to have high spatial and temporal resolution in measuring changes in cerebral activity during various cognitive, sensory, and motor activation tasks (Binder et al., 1994; Hammeke et al., 1994; McCarthy et al., 1994; Rao et al., 1995; Sergent, 1994). Thus, activation studies with the functional imaging techniques have been employed to determine the areas in the brain that are involved in the production and understanding of language, visual processing, and pain reception and sensation (Friston,

Table 2.1 A Partial Listing of Radioligands Used in Neurological SPECT Imaging

Compound	Application
HMPAO, IMP, ECD	Cerebral blood flow
3-quinuclidinyl benzilate (IQNB)	Muscarinic cholinergic receptor
Iodopride, IBZM, iodospiperone	Dopamine receptor activity
AMIK, DOI	Serotonin receptor activity
Iomazenil	Benzodiazepine activity
2-iodomorphine	Opioid receptor activity
I-d(CH2)5[Tyr(Me)2, Tyr(NH2)9]AV	Vasopressin activity

AMIK = 7-amino-8-iodo-ketanserin
DOI = 1-(2,5-dimethoxy-4-iodophenyl)-2-aminopropane
ECD = Ethylene Cystinate Dimer
HMPAO = Technetium 99m hexamethyl propylene amine oxime
IBZM = 3-iodo-N-[(1-ethyl-2-pyrrolidinyl)] methyl-2-hydroxy-6-methoxybenzamide
IMP = Iodine-123-N-N', N, -trimethyl-N'-[2-hydroxyl-3-methyl-5-iodo-benzyl]- 1, 3 propane diamine

Frith, Passingham, Liddle, & Frackowiak, 1992; Phelps, Huhl, & Mazziotta, 1981; Phelps & Mazziota, 1985).

With regard to the functional imaging techniques of PET and SPECT, it is important to note that a large number of radiopharmaceuticals have been developed over the past 30 years that may be of use for studying the effects of meditative and related experiences. Tracers have now been developed that are specific for glucose and oxygen metabolism as well as cerebral blood flow. One of the most important strengths of PET and SPECT imaging is in the evaluation of neurotransmitter systems. Radioactive analogues of almost every neurotransmitter have been developed including those related to the dopamine, benzodiazepine, opiate, and cholinergic receptor systems (Diksic & Reba, 1991; Frost, 1992; Gatley, DeGrado, Kornguth, & Holden, 1990; Kung, 1991; Maziere & Maziere, 1991). As more and more tracers are developed, we will continue to expand our understanding of what each system does and how they interact during various mental states. This has important implications for the study of spiritual practices and experiences.

Each of the functional imaging techniques provides different logistical advantages and disadvantages in the study of meditation and other spiritually related experiences. Functional MRI, while having improved resolution over SPECT and the ability of immediate anatomic correlation, would be very difficult to utilize for the study of meditation because of the noise from the machine and the problem of having to lie prone in the machine. In fact, we attempted the use of fMRI with our initial subject to determine feasibility, but the subject found it extremely difficult to carry out the meditation

Table 2.2 A Partial Listing of Radioligands Used in Neurological PET Imaging

Compound	Application
[15O] H2O	Blood flow
[18F] fluorodeoxyglucose	Glucose metabolism
15O2	Oxygen metabolism
[11C] l-methionine	Amino acid metabolism
[11C] raclopride, [11C] methylspiperone, 6-[18F] fluorodopamine, [18F] spiperone,	Dopamine receptor activity
[11C] carfentanil, [11C] etorphine	Opiate receptor activity
[11C] flunitrazepam	Benzodiazepine receptor activity
[11C] scopolamine, [11C] quinuclidinyl benzilate	Muscarinic cholinergic receptors
6-[18F] fluoro-L-DOPA, 4-[18F] flouro-m-tyrosine	Presynaptic dopaminergic system
[11C] ephedrine, [18F] fluorometaraminol	Adrenergic terminals

practice. Other investigators have attempted to acclimate patients prior to performing the fMRI scan with varying degrees of success. While PET imaging also provides better spatial resolution than SPECT, if one strives to make the environment relatively distraction free to maximize the chances of having as strong a meditative experience as possible, it is sometimes beneficial to perform these studies off hours (especially if there is a busy clinical service). This may complicate the use of PET because the radiopharmaceuticals often require preparation close to the time of use. The SPECT tracers have longer half lives and thus can be prepared in advance and then used when needed. Thus, while PET and fMRI offer certain technical advantages, SPECT appeared to provide the best option for our initial study of Tibetan Buddhist meditation (Newberg et al., 2001). In this study, patients had an intravenous line placed and were injected with a cerebral blood flow tracer while at rest to acquire a baseline image. They then meditated for approximately one hour until they experienced a peak in their meditation that was indicated by a signal from the subject during the meditation. The patients were again injected with the tracer while they continued to meditate. The tracer is fixed in the brain at the time of injection so that when the images were acquired approximately 20 minutes later, they reflected the cerebral blood flow during the peak meditation. The baseline and meditation images were then compared to determine changes in cerebral blood flow.

The findings of this study showed marked increases in the bilateral frontal cortices, cingulate gyrus, and thalami. A decrease in blood flow was noted in the superior parietal lobes bilaterally with the left more affected than the right. Interestingly, the decreases in the superior parietal lobes correlated with the increases in the thalami, suggesting a complex network that affects multiple brain areas.

The other brain imaging studies of spiritual practices have utilized the different functional imaging modalities of fMRI and PET. The fMRI study by Lazar et al. and the PET study by Herzog et al. both demonstrated increased activity in the frontal areas, particularly the prefrontal cortex (Herzog et al., 1990–1991; Lazar et al., 2000). They also demonstrated some decreases in the parietal regions. The study by Lazar took an interesting approach to avoiding the distraction of the MRI noise by having patients practice ahead of time with a tape of the MRI machine. However, the results from both of these studies are not inconsistent with our results. One PET study by Lou et al. did not demonstrate increased prefrontal activity (Lou et al., 1999). However, this may have been due to the fact that patients were following a tape guiding them through the meditation, which is different from our study during which the meditation was self-initiated and maintained. In a similar manner, internally generated words activate the prefrontal cortex while guided word generation does not, so whether or not the PFC is activated during meditation may have to do with the type of approach used by the practitioner.

PHYSIOLOGICAL STUDIES OF SPIRITUAL PRACTICES

In studies of the physiological correlates of practices such as meditation, investigators have examined both specific neurophysiological function as well as the relation of that function to various aspects of body physiology (please see Figure 2.1 for an overall diagram of the potential neurophysiological

Figure 2.1 Schematic Overview of the Neurophysiological Network Possibly Associated with Meditative States

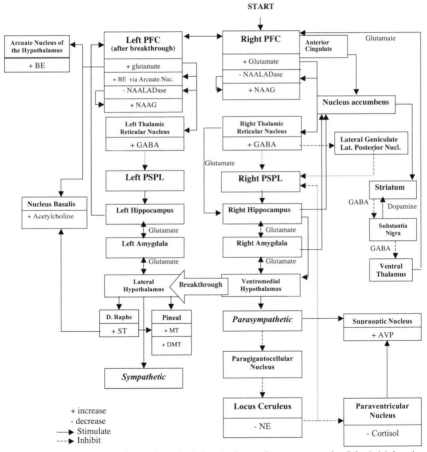

Note: The circuits generally apply to both hemispheres, however, much of the initial activity is on the right.

effects related to meditation practices; Newberg & Iversen, 2003). The autonomic nervous system's responses to meditation include decreases in blood pressure, heart rate, respiratory rate, and galvanic skin responses (Jevning, Wallace, & Beidebach, 1992; Wallace, 1970). Investigators have also performed a number of studies that measured changes in the body's neurochemistry as a result of meditation. The vast majority of these studies were performed on patients practicing transcendental meditation. In this type of practice, originally derived from Hindu practice, the individual focuses on a particular word or phrase (the mantra) that has significant meaning to the individual. The result is a feeling of calmness, a loss of the sense of self, and the diminishment of the perception of external stimuli.

Several studies have demonstrated an increase in gamma aminobutyric acid (GABA) in the blood serum of individuals during meditation (Elias, Guich, & Wilson, 2000; Elias & Wilson, 1995). Interestingly, GABA is the principal inhibitory neurotransmitter in the brain. Serotonin (ST) is a neuromodulator that densely supplies the visual centers of the temporal lobe, where it strongly influences the flow of visual associations generated by this area (Foote, 1987). The cells of the dorsal raphe produce and distribute ST when innervated by the lateral hypothalamus (Aghajanian, Sprouse, & Rasmussen, 1987). Moderately increased levels of ST appear to correlate with positive affect, while low ST often signifies depression (Van Praag & De Haan, 1980). This has clearly been demonstrated with regard to the effects of the selective serotonin reuptake inhibitor medications such as Prozac or Zoloft, which have been widely used for the treatment of depression. When cortical ST2 receptors (especially in the temporal lobes) are activated, however, the stimulation can result in a hallucinogenic effect. Tryptamine psychedelics such as psylocybin and LSD seem to take advantage of this mechanism to produce their extraordinary visual experiences (Aghajanian & Marek, 1999). Interestingly, after practices such as meditation, breakdown products of ST in urine have been found to significantly increase, suggesting an overall elevation in ST during meditation (Bujatti & Riederer, 1976; Walton, Pugh, Gelderloos, & Macrae 1995). The neurohormone melatonin (MT) is produced by the pineal gland, which can convert ST into MT when innervated by the lateral hypothalamus (Moller, 1992). MT has been shown to depress the central nervous system and reduce pain sensitivity (Shaji & Kulkarni, 1998). During meditation, blood plasma MT has been found to increase sharply, but it is not clear whether this is directly related to the experiences that arise during such practices (Coker, 1999; Tooley, Armstrong, Norman, & Sali, 2000)

The neurochemical arginine vasopressin (AVP), produced in the supraoptic nucleus of the hypothalamus, serves many functions in the brain and body. It is a vasoconstrictor that tightens blood vessels, but also it decreases self-perceived fatigue and arousal and appears to contribute to the general maintenance of positive affect (Pietrowsky, Braun, Fehm, Pauschinger, & Born, 1991). Increases in AVP have also been found to significantly improve the consolidation of new memories and learning (Reghunandanan, Reghunandanan, & Mahajan, 1998; Weingartner et al., 1981). In meditators, blood plasma AVP has been found in exponentially higher levels (O'Halloran et al., 1985). Of course, whether this translates into central effects of AVP remains to be seen.

Norepinephrine (NE) is a neuromodulator produced by the locus ceruleus of the pons (Foote, 1987). NE increases the susceptibility of brain regions to sensory input by amplifying strong stimuli, while simultaneously gating out weaker activations and cellular "noise" that fall below the activation threshold (Waterhouse, Moises, & Woodward, 1998). The breakdown products of catecholamines such as NE and epinephrine have generally been found to be reduced in the urine and plasma during meditation (Bujatti M. & Riederer, 1976; Infante et al., 2001; Walton, Pugh, Gelderloos, & Macrae, 1995). Cortisol is a hormone associated with the stress responses. Cortisol is produced when the paraventricular nucleus of the hypothalamus secretes corticotropin-releasing hormone (CRH) in response to innervation by NE from the locus ceruleus (Ziegler, Cass, & Herman, 1999). This CRH stimulates the anterior pituitary to release adrenocorticotropic hormone (ACTH; Livesey, Evans, Mulligan, & Donald, 2000). ACTH, in turn, stimulates the adrenal cortex to produce cortisol (Davies, Keyon, & Fraser, 1985). Thus, cortisol is released during stress states, but most studies have found that urine and blood plasma cortisol levels are decreased during meditation (Jevning, Wilson, & Davidson, 1978; Sudsuang, Chentanez, & Veluvan, 1991; Walton, Pugh, Gelderloos, & Macrae, 1995). In fact, this has led a number of investigators to examine the ability of practices such as meditation to attenuate the effects of stress.

Beta-endorphin (BE) is an endogenous opioid produced primarily by the arcuate nucleus of the medial hypothalamus and distributed to the brain's sub-cortical areas (Yadid, Zangen, Hezberg, Nakash, & Sagen, 2000). The arcuate nucleus releases BE in response to the excitatory neurotransmitter glutamate, to which it is extremely sensitive (Kiss, Kocsis, Csaki, Gorcs, & Halasz, 1997). BE depresses respiration, reduces fear, reduces pain, and produces sensations of joy and euphoria (Amano et al., 1982; Campbell, Weinger, & Quinn, 1995; Janal, Colt, Clark, & Glusman, 1984; Kalin, Shelton, & Barksdale, 1988). Meditation has been found to disrupt diurnal rhythms of BE and ACTH, while not affecting diurnal cortisol rhythms (Infante et al., 1998). Thus, the opiate system may play some role in spiritual states, but it is unlikely to be the primary neurotransmitter involved.

NEUROCHEMICAL CORRELATES OF SPIRITUAL PRACTICES

Activation of the Prefrontal Cortex and Cingulate Gyrus

Brain imaging studies suggest that willful acts are initiated via activity in the prefrontal cortex along with the anterior cingulate gyrus and are mediated by the excitatory neurotransmitter glutamate (Ingvar, 1994). Since the prefrontal cortex (PFC) in particular appears to mediate intense concentration, it thus should be essential for all meditative practices. Using PET imaging, investigators have shown that when patients performed purposely willed tasks or tasks that required sustained attention, there was activation of the PFC (Frith, Friston, Liddle, & Frackowiak, 1991; Pardo, Fox, & Raichle, 1991). Activation of the PFC and cingulate gyrus has been further validated by the increased activity observed in this region on several of the brain imaging studies of meditation (Herzog et al., 1990–1991; Lazar et al., 2000; Newberg et al., 2001). Therefore, meditation appears to start with activating the prefrontal cortex and possibly the cingulate gyrus associated with the will or intent to clear the mind of thoughts.

Thalamic Activation

The thalamus governs the flow of sensory information to cortical processing areas via the inhibitory effects of the neurotransmitter GABA on structures such as the lateral geniculate and lateral posterior nuclei. The lateral geniculate nucleus receives raw visual data from the optic tract and routes it to the striate cortex for processing (Andrews, Halpern, & Purves, 1997). The lateral posterior nucleus of the thalamus provides the posterior superior parietal lobule (PSPL) with the sensory information it needs to determine the body's spatial orientation (Bucci, Conley, & Gallagher, 1999). During meditation, if the activation of the right PFC causes increased activity in the reticular nucleus, the result may be decreased sensory input entering into the PSPL and visual center. While brain imaging studies of meditation have not had the resolution to distinguish the reticular nuclei, our recent SPECT study did demonstrate a general increase in thalamic activity that was proportional to the activity levels in the PFC (Newburg et al., 2001). However, further studies will be necessary to clarify the role of the thalamus in spiritual practices.

PSPL Deafferentation

The PSPL (Brodmann's area 7) is heavily involved in the analysis and integration of higher-order visual, auditory, and somaesthetic information.

Through the reception of auditory and visual input from the thalamus, the PSPL is able to generate a three-dimensional image of the body in space and may actually be crucial in distinguishing self from other (Joseph, 1990; Lynch, 1980). It should be noted that a recent study has suggested that the superior temporal lobe may play a more important role in body spatial representation, although this has not been confirmed by other reports. However, it remains to be seen what is the actual relationship between the parietal and temporal lobes in terms of spatial representation. Regardless, deafferentation of these orienting areas of the brain, we propose, is an important concept in the physiology of spiritual practices ranging from ritual to intense meditative states. If, for example, deafferentation of the PSPL by the reticular nucleus's effect on the posterior thalamic nucleus occurs to a significant degree, the person may begin to lose their usual ability to spatially define the self and help to orient that self. Deaffentation of the PSPL has been corroborated by several functional imaging studies of meditation that have demonstrated decreased activity in this area during intense meditation.

Limbic Activation

The hippocampus acts to modulate and moderate cortical arousal and responsiveness, via rich and extensive interconnections with the prefrontal cortex, other neocortical areas, the amygdala, and the hypothalamus (Joseph, 1990). Hippocampal stimulation has been shown to diminish cortical responsiveness and arousal; however, if cortical arousal is initially at a low level, then hippocampal stimulation tends to augment cortical activity (Redding, 1967). Thus, the hippocampus functions in conjunction with the thalamus, hypothalamus, and septal nuclei to prevent extremes of arousal, thereby maintaining a state of quiet alertness (Joseph, 1990).

The hippocampus greatly influences the amygdala, such that they complement and interact in the generation of attention, emotion, and certain types of imagery (Joseph, 1990). It seems that much of the prefrontal modulation of emotion is via the hippocampus and its connections with the amygdale (Poletti & Sujatanond, 1980). Because of this reciprocal interaction between the amygdala and hippocampus, the activation of the right hippocampus likely stimulates the right lateral amygdala as well.

Parasympathetic Activation and Resulting Effects

Stimulation of the right amygdala can cause a stimulation of the ventromedial portion of the hypothalamus with a subsequent activation of the peripheral parasympathetic system (Joseph, 1990). This activation may result in the subjective sensation first of relaxation, and eventually, of a more profound quiescence. Activation of the parasympathetic system would cause a reduction in heart rate and respiratory rate, an involuntary decrease combined with the voluntary attempt of the meditator to steady and slow breathing and movement. The locus ceruleus, which produces and distributes NE, receives most of its excitatory input from the medulla's lateral paragigantocellular nucleus, which monitors breathing and heart rate (Van Bockstaele & Aston-Jones, 1995). During a meditative practice, decreased heart rate and breathing associated with parasympathetic activation, then, should theoretically reduce the firing of the paragigantocellular nucleus of the medulla and cut back its innervation of the locus ceruleus, which densely and specifically supplies the PSPL and the lateral posterior nucleus with NE (Foote, 1987). Less innervation would mean a decrease in the quantity of NE delivered to these regions, where it normally serves to increase their susceptibility to sensory input by amplifying strong stimuli and gating out noise that falls below the activation threshold (Waterhouse, Moises, & Woodward, 1998). Thus, a reduction in NE decreases the impact of sensory input on the PSPL, contributing to its deafferentation.

The parasympathetic activity should also result in the hypothalamic paraventricular nucleus, decreasing its production of CRH, ultimately lowering the adrenal cortex's production of cortisol, a finding observed in the majority of meditation studies. The drop in blood pressure associated with meditation should induce the hypothalamic supraoptic nucleus to release the vasoconstrictor AVP, which has been shown to increase during meditation (Renaud, 1996).

Positive-Feedback Circuit Formation

As the meditation practice continues, there should theoretically be increasing activity in the PFC associated with the ever persistent will to focus attention. Most of the neurons of the PFC are glutamatergic, meaning that they produce and employ the excitatory neurotransmitter glutamate to communicate among themselves and to innervate other brain structures (Cheramy, Romo, & Glowinski, 1987). In general, as PFC activity increases, it produces ever-increasing levels of free synaptic glutamate in the brain. This glutamate can stimulate the hypothalamic arcuate nucleus to release BE, depressing respiration, reducing fear and pain, and producing sensations of joy and euphoria, feelings that have been described during meditation. However, it is unlikely that BE is the sole mediator in such experiences because simply taking morphine-related substances does not produce equivalent experiences, and one very limited study demonstrated that blocking the opiate receptors with naloxone did not effect the experience or EEG pattern associated with meditation (Sim & Tsoi, 1992).

Glutamate activates NMDA receptors (NMDAr), but excess glutamate can kill these neurons through excitotoxic processes (Albin & Greenamyre,

1992). We propose that, as glutamate levels approach excitotoxic concentrations, the brain might limit its production of NAALADase, which converts the endogenous NMDAr antagonist NAAG into glutamate (Thomas, Vornov, Olkowski, Merion & Slusher, 2000). The resultant increase in NAAG would protect cells from excitotoxic damage. There is an important side effect, however, since the NMDAr inhibitor NAAG is functionally analogous to the disassociative hallucinogens ketamine, phencyclidine (PCP), and nitrous oxide. These NMDAr antagonists produce a variety of states that may be characterized as either schizophrenomimetic or mystical, such as out-of-body and near-death experiences (Ellison, 1995; Jansen, 1995).

Complex Autonomic Activity

Our original model was based to some extent on the work of Gellhorn and Kiely, who suggested that intense stimulation of either the sympathetic or parasympathetic system, if continued, could ultimately result in simultaneous discharge of both systems (Gellhorn & Kiely, 1972). A recent study corroborated the notion of mutual activation of parasympathetic and sympathetic systems by demonstrating an increase in the variability of heart rate during meditation (Peng et al., 1999). The increased variation in heart rate was hypothesized to reflect activation of both arms of the autonomic nervous system. This notion also fits the description people have of these experiences in that they feel both a sense of overwhelming calmness as well as significant alertness.

It is interesting to note that stimulation of both systems can result in intense stimulation of structures in the lateral hypothalamus and median forebrain bundle, which are known to produce both ecstatic and blissful feelings when stimulated (Olds & Forbes, 1981). This may be associated with the lateral hypothalamus stimulation of the dorsal raphe to deliver more ST to the temporal lobe visual association areas. When ST is produced by the dorsal raphe, it also inhibits the lateral geniculate nucleus, greatly reducing the amount of visual information that can pass through (Funke & Eysel, 1995; Yoshida, Sasa, & Takaori, 1984). Combined with reticular and ST inhibition of the lateral geniculate nucleus of the thalamus, ST would increase the fluidity of temporal visual association in the absence of sensory input. The result would likely be the generation of internally derived imagery that has also been utilized during certain meditative states. Greatly increased ST levels might also act as agonists on ST2 receptors, provoking hallucinations in the manner of the tryptamine psychedelics.

These increased ST levels, combined with lateral hypothalamic innervation, may lead the pineal gland to increase MT production, decreasing pain sensitivity and producing a sensation of tranquility. Under circumstances of heightened activation, pineal enzymes can also endogenously synthesize the powerful hallucinogen 5-methoxy-dimethyltryptamine (DMT) (Guchhait,

1976). Strassman has extensively linked DMT to a variety of mystical states, including out-of-body experiences, distortion of time and space, and interaction with supernatural entities (Strassman, 2001).

FUTURE DIRECTIONS IN THE STUDY
OF SPIRITUAL PRACTICES AND EXPERIENCES

The future study of meditative practices, other religious experiences, and experiences of distant intentionality may offer a number of fascinating possibilities. The focus of initial studies will need to be on the specific neuroscientific techniques that will be most useful in the study of such phenomena. Imaging techniques, including PET, SPECT, and MRI, can be evaluated for their capacity to study the neurobiological correlates of meditative practices and spiritual phenomena. Specifically, such neurobiological correlates as cerebral metabolism, blood flow, and neurotransmitter receptor levels can be analyzed. Logistical issues and problems of the various techniques need to be considered to assess which techniques may offer the most appropriate methodology for the study of such experiences. Care should be taken so that confounding variables can be minimized and the possibility of identifying an effect is maximized. Experimental interventions should be simple, well-defined, and distinct from other types of interventions to exclude possible extraneous effects. Interventions that use only one form of activity such as meditation or prayer might be the most appropriate. Interventions requiring a combination of techniques (i.e., combining praying, dancing, and singing) might be too complicated for studying individual components of the intervention and may complicate careful analysis of the effects. Thus, interventions that allow for the simplified study of specific aspects of spiritual experience will have the highest yield in initial experiments. Homogeneity of spiritual interventions also will improve the results obtained from small, preliminary studies. Other variables such as electroencephalography, autonomic activity, and neuroendocrine and immunological markers may also help elucidate the overall interaction between the brain and the body during such states.

Ultimately, scientific methods such as functional brain imaging techniques may offer the best window into exploring how the human brain works during spiritual experiences and how it may be able to interact with the world in complex and remarkable ways.

REFERENCES

Aghajanian, G. K., & Marek, G. J. (1999). Serotonin and hallucinogens. *Neuropsychopharmacology, 21*(2 Suppl), 16S–23S.
Aghajanian, G. K., Sprouse, J., & Rasmussen, K. (1987). Physiology of the midbrain serotonin system. In H. Meltzer (Ed.), *Psychopharmacology: The third generation of progress* (pp. 141–149). New York: Raven Press.

Albin, R., & Greenamyre, J. (1992). Alternative excitotoxic hypotheses. *Neurology*, *42*, 733–738.

Amano, K., Tanikawa, H., Kawamura, H., Iseki, H., Notani, M., Kawabatake, H., et al. (1982). Endorphins and pain relief. *Applied Neurophysiology*, *45*, 123–135.

Andrews, T. J., Halpern, S. D., & Purves, D. (1997). Correlated size variations in human visual cortex, lateral geniculate nucleus, and optic tract. *Journal of Neuroscience*, *17*(8), 2859–2868.

Binder, J. R., Rao, S. M., Hammeke, T. A., Yetkin, F. Z., Jesmanowicz, A., Bandettini, P. A., et al. (1994). Functional magnetic resonance imaging of human auditory cortex. *Annals of Neurology*, *35*, 662–672.

Bucci, D. J., Conley, M., & Gallagher, M. (1999). Thalamic and basal forebrain cholinergic connections of the rat posterior parietal cortex. *Neuroreporting*, *10*(5), 941–945.

Bujatti, M., & Riederer, P. (1976). Serotonin, noradrenaline, dopamine metabolites in transcendental meditation-technique. *Journal of Neural Transmission*, *39*(3), 257–267.

Campbell, C., Weinger, M. B., & Quinn, M. (1995). Alterations in diaphragm EMG activity during opiate-induced respiratory depression. *Respiratory Physiology*, *100*(2), 107–117.

Cheramy, A., Romo, R., & Glowinski. (1987). Role of corticostriatal glutamatergic neurons in the presynaptic control of dopamine release. In M. Sandler, C. Feuerstein, & B. Scatton, (Eds.), *Neurotransmitter Interactions in the Basal Ganglia* (pp. 131–133). New York: Raven Press.

Coker, K. H. (1999). Meditation and prostate cancer: integrating a mind/body intervention with traditional therapies. *Seminars in Urological Oncology*, *17*(2), 111–118.

Davies, E., Keyon, C. J., & Fraser, R. (1985). The role of calcium ions in the mechanism of ACTH stimulation of cortisol synthesis. *Steroids*, *45*, 557.

Diksic, M., & Reba, R. C. (Eds.). (1991). *Radiopharmaceuticals and brain pathology studied with PET and SPECT.* Boca Raton, FL: CRC Press.

Ellison, G. (1995) The N-methyl-D-aspartate antagonists phencyclidine, ketamine and dizocilpine as both behavioral and anatomical models of the dementias. *Brain Research Reviews*, *20*(2), 250–267.

Elias, A. N., Guich, S., & Wilson, A. F. (2000). Ketosis with enhanced GABAergic tone promotes physiological changes in transcendental meditation. *Medical Hypotheses*, *54*(4), 660–662.

Elias, A. N., & Wilson, A. F. (1995). Serum hormonal concentrations following transcendental meditation—potential role of gamma aminobutyric acid. *Medical Hypotheses*, *44*(4), 287–291.

Foote, S. (1987). Extrathalamic modulation of cortical function. *Annual Review of Neuroscience*, *10*, 67–95.

Frost, J. J. (1992). Receptor imaging by positron emission tomography and single-photon emission computed tomography. *Investigative Radiology*, *27*, S54–S58.

Friston, K. J., Frith, C. D., Passingham, R. E., Liddle, P. F., & Frackowiak, R. S. (1992). Motor practice and neurophysiological adaptation in the cerebellum. A positron emission tomography study. *Proceedings of the Royal Society of London, series B*, *248*(1323), 223–228.

Frith, C. D., Friston, K., Liddle, P. F., & Frackowiak, R. S. (1991). Willed action and the prefrontal cortex in man. A study with PET. *Proceedings of the Royal Society of London, series B, 244*(1311), 241–246.

Funke, K., & Eysel, U. T. (1995). Possible enhancement of GABAergic inputs to cat dorsal lateral geniculate relay cells by serotonin. *Neuroreporting, 6*(3), 474–476.

Gatley, S. J., DeGrado, T. R., Kornguth, M. L., & Holden, J. E. (1990). Radiopharmaceuticals for positron emission tomography. Development of new, innovative tracers for measuring the rates of physiologic and biochemical processes. *Acta Radiologica Supplement, 374*, 7–11.

Gellhorn, E., & Kiely, W. F. (1972). Mystical states of consciousness: Neurophysiological and Clinical aspects. *Journal of Nervous Mental Disorders, 154*, 399–405.

Guchhait, R. B. (1976). Biogenesis of 5-methoxy-N,N-dimethyltryptamine in human pineal gland. *Journal of Neurochemistry, 26*(1), 187–190.

Hammeke, T. A., Yetkin, F. Z., Mueller, W. M., Morris, G. L., Haughton, V. M., Rao, S. M., et al. (1994). Functional magnetic resonance imaging of somatosensory stimulation. *Neurosurgery, 35*, 677–681.

Herzog, H., Lele, V. R., Kuwert, T., Langen, K. J., Kops, E. R., & Feinendegen, L. E. (1990–1991). Changed pattern of regional glucose metabolism during Yoga meditative relaxation. *Neuropsychobiology, 23*, 182–187.

Infante, J. R., Peran, F., Martinez, M., Roldan, A., Poyatos, R., Ruiz, C., et al. (1998). ACTH and beta-endorphin in transcendental meditation. *Physiology and Behavior, 64*(3), 311–315.

Infante, J. R., Torres-Avisbal, M., Pinel, P., Vallejo, J. A., Peran, F., Gonzalez, F., et al. (2001). Catecholamine levels in practitioners of the transcendental meditation technique. *Physiology snd Behavior, 72*(1–2), 141–146.

Ingvar, D. H. (1994). The will of the brain: Cerebral correlates of willful acts. *Journal of Theoretical Biology, 171*, 7–12.

Janal, M., Colt, E., Clark, W., & Glusman, M. (1984). Pain sensitivity, mood and plasma endocrine levels in man following long-distance running: Effects of naxalone. *Pain, 19*, 13–25.

Jansen, K. L. R. (1995). Using ketamine to induce the near-death experience: mechanism of action and therapeutic potential. *Yearbook for Ethnomedicine and the Study of Consciousness*[Jahrbuch furr Ethnomedizin und Bewubtseinsforschung], *4*, 55–81.

Jevning, R., Wallace, R. K., & Beidebach, M. (1992). The physiology of meditation: A review. A wakeful hypometabolic integrated response. *Neuroscience Biobehavioral Review, 16*, 415–424.

Jevning, R., Wilson, A. F., & Davidson, J. M. (1978). Adrenocortical activity during meditation. *Hormones and Behavior, 10*(1), 54–60.

Joseph, R. (1990). *Neuropsychology, neuropsychiatry, and behavioral neurology.* New York: Plenum.

Kalin, N., Shelton, S., & Barksdale, C. (1988) Opiate modulation of separation-induced distress in non-human primates. *Brain Research, 440*, 285–292.

Kiss, J., Kocsis, K., Csaki, A., Gorcs, T. J., & Halasz, B. (1997). Metabotropic glutamate receptor in GHRH and beta-endorphin neurons of the hypothalamic arcuate nucleus. *Neuroreporting, 8*(17), 3703–3707.

Kung, H. F. (1991). Overview of radiopharmaceuticals for diagnosis of central nervous disorders. *Critical Review of Clinical Laboratory Science, 28*, 269–286.

Lazar, S. W., Bush, G., Gollub, R. L., Fricchione, G. L., Khalsa, G., & Benson, H. (2000). Functional brain mapping of the relaxation response and meditation. *Neuroreporting, 11*, 1581–1585.

Livesey, J. H., Evans, M. J., Mulligan, R., & Donald, R.A. (2000). Interactions of CRH, AVP and cortisol in the secretion of ACTH from perifused equine anterior pituitary cells: "Permissive" roles for cortisol and CRH. *Endocrine Reviews, 26*(3), 445–463.

Lou, H. C., Kjaer, T. W., Friberg, L., Wildschiodtz, G., Holm, S., & Nowak, M. (1999). A 15O-H2O PET study of meditation and the resting state of normal consciousness. *Human Brain Mapping, 7*, 98–105.

Lynch, J. C. (1980). The functional organization of posterior parietal association cortex. *Behavior Brain Science, 3*, 485–499.

Maziere, B., & Maziere, M. (1991). Positron emission tomography studies of brain receptors. *Fundamental Clinical Pharmacology, 5*, 61–91.

McCarthy, G., Blamire, A. M., Puce, A., Nobre, A. C., Bloch, G., Hyder, F., et al. (1994). Functional magnetic resonance imaging of human prefrontal cortex activation during spatial working memory task. *Proceedings of the National Academy of Sciences of the United States of America, 91*, 8690–8694.

Moller, M. (1992). Fine structure of pinealopetal innervation of the mammalian pineal gland. *Microscopic Research Techniques, 21*, 188–204.

Newberg, A. B., Alavi, A., Baime, M., Pourdehnad, M., Santanna, J., & d'Aquili, E. G. (2001). The measurement of regional cerebral blood flow during the complex cognitive task of meditation: A preliminary SPECT study. *Psychiatry Research: Neuroimaging, 106*, 113–122.

Newberg, A. B., & Iversen J. (2003). The neural basis of the complex mental task of meditation: Neurotransmitter and neurochemical considerations. *Medical Hypothesis, 61*(2), 282–291.

O'Halloran, J. P., Jevning, R., Wilson, A. F., Skowsky, R., Walsh, R. N., & Alexander, C. (1985). Hormonal control in a state of decreased activation: potentiation of arginine vasopressin secretion. *Physiology and Behavior, 35*(4), 591–595.

Olds, M. E., & Forbes, J. L. (1981). The central basis of motivation: intracranial self-stimulation studies. *Annual Review of Psychology, 32*, 523–574.

Pardo, J. V., Fox, P. T., & Raichle, M. E. (1991). Localization of a human system for sustained attention by positron emission tomography. *Nature, 349*, 61–64.

Peng, C. K., Mietus, J. E., Liu, Y., Khalsa, G., Douglas, P. S., Benson, H., et al. (1999). Exaggerated heart rate oscillations during two meditation techniques. *International Journal of Cardiology, 70*, 101–107.

Phelps, M. E., Huhl, D.E., & Mazziotta, J.C. (1981). Metabolic mapping of the brain's response to visual stimulation. Studies in man. *Science, 211*, 1445–1448.

Phelps, M. E., & Mazziota, J. C. (1985). Positron emission tomography. Human brain function and biochemistry. *Science, 228*, 799–809.

Pietrowsky, R., Braun, D., Fehm, H. L., Pauschinger, P., & Born, J. (1991). Vasopressin and oxytocin do not influence early sensory processing but affect mood and activation in man. *Peptides, 12*(6), 1385–1391.

Poletti, C. E., & Sujatanond, M. (1980). Evidence for a second hippocampal efferent pathway to hypothalamus and basal forebrain comparable to fornix system: A unit study in the monkey. *Journal of Neurophysiology, 44,* 514–531.

Rao, S. M., Binder, J. R., Hammeke, T. A., Bandettini, P. A., Bobholz, J. A., Frost, J. A., et al. (1995). Somatotopic mapping of the human primary motor cortex with functional magnetic resonance imaging. *Neurology, 45,* 919–924.

Redding, F. K. (1967). Modification of sensory cortical evoked potentials by hippocampal stimulation. *Electroencephalography and Clinical Neurophysiology, 22,* 74–83.

Reghunandanan, V., Reghunandanan, R., & Mahajan, K. K. (1998). Arginine vasopressin as a neurotransmitter in the brain. *Indian Journal of Experimental Biology, 36*(7), 635–643.

Renaud, L. P. (1996). CNS pathways mediating cardiovascular regulation of vasopressin. *Clinical and Experimental Pharmacology and Physiology, 23*(2), 157–160.

Sergent, J. (1994). Brain-imaging studies of cognitive functions. *Trends in Neuroscience, 17,* 221–227.

Shaji, A. V, & Kulkarni, S. K. (1998). Central nervous system depressant activities of melatonin in rats and mice. *Indian Journal of Experimental Biology, 36*(3), 257–263.

Sim, M. K., & Tsoi, W. F. (1992). The effects of centrally acting drugs on the EEG correlates of meditation. *Biofeedback Self-Regulation, 17,* 215–220.

Strassman, R. J. (2001). *DMT: The spirit molecule.* Rochester: Park Street Press.

Sudsuang, R., Chentanez, V., & Veluvan, K. (1991). Effects of Buddhist meditation on serum cortisol and total protein levels, blood pressure, pulse rate, lung volume an reaction time. *Physiology and Behavior, 50,* 543–548.

Thomas, A. G., Vornov, J. J., Olkowski, J. L., Merion, A. T., & Slusher, B. S. (2000). N-Acetylated alpha-linked acidic dipeptidase converts N-acetylaspartylglutamate from a neuroprotectant to a neurotoxin. *Journal of Pharmacology and Experimental Therapeutics, 295*(1), 16–22.

Tooley, G. A., Armstrong, S. M., Norman, T. R., & Sali, A. (2000). Acute increases in night-time plasma melatonin levels following a period of meditation. *Biological Psychology, 53*(1), 69–78.

Van Bockstaele, E. J., & Aston-Jones, G. (1995). Integration in the ventral medulla and coordination of sympathetic, pain and arousal functions. *Clinical and Experimental Hypertension, 17*(1–2), 153–165.

Van Praag, H., & De Haan, S. (1980). Depression vulnerability and 5-Hydroxytryptophan prophylaxis. *Psychiatric Research, 3,* 75–83.

Wallace, R. K. (1970). Physiological effects of transcendental meditation. *Science, 167,* 1251–1254.

Walton, K. G., Pugh, N. D., Gelderloos, P., & Macrae, P. (1995). Stress reduction and preventing hypertension: Preliminary support for a psychoneuroendocrine mechanism. *Journal of Alternative and Complementary Medicine, 1*(3), 263–283.

Waterhouse, B. D., Moises, H. C., & Woodward, D. J. (1998). Phasic activation of the locus coeruleus enhances responses of primary sensory cortical neurons to peripheral receptive field stimulation. *Brain Research, 790*(1–2), 33–44.

Weingartner, H., Gold, P., Ballenger, J. C., Smallberg, S. A., Summers, R., Rubinow, D. R., et al. (1981). Effects of vasopressin on human memory functions. *Science, 211*(4482), 601–603.

Yadid, G., Zangen, A., Herzberg, U., Nakash, R., & Sagen, J. (2000). Alterations in endogenous brain beta-endorphin release by adrenal medullary transplants in the spinal cord. *Neuropsychopharmacology, 23*(6), 709–716.

Yoshida, M., Sasa, M., & Takaori, S. (1984). Serotonin-mediated inhibition from dorsal raphe nucleus of neurons in dorsal lateral geniculate and thalamic reticular nuclei. *Brain Research, 290,* 95–105.

Ziegler, D. R., Cass, W. A., & Herman, J. P. (1999). Excitatory influence of the locus coeruleus in hypothalamic-pituitary-adrenocortical axis responses to stress. *Journal of Neuroendocrinology, 11*(5), 361–369.

CHAPTER 3

NEUROIMAGING STUDIES OF RELIGIOUS EXPERIENCE: A CRITICAL REVIEW

Nina P. Azari

INTRODUCTION

What makes an experience *religious*, as opposed to *nonreligious?* This question continues to be a challenge in the study of religion (Martin, 1987). One dimension of all human experience is the body, of which the brain is a part. Accordingly, one place to look for a distinctive signature of religious experience—that which makes an experience *religious*—is at the level of the human neurophysiology, the human brain. The role the human brain plays in any experience cannot be assessed without recourse to the human neurosciences. Hence, neuroscience, specifically, studies of the live human brain, may have something important to contribute to the non-neuroscientific literature on the topic of religious experience. The question of interest from a neuroscientific perspective is: "What's going on in the brain when a person reports having a religious experience?"

In this chapter, I offer a critical review of the functional neuroimaging studies that have investigated religious experience (broadly conceived).[1] The purpose of this review is to explore the extent to which neuroimaging studies may provide new insight into the nature and structure of religious experience.

Toward that end, first I will describe the human brain functional imaging techniques that have been used for such studies. Second, I consider the interpretive limits of any neuroimaging study (regardless of the topic of inquiry) and explore how they apply in the case of religious experience. Third, I will describe each study (i.e., methods, results, conclusions) and offer a critical examination of the assumptions associated with those studies (especially as regards the concepts "religious" and "experience"). Finally, I will discuss how the recent neuroimaging studies, taken together, stand in relation to current non-neuroscientific theorizing about the nature and structure of religious experience. I conclude the chapter by considering prospects for future research.

FUNCTIONAL NEUROIMAGING TECHNIQUES

The most recent and direct way to study the living human brain is with functional imaging technologies, such as single photon computed emission tomography (SPECT), positron emission tomography (PET), and functional magnetic resonance imaging (fMRI). These techniques are referred to as functional imaging methods because they afford an assessment of brain *activity* (i.e., function), not just *structure*—as opposed to MRI and CT (computerized tomography), both of which are structural imaging techniques. Thus, SPECT, PET, and fMRI can be used to examine what is going on in the brain when a person is engaged in doing something (i.e., performing a task, or just lying still). Functional neuroimaging techniques have made it possible, for the first time, to study brain function in normal, living humans, so afford an opportunity to investigate phenomena considered unique to human beings, more specifically, "higher-order" cognitive functions.[2]

Human brain functional imaging techniques all rely on the fact that the brain (specifically, neural tissue, tissue in which there are brain cells, or neurons) uses energy when it is working, and energy utilization requires both glucose (a simple sugar) and oxygen consumption.

Broadly speaking, there are two approaches to analyzing functional imaging data. On one approach (so-called categorical analysis), images acquired for one condition (e.g., control, baseline, or rest condition) are subtracted from those for another condition (e.g., experimental or activation condition). The resulting subtraction image is thought to provide information about discrete areas of salient brain activity that are greater in one condition as compared to another. On another approach (so-called network-type analysis), information is obtained not only about areas of task-related brain activity increases, but also about areas that participate in this function but do not increase their metabolic or blood flow level as compared with the respective control state. It is thought that these areas may be as important as the areas that show an enhanced metabolic or blood flow levels correlated with mental states (McIntosh, 2000).

While PET, SPECT, and fMRI all can measure indirect correlates of neuronal activity in the live human brain, the principles of measuring brain energy utilization are different for each imaging technique.

PET and SPECT

Similarities: PET can be used to measure rates of glucose or oxygen metabolism (called PET-rCMR$_{glc}$), or—as can SPECT—regional cerebral blood flow (called PET-rCBF). All SPECT and PET studies require the use of radioactive tracers or isotopes (such as hexamethyl propyleneamine oxamine [^{99m}Tc-HMPAO] in the case of SPECT; fluorine-18-deoxyglucose, in the case of PET-rCMR$_{glc}$; or oxygen-15-labeled [^{15}O-] water or butanol, in the case of PET-CBF). Correspondingly, SPECT and PET studies are considered invasive in the sense that the subject is injected with a small amount of the radiotracer. The radiotracers that are used for these two functional neuroimaging techniques work like substances that naturally occur in the brain (e.g., water or glucose [a simple sugar]). That is, they must be able to travel efficiently from peripheral organs (i.e., the injection site, such as the arm) into the brain (cross the so-called blood-brain barrier), and they must be able follow the path of blood to the brain. Tracers labeled with the positron-emitting isotopes, such as [^{15}O], allow one to estimate rCBF in quantitatively (Herzog et al., 1996), or semi-quantitatively (Friston et al., 1994; Fox & Raichle, 1984).

Techniques such as SPECT or PET rely on the emission of positrons or photons of light (what radioactive tracers emit). In the case of PET, for example, when the brain is active, positrons are emitted in the brain areas that are using energy, and the positrons are localized in the brain with the use of external detectors surrounding the experimental subject's head. A special camera detects the emitted photons, and via subsequent computer processing steps, the pictures or images acquired are converted into three-dimensional representations of the brain (Raichle, 1998).

Differences: Notable differences between SPECT and PET include how long the radiotracer stays in the brain (longer for SPECT) and how accurately one can locate the areas of activation—referred to as spatial resolution (PET has better spatial resolution). Because the radiotracers used in SPECT studies are long-lived, the subject can be injected with the tracer and engage in the task/state that is being studied outside of the scanner. The actual brain scan is performed later. In contrast, since the radiotracers used in PET studies stay in the brain for less than 2 minutes, the subject must be in the scanner when injected with the tracer, and while engaging in the task/state of interest.

fMRI

For fMRI studies, changes in blood oxygenation level-dependent (BOLD) contrast is used as an indirect marker of cerebral blood flow changes (Calamante, Thomas, Pell, Wiersma, & Turner, 1999). Due to the excess of blood flow increase relative to oxygen consumption in activated brain areas, the amount of diamagnetic oxygenated blood becomes locally enhanced. Thus, the paramagnetic deoxy-haemoglobin decreases, which results in a signal increase in the fMRI images. In proportion to the fast-evolving hemodynamics, this signal builds up in about 8 seconds, which can be followed with what are known as fast MR sequences, including echo-planar imaging (Bandettini et al., 1997; Frahm, Bruhn, Merboldt, & Hänicke, 1992; Kleinschmidt, Büchel, Zeki, & Frackowiak, 1998).

While image evaluation of PET-rCBF capitalizes on identifying significant changes that persist in the steady-state during the scanning interval compared to the control steady-state, fMRI exploits the consistency of activation-related signal changes over a couple of subsequent activation vs. control cycles. Importantly, this means that fMRI does not provide information for a single activation or nonactivation state as such (e.g., for a rest state) but, rather, provides information in changes in blood flow from one state to another (e.g., activation vs. control/baseline).

An fMRI scanner is essentially a large magnet in the form of a tunnel, inside of which is a strong magnetic field. For a typical fMRI investigation, subjects are put into the fMRI scanner tunnel. Accordingly, subjects must be free of any metal objects (e.g., watches, keys, coins, credit cards) before being scanned with fMRI.

Studies that use fMRI do not involve the use of radioactive tracers. In this regard, fMRI is a relatively noninvasive technique as compared to PET and SPECT. However, fMRI scanning involves subjecting the study participant to a loud knocking sound within the scanner, which is a consequence of how fMRI detects changes in brain function. That is, the technique of fMRI involves detection of rapid changes of magnetic fields, which allows the magnet to pick up signals from the brain. These changes in the magnetic field produce a moderately loud metallic-like noise for the individual who is in the MRI scanner. Thus, for acoustic protection, subjects are usually provided ear pads or plugs.

fMRI vs. PET and SPECT

The fact that fMRI does not require the use of radiotracers means that, in principle, one can perform an unlimited number of scans on the same subject (i.e., have the subject perform multiple tasks repeatedly). Of course, this is not practicable. Nonetheless, the relative noninvasiveness of fMRI as compared to PET and SPECT affords study designs that render greater statistical power (i.e., repeated measurements on a single subject). Further, subject recruitment is usually easier for fMRI studies. Thus, the sample size for fMRI studies is usually larger, another statistical advantage. As already noted, unlike PET, fMRI cannot provide information on what's going on in a subject's brain when the subject is not engaged in any specific task (i.e., during the so-called rest state). As explained, this is because fMRI measures *changes* in BOLD effects (i.e., changes in brain function between different activation conditions). Finally, fMRI, but not PET and SPECT, now can provide information about the time-course of information processing in the brain (i.e., fMRI has better temporal resolution than PET and SPECT).

Functional imaging techniques—most especially PET and fMRI—have been used to investigate a wide variety of human mental phenomena (e.g., mental imagery, arithmetic, abstract problem solving, and memory recall [Binkofski et al. 2000; Cabeza et al. 1997; Dehaene, Spelke, Pinel, Stanescu, Tsivkin, 1999; Duncan et al. 2000; Kosslyn, Behrmann, Jeannerod, 1995]). Now, there are reports on the neural correlates of two different kinds of religious experience (Azari et al., 2001a, 2001b; Newberg et al., 2001; Newberg, Pourdehnad, Alavi, & d'Aquili, 2003).

FUNCTIONAL NEUROIMAGING STUDIES OF RELIGIOUS EXPERIENCE

Christian

Methods

Azari et al. (2001b) used PET-CBF to study a group of self-identified religious subjects, who were Protestant Christians, and a group of control subjects, who were self-identified as nonreligious. Specifically, the subjects in that study were 12 normal, healthy adults aged 28+/−5 years (mean +/− standard deviation). All were right-handed, native German speakers. Six subjects (2 women, 4 men) were self-identified as religious and were members of a Christian Free Evangelical Fundamentalist Community. They were teachers at a private Christian secondary school and had been selected for their teaching posts on the basis of rigorous faith-based criteria. Each of them reported having had a documented conversion experience and interpreted biblical text literally as the word of God. According to those religious subjects, the first verse of Psalm 23 (i.e., The Lord is my shepherd . . .) was essential for each to get into and sustain a religious state, defined as "being in a personal relationship with God as Jesus Christ." Six subjects (2 women, 4 men) were self-identified as nonreligious and were students at the University of Duesseldorf, studying various subjects in the natural sciences. For those subjects, religion did not play any significant role in their daily life, and, in fact, they reported feeling somewhat indifferent to religious matters (i.e., none was a committed atheist, none felt strongly about any particular set of religious beliefs or practices). The two groups were matched on age, gender, and level of education.

Azari et al. employed a self-induction functional neuroimaging paradigm, which involved asking the subjects to induce in themselves a religious state (as they understood that to mean) with the help of biblical text that the religious subjects themselves suggested would be most effective, namely, Psalm 23.

Subjects were PET-scanned in six conditions (occurring in a different order for each subject).[3] For each scan, the subjects were asked to induce in themselves the requisite target state, with the help of particular textual material (i.e., cues). Directly before and after each scan, the felt-quality of each target state was assessed objectively, using a standardized questionnaire (called the Positive Affect Negative Affect Scale, or PANAS; Watson, Clark, & Tellegren, 1988). In addition, after each PET scanning session, the subjects were asked to assess the extent to which each felt he/she had attained the requisite target state (i.e., religious, happy, neutral; these self-assessment ratings ranged on a scale of 0–10 [10 max]). The scanning conditions were as follows: (1) religious-read, (2) religious-recite, (3) happy-read, (4) happy recite, (5) neutral-read, (6) rest. The textual cues used for the different task conditions were: religious— the first verse of biblical Psalm 23; happy—a well-known German children's nursery rhyme; and neutral—instructions on using a phone card, taken from the Duesseldorf, Germany telephone book. Texts were matched on length, and the rhyme was not associated with music. All subjects were able to recite from memory both the religious and happy texts at the time of the PET scanning. In the read conditions, the texts were presented on a screen that was visible to the subjects as they lay on the scanner bed. In the recite conditions, the subjects had their eyes covered and recited the textual material silently to themselves. In the rest condition, they lay quietly with their eyes covered.[4]

Results

According to their self-assessment ratings, only the religious subjects achieved the religious state (while reciting the religious text). These Christian subjects described their personal religious experiences as being in a close interpersonal relationship with God as Jesus Christ. The functional brain imaging results during their religious state showed a brain activation pattern that corresponded to their individual self-perspectives.

The PET images acquired in the religious subjects in the religious state showed peak blood flow activation in the right dorsolateral prefrontal cortex as compared to the nonreligious subjects. This activation pattern was observed also in contrast to the happy state and the neutral read condition. Other activations in the religious state were the dorsomedial frontal cortex (or, pre-SMA) and a posterior parietal area identified as the right precuneus. Increased blood flow in the left amygdala (i.e., a limbic structure) was observed only for the happy emotion state; no significant changes in blood flow involving limbic structures was evident for the religious state.

To further explore the distinctiveness of religious experience, a network-type analysis was recently applied to the PET-CBF data of the Christian religious experience and the happy emotion (Azari, Missimer, & Seitz, 2005).[5] The results indicated that the religious experience and the happy emotion were mediated by distinctive neural patterns, involving the areas identified in the prior categorical analysis of the PET data.

Conclusions

Neuroscientific studies different from that of Azari et al. have shown that areas that were associated with the Christian religious experience participate in complex cognitive processes. Specifically, the dorsolateral prefrontal cortex has been shown to play a central role inferential reasoning and belief (Iacaboni, 2000) and seems also to be critical for managing memories stored in posterior areas of the brain, as well as for the conscious monitoring of thought (Duncan et al., 2000; Fletcher, Shallice, Frith, Frackowiak, & Dolan, 1998; McIntosh, 1999). Although little as yet is known about the function of the pre-SMA, the most current understanding is that it is involved in controlling and sustaining a readiness to act based on the current contents of working memory (Deiber et al., 1991; Tanji & Mushiake, 1996). The precuneus has been shown (in independent neuroimaging studies) to play a key role in visual memory, that is, storing memories in the form of visual images or representations (Fletcher et al., 1995).

On this basis, the investigators proposed that religious experience (at least one kind) may be a cognitively structured phenomenon, for which thoughts-beliefs play a central role. This proposal challenges an alternative, highly popularized (e.g., Alper, 2001) view of religious experience, according to which religious experience is marked by (dysfunctional) brain activity involving limbic structures, that is, the so-called limbic marker hypothesis of religious experience (Joseph, 2001).[6]

In addition, the investigators suggested that the network analysis findings not only support the view that religious experience may be cognitively structured, but also further the conviction that religious experience and emotion, while necessarily related (Azari & Birnbacher, 2004), are not exactly the same thing (Dewey, 1969; James, 1902). The authors concluded that network analysis also suggested something *in common* between religious and nonreligious emotion experiences, namely, an essential cognitivity. That is, the investigators called attention to the fact that the religious experience and the emotion were distinguishable in virtue of *a single neural network* that evidenced *two distinctive forms* of expression—one corresponding to the religious experience, the other corresponding to the happy emotion—and the brain structures that were important to that single neural network (expressed differentially for the religious experience and happy emotion) have been shown to participate in complex cognitive functions. In this way, the network analysis indicated that *both* religious experience *and* emotion may be cognitively structured.[7]

Buddhist

Methods

In another recent neuroimaging investigation, Newberg et al. (2001, 2003) used SPECT to study a Tibetan Buddhist meditation experience. They, like Azari et al., employed a self-induction neuroimaging paradigm in which they asked their subjects—four men and four women, self-described as experienced, practicing Tibetan Buddhist meditators—to meditate and try to achieve the most intense state of their meditative experience. Included in this study were nine nonmeditator controls subjects. The Buddhist participants were allowed to use incense (i.e., cues) to help them achieve the peak meditative state. Due to the special characteristics of SPECT scanning (discussed above), the subjects could meditate outside the scanner when the SPECT blood flow tracer was injected. The tracer accumulation in the brain reflected the activation during meditation and could be scanned thereafter. In the control condition the subjects were at rest.

Results

Newberg et al. (2001) reported brain activations in the cingulate cortex, superior frontal cortex, dorsolateral prefrontal cortex, orbitofrontal cortex, precuneus, thalamus, and cerebellum during the peak meditative state in the Buddhist subjects. In addition, the investigators found slightly decreased blood flow in the superior parietal cortex. This decrease was small in magnitude and not significant but correlated with the blood flow increase observed in dorsolateral prefrontal cortex. No blood flow changes in limbic structures were observed during the religious experience of the Buddhist meditators.

Conclusions

Similar to the findings from the study by Azari et al. (2001b), the brain structures that showed salient changes in blood flow during the Buddhist religious experience play a role in complex cognitive processes. Newberg et al. (2001) considered it likely that the negative correlation between prefrontal cortex and superior parietal cortex was of special significance for the Buddhist meditative experience they were investigating. They speculated that the sense of unity (one's own body with the external world) that is commonly reported for such peak meditative experiences may be mediated by relative decreased brain activity in superior parietal cortex, an areas thought to be important for creating mental representations of bodily-self orientation in space.

Summary and Assumptions

Taken together, the neuroimaging results from two very different kinds of religious experience suggest that complex cognitive processes are central to at least some kinds of religious experience. Further, the results of the recent network analysis of the PET data suggest that at least one kind of religious experience is distinguishable from at least one kind of emotion.

At this point it is important to note how the two studies described above conceptualized the terms "religious" and "experience," for doing so will serve to introduce some of the limitations inherent to any neuroimaging study, which will be discussed in greater detail below.

First, the term "experience" was conceptualized in both studies as a short-lived event. However, experience also can be conceptualized as occurring over a lifetime. Correspondingly, a religious experience could refer to one's entire life span.

Second, in so far as both studies employed a self-induction paradigm, they both assumed that an experience is "religious" if the subject says it is. Accordingly, a religious experience is an experience that is consciously available to the subject, has reportable content, and can be self-induced. Clearly, there are religious experiences that do not meet these criteria (e.g., ineffable experiences, conversion experiences). Third, studies also assumed that religious experience is a normal, healthy phenomenon (i.e., normal, healthy people have them). There are cases, however, when people who are unwell report intense religious experiences.[8] Note, because both studies assume that religious experience is a normal phenomenon, the results of neither study can be used to establish that religious experiences are *in fact* normal, healthy phenomena. Finally, in the Azari et al. (2001b) study, it was assumed that religious experience is accessible to nonexperts.

These assumptions limit interpretations of the neuroimaging data obtained for the neuroimaging studies of religious experience described in this chapter. It turns out that there are interpretive limits for *any* functional neuroimaging study regardless of the topic of inquiry. Gaining clarity on such limits will make the positive contributions that functional neuroimaging can make on the topic of religious experience all the more evident.

INTERPRETATIVE LIMITS

First, the strongest statements that can be made about the results from brain imaging studies are correlational, not causal.[9] Functional neuroimaging techniques measure brain activity and mental activity concurrently; and, this amounts to detecting a correlation between brain events (i.e., brain activity) and mind events. Correspondingly, one cannot appeal directly to neuroimaging data to establish the origins (or, causal root) of mental phenomena as such (i.e., determine why mental events occur or exists *at all*). Thus, the results of functional imaging studies of religious experience cannot properly be used to fund causal explanations for religious experience (i.e., why people have them at all), let alone explanations for religion (why there is religion at all; or, what the origins of religion are).

Second, functional neuroimaging data are not interpreted in terms of identifying special spots in the brain for particular mental processes or phenomena (see especially, McIntosh, 2000). Thus, it would be inappropriate to conclude, on the basis of functional imaging studies of religious experience, that there is a religious- or God-spot in the brain (versus, e.g., Alper, 2001).

Third, the proper object of study in functional imaging investigations is the human being. Such studies, then, can legitimately make statements only about the human experience or perception, not about the specific objects experienced or perceived (or about any perceived relationship therewith).[10] Thus, in the PET study of the Christian religious experience, for example, just because the brain activity patterns of those Christians corroborated their belief that they were in a personal relationship with God (as Jesus Christ), this does not lead to the conclusion that the brain imaging findings prove that these Christians were *in fact* in such a relationship. Along the same lines, functional imaging studies cannot prove the *necessity* of any object of experience, or of any belief. In the PET study of the Christian religious experience, then, the functional imaging results cannot speak to the necessity of God, of a belief in God, or of the religious experiences of the Christian subjects (here, a personal interaction with God). In fact, the answer to the question of God's necessity depends on one's understanding of the nature of God in the first place. Does God change? Is God conditioned by human experience? Or is God unconditioned? Those questions call for conceptual analyses—or, perhaps, for recourse to faith.[11] Functional neuroimaging studies of religious experience have no contribution to make to that discussion.[12]

Finally, it is assumed for any functional neuroimaging studies that both brain events and mental events exist (i.e., both are real). Neuroimaging data, therefore, cannot be used to argue for the reality of mental phenomena. In other words, that there are observed neural correlates of a given mental phenomenon cannot be taken as proof of the existence or reality of that mental event. Thus, functional imaging studies of religious experience cannot establish the reality of such experiences (versus, e.g., Newberg & d'Aquili, 2001).[13] In line with what has just been said, functional imaging studies cannot address the truth or falsity of mental states (e.g., thought-belief); the question, in fact, is never even raised in such studies.[14] Thus, the PET and SPECT studies described in this chapter cannot be used to adjudicate between the religious beliefs held by Christian and those held by Buddhists.

With these interpretive limits in mind, we can now ask what the functional imaging findings reviewed in this chapter have to say about the nature and structure of religious experience.

NATURE AND STRUCTURE OF RELIGIOUS EXPERIENCE: CONTRIBUTIONS FROM FUNCTIONAL NEUROIMAGING

Taken together, the recent human brain functional findings reviewed in this chapter provide support for the view (current among scholars of religion) that religious experience is a cognitively structured phenomenon for which thoughts and beliefs are central (Dupre, 1998; Gelphi, 1994; Henry, 1991; McIntosh, 1995; Proudfoot, 1985; Schlitt, 2001; Spilka, Brown, & Cassidy, 1992; Spilka, Ladd, McIntosh, & Milmoe, 1996; Spilka & McIntosh, 1995; Spilka, Shaver, & Kirkpatrick, 1985). Moreover, the findings suggested that the cognitivity of religious experience may apply across at least two, quite different religious traditions—Buddhist and Christian. In this way, recent functional neuroimaging studies of religious experience challenge an alternative, highly popularized view that religious experience is entirely a matter of a pre-cognitive, arousal-type brain response localized to the limbic system. Instead, the studies reviewed in this chapter lead to the conclusion that what makes an experience *religious* as opposed to *nonreligious* has to do with complex cognitive factors. Further, the results of the recent network analysis (described above) imply that the distinctiveness of religious experience—what makes an experience religious versus nonreligious—has to do with a specific kind of cognitivity.

Relational Cognitivity and Religious Experience

The prefrontal cortex—a structure whose connectivity patterns were associated with the religious experience—is most recently understood to play an especially important role in particular kinds of social-relational cognitive processes (e.g., mentalizing or theory of mind) (Adolphs, 2003a, 2003b). Specifically, findings from recent functional imaging studies suggest that widespread connections involving especially the prefrontal and medial-frontal cortex are critical for reasoning processes that are necessary for social interactions, namely, those that involve mentalizing—that is, attributing independent mental states to oneself and others; reflecting on one's own inner states and reading another's mind (Calarge, Andreasen, & O'Leary, 2003; Fletcher et al., 1995; Goel, Grafman, Sadato, & Hallett, 1995; Happe, 2003; Kampe, Frith, & Frith, 2003; Siegal & Varley, 2002; Vogeley et al., 2001); agency detection (Blakemore et al., 2003); intentional (vs. incidental) self-processing (Kirchner et al., 2002); decision-making in social context (Sanfey, Rilling, Aronson, Nystrom, & Cohen, 2003); and complex emotions such as empathy and sympathy (Decety & Chaminade, 2003; Wicker, Perrett, Baron-Cohen, & Decety, 2003).

As already noted, the Christian religious subjects in the PET study described their individual religious experiences in terms of an inter-personal relationship with God (in the person Jesus Christ). In other words, the cognitivity that played into the Christian religious experience for those religious subjects seemed to have been structured in terms of a perceived social *relationship*. Also mentioned above, the authors of the SPECT study of the Buddhist meditation experience concluded that the brain areas most important to mediating that experience were those that mediate perceived changes in the orientation of the body/self in space (Newberg et al., 2001). This interpretation corresponded to the descriptions of such experiences within the Buddhist tradition relevant to that SPECT study, that is, a perceived change in the *relation* between the experient's body/self and the rest of space.

These observations, taken together, provide neuroscientific support for the notion, proposed much earlier by scholars of religion, that religious-*ness* of an experience is more a matter of the how or quality of the experience, than of the what or presumed object experienced (e.g., Dewey, 1934). This would imply that an experience is religious because of a particular kind of perceived relationship and not in virtue of some specific perceptual object as such (e.g., God). On this interpretation, God *as such* (or as an object) would not be what a Christian religious experience, for example, is about in the first place; God *as such* (or any other presumed object) is not what makes the experience specifically religious (e.g., Tillich, 1951). Rather, a perceived *relationship with*, for example, God would be what makes that experience religious (for a Christian) as opposed to nonreligious.

Cross-cultural Similarities and Differences

Recent functional neuroimaging findings on religious experience may point to a possible cross-cultural invariance of religious experience, namely, an essential relational cognitivity. Correspondingly, what may be common across religious traditions is a cognitivity that has to do with perceived rela-tionality. This, then, would suggest that there is a universal factor that runs across a wide variety of experiences, all of which may belong to a broader family called religious experience. At the same time, cross-cultural differences in religious experience may show up in terms of different kinds of relational cognitivity (and distinctive neural networks thereof), rather than in terms of different kinds of perceived objects of experience.

PROSPECTS FOR FUTURE RESEARCH

Varieties of Religious Experience

What has emerged from recent neuroimaging studies so far is that the neurophysiological correlates of religious experience seem to involve cognitive brain structures and that such a fundamentally cognitive pattern seems to apply across at least two different and diverse kinds of religious experience (Christian and Buddhist). Furthermore, given the conclusions drawn in this chapter, religious experience seems to involve a particular kind of cognitivity, namely, that having to do with a perceived relationality, but that relational cognitivity does not seem to be monolithic in terms of correlated neural activation patterns. That is, different kinds of perceived relationality (e.g., inter-personal, orientation of body in space) seem to have different patterns of correlated neural activity. More neuroscientific studies along the lines of what has already been done on varieties of religious experience itself are needed to see if the results obtained so far will have any significant power as regards broader generalizations.

Religious Versus Nonreligious Experiences

So far, brain imaging findings suggest that the neural expression of at least one kind of Christian religious experience seems to be different to that of at least one kind of nonreligious emotion experience, a happy emotion. At the same time, that particular religious experience showed similarities with that particular emotion experience in the sense that both phenomena had neural correlates that involved brain areas that can participate in higher-order cognitive processes and behaviors, even as the extent of activation of those cognitive brain structures was different between the religious and emotion states. Clearly, there need to be more neuroscientific studies comparing religious and nonreligious experiences (e.g., different kinds of emotion). There are, of course, many nonreligious experiences, besides commonly characterized emotions, that have yet to be explored neuroscientifically on their own merits, let alone being compared and contrasted with religious experience (e.g., aesthetic experiences, such as listening to a favorite piece of music, viewing a particular painting, or listening to/reading poetry). How would these kinds of neural patterns compare to those correlated with different kinds of religious experience? Alternatively, there are phenomena that appear to have something in common with religious phenomena on a seemingly different level, namely, the level of feelings of conviction. So, one could ask, how would the neural correlates of, for example, feelings of nationalism-patriotism or political affiliation compare to those of feelings that go with particular kinds of religious conviction?

Neural Correlates of Relational Cognitivity

There is much work to be done also in terms of describing the neurophysiology of relational cognitivity. That is, mapping the neural bases of complex kinds of relational cognitivity (e.g., the neural correlates and functional connectivity patterns of different kinds of perceived causal relations) may be critical for gaining further insight into the neural bases of religious experience. The results of such studies, taken together with results of new neuroscientific studies of different kinds of religious and nonreligious experience, may provide new insight into cross-cultural similarities and differences in the embodied nature of the cognitivity of religious experience, as well as new insight into similarities and differences between religious and nonreligious phenomena. For example, one may conceive of different kinds of inter-personal relationality that may or may not map to different neural patterns. In the case of the neuroimaging study of the Christian religious experience, the perceived "other" with whom the Christian subjects reported experiencing a close relation was God (an objectively nonobservable being) personified as Jesus Christ. Hence, the character of that relationality was perceived as inter-personal. What kind of neural pattern might correlate with a perceived inter-personal relation with an objectively observable other not objectively a person, for example, experiencing a close relation with the family dog? Interestingly, there is some preliminary evidence to suggest that there is a common neural network involved in the recognition of beloved familiar faces, regardless of species (Shinozaki, Hanakawa, & Fukuyama, 2005). Ultimately, one may be able to describe varieties of perceived relationality in terms of varieties of correlated neural patterns and to identify correspondences between those neural patterns and varieties of religious and nonreligious experiences.

Neuroplasticity and Religious Experience

Finally, the topic of neuroplasticity—the capacity of the brain to change (Azari & Seitz, 2000)—may be of special relevance to the study of religious experience, specifically, types of conversion experiences (Richardson, 1985) or a "falling into" religion, which is described in terms of some kind of change (sudden or gradual). Might there be corresponding changes at the neural level? Similarly, might different kinds of apostasy (Bromley, 1988)— "falling out of" religion—map to different neural patterns? No doubt, such studies will be especially challenging for the imaging data would have to capture the critical switch (i.e., to or from religion) involved in such experiences.

NOTES

1. The adjective "religious" can classify an experience in terms of its subject matter (i.e., its contents), or in terms of a judgment made by the experient regarding the religious significance of the experience (Martin, 1987; Smith, 1995). The same can be said of two other, closely related terms: "spiritual" and "mystical." While the non-neuroscientific literature in study of religion has highlighted important differences among the terms religious, spiritual, and mystical (Hood, 2003; Katz, 1977; McGinn, 1991; Pargament, 1999; Zinnbauer et al., 1997), the neuroscientific literature tends to use these adjectives interchangeably. I do not include in this review studies that do not at all refer to the phenomenon under investigation as religious (e.g., studies of meditation, with no reference to the term religious [i.e., Herzog et al., 1990; Lazar et al., 2000; Lou et al., 1999]).

2. In contrast to electroencephalography (EEG) and magnetoencephalography (MEG), the techniques of PET, SPECT, and fMRI do not assess brain electrical activity directly, but, rather, they assess activity-related changes in cerebral hemodynamics. In addition to activation studies, these techniques also can be used to investigate neuroreceptor and neurotransmitter systems in the live human brain.

3. The neuroimaging (PET-rCBF) data were acquired with a 24-ring ECAT EXACT-HR camera. Resolution 4mm in-plane, 9mm FWHM, slice distance 2.4 mm.

4. For each scan, 555 MBq of ^{15}O butanol were injected into the right brachial vein, flushed with saline. PET scanning began at the moment of the injection, and lasted for 60 sec. The 40 sec of dynamically recorded head uptake were used for calculation of the rCBF data. PET images slices were reconstructed using a Hanning filter to an effective image resolution of 9mm (FWHM) with slice distance of 2.425 mm (see also, Duncan et al., 2000; Herzog, Seitz, Tellmann, & Müller-Gärtner, 1996).

5. There is a long tradition in religious and theological studies of trying to elucidate what makes an experience distinctly religious—as opposed to nonreligious—by comparing religious experience to, or analyzing it in terms of, emotion (Dewey 1969; James 1902; Martin 1987; Smart 1997; Smith 1995).

6. The limbic marker hypothesis maintains that limbic activity is *necessary* for (any and all) religious experience. Correspondingly, there have been suggestions that direct stimulation (electrically or magnetically) of the limbic system will artificially generate a religious experience (Persinger, 1983), and that removing limbic structures will render someone incapable of having religious experiences (Ramachandra & Blakeslee, 1998). These suggestions have furthered the notion—inherent to the limbic marker hypothesis—that what makes an experience religious, as opposed to nonreligious, has to do with a pre-cognitive, automatic-type brain response in the limbic system. There has been considerable evidence cited against this hypothesis (Tucker, Novelly, & Walker, 1987), and, most serious scholars of religion—in particular, those concerned with the neurophysiological processes of religious phenomena—do not endorse this view of religious experience (Austin, 1998; Glassman, 2002; Hood, Spilko, Hunsberger, & Gorsuch, 1996;

McNamara, 2002; Peterson, 2001, 2002; Teske, 2001). Nonetheless, the limbic marker hypothesis of religious experience persists.

7. This finding fits well with current theorizations on emotion, all of which conceptualize emotion as essentially cognitive (Ben Ze'ev, 2000; Damasio, 1999, 2003; Eich, Kihlstrom, Bower, Forgas, & Niedenthal, 2000; LeDoux, 2000; Nussbaum, 2001; Ochsner & Barrett, 2001; Rolls, 2001; Scherer, Schorr, & Johnstone, 2001). Moreover, the results suggest that emotion may play a role in religious experience at a complex cognitive level, and not necessarily (if at all) at the level of a basic arousal response or pre-cognitive feeling (Azari & Birnbacher, 2004).

8. An opposite view of religious experience (i.e., that it is abnormal) is associated with studies using particular patient populations (i.e., TLE, schizophrenia [cf., Bear, 1979; Bear & Fedio, 1977; Bear, Levin, Blumer, Chetham, & Ryder, 1982; Dewhurst & Beard, 1970; Puri, Lekh, Nijran, Bagary, & Richardson, 2001; Ramachandran & Blakeslee, 1998; Stifler, Greer, Sneck, & Dovenmuehle, 1993]), as well as those using healthy volunteers (Persinger, 1983, 1984). On this view, the neurophysiological basis of religious phenomena is fundamentally a matter of an abnormal brain state, localized to the limbic system (Persigner, 1983, 1987).

9. The word "cause" can take many meanings (Hulswitt, 2002). Here, I use the term to refer to the most common understanding of cause, especially as it has been applied in the natural sciences, namely, efficient cause. This interpretive limitation is a consequence of a foundational assumption that is made for any functional brain imaging study, namely, that mental events emerge from brain events—the character of that emergence, however, is left unspecified.

10. For example, one cannot prove or disprove that there is *in fact* a bear out there, simply by looking at the neural activity of a person's brain when that person reports having an experience of, or perceiving, a bear. All one can do is conclude that the observed brain activity corresponds to a person's conviction that what he or she perceived was something he or she took to be a bear.

11. What about the necessity of *belief in God*—regardless of the truth of such belief (i.e., of whether God exists or not)? As explained above, the brain areas that have so far been involved in religious experience can serve a variety of cognitive functions. Thus, there is as yet no neuroscientific evidence to support the claim that such activation patterns *must* involve belief *in God*. Further, claiming that the neuroimaging findings can establish the necessity of religious belief (e.g., in God) is based on reducing such belief to something evolutionarily useful. There may not be a necessary evolutionary function for religious belief, specifically (Boyer, 1994).

12. In effect, what this means is that results from functional neuroimaging studies of religious experience do not reduce away religious belief, religion, or God. That being said, there is another kind of reductionism that may pose a challenge to theology, namely, that of the reduction of traditional theological concepts to cognitive neuroscientific ones. That is, one can talk about religious experience in traditional cognitive neuroscientific terms. Does this mean that neuroscience has reduced religious experience, not to brain stuff, but to a collection ordinary, everyday cognitive functions? If cognitive functions and capacities that are traditionally attributed to the soul—for example, emotion, rationality, morality—are now described neuroscientifically, what does this imply for the concept of soul?

13. Further, a claim that neuroimaging studies of religious experience can establish the reality of such experiences *just because* there are observed (i.e., real) neural correlates thereof is equally untenable. For, it is already assumed that for *any* given mental event, there will be *some kind of* brain correlate/event (i.e., in keeping with current thought, the human neurosciences assume that all human experiences are embodied). In fact, it is difficult to conceive of a functional neuroimaging study, the results of which could support the conclusion that there simply *are* no brain correlates for mental phenomenon X, say.

14. On a pragmatic understanding of truth, the truth of a thought-belief, for example, is determined by the (long term) consequences of holding that thought or belief (cf., James, 1902). An inquiry into mental phenomena using functional neuroimaging techniques (currently available today) is constrained to talk about mental phenomena in terms of brain activity that happens (begins and ends) within a relatively short window of time. Functional neuroimaging studies cannot consider the pragmatic consequences of what is observed in the brain for any given mental phenomenon.

REFERENCES

Adolphs, R. (2003a). Cognitive neuroscience of human social behavior. *Nature Reviews Neuroscience, 4,* 165–178.

Adolphs, R. (2003b). Investigating the cognitive neuroscience of social behavior. *Neuropsychologia, 41,* 119–126.

Alper, M. (2001). *The 'God' part of the brain: A scientific interpretation of human spirituality and God.* New York: Rogue Press.

Austin, J. H. (1998). *Zen and the brain.* Boston: MIT Press.

Azari, N. P., & Birnbacher, D. (2004). The relation between emotion and religious experience: An interdisciplinary inquiry. *Zygon, 43*(9), 901–918.

Azari, N. P., Missimer, J., & Seitz, R. J. (2005). Religious experience and emotion: Evidence for distinctive cognitive neural patterns. *International Journal for the Psychology of Religion, 15*(4), 263–281.

Azari, N. P., Nickel, J. P., Wunderlich, G., Niedeggen, M., Hefter, H., Tellmann, L., et al. (2001a). Neural circuitry of religious experience. In *Proceedings of the 31st Annual Meeting of the Society for Neuroscience, 1,* 382. San Diego: Society for Neuroscience.

Azari, N. P., Nickel, J. P., Wunderlich, G., Niedeggen, M., Hefter, H., Tellmann, L., et al. (2001b). Neural correlates of religious experience. *European Journal of Neuroscience, 13,* 1649–1652.

Azari, N. P., & Seitz, R. J. (2000). Brain plasticity and recovery from stroke. *American Scientist* (Sept–Oct), 426–431.

Bandettini, P. A., Kwong, K. K., Davis, T. L., Tootell, R. B. H., Wong, E. C., Fox, P. T., et al. (1997). Characterization of cerebral blood oxygenation and flow changes during prolonged brain activation. *Human Brain Mapping, 5,* 93–109.

Bear, D. M. (1979). Temporal lobe epilepsy: A syndrome of sensory-limbic ypercon-nection. *Cortex, 15,* 357–384.

Bear, D. M., & Fedio, P. (1977). Quantitative analysis of interictal behavior in tempo-ral lobe epilepsy. *Archives of Neurology, 34*, 454–467.

Bear, D., Levin, K., D. Blumer, D., Chetham, D., & Ryder, J. (1982). Interictal behav-ior in hospitalized temporal lobe epileptics: Relationship to idiopathic psychiatric syndromes. *The Journal of Neurology, Neurosurgery, and Psychiatry, 45*, 481–488.

Ben-Ze'ev, A. (2000). *The subtlety of emotions* (1st ed.). Cambridge, MA: MIT Press.

Binkofski, F., Amunts, K., Stephan, K. M., Posse, S., Schormann, T., Freund, H. J., et al. (2000). Broca's region subserves imagery of motion: A combined cytoarchitectonic and fMRI study. *Human Brain Mapping, 11*, 273–285.

Blakemore, S. J., Boyer, O., Pachot-Clouard, M., Meltzoff, A., Segebarth, C., & Decety, J. (2003). The detection of contingency and animacy from simple animations in the human brain. *Cerebral Cortex, 13*, 837–844.

Boyer, P. (1994). *The naturalness of religious ideas: A cognitive theory of religion.* Berkeley: University of California Press.

Bromley, D. G. (1988). Religious disaffiliation: A neglected social process. In D. G. Bromley (Ed.), *Falling from the faith: Causes and consequences of religious apos-tasy* (pp. 9–25). Newbury Park, CA: Sage.

Cabeza, R., Grady, C. L., Nyberg, L., McIntosh, A. R., Tulving, E., Kapur, S., et al. (1997). Age-related differences in neural activity during memory encoding and retrieval: A positron emission tomography study. *Journal of Neuroscience, 17*, 391–400.

Calarge, C., Andreasen, N. C., & O'Leary, D. S. (2003). Visualizing how one brain understands another: A PET study of theory of mind. *American Journal of Psychiatry, 160*, 1954–1964.

Calamante, F., Thomas, D. L., Pell, G. S., Wiersma, J., & Turner, R. (1999). Measuring cerebral blood flow using magnetic resonance imaging techniques. *Journal of Cerebral Blood Flow and Metabolism, 9*, 701–735.

Damasio, A. R. (1999). *The feeling of what happens: Body and emotion in the making of consciousness* (1st ed.). Orlando: Harcourt.

Damasio, A. R. (2003). *Looking for Spinoza.* Orlando: Harcourt.

Decety, J., & Chaminade, T. (2003). Neural correlates of feeling sympathy. *Neuropsychologia, 41*, 127–138.

Dehaene, S., Spelke, E., Pinel, P., Stanescu, R., & Tsivkin, S. (1999). Sources of math-ematical thinking: Behavioral and brain-imaging evidence. *Science, 284*, 970–974.

Deiber, M. P., Passingham, R. E., Colebatch, J. G., Friston, K. J., Nixon, P. D., & Frackowiack, R. S. J. (1991). Cortical areas and the selection of movement: A study with positron emission tomography. *Experimental Brain Research, 84*, 393–402.

Dewey, J. (1934). *A common faith.* New Haven, CT: Yale University Press.

Dewey, J. (1969). The place of religious emotion. In J. Boydston (Ed.), *John Dewey: The early works, 1882–1898, Vol. 1: 1882–1888.* London: Southern Illinois University Press, Feffer & Simons.

Dewhurst, K., & Beard, A. W. (1970). Sudden religious conversions in temporal lobe epilepsy. *The British Journal of Psychiatry, 117*, 497–507.

Duncan, J., Seitz, R. J., Kolodny, J., Bor, D., Herzog, H., Ahmed, A., et al. (2000). A neural basis for general intelligence. *Science, 289*, 457–460.

Dupre, L. (1998). *Religious mystery and rational reflection: Excursions in the phenomenol-ogy and philosophy of religion.* Grand Rapids, MI: Eerdmans Publishing.

Eich, E., Kihlstrom, J. F., Bower, G. H., Forgas, J. P., & Niedenthal, P. M. (Eds.). (2000). *Cognition and emotion.* New York: Oxford University Press.

Fletcher, P. C., Happe, F., Frith, U., Baker, S. C., Dolan, R. J., Frackowiak, R. S. J., et al. (1995). Other minds in the brain: A functional imaging study of "theory of mind" in story comprehension. *Cognition, 57,* 109–128.

Fletcher, P. C., Shallice, T., Frith, C. D., Frackowiak, R. S. J., & Dolan, R. J. (1998). The functional roles of the prefrontal cortex in episodic memory. II. Retrieval. *Brain, 121,* 1249–1256.

Fox, P. T., & Raichle, M. E. (1984). Stimulus rate dependence of regional cerebral blood flow in human striate cortex, demonstrated by positron emission tomography. *Journal of Neurophysiology, 51,* 1109–1120.

Frahm, J., Bruhn, H., Merboldt, K. D., & Hänicke, W. (1992). Dynamic MR imaging of human brain oxygenation during rest and photic stimulation. *Journal of Magnetic Resonance Imaging, 2,* 501–505.

Friston, K. J., Holmes, A. P., Worsley, K. J., Poline, J. P., Frith, C. D., & Frackowiak, R. S. J. (1994). Statistical parametric maps in functional imaging: A generalized linear approach. *Human Brain Mapping, 2,* 189–210.

Gelphi, D. L. (1994). *The turn to experience in contemporary theology.* Mahwah, NJ: Paulist Press.

Glassman, R. B. (2002). "Miles within millimeters" and other awe-inspiring facts about our "mortarboard" human cortex. *Zygon, 37,* 255–277.

Goel, V., Grafman, J., Sadato, N., & Hallett, M. (1995). Modeling other minds. *Neuroreport, 6,* 1741–1746.

Happe, F. (2003). Theory of mind and the self. *Annals of the New York Academy of Sciences, 1001,* 134–144.

Henry, C. F. H. (1991). Theology: 20th-century trends. In J. D. Douglas, (Ed.), *New 20th-century encyclopedia of religious knowledge* (pp. 820–824). Grand Rapids, MI: Baker Bookhouse.

Herzog, H., Seitz, R. J., Tellmann, L., & Müller-Gärtner, H. W. (1996). Quantitation of regional cerebral blood flow using an autoradiogaphic-dynamic approach in positron emission tomography. *Journal of Cerebral Blood Flow and Metabolism, 16,* 645–649.

Herzog, H., Lele, V. R., Kuwert, T., Langen, K. J., Kops, E. R., Feinendegen, L. E. (1990). Changed pattern of regional glucose metabolism during yoga meditative relaxation. *Neuropsychobiology, 24,* 182–187.

Hood, R. W. (2003). The relationship between religion and spirituality. In D. Bromley (Series Ed.) & A. L. Griel & D. Bromley (Vol. Eds.), *Defining religion: Investigating the boundaries between the sacred and the secular: Vol. 10. Religion and the social order* (pp. 241–265). Amsterdam, The Netherlands: Elsevier Science.

Hood, R. W., Jr., Spilka, B., Hunsberger, B., & Gorsuch, R. (Eds.). (1996). *The psychology of religion: An empirical approach.* New York: Guilford Press.

Hulswit, M. (2002). From cause to causation: A piercean perspective (Vol. 90). In K. Leher, (Ed.), *Philosophical studies.* Dordrecht: Kluwer Academic Publishers.

James, W. (1902). *The varieties of religious experience* (Foreword by J. Barzun). New York: New American Library, Penguine Putnam.

Joseph, R. (2001). The limbic system and the soul: Evolution and neuroanatomy of religious experience. *Zygon, 36,* 105–136.

Kampe, K. K. W., Frith, C. D., & Frith, U. (2003). "Hey John": Signals conveying communicative intention toward the self activate brain regions associated with mentalizing, regardless of modality. *Journal of Neuroscience, 23,* 5258–5263.

Katz, S. T. (1977). *Mysticism and philosophical analysis.* New York: Oxford University Press.

Kirchner, T. T. J., Brammer, M., Bullmore, E., Simmons, A., Bartels, M., & David, A.S. (2002). The neural correlates of intentional and incidental self processing. *Neuropsychologia, 40,* 683–692.

Kleinschmidt, A., Büchel, C., Zeki, S., & Frackowiak, R. S. J. (1998). Human brain activity during spontaneously reversing perception of ambiguous figures. *Proceedings of the Royal Society of London, series B, 265,* 2427–2433.

Kosslyn, S. M., Behrmann, M., & Jeannerod. M. (1995). The cognitive neuroscience of mental imagery. *Neuropsychologia, 33,* 1335–1344.

Lazar, S. W., Bush, G., Gollub, R. L., Fricchione, G. L., Khalsa, G., & Benson, H. (2000). Functional brain mapping of the relaxation response and meditation. *Neuroreport, 11,* 1581–1585.

Lou, H. C., Kjaer, T. W., Friberg, L., Wildschiodtz, G., Holm, S., & Nowak, M. (1999). A ^{15}O-H$_2$O PET study of meditation and the resting state of normal consciousness. *Human Brain Mapping, 7,* 98–105.

LeDoux, J. E. (2000). Emotion circuits in the brain. *Annual Review of Neuroscience, 23,* 155–184.

Martin, J. A. (1987). Religious experience. In M. Eliade (Ed.), *The encyclopedia of religion* (12th ed., pp. 323–330). New York: MacMillan Publishing.

McGinn, B. (1991). Appendix: Theoretical foundations: The modern study of mysticism. In: B. McGinn (Ed.), *The foundations of mysticism* (pp. 265–343). New York: Crossroads.

McIntosh, A. R. (1999). Interactions of prefrontal cortex in relation to awareness in sensory learning. *Science, 284*(5419), 1531–1533.

McIntosh, A. R. (2000). Towards a network theory of cognition. *Neural Networks, 13,* 861–870.

McIntosh, D. N. (1995). Religion as schema, with implications for the relation between religion and coping. *The International Journal for the Psychology of Religion, 5,* 1–16.

McNamara, P. (2002). The motivational origins of religious practices. *Zygon, 37,* 143–160.

Newberg, A., Alavi, A., Baime, M., Pourdehnad, M., J. Santanna, J., & d'Aquili, E. (2001). The measurement of regional cerebral blood flow during the complex cognitive task of meditation: A preliminary SPECT study. *Psychiatry Research, 106,* 113–122.

Newberg, A. B., & d'Aquili, E. (2001). *Why God won't go away: Brain science and the biology of belief.* New York: Ballantine Books.

Newberg, A., Pourdehnad, M., Alavi, A., & d'Aquili, E. G. (2003). Cerebral blood flow during meditative prayer: Preliminary findings and methodological issues. *Perceptual Motor Skills, 97,* 625–630.

Nussbaum, M. C. (2001). *Upheavals of thought: Intelligence of emotions.* New York: Cambridge University Press.

Ochsner, K. N., & Barrett, L. F. (2001). A multiprocess perspective on the neuroscience of emotion. In T. J. Mayne, G. A. Bonnano, & P. Salovey (Ed.), *Emotions:
Current issues and future directions* (pp. 38–81). New York: Guilford Press.

Pargament, K. I. (1999). The psychology of religion and spirituality? Yes and no.
International Journal for the Psychology of Religion, 9, 3–16.

Persinger, M. A. (1983). Religious and mystical experiences as artifacts of temporal
lobe function: A general hypothesis. *Perceptual Motor Skills, 57, 1255–1262.*

Persinger, M. A. (1984). People who report religious experiences may also display
enhanced temporal-lobe signs. *Perceptual Motor Skills, 58, 963–975.*

Persinger, M. A. (1987). *Neurophysiological bases of God beliefs.* New York: Praeger.

Peterson, G. R. (2001). Think pieces: Religion as orienting worldview. *Zygon,
36, 5–19.*

Peterson, G. R. (2002). Thinkpieces: Mysterium tremendum. *Zygon, 37, 237–253.*

Proudfoot, W. (1985). *Religious experience.* Berkeley: University of California Press.

Puri, B. K., Lekh, S. K., Nijran, K. S., Bagary, M. S., & Richardson, A. J. (2001). Spect
neuroimaging in schizophrenia with religious delusions. *International Journal of
Psychophysiology, 40, 143–148.*

Raichle, M. E. (1998). Behind the scenes of functional brain imaging: A historical
and physiological perspective. *Proceedings of the National Academy of Sciences, 95,
765–772.*

Ramachandran, V. S., & Blakeslee, S. (1998). *Phantoms in the brain.* New York: William
Morrow.

Richardson, J. T. (1985). The active vs. passive convert: Paradigm conflict in con-
version/recruitment research. *Journal for the Scientific Study of Religion, 24,
163–179.*

Rolls, E. T. (2001). *The brain and emotion.* Oxford, UK: Oxford University Press.

Sanfey, A. G., Rilling, J. K., Aronson, J. A., Nystrom, L. E., & Cohen, J. D. (2003). The
neural basis of economic decision-making in the ultimatum game. *Science, 300,
1755–1758.*

Scherer, K. R., Schorr, A., & Johnstone, T. (Eds.). (2001). *Appraisal processes in emotion.*
New York: Oxford University Press.

Schlitt, D. M. (2001). *Theology and the experience of God.* New York: Peter Lang.

Shinozaki, J., Hanakawa, T., & Fukuyama, H. (2005). The neural correlates of common affection to human and animal family members studies by fMRI. Abstract.
OHBM June 2005 Meeting, Toronto, Canada.

Siegal, M., & Varley, R. (2002). Neural systems involved in "theory of mind." *Nature
Reviews Neuroscience, 3, 463–471.*

Smart, N. (1997). *The religious experience.* Upper Saddle River, NJ: Prentice Hall.

Smith, J. Z. (Ed.). (1995). *The HarperCollins dictionary of religion.* San Francisco:
Harper San Francisco.

Spilka, B., Brown, G. A., & Cassidy, S. A. (1992). The structure of religious mystical experience in relation to pre-and post-experience lifestyles. *The International
Journal for the Psychology of Religion, 2, 241–257.*

Spilka, B., Ladd, K. L., McIntosh, D. N., & Milmoe, S. (1996). The contents of religious experience: The roles of expectancy and desirability. *International Journal
for the Psychology of Religion, 6, 95–105.*

Spilka, B., & McIntosh, D. N. (1995). Attribution theory and religious experience. In R. W. Hood (Ed.), *Handbook of religious experience* (pp. 421–445). Birmingham, AL: Religious Education Press.

Spilka, B., Shaver, P., & Kirkpatrick, L. A. (1985). A general attribution theory for the psychology of religion. *Journal for the Scientific Study of Religion, 24,* 1–20.

Stifler, K., Greer, J., Sneck, W., & Dovenmuehle, R. (1993). An Empirical Investigation of the discriminability of reported mystical experiences among religious contemplatives, psychotic in-patients, and normal adults. *Journal for the Scientific Study of Religion, 32,* 366–372.

Tanji, J., & Mushiake, H. (1996). Comparison of neuronal activity in the supplementary motor area and primary motor cortex. *Brain Research. Cognitive Brain Research, 3,* 143–150.

Teske, J. A. (2001). Neuroscience and spirit: The genesis of mind and spirit. *Zygon, 36,* 93–103.

Tillich, P. (1951). *Systematic theology* (Vol. I). Chicago: University of Chicago Press.

Tucker, D. M., Novelly, R. A., & Walker, P. J. (1987). Hyperreligiosity in temporal lobe epilepsy: Redefining the relationship. *Journal of Nervous and Mental Disease, 175,* 181–184.

Vogeley, K., Bussfeld, P., Newen, A., Herrmann, S., Happe, F., Falkai, P., et al. (2001). Mind reading: Neural mechanisms of theory of mind and self-perspective. *NeuroImage, 14,* 170–181.

Watson, D., Clark, L. A., & Tellegren, A. (1988). Development and validation of brief measures of positive and negative affect: The PANAS Scales. *Journal of Personality and Social Psychology, 54,* 1063–1070.

Wicker, B., Perrett, D. I., Baron-Cohen, S., & Decety, J. (2003). Being the target of another's emotion: A PET study. *Neuropsychologia, 41,* 139–146.

Zinnbauer, B. J., Pargament, K. I., Cole, B., Rye, M. S., Butter, E. M., Belavich, T. G., et al. (1997). Religion and spirituality: Unfuzzying the fuzzy. *Journal for the Scientific Study of Religion, 36,* 549–564.

CHAPTER 4

RELIGION AND THE LIFE COURSE: IS ADOLESCENCE AN "EXPERIENCE EXPECTANT" PERIOD FOR RELIGIOUS TRANSMISSION?

Candace S. Alcorta

When that sign is carved on the body the abstract is not only made substantial but immediate . . . and if the mark is indelible, as in the case of the subincision, the excised canine, the lopped finger, the scarified face, chest or back, it is ever-present. As the abstract is made alive and concrete by the living substance of men and women, so are men and women predicated by the abstractions which they themselves realize. (Rappaport, 1999)

The incessant drizzle did little to dampen the spirits of the 100 disheveled teenagers that filed onto the powder blue, 1960s vintage school buses. It was early and uncharacteristically quiet. Most of the teens had been up late socializing on the first night of this week-long mission program and had still not fully awakened, but they smiled and nodded as they grabbed their rakes and shovels and climbed onboard.

This was my first morning with the group. As an anthropologist conducting research on adolescent religiosity, I had been invited to come and observe this fledgling youth mission program, now in its second year of existence. The project had been initiated by a local minister who saw it as an opportunity to bring together urban and suburban teens while addressing inner city needs. Over the course of the next week, the teens participating in the program would spend the majority of their time cleaning, shoveling, raking, and hammering as helpers at Habitat for Humanity and Head Start projects throughout the city. The 100 teens in the mission group included Latino,

African-American and Anglo adolescents from seven different suburban and urban churches. Although clothing and hairstyles differed throughout the group, all of the youth participants shared a common aversion to the daily 6:00 A.M. wake-up call and a common belief in the importance of the project.

What I observed over the next several days was, from an anthropological perspective, a classic example of adolescent rites of passage. The work teams of the mission project didn't create ancestral clans, but they soon created their own fictive kin groups, aided by organized team-building activities that included team names and badges, ropes course training, and inter-group competitions. There were no psychological ordeals, although sleep deprivation was very real as the teenagers struggled to be on time for their early morning bus departure each day. The beatings, scarification, and bodily mutilation that are central elements of adolescent initiation rites among such groups as the Ndembu of Africa and the Baktaman of New Guinea were noticeably absent here. The physical labor required of team members each day was, however, clearly a novel and painful physical ordeal. The communal song, dance, and ritual that feature prominently in rites of passage across traditional cultures were all integral parts of the mission program as well. Every evening after returning from their mission work, team members spent several hours practicing for a talent show to be performed at the final ceremony of the week's activities. Each day ended in the hushed and darkened seminary chapel where all the teens shared their project experiences, recounted their "highs" and "lows," and joined together in prayer and song. By the end of the week, the adolescent volunteers who had arrived with 100 different backgrounds, personalities, and beliefs had become a single, cohesive unit. The mission project had succeeded in generating what anthropologist Victor Turner called "communitas"—an intensely shared feeling of community among this previously diverse group of American adolescents.

For an evolutionary anthropologist steeped in the selfish gene theories of Dawkins and the inclusive fitness models of Hamilton and Trivers, the mission program was puzzling. Why would 100 unrelated American teenagers who didn't know one another or those they were helping give up a week of their summer vacations to live in a cramped seminary dorm room and perform hard physical labor? Certainly, some of the youth who participated in the program had been encouraged by their parents to do so. For the majority of the adolescents, however, the decision to volunteer for the mission program had been an individual choice. Whether involvement was self-initiated or parentally inspired, parents clearly approved of their teen's participation in the program, even though this entailed both time and monetary costs. In many cases, parents not only supported their child's participation, but actively participated themselves.

Mission programs are but one aspect of American adolescents' religious involvement. A recent national survey conducted by sociologist Christian

Smith (2005) found that many American teens are actively involved in religious youth groups, church and synagogue activities, and an active program of religious youth camps throughout the nation. Adolescence is also the time when American youth attend confirmation classes, participate in bar/bat mitzvahs, and publicly assert and acknowledge their religious beliefs. Americans are not unique in their focus on adolescence as a significant life period for "learning and living" religion. Most cultures throughout the world consider adolescence to be the appropriate life period for religious initiation. Nearly three-quarters of the societies studied by anthropologists have formalized adolescent initiation rites for the express purpose of transmitting religious knowledge (Lutkehaus & Roscoe, 1995). Numerous anthropological accounts describe these "rites of passage" as the most elaborate and significant religious ceremonies performed within a culture. Religious systems as different as those of Arapesh animists, American Protestants, and Asian Buddhists all include such rites and focus on adolescence as the developmental period most appropriate for religious transmission.

This universal focus on adolescence as the most important time of life for the transmission of religious beliefs and behaviors is taken for granted by most of us. Like learning music or learning language, it is something that comes naturally and is seldom questioned. But why does learning religion during adolescence come naturally? Why don't we learn religion when we learn language? If beliefs are the critical element of religious systems, then humans should be able to learn religion once language skills are mastered. Yet, there are no societies reported to conduct "childhood rites of initiation." Why is adolescence the preferred developmental period for religious transmission across cultures as different as those of Australian Arunta hunter-gatherers, African Ashanti agriculturalists, and American industrial Protestants? Is religion, like music and language, a universal human capacity that is best developed during a particular life stage? If so, what happens in the absence of such development? We still do not have answers to many of these questions, but new research is beginning to provide intriguing insights into possible answers and to expand our understanding of both the neurophysiology and the evolutionary function of religion.

MAKING THE ABSTRACT IMMEDIATE: MUSIC, LANGUAGE AND RELIGION

Anthropological and archaeological research indicates that religion is a universal human trait with a long history. Every culture known includes religious beliefs and behaviors that are recognizable as religion, even to outsiders unfamiliar with the language and customs of that culture. Like music and language, religion is both culturally specific and species universal. Music, language, and religion are all cultural constructions that must be learned through social transmission; however, both the capacity for and constraints on such learning appear to be hard wired in all human brains. Whether we enjoy the sitar or the sousaphone, speak Hindi or English, and worship Vishnu or the Holy Trinity depends on the culture in which we are socialized. Yet our ability to speak any language, enjoy any musical tradition, or engage in any religious experiences all appear to derive from genetically encoded neural capacities common to all humans.

We not only possess the ability to learn music, language, and religion; we also exhibit innate predispositions to do so. These innate predispositions structure our experiences and bias our learning. As a result, what we learn is highly influenced by predispositions to attend to and process particular classes of stimuli during specific developmental periods. What we learn is culturally prescribed. When we learn appears to be a function of brain growth patterns.

Much of human brain growth occurs after birth. The brain of a human newborn continues to grow at a rapid fetal rate throughout the first year of life. By the second year of the human infant's life, only about 50 percent of brain development is complete. The human brain does not reach its maximum size until adolescence. This brain growth is not uniform. Different parts of the human brain mature at different times. Sensory cortices, including those for sight and hearing, mature relatively early in development, while other brain regions, such as those involved in language processing and abstract thought, mature much later. During development, periods of high dendrite and synapse proliferation are interspersed with periods of pruning in which the total number of neurons and their interconnections are reduced (Kolb, Forgie, Gibb, Gorny, & Rontree, 1998). The neuronal interconnections that remain are enhanced through the formation of lipid sheaths around axons that speed neuronal transmissions. This process of myelination creates the white matter of the brain and is one of the last stages of neuronal maturation.

The prolonged pattern of brain development in humans and the differential maturation rates of various brain regions have profound implications for learning and behavior. During brain growth, neuronal dendrites proliferate. Each of these dendrites has the potential to interconnect with other neurons through the creation of synapses. Synapses link the axons and dendrites of one neuron with another. Environmental stimuli that activate specific neurons cause these synapses to fire, thereby strengthening the inter-neuronal connections. This process creates associational networks within the brain. Synapses that are seldom fired are eliminated, and their energetic resources are reallocated to active networks. Since the maturation rates of various brain structures differ, the optimal developmental periods for shaping neural interconnections through experientially based firing of synapses differ as well. As a result, environmental stimuli are processed differently and have different impacts on the brain at various stages of development (Kolb et al., 1998). The human capacity to learn music offers a glimpse into this process.

MUSIC: A DEVELOPMENTAL MODEL

Throughout the world, mothers and other caregivers sing to newborns. These songs are sung in hundreds of different languages, but the style in which they are sung is universal. Songs sung to infants are slower, higher pitched, and have an exaggerated rhythm when compared to noninfant songs. No matter what the language, these are the songs infants prefer. Even two-day-old infants born from congenitally deaf parents who sign and do not speak or sing prefer infant-directed singing to adult-directed singing. Videotaped studies of infants as young as six months old demonstrate that even at this early age humans perceive and attend to both the structural and emotional features of musical sounds (Trehub, 2001). These apparently innate musical capacities and preferences are shaped during early childhood through cultural exposure and socialization. By age 3 children are able to recognize "happiness" as represented by the musical forms of their culture, and by age 5 they are able to discriminate between happy and sad musical excerpts on the basis of tempo differences. By 6 years of age children readily employ both tempo and mode to identify sadness, fear, and anger in music (Trehub, 2001). Once developed, this ability to read the emotions encoded in a culture's musical conventions seems to remain unchanged throughout the remainder of life. Psychologist Sandra Trehub (2001) compares this culturally patterned learning of music's emotional meaning to that which occurs in relation to facial expressions. Both appear to derive from basic innate predispositions and encompass several apparently universal features, but both also require socialization experiences within a particular developmental window in order for the culturally defined components to be fully developed.

For music, the development of these innate abilities is directly linked to the neural maturation of specific brain areas. The ability of young infants to distinguish pitch is dependent upon the maturation of neurons that make up "tonotopic" maps of the right temporal lobe that associate sound frequencies with pitch. Similar processing of time intervals in music occurs in the homologous region of the left temporal lobe, resulting in perceptions of rhythm (Liegeois-Chauvel, Giraud, Badier, Marquis, & Chauvel, 2001). These initial functions perceptually organize and structure sound such that infants enter the world with a brain capable of organizing sound frequencies in relation to rhythm and pitch. The association of these components with culturally prescribed meaning occurs later. The songs sung to infants begin this experiential process of shaping associational networks between the auditory processing areas of the temporal lobes and limbic structures, such as the anterior cingulate cortex, involved in investing them with emotional meaning. Although the capacity to create these interconnections is innate, the development of these capacities depends on, and is shaped by, the social experiences in the infant's world.

Language learning, like music, also involves the social development of innate predispositions. The development of language capacities occurs slightly after that of music and may actually build on several of the capacities developed during music acquisition. The associations between sound patterns and meaning and the correlations between sound patterns and syntactic structure that are critical elements in language are first developed in relation to music (Koelsch & Friederici, 2003). The pitch, tone, and cadence of speech, collectively referred to as speech prosody, are the first elements attended to in linguistic communication. In contrast to the left-hemisphere processing of all other language features, these elements of language are processed in the right "musical" side of the brain. Likewise, the predominant rhythms of a culture's speech sounds reflect the predominant musical rhythms of the culture (Patel, 2003). Brain studies show that children first learn to process structure in music around the age of 5. The processing of structure in language follows a similar developmental trajectory but occurs approximately four years later.

Brain imaging studies clearly demonstrate the existence of dedicated neural structures underlying innate human capacities for both music and language. Full development of these capacities, however, depends on the maturation of functional brain regions responsible for specific components of these capacities, as well as development of the neural networks that link these regions together. At each specific stage of development, associations among regions are shaped by activation of specific neurons that occurs in response to social and cultural experiences. Our innate predispositions to learn the music and language of our culture reflect the existence of neural structures specific to music and language. Maturation of these various structures at different times during development creates what neurophysiologist William Greenough (1986) has called "experience expectant" periods for learning. Infancy appears to be such a period for learning culturally encoded meanings of musical rhythm and pitch. These learned capacities then provide a basis for the development of language skills during childhood. What about religion? Do we also possess an innate predisposition to learn religion? Does the development of our religious capacity build on previously learned skills? Is there an experience expectant period for religion, as there is for music and language? There is considerable evidence that the answer to many of these questions is "yes."

THE "DEEP STRUCTURE" OF RELIGION

Religion, like music and language, is a universal human trait that is at once individual and social, innate and learned. Like music and language, religion exhibits structural features that are universal and allow us to recognize religion in cultures very different from our own. These features include: (a) a belief in socially omniscient supernatural agents; (b) separation of the sacred from the profane; and, (c) music-based communal ritual.

Across cultures, religious systems include supernatural agents that regularly violate natural categories and laws and also possess extraordinary powers. These agents are conceived of in different forms across cultures. The supernatural agents of some religions, such as those of the Arctic Inuit and the Australian Arunta, are embodied in animal totems. In other cultures, as among the Ilahita Arapesh of New Guinea, such agents may be the ghosts of the recently deceased. In monotheistic religions, such as Islam, Christianity and Judaism, a single god is considered to have omnipresent, omnipotent, and omniscient powers. This omniscience is a distinguishing feature of the supernatural agents of all religions. Whatever form these agents take, they are always knowledgeable about human social behaviors and human affairs. People everywhere seem to possess an innate predisposition to believe in such socially omniscient agents. When they are not formally incorporated into the religion of a culture, as in Buddhism, they tend to sneak in through the back door, or,—as evident from the spirit houses commonly found throughout southeast Asia,—the front door. Cognitive scientist Scott Atran notes that "Even Buddhist monks ritually ward off malevolent deities by invoking benevolent ones" (Atran & Norenzayan, 2004, p. 714). A common human proclivity to believe in such agents may be a part of our make-up. Experiments conducted by psychologist Jesse Bering (2004) found that young children innately believe in such omniscient supernatural agents. These agents retain their omniscience throughout childhood, even as initial childhood perceptions of parents as omniscient begin to fade. By adolescence not only do these beliefs persist, but they also expand to include the belief that such agents are able to act on their knowledge. Not only do the gods and ancestors know what we're doing; they can also let us know that they are displeased.

Throughout the world these innate predispositions to believe in powerful, socially omniscient supernatural agents are shaped by the cultures in which they occur. They are transmitted from generation to generation through the use of highly memorable images, concepts, and narratives. Totemic animals that talk, incorporeal spirits that eat, and powerful gods capable of transforming themselves into swans and volcanoes are not quickly forgotten. Such supernatural agents grab our attention because they violate universal expectations about the world's everyday structure. At the same time, they engage sets of cultural beliefs about these agents that derive from their real life counterparts. When these counterintuitive concepts are embedded within memorable narrative frameworks, they are easy to learn and remember (Atran & Norenzayan, 2004). And when they are associated with emotionally arousing rituals, they are almost impossible to forget.

Anthropologist Maurice Bloch (1989) has identified music, chanting, and dance as "distinguishing marks of ritual" in all cultures known. These features of ritual are found in the traditional societies studied by anthropologists, but they are also basic components of religion in contemporary Western cultures. In their recent nationwide survey of U.S. congregations, sociologist Mark Chaves and his colleagues (Chaves, Konieszny, Beyerlein, & Barman, 1999) found music to be the single most consistent feature of contemporary worship across all faiths studied in the United States. Even fundamentalist sects retain music as an essential element of religion. Cognitive scientists Scott Atran and Ara Norenzayan note that "even the Taliban, who prohibited nearly all public displays of sensory stimulation, promoted a cappella religious chants" (Atran & Norenzayan, 2004, p. 717). Throughout human history music and religious ritual have been inseparable, and in some cultures, such as that of the Igbo of Africa, a single word, "nkwa," refers to both (Becker, 2001). It is only within the last 200 years of Western civilization that secular music has emerged as an entity separate from religious ritual. Even this music, however, is rooted in the monastic Gregorian chants of Medieval Europe (Cross, 2003). Music appears to be an integral part of religions throughout the world. It is capable of eliciting joy, awe and ecstasy, as described by the eleventh century Persian Sufi mystic Ghazzali:

> The heart of man has been so constituted by the Almighty that, like a flint, it contains a hidden fire which is evoked by music and harmony, and renders man beside himself with ecstasy. These harmonies are echoes of that higher world of beauty which we call the world of spirits, they remind man of his relationship to that world, and produce in him an emotion so deep and strange that he himself is powerless to explain it. (Becker, 2001, p. 145)

This sense of the infinite, eternal, and sacred described by Ghazzali is not unique to Sufi mystics. A contemporary American woman describes very similar responses to a performance of Mahler's Tenth Symphony:

> I remember tears filling my eyes. I felt as if I understood a message, from one time to another, from one human to another. . . . The way through the symphony had been hard and frightening, even shocking, but it was a great happiness—almost an honor—having had the opportunity to experience this. . . . now all words would have been superfluous, even my own. My thoughts had nothing to do with words. (Gabrielsson, 2001, p. 441)

These emotions elicited by music appear to be common to humans across both time and space. Just as music is a central feature across religions, the emotions music evokes are also a critical element in the experience of "the sacred." The ability of religious ritual to evoke such emotions in the creation of the sacred is the second feature common to all religions.

In all cultures religious ritual is the means by which people, places, objects, and beliefs are sanctified (Eliade, 1958; Rappaport, 1999). As a result of participation in religious ritual, adherents come to view the ordinary as extraordinary and to invest special meanings and powers in sacred things. Among the Mbuti pygmies of the African Congo, the religious "molimo" festival transforms a rusty pipe that remains submerged beneath river water throughout most of the year into a sacred flute capable of eliciting reverence and awe (Turnbull, 1962). Likewise, canonization rituals of the contemporary Roman Catholic Church transform ordinary men and women into saints invested with miraculous abilities. Things perceived to be sacred—whether pipes or people—are also perceived to have power. The source of this power lies in the ability of sacred things to evoke strong emotions of joy, fear, awe, and danger in those who believe. These intense emotions influence choices and motivate individual behaviors. Mbuti men who hear the voice of the forest spirit in the molimo flute not only feel a sense of awe, but also feel a sense of dread if there is reason to believe that the forest spirit may be displeased or angry with their conduct in human affairs. These feelings have the power to change behaviors, making the lazy more energetic and the stingy more generous. Studies conducted on Israeli kibbutzim by anthropologist Richard Sosis and economist Bradley Ruffle (2003) provides empirical evidence of the effects of religious participation on individual behaviors. This research demonstrated a positive and significant correlation between regular participation in religious ritual and measures of cooperation. Music and other elements of religious ritual, such as candle-lit cathedrals, life-like statues, and stylized movements that heighten our emotional engagement, better prepare us to experience the sacred. These elements of religion elicit emotions capable of transforming ordinary objects, places, and beliefs into sacred things by investing them with extraordinary emotional meaning for ritual participants.

These three structural features of religion—belief in supernatural agents, music-based communal ritual, and the emotional significance of the sacred—are elements common to all religions (Alcorta & Sosis, 2005). Humans exhibit an innate predisposition to develop culturally defined emotional responses to music during infancy. Humans also appear to possess an innate predisposition to believe in socially omniscient supernatural agents during childhood. It is, however, during adolescence that these developed capacities and beliefs are integrated into religious systems in the creation of the sacred. Cross-cultural studies suggest that adolescence may be a particularly important developmental period for shaping this experience and for associating it with the symbols and beliefs of religion.

ADOLESCENT RITES OF PASSAGE

Adolescent rites of passage are found in 70 percent of the world's cultures and vary widely from culture to culture. In some societies only males participate in adolescent initiation rites. Other societies restrict these rites to females. In cultures that do practice male rites of passage, approximately one-half of such rites are group rites. In contrast, nearly 90 percent of female rites of passage are individual (Lutkehaus & Roscoe, 1995).

There is considerable cross-cultural variation in the duration of adolescent rites of passage. In some societies, such as the Ndembu of Zambia, adolescent initiation begins for boys around the age of ten, as they are forcibly kidnapped from their mother's hut and taken to a secluded initiation site where they remain for the next several years. In other cultures, rites are brief. The Sunrise Ceremony of the Apache was celebrated when a girl began menstruation and lasted only a few days (Eliade, 1958; Paige & Paige, 1981). Adolescent initiation rites may be relatively simple and consist of little more than the transmission of sacred knowledge, as among the Yamana and Halakwulup of Tierra del Fuego, or they may be prolonged, intense, and psychologically and physically painful. Among the Baktaman of New Guinea, male initiates are routinely deprived of food, water, and sleep, repeatedly beaten and tortured, forced to dance to the point of exhaustion, and required to eat things initiates consider disgusting (McCauley, 2001). Many adolescent rites of passage include the permanent excision or mutilation of body parts, including removal of teeth or fingers, scarification, and genital mutilation (Glucklich, 2001). Initiation rites can and sometimes do result in permanent disfigurement, infertility, and even the death of initiates (Glucklich, 2001; Paige & Paige, 1981; Turner, 1967).

Anthropologists have traditionally viewed adolescent initiation rites as social institutions that function to redefine social roles and identities within society. Initiates who participate in these rites learn both the sacred and secular aspects of their new roles as men and women and are psychologically transformed from children to adults. This function is explicitly acknowledged. In most societies that conduct these rites, it is only after the successful completion of initiation that adolescents assume the culturally defined roles of adulthood. Only then can successful initiates enter into marriage and assume other reproductive, economic, political, and religious rights and responsibilities within their societies.

Although adolescent initiation rites exhibit considerable variation across groups, the underlying structure of these rites is highly consistent in every culture known. Nearly a century ago Arnold van Gennep (1960) identified three distinct phases of initiation rites, including separation, transition, and incorporation. He viewed these phases as psychological mechanisms that play an important role in the transformation of the initiate. Van Gennep maintained that the separation of initiates from the safety and security of the familiar was an important first step in their psychological transformation. The separation of initiates may be as simple as a week voluntarily spent at an urban seminary. Alternatively, separation may involve forcible kidnapping and seclusion for several years. Although there are clear differences in the emotional impacts of these two experiences, in both cases the separation of the initiate from the familiar psychologically "primes" the individual for the transformation that occurs during the second phase.

The second phase of initiation rites is the transition or "liminal" phase. In this stage of initiation, participants are stripped of their old identities to recreate them anew. Anthropologist Victor Turner (1967) described this phase as "a moment in and out of time," For Turner this state of liminality was a key element in preparing the initiate to realize and integrate the symbolic, imaginative, and emotional aspects of ritual. Across religions, ritual practices that alter normal body states and perceptions are a fundamental part of achieving the liminal state. Food and sleep deprivation, psychological and physical ordeals, and pain experienced by initiates serve to "grind (initiates) down to a uniform condition to be fashioned anew and endowed with additional powers to enable them to cope with their new station in life" (p. 95). This stripping away of external social identities and the "grinding down" of individual psyches promotes egalitarianism among initiates and allows the recognition of a generalized social bond. Once recognized, this bond can be enhanced and strengthened through joint participation in music-based communal ritual. The result is the development of "communitas," a deeply felt, spiritually binding, and long-lasting communion among the initiates.

The nature, duration, and intensity of transition phase activities have a direct impact on both the loss of individual initiate identity and on the strength of group cohesion achieved. In the church mission group I observed, the ropes training course, the daily physical labor, and the evening social and communal worship activities all helped create the experience of "communitas" among participants. The emotional depth of these experiences, however, was far removed from that of Ndembu adolescent males who participate in that society's Mukanda rites. For these adolescents the emotional intensity evoked by forcible kidnapping, prolonged seclusion, repetitive sleep and food deprivation, psychological and physical ordeals, and the excruciating pain of circumcision performed with a sharpened stone in the absence of anesthesia significantly intensify the psychological impacts of the liminal phase experience. Among the Ndembu these rites are especially traumatic as a result of the very close mother-child bond that exists in this society prior to kidnapping. This is also true for many of the patrilineal, patrilocal societies that practice highly intense and painful initiation rites. The intensity of these emotionally charged experiences have indelible psychological and neurological effects. In her book *Sacred Pain*, author Ariel Glucklich (2001) argues that the pain experienced by initiates as a result of such practices as circumcision "is meant to produce a unity on the level of moral order instead of the particularistic order based on birth and motherhood" (p. 141). Initiates who share such extremely intense experiences together forge a bond. In initiation ceremonies this bond is further strengthened through joint participation in ritual, song, and dance. As a result, such highly intense group initiation ceremonies not only transform individual initiates, but also bring into being a new social body that did not previously exist.

The last phase of adolescent rites of passage involves the reintegration of initiates back into society. In this phase individuals re-enter the social group, but they do so as a new person who has been both psychologically and socially transformed. In many cultures initiation rites underscore this transformation through the symbolic death and rebirth of the initiate. In cultures that practice intense male group rites, such as the Baktaman and Ndembu, reintegration also involves the reintegration of the new social group that has been forged through the ritual process. The use of physical "badges," including scarification, circumcision, and other alterations of physical appearance, serve as indelible testaments of the individual's new identity as a member of this newly created social body.

Adolescent rites of passage clearly serve to signal a change in the social roles and statuses of initiates. The bar/bat mitzvahs of Judaism, Christian confirmation classes, and the Mukanda ceremony of the Ndembu all visibly and publicly announce the status change of initiates to all other members of society. The new powers and the responsibilities of initiates are announced and clarified, both to the initiates and to all others with whom they interact. Rites of passage transmit new knowledge, new skills, new beliefs, and new values and prepare initiates for new social roles, both cognitively and emotionally. Empirical evidence demonstrates that participation in such religious rituals creates social and moral bonds that strengthen group commitment and promote cooperative group behaviors (see Sosis, this volume). Increasing the "costs" of these rituals also increases the degree of commitment and cohesion among the ritual participants. Rites of passage that are most prolonged, intense, and painful should engender the greatest long-term cohesion and cooperation among initiates. A cross-cultural study of male rites of initiation and warfare conducted by anthropologist Richard Sosis and his colleagues (Sosis this volume, chap. 4) confirms this prediction. Non-state societies that most frequently engage in external warfare are also those societies that practice the most prolonged, intense, and painful male group initiation rites. Such rites appear to promote the highest levels of individual altruism and achieve greatest adherence to cooperative group goals—precisely the motivation and commitment you would want if you were frequently counting on your fellow initiates during war.

The initiation experience is one which adolescents never forget. This is certainly true for Ndembu males who bear bodily, as well as mental signals, of their initiation experience. It is also true for American teenagers who have participated in church mission trips. In my interviews with these youths, they consistently report mission trips as the most memorable of all their religious experiences. They also assert that these trips have changed the way they see the world. Although it is certainly not surprising that Ndembu initiates would be transformed by the intense, prolonged and painful experiences they undergo during rites of passage, it is somewhat more difficult to understand the impact of church mission trips on contemporary American teenagers. Such trips do not include memorably painful experiences, yet they appear to have a significant effect on adolescent perceptions of self and others. What is it about adolescent rites of passage that make such an impact on adolescents? And what is it about adolescence that render these rites particularly powerful?

ADOLESCENCE AS A LIFE STAGE

In many species adolescence is a relatively brief period between the juvenile and adult phases of the organism. In humans this transitional period between childhood and adulthood extends over several years and in some cultures, such as our own, may span more than a decade. Adolescence differs from puberty. Puberty refers to the attainment of sexual maturation and is defined in relation to specific neuroendocrine changes. Adolescence encompasses a gradual process that includes puberty, but also involves a series of "soft events," both behavioral and physiological (Spear, 2000). Not long ago adolescence was viewed largely as a cultural creation of wealthy developed nations. Proponents of this view argued that the lengthy period of adolescence that typifies contemporary industrialized nations did not occur in traditional societies in which children were quickly transitioned from childhood to adult status at the onset of puberty. Accumulating neurophysiological evidence refutes this view and indicates that the psychological and behavioral changes that define adolescence are not simply cultural constructions, but instead include significant physiological events that occur in nonhuman, as well as human species. Neuroscientists, biologists, and physicians increasingly view adolescence as a critical period of brain development. Although cultural variables clearly influence the duration of adolescence, the behavioral, neural, and physiological changes that occur during adolescence are not merely cultural creations. One leading interdisciplinary research group of scientists has defined adolescence as "that awkward period between sexual maturation and the attainment of adult roles and responsibilities" (Dahl, 2004, p. 9). This definition of adolescence applies to nonhuman species but is particularly relevant for human cultural systems in which both ecological and social factors are critical in determining when adult status is attained. Cross-cultural research demonstrates that nutritional and ecological factors impact the onset and length of adolescence. In many traditional societies the average two-year period between puberty and marriage defines a relatively short adolescence for females, with a somewhat longer four-year average for males (Schlegel & Barry, 1991). In societies afflicted with poverty, stress, and poor nutrition, adolescence, like life itself, may be brief. In contrast, wealthy societies that benefit from good nutrition and healthy living conditions may extend adolescence across a decade as a result of both earlier physical and reproductive maturation and later social maturation (Dahl, 2004). Yet, whether adolescence occurs earlier or later in the life span, and whether it is brief or prolonged, there are universal changes in behavior, psychology, and neurophysiology that define this developmental period.

Adolescence has been called "a chronic state of threatened homeostasis" (Dorn & Chrousos, 1993). Adolescents react more quickly and with greater intensity to environmental stimuli than do either children or adults. Adolescents also perceive events as relatively more stressful than individuals at other life stages (Laviola, Adrianni, Terranova, & Gerra, 1999). Basal levels of circulating stress hormones, such as cortisol, are greater during adolescence than during any other period throughout the lifespan. Adolescents exhibit increased physiological responses to stressors, such as blood pressure and cardiac output response, as well. During adolescence metabolism and growth rates accelerate and appetitive behaviors increase (Spear, 2000). Total sleep time and slow wave sleep decrease and a phase delay occurs in the sleep pattern. As parents of teens can attest, adolescents eat more, sleep less, and sleep later than both children and adults.

Social behaviors also change during the adolescent period, as peer relationships, romantic interests, and sexual motivations become increasingly important. Inter-individual play behaviors decline and coordinated group behaviors, such as organized sports activities and dance, increase.

Adolescence is also marked by emotional intensity. Ronald Dahl (2004), a leader in pediatric psychiatry, has characterized adolescence as a period "prone to erratic . . . and emotionally influenced behavior" (p. 3). This change in emotional intensity during adolescence is accompanied by a heightened risk for emotional disorders, particularly in females. Increased risk taking and novelty seeking are characteristics of this life phase and are more pronounced in males (Dahl, 2004). Human sensation-seeking scores peak in late adolescence, as does vulnerability to drug and alcohol abuse (Spear, 2000). Even though adolescents are physically and immunologically more robust and resilient than younger children, mortality rates rise by nearly 200 percent during the teenage years. This is largely due to increases in "homicides, suicides, and accidents (that) collectively account for more than 85 percent of all adolescent deaths" (Spear, 2000, p. 421).

In addition to being a time of increased risk taking, novelty seeking, and emotional intensity, adolescence is also the developmental period when mental processing speeds increase and abstract reasoning develops. On experiments designed to test mental processing speed, scientific reasoning, and the ability to focus on task-relevant information show adolescents consistently outperform younger children (Kwon & Lawson, 2000).

ADOLESCENT BRAIN DEVELOPMENT

These various adolescent behaviors and abilities derive from widespread changes in neuroendocrine systems and reflect brain development patterns. During pre-adolescence, there is a large increase in the cortical gray matter of the brain. This increase is particularly dramatic in the frontal and parietal lobes. Although the parietal lobe has attained its maximum size in both males and females by age 12, localized growth in specific areas of the prefrontal cortex continues over the next several years (Sowell, Thompson, Holmes, Jernigan, & Toga, 1999). The temporal cortex also continues to increase in size during early adolescence and does not attain its maximum volume until around 16.5 years of age for males and 16.7 years for females (Giedd et al., 1999).

The frontal and temporal cortices of the brain are particularly important in relation to social behaviors and activities. The extensive changes that occur in these brain areas during adolescence impact these behaviors and activities. While the temporal lobe functions in music and language processing, and in facial recognition, the prefrontal region of the frontal cortex is responsible for various "executive" functions of the brain. It receives and integrates information from emotional processing and reward areas of the brain with input received from other brain regions. Processing of this information by the prefrontal cortex is important in planning, impulse control, abstract and symbolic reasoning, and social judgment. The development of these capacities throughout adolescence reflects the ongoing maturation of this brain region.

The cortex is not the only area of the brain that increases during adolescence. Limbic structures, including the amygdala and the hippocampus, also show volume increases during this time (Walker & Bollini, 2002). The hippocampus functions in memory processing and the amygdala is critical to the perception and processing of emotions. The amygdala projects to and influences the hypothalamus, which regulates autonomic functions in the body, such as heart rate, blood pressure, and respiration. Interconnections between the amygdala and the hypothalamus are important for mobilizing body functions in response to threatening and potentially harmful stimuli. The amygdala is also closely interconnected with both the prefrontal cortex and the reward systems of the brain. These interconnections are crucial in providing emotional inputs to the prefrontal cortex that weight behavioral choices. Individuals whose prefrontal cortex and amygdala are both intact but disconnected from one another can solve abstract problems but lack the ability to apply these solutions to their personal lives (Damasio, 1994).

Adolescence is clearly a critical developmental period for limbic, temporal, and prefrontal regions of the brain. During adolescence neuronal connections between these structures are being shaped and defined through both growth and pruning processes. These connections play a role in the integration of emotional behaviors with cognitive processes (Walker & Bollini, 2002). The gray matter increases that occur during adolescence are followed by a decline that ultimately results in a net decrease in brain volume. Synaptic pruning eliminates as much as one half of the cortical synapses per neuron during this process (Spear, 2000). Synapses that are frequently activated are retained while those that are not are eliminated. Neuroscientist Jay Giedd and colleagues (1999) describe the process as one in which "the environment or activities of the teenager may guide selective synapse elimination during adolescence" (p. 863).

At the same time that gray matter is being decreased through synaptic pruning, white matter increases through myelination. This occurs predominantly in the tracts connecting frontal and temporal areas of the brain and in limbic structures. These changes in both gray and white matter streamline adolescent brain function by eliminating infrequently activated interconnections and enhancing those that remain. Biologist Linda Spear (2000) sees this process as increasing "focal activation of the brain, with less widespread activation of brain function during task performance as development proceeds through childhood and adolescence" (p. 439).

Neurotransmitter systems are also undergoing change during adolescence, as receptors for various neurotransmitters are pruned from their pre-adolescent over-production. Most such pruning eliminates excitatory stimulation reaching the cortex. This results in a decline in brain activity. During adolescence, prefrontal cortex activity is further suppressed as dopamine inhibitory input to the prefrontal cortex peaks. This affects judgment, decision-making, and impulse control. At the same time that dopamine inhibitory input to the prefrontal cortex reaches its maximal levels, dopamine inhibition of limbic activity, including that of the amygdala, is apparently lowest. Brain imaging studies show that when adolescents are tested on tasks that require them to identify the emotional state of others based on facial expressions, they exhibit much greater activity in the amygdala than in the frontal lobe while completing this task. Adults, however, exhibit greater activation in the frontal lobe than in the amygdala when engaged in the same activity (Spear, 2000). The adolescent shift in dopaminergic dominance may underlie these differences.

The shift in the dopaminergic systems that takes place during adolescence affects the "reward circuitry" of the brain, as well. This shift is implicated in the increased vulnerability of adolescents to drug and alcohol abuse. It may also provide the neurophysiological basis for "developing" religion. The reward circuitry is responsible for assigning incentive value to stimuli. As a result, it is important in translating motivational stimuli into adaptive behaviors. Some things, such as food, sex, and psychoactive drugs, have intrinsic reward value. They initiate approach and goal-seeking behaviors by activating the reward system. It is possible for stimuli with no intrinsic reward value to acquire incentive value through a process of learning. This has been demonstrated in individuals addicted to such drugs as cocaine. Brain imaging studies of these individuals have shown that, over time, the places and paraphernalia associated with cocaine are capable of activating the brain's "reward circuitry" even in the absence of the drugs themselves.

During adolescence the shift in the brain's reward system and the simultaneous maturation of the prefrontal cortex create an important opportunity for such learning to occur. The simultaneous shift in the dopaminergic reward system and the emergence of symbolic thought provides a developmental window for assigning reward value to social and symbolic stimuli. Changes in interconnections between the amygdala and the prefrontal cortex create an opportunity for integrating emotional valuations of these stimuli, as well. During adolescence emotional reactivity is at its peak, reward systems are in flux, and the prefrontal cortex itself is undergoing changes that introduce capacities for abstract and symbolic thought. Music, language, and social networks constitute the most important symbolic systems in human cultures. The maturation of the prefrontal and temporal cortices during adolescence allows the integration of these capacities with the brain's emotional and reward systems. The simultaneous shift in the brain's dopaminergic reward system, the change in amygdala limbic and prefrontal inter-connections, and the maturation of temporal and prefrontal cortices provide a unique developmental window for investing abstract and symbolic constructs with both incentive value and emotional meaning.

THE EMOTIONS AND SYMBOLS OF RELIGION

Religion is well suited to this task. The creation of "the sacred" depends on the formation of emotionally valenced association networks (Alcorta & Sosis, 2005). In religious systems highly memorable symbols make up the nodes of these networks. The settings, rituals, and beliefs of religion purposefully elicit emotions, both positive and negative. Darkened caves, chapels and cathedrals, grotesque masks, bleeding statues, and powerful supernatural agents that violate our normal expectations all activate our evolved vigilance systems and evoke an emotional response. These elements of ritual alert us, focus our attention, and emotionally engage us. Adolescent rites of passage that involve deprivation, pain, and fear further intensify these emotions. Such powerful emotions result in indelible memories that may be repressed but are never erased (Adolphs, 2002).

Of course, religion also evokes positive emotions. The awe-inspiring temples of Buddhism, the beautiful paintings that adorn Renaissance churches, and the engaging lyricism of Judeo-Christian psalms, Sufi poetry, and the Koran evoke emotions of peace and joy. Most significantly, in every religion known, music plays a central role in eliciting and entraining the positive emotions of sacred joy and ecstasy in adherents.

Music not only evokes such emotions, it also conjoins and entrains those who experience these emotions. Individuals listening to the same music share elicited emotions. They also share the autonomic changes in heart rate, respiration, skin conductance, and pulse rate engendered by those emotions. Studies by neuropsychologist Robert Levenson (2003) show that such shared autonomic functions highly correlate with the ability to empathize, an important element in cooperation. Music is highly symbolic. It not only elicits emotion, it also evokes social meaning. A musical phrase, like Proust's madeleines, can instantly recall a person, an event, or a year. This ability of music to simultaneously elicit emotions, entrain listeners, and symbolize events situates it in a unique position as a "proto-symbolic" system. The pivotal role of music in religions everywhere suggests that these attributes of music play a significant role in the ability of religious ritual to promote cooperation and unify groups.

ADOLESCENCE, RELIGION, AND BEHAVIOR

Adolescent rites of passage are a particularly effective mechanism for the experiential sculpting of emotionally valenced social-symbolic networks. As adolescents transition from the predominantly kin-based world of childhood to the expanded adolescent peer group encompassing unrelated individuals, they face the difficult task of sorting potential allies from adversaries. Biologist Norbert Sachser (1998) notes that in humans and other mammalian species, "the time around puberty seems to be essential for the acquisition of those social skills needed to adapt to unfamiliar conspecifics in a non-stressful and non-aggressive way" (p. 891). Religions throughout the world address this need by creating emotionally weighted value systems that guide social interactions. During the "experience expectant" period of adolescence, religion is particularly salient in integrating emotions and social-symbolic systems.

Can we find empirical evidence that religious participation does impact adolescent values and social behaviors? The traditional societies studied by anthropologists certainly support this argument. Adolescent rites of passage in these societies clearly and effectively shape adolescent values. The psychosocial changes in novices found in a longitudinal study of Thai adolescents participating in a Buddhist ordination program support this thesis (Thananart, Tori, & Emavardhana, 2000). The significant positive relationship between external warfare and highly intense and painful adolescent rites of passage provides additional empirical support for this argument (Sosis, Kress, & Boster, 2005). In traditional societies, however, alternative choices for adolescents are limited, and values may be dictated as much by the possibilities of everyday existence as by individual choice.

Contemporary developed nations provide a more rigorous testing ground for assessing the impacts of religious participation on values and social relationships. The wider religious diversity and the greater economic and political opportunities available to adolescents in these societies offer alternative secular lifestyles not available in traditional cultures. Recent sociological studies conduced in the United States have also found a significant positive relationship between adolescent religious involvement and pro-social values (Donahue & Benson, 1995; Smith, 2005). Adolescents who regularly attend religious services are significantly less likely to engage in delinquent behaviors, and less likely to use tobacco, alcohol, or drugs; they are also less likely to engage in premarital sex and risky sexual behaviors. Studies of the relationship between adolescent religious participation and sexual attitudes and activity in U.S. Christian populations have consistently found that young people who attend church frequently are less likely to hold permissive sexual attitudes and are as much as 50 percent less likely to engage in sexual behavior than nonattending teens (Donahue & Benson, 1995; Smith, 2005). Early life course exposure to religion also impacts adolescent predispositions toward childbearing. Sociologist Linda Pearce (2002) conducted an 18-year intergenerational panel study of mothers and children and found that "religion seems to act as a cultural system for these young adults that influences their larger views on childbearing, as well as their personal plans" (p. 232). These influences are both psychological and physiological. C.T. Halpern and his colleagues from the University of North Carolina (Halpern, Udry, & Campbell, 1994) conducted a study that looked at religious attendance, male adolescent testosterone levels, and sexual activity. They found a significant negative correlation between church attendance and sexual activity. They also found a significant negative correlation between church attendance and male testosterone indices. The effects of religious participation on adolescents clearly go beyond the psychological and include neuroendocrine changes, as well.

An accumulating health literature comparing the mental and physical health of adolescents who regularly participate in religious worship with those who do not also supports these conclusions (Regnerus, 2003). If religion is important in the development of emotionally anchored values that effectively guide behavior, then adolescents who participate in religion should experience less cognitive dissonance, and thus, less psychological distress, than nonparticipating teens. Accumulating research "confirms that religiosity is inversely related to depression and suicide ideation among adolescents" (Nooney, 2005, p. 341). Additionally, suicide rates are significantly lower for youth who regularly attend worship services as compared to those who do not (Donahue & Benson, 1995).

RELIGION AND THE LIFE COURSE

Human adolescence appears to be an "experience expectant" period of brain development for learning emotionally weighted social-symbolic schema. The structural elements of religious systems, and particularly those of adolescent rites of passage, incorporate elements that optimize the learning of such schema. Contemporary adolescent suicide bombers willing to give their lives for a perceived religious cause is testimony to the efficacy of religion in inculcating such emotionally valenced values.

Religion may be of particular importance during adolescence, but in most societies and religions throughout the world, religious participation is not confined to adolescence. A peek inside any Christian church on a Sunday morning will reveal attendance by men, women, and children of all ages. A closer look at the "average" American congregation would reveal more women than men and more elderly than adolescent participants. Young children and teens, when present, would be accompanied by other family members, and young unmarried adults would be conspicuous by their absence (Argue, Johnson, & White, 1999). Most adult men in attendance would be married, employed full-time, and have young or teenage children. The majority of women in attendance would also be parents of school-age children. However, the single mothers surveyed would be more likely than married mothers to be full-time employees (Becker & Hofmesiter, 2001; Sherkat, 2001). These patterns of religious attendance recur in other contemporary developed nations as well and have been assumed by many sociologists to represent universal patterns of religious participation. A review of the anthropological literature refutes this assumption, however. These patterns are specific to modern Western cultures. They do not typify religious attendance across all cultures and all times.

In many traditional societies participation in religious ritual is predominantly the province of adult males. In some cultures, such as that of the Ilahita Arapesh of New Guinea, religious participation is restricted exclusively to males who have successfully completed adolescent initiation rites (Paige & Paige, 1981). In these societies the exclusion of children and females from religious rituals contributes to their perceived danger and awe. Sacred names softly whispered, fearsome masks barely glimpsed, and powerful spirits summoned by eerily haunting music all foster innate predispositions of children to believe in the socially omniscient supernatural agents of their cultures and enforce cultural proscriptions and beliefs.

A rigorous cross-cultural comparison of religious participation patterns has yet to be conducted. Participation patterns reported for many traditional societies, as well as the patterns found by sociologists in contemporary American cultures, strongly suggest a relationship between religious participation and trust-based social affiliation. In traditional, non-state societies, such participation creates and reinforces political, as well as social, relationships in the absence of formalized political institutions (Paige & Paige, 1981). Religion may also serve this role for disenfranchised subcultures within modern nation-state societies. The importance of religion in mobilizing the African-American Civil rights movement of the 1960s, the growing political role of Pentecostalist churches throughout Latin America, and the increasing clout of the conservative religious right in U.S. politics all provide evidence of such a role for religion. The ability of religion to create cooperative, trust-based social groups also goes far in explaining the higher religious participation rates of females, and specifically of single working mothers, in contemporary U.S. religions, as well as the high participation rates of the elderly. Both of these groups lack a clearly defined power base within the dominant economic institutions of the United States, and both experience trust-based cooperative needs, such as childcare and social integration, that are not being met by either the kin systems or political institutions of the society. In my own research with American adolescents, I have found that one of the most important features of successful church youth groups is the creation of such trust-based social affiliations. The ability of religion to foster such affiliations may constitute the initial reason for its evolution and explain the ongoing importance of religion as a fundamental component of human cultural systems.

CONCLUSION

Do humans possess an innate predisposition to "learn" religion, and is there a sensitive developmental period for such learning to occur? There is mounting evidence that the answer to both of these questions is "yes." Much like music and language, religion appears to be an evolved capacity of humans with both a neurophysiological and genetic basis, but that is dependent upon socialization experiences for its development. Like music and language, religion is both an individual and social construction. The development of each of these human capacities requires the creation of neural networks shaped through cultural experiences. Music, language, and religion all exhibit "experience expectancy"; each is best developed during specific brain maturation periods. "Learning" religion, like learning music and language, is a cumulative process that incorporates previously developed capacities and builds upon them. The cultural encoding of emotional meaning in music, and the development of innate predispositions for language-based supernatural beliefs are part of this process. During adolescence music and language capacities are engaged in the construction of emotionally weighted symbolic systems that motivate individual behaviors and structure social relations. The shifting of neurotransmitter-based reward systems in the brain, and the maturation of brain regions responsible for planning, social judgment, abstract and symbolic thought, and individual impulse control create an "experience expectant" period for associating cultural symbols, individual emotions, and social relations. Religion generally, and adolescent rites of passage in particular, appear optimally selected to shape these associations.

Adolescence provides a particularly important developmental window for "learning" religion. Like music and language, religion appears to be a unique human adaptation made possible by the developmental plasticity of the human brain. This plasticity provides a substrate for the creation of emotionally valenced social-symbolic systems capable of integrating individual needs and social behaviors. The development of these emotionally weighted value systems plays a crucial role in the integration of individuals into larger cooperative social groups. The shared motivational force and meaning of religious symbols provide a foundation for both guiding and predicting social behaviors. In the absence of such a system, social interactions among unrelated individuals are fraught with misperceptions and predicated upon self-interest. Such circumstances simultaneously degrade social cooperation and increase individual stress. Religion's vital role in the developmental of emotionally anchored social-symbolic systems, and its ability to cohere and create cooperative social groups, establish the foundations for human culture.

REFERENCES

Adolphs, R. (2002). Social cognition and the human brain. In J. T. Cacioppo, G. G. Berntson, R. Adolphs, C. Carter, R. Davidson, M. McClintock, B. McEwen M. Meaney, D. Schacter, E. Sternberg, S. Suomi, & S. Taylor (Eds.), *Foundations in social neuroscience* (pp. 313–332). Cambridge: MIT Press.

Alcorta, C., & Sosis, R. (2005). Ritual, emotion and sacred symbols: The evolution of religion as an adaptive complex. *Human Nature, 16*(4), 323–359.

Argue, A., Johnson, D., & White, L. (1999). Age and religiosity: Evidence from a three-wave panel analysis. *Journal for the Scientific Study of Religion, 38*, 423–435.

Atran, S., & Norenzayan, A. (2004). Religion's evolutionary landscape: Counterintuition, commitment, compassion, communion. *Behavioral and Brain Sciences, 27*, 713–730.

Becker, J. (2001). Anthropological perspectives on music and emotion. In P. Juslin & J. Sloboda (Eds.), *Music and emotion* (pp. 135–160). Oxford: Oxford University Press.

Becker, P. E., & Hofmeister, H. (2001). Work, family and religious involvement for men and women. *Journal for the Scientific Study of Religion, 40*, 707–722.

Bering, J. M. (2004). The evolutionary history of an illusion: Religious causal beliefs in children and adults. In B. Ellis & D. Bjorklund (Eds.), *Origins of the social mind: Evolutionary psychology and child development* (pp. 411–437). New York: Guilford Press.

Bloch, M. (1989). *Ritual, history and power.* London: Athlone Press.

Chaves, M., Konieszny, M. E., Beyerlein, K., & Barman, E. (1999). The national congregations study: Background, methods and selected results. *Journal for the Scientific Study of Religion, 38*, 458–476.

Cross, I. (2003). Music as a biocultural phenomenon. In G. Avanzini, C. Faienza, D. Minciacchi, L. Lopez, & M. Majno (Eds.), *The neurosciences and music* (pp. 106–111). Annals of the New York Academy of Sciences, Vol. 999. New York: New York Academy of Sciences.

Dahl, R. E. (2004). Adolescent brain development: A period of vulnerabilities and opportunities. In R. E. Dahl & L. P. Spear (Eds.), *Adolescent brain development: Vulnerabilities and opportunities* (pp. 1–22). Annals of the New York Academy of Sciences, Vol. 1021. New York: New York Academy of Sciences.

Damasio, A. R. (1994). *Descartes' error: Emotion, reason, and the human brain.* New York: Avon Books.

Donahue, M. J., & Benson, P. L. (1995). Religion and the well-being of adolescents. *Journal of Social Issues, 51*, 145–160.

Dorn, L. D., & Chrousos, G. P. (1993). The endocrinology of stress and stress system disorders in adolescence. *Endocrinology and Metabolism Clinics of North America, 22*, 685–700.

Eliade, M. (1958). *Rites and symbols of initiation: The mysteries of birth and rebirth.* Dallas, TX: Spring Publications.

Gabrielsson, A. (2001). Emotions in strong experiences with music. In P. A. Justin & J. A. Sloboda (Eds.), *Music and emotion* (pp. 431–449). Oxford: Oxford University Press.

Giedd, J., Blumenthal, J., Jeffries, N. O., Catellanos, F. X., Liu, H., Zijdenbos, A., et al. (1999). Brain development during childhood and adolescence: A longitudinal MRI study. *Nature Neuroscience, 2*, 861–863.

Glucklich, A. (2001). *Sacred pain.* New York: Oxford University Press.

Greenough, W. T. (1986). What's special about development? Thoughts on the bases of experience sensitive synaptic plasticity. In W. T. Greenough & J. M. Juraska (Eds.), *Developmental neuropsychobiology* (pp. 387–408). New York: Academic Press.

Halpern, C. T., Udry, J. R., & Campbell, B. (1994). Testosterone and religiosity as predictors of sexual attitudes and activity among adolescent males: A biosocial model. *Journal of Biosocial Science, 26*, 216–234.

Koelsch, S., & Friederici, A. D. (2003). Toward the neural basis of processing structure in music. Comparative results of different neurophysiological investigation methods. In G. Avanzini, C. Faineza, D. Minciacchi, L. Lopez, & M. Majno (Eds.), *The neurosciences and music* (pp. 15–28). Annals of the New York Academy of Sciences, Vol. 999. New York: New York Academy of Sciences.

Kolb, B., Forgie, M., Gibb, R., Gorny, G., & Rontree, S. (1998). Age, experience and the changing brain. *Neuroscience & Biobehavioral Reviews, 22*, 143–159.

Kwon, Y. J., & Lawson, A. E. (2000). Linking brain growth with the development of scientific reasoning ability and conceptual change during adolescence. *Journal of Research in Science Teaching, 37,* 44–62.

Laviola, G., Adriani, W., Terranova, M. L., & Gerra, G. (1999). Psychobiological risk factors for vulnerability to psychostimulants in human adolescents and animal models. *Neuroscience and Biobehavioral Reviews, 23,* 993–1010.

Levenson, R. W. (2003). Blood, sweat and fears: the autonomic architecture of emotions. In P. Ekman, J. J. Campos, R. J. Davidson, & F.B.M. de Waal (Eds.), *Emotions inside out,* (pp. 348–366). Annals of the New York Academy of Sciences, Vol. 1000. New York: New York Academy of Sciences.

Liegeois-Chauvel, C., Giraud, K., Badier, J. M., Marquis, P., & Chauvel, P. (2001). Intracerebral evoked potentials in pitch perception reveal a functional asymmetry of the human auditory cortex. In R. J. Zatorre & I. Peretz (Eds.), *The biology of music* (pp. 117–132). New York Academy of Science, Vol. 930. New York: New York Academy of Sciences.

Lutkehaus, N. C., & Roscoe, P. B. (Eds.). (1995). *Gender rituals: Female initiation in Melanesia.* New York: Routledge.

McCauley, R. N. (2001). Ritual, memory and emotion: Comparing two cognitive hypotheses. In J. Andresen (Ed.), *Religion in mind* (pp. 115–140). Cambridge: Cambridge University Press.

Nooney, J. G. (2005). Religion, stress, and mental health in adolescence: Findings from ADD health. *Review of Religious Research, 46,* 341–354.

Paige, K. E., & Paige, J. M. (1981). *The politics of reproductive ritual.* Los Angeles: University of California Press.

Patel, A. D. (2003). Rhythm in language and music. Parallels and differences. In G. Avanzini, C. Faienza, D. Minciacchi, L. Lopez, & M. Majno (Eds.), *The neurosciences and music* (pp. 140–143). Annals of the New York Academy of Sciences, Vol. 999. New York Academy of Sciences, New York.

Pearce, L. D. (2002). The influence of early life course religious exposure on young adults' dispositions toward childbearing. *Journal for the Scientific Study of Religion, 41,* 325–340.

Rappaport, R. A. (1999). *Ritual and religion in the making of humanity.* London: Cambridge University Press.

Regnerus, M. D. (2003). Religion and positive adolescent outcomes: A review of research and theory. *Review of Religious Research, 44,* 394–413.

Sackser, N., Durschlagim, M., & Hirzel, D. (1998). Social relationships and the management of stress. *Psychoneuroendocrinology, 23*(8), 891–904.

Schlegel, A., & Barry, H. (1991). *Adolescence: An anthropological inquiry.* New York: Free Press.

Sherkat, D. E. (2001). Investigating the sect-church-sect cycle: Cohort-specific differences across African-American denominations. *Journal for the Scientific Study of Religion, 40*(2), 221–233.

Smith, C. (2005). *Soul searching. The religious and spiritual lives of American teenagers.* New York: Oxford University Press.

Sosis, R., Kress, H., & Boster, J. (2005). Scars for war: Evaluating alternative signaling explanations for cross-cultural variance in ritual costs. Unpublished manuscript, University of Connecticut.

Sosis, R., & Ruffle, B. (2003). Religious ritual and cooperation: Testing for a relationship on Israeli religious and secular kibbutzim. *Current Anthropology, 44*(5), 713–722.

Sowell, E. R., Thompson, P. M., Holmes, C. J, Jernigan, T. L., & Toga, A. W. (1999). In vivo evidence for post-adolescent brain maturation in frontal and striatal regions. *Nature Neuroscience, 2,* 859–861.

Spear, L. P. (2000). The adolescent brain and age-related behavioral manifestations. *Neuroscience and Biobehavioral Reviews, 24,* 417–463.

Thananart, M., Tori, C., & Emavardhana, T. (2000). A longitudinal study of psychosocial changes among Thai adolescents participating in a Buddhist ordination program for novices. *Adolescence, 35,* 285–293.

Trehub, S. E. (2001). Musical predispositions in infancy. In R. Zatorre, & I. Peretz, (Eds.), *The biological foundations of music* (pp. 1–16). Annals of the New York Academy of Sciences, Vol. 930. New York: The New York Academy of Sciences.

Turnbull, C. M. (1962). *The forest people.* New York: Simon and Schuster.

Turner, V. (1967). *The forest of symbols.* New York: Cornell University Press.

van Gennep, A. (1960). *The rites of passage.* Chicago: Chicago University Press. (Original work published in 1909)

Walker, E., & Bollini, A. M. (2002). Pubertal neurodevelopment and the emergence of psychotic symptoms. *Schizophrenia Research, 54,* 17–23.

CHAPTER 5

NEUROTHEOLOGY: A SCIENCE OF WHAT?

Matthew Ratcliffe

INTRODUCTION

There is considerable current interest in the question of what, if anything, neuroscience can tell us about religion. Discussion of the topic is not confined to academia, but has captured the public imagination and found its way into the popular press. For example, an article appeared in the *LA Times* on October 29, 1997 and, subsequently, in other publications announcing that a "God spot" had been found in the brain. The story referred to the finding reported by V. S. Ramachandran and colleagues that heightened emotional response in certain subjects with focal temporal lobe epilepsy was specific to stimuli of a religious nature (Ramachandran & Blakeslee, 1998). Some work by Michael Persinger has also received considerable attention.[1] Persinger used a device called a transcranial magnetic stimulator to focus a weak magnetic field on areas of the brain and reported that stimulation of a particular area often resulted in a religious experience (Persinger, 2002b). The growing field of research on religion and the brain, which has taken its lead from such findings, often goes by the name "neurotheology," a term that was in use at least as far back as the 1980s but has been employed increasingly during the last few years.

Why all the interest? The possibility of neural circuits specifically associated with religion raises all sorts of intriguing questions concerning the biological basis, function, and evolutionary history of religion. Perhaps it might even cast light on the question of God's existence. But before such questions can be coherently addressed, it is important to be clear about just what it is that is being studied. When claims are made about neural circuitry associated with "religion" or with "religious experience," how are those terms to be understood? My aim here is to explore this question and, in so doing, to raise a number of related philosophical concerns that arise in connection with some of the better known recent work in neurotheology.

If the claim were that certain brain areas are specifically associated with religion, it would be highly problematic. Studies such as those of Ramachandran and Persinger do not investigate the neural correlates of *religion* but of certain kinds of *experience*, and brief reflection suffices to make clear that there is a lot more to religion than just religious experience. Religions incorporate texts, rituals, roles, statuses, ceremonies, practices, and shared belief systems. They interact in numerous ways with a broader culture and allow for many different levels and kinds of commitment and conviction on the part of their diverse practitioners.

Much of the structure of religion cannot be understood in terms of the cognitive dispositions of religious individuals, given that religion is also a cultural-historical framework into which those individuals are born or introduced and shaped. Religion, it seems, is not just a matter of the properties of individual brains, but of a shared way of life through which words, deeds, and experiences are interpreted (Phillips, 1986). Furthermore, religions differ in all manner of ways and, even if an essence common to all religions could be distilled, it would most likely not be something that could be wholly captured in terms of the beliefs and experiences of individuals viewed in isolation from culture.

The way to avoid such tricky issues is to stress that these studies are concerned not with religions as historical and cultural phenomena, but with the religious experiences of individuals. Now it might well be that all religions were originally inspired by such experiences, or, alternatively, it could be that religious experience is only one contributing factor in the formation of religions. Turning to individual practitioners, some people's religious beliefs might originate in religious experience, while those of others might arise wholly from other sources, such as enculturation, indoctrination, or rational deliberation. However, regardless of the specifics, it is clear that religious experience is an important element of most, if not all, religions. Hence, discoveries about religious experience are likely to have at least some repercussions for a more general understanding of religion.

Unfortunately, focusing on religious experience does not dispense with the problem of identifying one's subject matter, since it is by no means clear what religious experience is or whether various religious experiences have anything interesting in common. One might reply that a religious experience is just an experience of God. For instance, Persinger (2002a) repeatedly refers to "the God experience," suggesting that a distinct kind of experience has indeed been identified. However, other authors have described several different kinds of religious experience, some of which do not seem to incorporate the presence of the God of monotheism. For example, Caroline Franks Davis (1989, chap. 2) offers the following taxonomy:

1. Interpretive experiences: Experiences, such as fortuitous co-incidences, which are interpreted in religious terms.

2. Quasi-sensory experiences: These include visions, voices, dreams and tactile sensations.

3. Revelatory experiences: Sudden moments of insight that seem to come from elsewhere.

4. Regenerative experiences: Profound feelings of strength, comfort or joy.

5. Numinous experiences: Feelings of insignificance before the majesty of God.

6. Mystical experiences: The experience of encountering ultimate reality, often associated with feelings of oneness, serenity and a loss of the sense of space and time.

These experiences need not be mutually exclusive, and they might combine in all sorts of ways. The question is what, if anything, they all have in common. If some are very different from others, the search for neural correlates of a single type of religious, mystical, or spiritual experience would be futile, analogous to looking for the neural correlates of metal object experience, hairy thing experience, car experience or any other category that arbitrarily brought together many different kinds of phenomena. Thus, if neurotheology is to get off the ground, it must have as its subject matter a distinct experiential category or set of experiential categories.

This is not just a hypothetical concern. Seemingly different kinds of experience *do* run together in some of the literature. For example, Persinger (2002b, p. 280) hypothesizes that an experience of the "'sensed presence' of a Sentient Being," as induced through weak magnetic stimulation of an area of the brain, is the prototype or experiential foundation for full-blown religious experiences. Why, he asserts this is unclear. Feelings of sensed presence often involve experiencing another being as utterly other than oneself, as detached and alien (Cheyne, 2001). In contrast, many religious experiences are characterized by a feeling of oneness with the cosmos, of a mystical union that is quite different from the sense that another sentient being, wholly distinct from oneself, is present.[2] So if such claims are to be made plausible, a clearer account is needed of why these experiences are similar in kind.

To demarcate its subject matter, neurotheology not only requires a plausible, explicit taxonomy of different religious, mystical, and spiritual experiences, but it also needs to draw a clear line between these and mundane, everyday experiences. If one is to study the neural correlates of *religious experience,* one must assume that there is such a thing as an intrinsically religious experience. An alternative possibility is that religious, mystical, or spiritual characteristics are not *part of* the experience at all but, rather, religious *interpretations* of experiences that possess no intrinsic religious elements. For example, it could be that many religious experiences are just emotionally charged experiences that are interpreted in religious terms by certain people.

Furthermore, many nonreligious experiences are far from mundane. Take intense feelings of grief, love, guilt, estrangement, and surreality. All of these can be very intense and utterly imbued with meaning, but they do not fall into the familiar categories of religious, spiritual, or mystical? Thus, there is the concern that attempts to study religious experience and the brain risk throwing a diverse range of experiences together while ignoring others, despite there being no arbitrary division between those studied and those cast aside.

All of this is not so say that religious experiences do not all have a common, underlying core. Perhaps they do. A well-known unitary account is that of William James. In his famous *Varieties of Religious Experience,* James (1902) suggests that there is a "nucleus" uniting superficially diverse religious experiences. This nucleus involves a sense that something is not quite right about oneself, the world, or one's relation with the world. The unease is followed by a solution, whereby one discovers a higher part of oneself, a part that is not isolated from the rest of the universe but is instead bound up with a higher power.

James (1902) claims that differences between religious experiences are the result of different "over-beliefs," by which he means culture-specific narratives through which the core experience is interpreted and communicated. God is not intrinsic to the experience but is just one over-belief in terms of which it can be interpreted and communicated to others (pp. 507–508).

Maybe neurotheology could adopt a description along similar lines. However, there might be a price. James's account explicitly focuses on those rare individuals for whom religion is an "acute fever," rather than a "dull habit" (p. 6), and it is perhaps not applicable to religious experiences more liberally construed. There may also be serious problems with James's view, which rests on his questionable prioritizing of individual experience over cultural expression. According to James, the over-beliefs are imposed *upon* the core experience. However, it seems that our habits, our practices, our abilities and so forth also feed into our experiences and shape them in all manner of ways. To give an obvious example, think about seeing a sign that says "no smoking." It is nearly impossible to look at this sign without comprehending its meaning, a grasp of which seems inseparable from one's *experience* of the sign. However, to experience it in that way, one must know how to read a particular language and also be a competent participant in a culture that recognizes both a practice known as smoking and the concept of an environment-specific prohibition applicable to all. Generalizing from any number of similar examples, it is arguable that the notion of a core experience, untainted by culture, is not sustainable. As Charles Taylor puts it:

> The ideas, the understanding with which we live our lives, shape directly what we could call religious experiences; and these languages, these vocabularies, are never those simply of an individual. (Taylor, 2002, p. 28)

Any account focusing solely on individuals, or indeed on brains, runs the risk of neglecting the shared social contexts through which experiences are structured. By analogy, if one were to study the nature of baseball, an account that referred solely to the biological capacities of individuals that dispose them to play baseball would not only be incomplete, but largely beside the point, given that the activity of playing baseball is only possible given a particular cultural context. It is this context that explains the *existence* of baseball, rather than "baseball areas" in people's brains.

Perhaps religious experiences are comparable. Even solitary meditation is performed in accordance with established norms and shared practices that are passed on from generation to generation via cultural, rather than biological, transmission. If historically stable cultural conditions are required before individuals can have experiences of a certain type, interpret their mundane experiences in a certain way, or categorize certain experiences as religious, spiritual, or mystical, then perhaps the brain is not the right place to start looking for answers.

Of course, just as there is variability in people's expertise at baseball, there may well be differing individual propensities for religious experience, which are explicable in neurobiological terms. However, one could never arrive at an understanding of what baseball *is* just by studying the biological traits of individuals. One would have to start with an understanding of the game before one could make sense of what individuals were doing, how they came to do it, and why they do it. The same may well be true of religious experience and the brain. Unless one already understands something of what religious experience is, studies of relevant brain processes run the risk of descending into confusion.

THE NEURAL CORRELATES OF SOMETHING RATHER VAGUE

So far, I have briefly sketched some problems concerning the nature of religious experience,[3] which will need to be addressed by any account of the relationship between religious experience and the brain. However, it is not unreasonable to suggest that, although neurotheologists need to be mindful of such problems, they are not required to solve them before they can start work. It might well turn out that scientific studies will themselves play a role in distinguishing and clarifying the different categories of experience. To give an overly simple example, if several subjects all volunteer similar verbal reports of an experience but it turns out that two quite different patterns of neural activity are involved, with roughly half the subjects exhibiting each pattern, we might look at their descriptions of the experience again, note subtle differences between them, and realize that what we previously thought was an experience of type A is actually two quite different types of experience, A and B. Neurotheology does not need to solve all the philosophical problems before it can even get off the ground. Instead, it can seek progressive clarification of its subject matter as it proceeds.

With this in mind, I will now look at some specific claims made on behalf of neurotheology. I will suggest that some of the best known work in the area has not satisfactorily resolved the kinds of problems mentioned above, with the consequence that many of the bolder claims made concerning the successes of neurotheology are premature. Although I will focus primarily on a well-known book by Andrew Newberg, Eugene d'Aquili, and Vince Rause (2001), many of the problems I discuss are common to work in neurotheology more generally.

Perhaps the strongest claim that Newberg et al. (2001) make on behalf of neurotheology is that neuroscience has demonstrated that religious, mystical, and spiritual experiences do indeed exist. As they put it, "mystical experience is biologically, observably, and scientifically real" rather than "wishful thinking" (p. 7). The claim is that, regardless of whether or not these experiences turn out to be veridical, they are at least shown to be real. By analogy, the experience of seeing a chocolate cake is a real experience, regardless of whether it is a dream or a veridical perception. But is this claim on behalf of neuroscience defensible? The suggestion seems to be that, without the intervention of science, there would be doubt concerning whether mystical experiences do in fact occur. However, such skepticism certainly does not apply to most other experiences. If I claim to be recalling the holiday I had in Tobago last summer, you would presumably not doubt my testimony until you had scanned my brain to check that the neural pattern was appropriate. And you would not suspend your belief that other people experience trees, stars, music, and the taste of curry until neuroscience had come to your assistance. But perhaps mystical experiences are different, in that they are outside the norm and cannot be supported by other evidence, such as several photographs of me in Tobago or a spoonful of meat vindaloo in the mouth of the person claiming to taste curry. Hence, it might be argued, they warrant a greater degree of skepticism.

Nevertheless, skepticism concerning their existence is still hard to defend. Religious, mystical, and spiritual experiences have been discussed and written about by many thousands of people over the course of thousands of years. Now it seems safe to assume that all these people have had some kind of experience, regardless of philosophical problems involved in specifying what, precisely, such experiences consist of. The alternative would be to brand them all liars or proclaim them incompetent to report in any way on what their experiences are like. So it is unclear why neural correlates should be required to corroborate such a substantial body of testimony. However, maybe neurotheology tells us something more specific about the *nature* of the experience, something absent from subjective reports. Newberg et al. (2001) state that ". . . neurology makes it clear that spiritual insights are born in startling moments of mystical transcendence" (p. 139) and that "[t]he wisdom of the mystics, it seems, has predicted for centuries what neurology now shows to be true: In Absolute Unitary Being, self blends into other; mind and matter are one and the same" (p. 156).

Is this so? Imagine that you had never had a religious experience and had never heard of religious experience. In fact, all you had to go on was the neurobiological data. What could you ascertain about experience from this alone? Could you look at the results of brain imaging studies and conclude that "Absolute Unitary Being" was experienced or that "mystical transcendence" was occurring? The answer is no. Newberg et al. *presuppose* a conception of what the relevant experiences consist of. They claim to discover specific patterns of neural activity correlated with an experiential type, but this discovery clearly does *not* underlie their understanding of what the experiential type consists of or their belief that it exists.

Furthermore, suppose that someone claimed to be having a religious experience and that her pattern of neural activity differed from what is the norm in such cases. Would this be reason enough to dismiss her claim? I suspect not. Consider a fictional scenario where 100 people have their brains scanned in all manner of ways while entertaining the belief that "the Eiffel Tower is in Paris." Now suppose that in 99 of these people, a specific area of the brain is active while they claim to entertain the belief. In the other person, that area is comparatively inactive, and several other areas are "lit up" instead. Would this be sufficient warrant for maintaining that the anomalous person had a different belief to the others? It would not, given that nobody claims that specific belief contents—such as "*Revenge of the Sith* is a *Star Wars* film," "Santa Claus exists," or "Sydney is warmer than the North Pole"—require the same patterns of brain activity in all people. Hence, there are clearly cases where we would not want to say that neuroscience overrides personal testimony. But, one might reply, Paris beliefs are not an appropriate object of study at all, given that they do not comprise an informative psychological kind. Anything one might learn about Paris beliefs would be equally informative with respect to just about any other belief content; Paris and The Eiffel Tower are incidental. It could be added that Paris beliefs can be associated with all sorts of very different experiences and that neurotheology is preoccupied with certain kinds of experience, rather than abstract beliefs stripped of their connection to concrete experience.

However, the same concern about psychological kinds arises in relation to experience. Suppose one were to study cat experiences in constrained laboratory conditions. A variety of subjects are asked, one after the other, to sit in a chair in the corner of a monochrome square room. At the other end of the room is a large white cat, asleep in a basket. Participants are asked to focus solely on the cat for one minute, and, during that time, their patterns of brain activity are recorded, using whatever technique you like. Now suppose that there are common patterns of activity associated with the experience in all participants. What would this tell us about cat experience? Such studies might well tell us something about *experience and the brain*, but they would not tell us anything about specifically catty experiences because cat experience is not an informative experiential category. We do not ordinarily identify distinct kinds of experience by identifying different kinds of experiential objects, such as dogs, cats, chainsaws, and oranges, given that anything we learn about the structure of experience more generally will be equally applicable to experiences of all these things. Thus, a correlation between experience of entity X and brain activity A need not be remotely informative with respect to the experiential content X.

If correlations between neural activity and religious experience are to be informative, it must be the case that religious experiences, unlike cat experiences, comprise an experiential type about which illuminating generalizations can be made. So, what makes an experience religious? The obvious answer is its content, what it is about, as indicated by Persinger's (2002a) references to the God experience. However, we have just seen that, in other cases, types of experiential object, such as cats and dogs, do not serve to distinguish experiential types. Now, it may be contested that other types of experiential object are different. Take an experience of emotion. Surely this is a common *kind* of experience in a way that a cat experience is not. However, the comparison does not work. Experiences of emotions are not generally experiences of objects called emotions. One experiences objects *emotionally*, rather than experiencing the emotions themselves as objects. Perhaps one might similarly maintain that religious, spiritual, and mystical experiences are ways of experiencing things or forms of experience rather than categories of experiential objects. But this is hard to reconcile with the fact that many such experiences are described as experiences *of* something. So neurotheology seems to be caught on the horns of a dilemma. If the experiences it explores constitute a type in virtue of their objects, then it is hard to see why that type would be worthy of study in its own right.

And, if they involve a way of experiencing, the question arises as to how they can be described so as to make clear what binds them together as a group, without appealing to their objects.

Do Newberg et al. (2001) manage to say anything in support of mystical experience being a distinctive experiential type with informative neural correlates? Consider the following passage:

[humans] are natural mystics blessed with an inborn genius for effortless self-transcendence. If you ever "lost yourself" in a beautiful piece of music, for example, or felt "swept away" by a rousing patriotic speech, you have tasted in a small but revealing way the essence of mystical union. (p. 113)

This seems to indicate that mystical experiences form a continuum with everyday experiences. Now, all our experiences are intricately structured and incorporate different elements to differing degrees and so the question arises as to what makes mystical elements stand out from the rest in such a way that they can be regarded as a distinctive experiential type. Newberg et al. emphasize a sense of oneness with things as the core characteristic and state that in everyday life, by contrast, "we experience that world as something from which we are clearly set apart" (p. 115). However, such pronouncements about everyday experience are simplistic to say the least. In a recent paper (Ratcliffe, 2005b), I try to make explicit some of the many different ways in which we experience our relationship with the world during the course of our everyday lives. Consider feeling detached from things, at home in the world, slightly lost, removed from it all, abandoned, disconnected, empty, powerless, in control of things, trapped and weighed down, at one with nature, part of a greater whole, out of it, at one with life, there, not quite there, part of things, cut off from reality, brought down to earth or unreal. And the list seems to go on indefinitely. There are feelings of strangeness, unreality, oneness, intangibility, belonging, familiarity, completeness, power, fragility, disjointedness, coherence, meaningfulness, emptiness, mystery, unintelligibility, separation and so forth. Some of these terms are synonyms for others, whereas others seem to point to subtly distinct experiences. But the bottom line is that any attempt to force all our experiences into the categories of either mundane separation or mystical oneness would fail to do justice to the varieties of experience and their complex relations to each other.

Even if we assume that mystical oneness is a distinctive way of experiencing, it is clear that we have drifted a long way from specifically religious experience and thus from anything warranting the name neurotheology. In discussing ritual, Newberg et al. (2001) state that "when the unitary states generated by the neurobiology of ritual occur in a religious context, they are usually interpreted as a personal experience of the closeness of God" (p. 90). This suggests that God, religion, and all manner of other contents are not part of the mystical experience of unity, but are imposed upon it through acts of interpretation. So we seem to have arrived at a rather Jamesian view, according to which multifarious interpretations rest upon an underlying way of experiencing one's relationship with things.

Can worthwhile neurobiological generalizations be made with regard to this way of experiencing? In an earlier publication, Newberg and d'Aquili (2000) acknowledge that the experiences in question are not simple states:

> Religious and spiritual experiences are highly complex states that likely involve many brain structures including those involved in higher order processing of sensory and cognitive input as well as those involved in the elaboration of emotions and autonomic responses. (p. 251)

This suggests a recurrence of the cat experience problem, which is not avoided by a shift in emphasis from the objects of experience to oneness as a way of experiencing. Suppose that all the constituents of mystical, religious, or spiritual experiences are common to other kinds of experiences and that there are no neural correlates specific to these experiences and only these experiences. Consider a type of experience A, which is already known to incorporate elements B, C, D, and E, these elements also being present to varying degrees in many other kinds of experience. Now assume that there are neural correlates of B, C, D, and E. Will this tell us anything specific about A? The answer is no. A common pattern of argument in neurotheology is as follows:

1. A incorporates B.
2. There are interesting neural correlates of B.
3. Therefore there are interesting neural correlates of A.

However, what is true of B here need not be true of A. For example, there are all sorts of neural processes specific to visual experiences but that does not make them informative with respect to visual experiences of cats.

Consider Newberg, d'Aquili, and Rause's work on meditating subjects. They report that unusual neural activity is consistently found in the "posterior superior parietal lobe" at the peak of meditation (p. 4). This area is associated with a sense of spatial orientation and so Newberg et al. (2001) hypothesize that the area is starved of input during prolonged periods of physically inactive meditation, resulting in a breakdown of spatial boundaries and a sense of oneness (p. 28). Now it is clear from subjective reports that certain mystical experiences involve a loss of spatial and temporal locatedness. Thus, it should come as no surprise that brain areas associated with spatial and temporal locatedness are implicated in the experience. However, there is no evidence to suggest the experience is wholly constituted by a loss of spatial and temporal boundaries. Newberg et al. do not enquire as to whether similar brain activities can be found in other unremarkable or very different experiences. So it is not clear that the correlations discovered through such studies pick up on something specific to mystical experience, as opposed to an element common to many, although not all, kinds of experience.

The problem is illustrated more clearly in other claims made by Newberg et al. (2001). For example, they state that "the visual association area may . . . play a prominent role in religious and spiritual experiences that involve visual imagery" (p. 27). It will, presumably, play a role in any experience associated with visual imagery. That neural circuits are specific to B and that B is involved in A need not say anything remotely informative about A. The same kind of logic could be applied equally to experiences of cups of tea. There are plenty of similar examples. For example:

> We believe that part of the reason the attention association area is activated during spiritual practices such as meditation is because it is heavily involved in emotional responses—and religious experiences are usually highly emotional. (Newberg et al., p. 31)

If the claim were simply that many religious experiences are emotional, it would hardly come as a surprise. The fact that certain religious experiences are highly emotional is readily apparent from a huge body of testimony and from observation of people lying prostrate on the floor wailing, with tears streaming down their faces, to cite but one of many obviously emotional behaviors that are frequently associated with religious experience. The claim is instead about the neural basis of religious experience. However, it actually relates to emotion and only trivially to the many experiences that involve emotion. All it amounts to, so far as I can see, is that religious experiences have similar constituents to other experiences and will involve brain areas that are associated with those constituents. It says nothing informative about the category "religious experience" and does nothing to address the still unresolved question of whether such experiences even comprise a distinctive experiential category.

This explanatory pattern is not just evident in the work of Newberg and colleagues. Consider one of the best known studies of the neural basis of religious dispositions, carried out by Ramachandran and colleagues (Ramachandran & Blakeslee, 1998). Ramachandran's findings show that heightened affective response in certain subjects is not stimulus-general, but specific to religious words and icons. Given this finding, Ramachandran goes on to speculate about there being neural structures dedicated to the mediation of religious experiences. Now, what the study certainly does achieve is a clear distinction between two possibilities, "globally heightened affect" and "specific affective responsiveness," plus a good empirical case for the latter. What it does not do is tell us anything at all about the relationship between specifically *religious* tendencies and the brain. How can that be? Well, it seems safe to assume that affective responsiveness to particular religious icons is not hard-wired from birth but learned. With this in mind, consider an alternative scenario. Throughout his life, Arnold, who perhaps suffers from focal temporal lobe seizures, has been obsessed by the films of Steven Seagal. Indeed, such is the extent of Arnold's obsession that his interest in all other stimuli is rather diminished. One day Arnold is taken into a laboratory, and his galvanic skin response is monitored while he is presented with various stimuli.[4] Among these stimuli are the DVD covers of several as yet unreleased Steven Seagal films, none of which Arnold has yet acquired or even heard of. Sure enough, we find that Arnold's skin response to these stimuli is far higher than his response to any of the others, including stimuli of a horrific, religious, or sexual nature. What can we conclude from this? Well, we can certainly say something about response specificity, but the content of the stimulus is utterly contingent; it could have been anything. One would certainly not be justified in speculating about a Steven Seagal spot in the brain or embarking on the new science of neuroStevenSeagalology.

What is the difference between the two cases? Granted, the structure of our culture and the significance attached by many people to religious iconography and language make it more likely that Arnold will be aroused by religious stimuli than by Steven Seagal. However, in both cases, I do not think the results tell us anything informative about the relationship between the stimulus *content* and brain biology. Areas of the brain associated with emotion are only contingently related to religion, and studies that tell us something about emotion and the brain need not tell us anything interesting about religion and the brain.

In summary, it seems that certain work in the general area of neurotheology suffers from confusion about its subject matter. It is difficult to see how this science can make significant progress unless these problems can be sorted out or at least lessened. Unless one has a reasonably good sense of the experiential category that one is studying, one's conclusions will either turn out to be vague or about something else altogether.

Further problems may well arise due to this lack of clarity. For example, without a good sense of what religious experience is, it is difficult to draw a clear line between genuine cases of religious experience and other, perhaps pathological, cases that resemble religious experiences in some superficial respect. For example, the serial killer Peter Sutcliffe, who terrorized the North of England in the 1970s, notoriously claimed that he heard voices of Divine origin ordering him to kill women (Mackie, 1982, p. 180).

Presumably one would want to distinguish Sutcliffe's experiences (if he indeed had these experiences) from those of a meditating Buddhist monk. Perhaps one could restrict talk of religious experiences to nonpathological cases. For instance, Franks Davis (Chapter 8 of this volume) suggests that it is possible to distinguish between healthy religious experiences from various pathologies that are superficially similar. William James (1902, Lecture 1), in contrast, argues that religious experiences are both inextricably entangled with psychopathology *and* of profound spiritual significance. So the issue is not an easy one to resolve. Of more direct relevance to neurotheology is the worry that laboratory studies of religious experience might be exploring artifacts brought about by experimental conditions, experiences that differ from genuine religious experiences had by people in their natural environments. Without a clear sense of what the relevant experiences are, the boundary cannot be drawn.

FUNCTIONS, FABLES AND FAITH

I do not wish to suggest that the problems discussed above are *irresolvable*. Indeed, it is at least conceivable that religious experience will turn out to be a quite distinctive way of experiencing things, supported by dedicated neural circuitry. My conclusion is, rather, that there is insufficient evidence for such a view and, more importantly, that the issue is obscured by substantial conceptual problems. In this section, I want to look at further issues that would arise should the claim turn out to be true. Once we have identified a type of experience and an associated neural structure, where do we go next?

One important question is whether the structure in question has the *function* of generating religious experiences. In addressing this question, it must be kept in mind that, even if there are certain circuits associated with religious experience, they may not comprise a discrete system that does most of the work of generating religious experience. Instead, they could be part of a much larger system. By analogy, my hands are very active when I type but do not constitute an autonomous typing system, the operation of which can be understood in isolation from a plethora of other capacities. Thus, if A plays a role in generating B, it should not be assumed that A is primarily or wholly responsible for B. But let us suppose for now that some such system does exist. What might the function of a biological capacity for religious experience be?

I will start by looking at a currently popular hypothesis concerning the function of religious experience and will suggest that it is problematic in a number of respects, some of which are also likely to plague rival hypotheses. I will then address the question of whether a functional account of the capacity for religious experience could, in principle, tell us anything about whether such experiences are veridical or illusory, that is, whether they reveal something real or whether they are merely psychological in nature.

Accounts of function are intimately connected with evolutionary accounts of how a biological structure evolved. Indeed, the function of X is taken by many to be synonymous with what X was selected or adapted for. Thus, functional accounts of religious experience often take the form of evolutionary narratives, which explain how a biological structure evolved and why it was favored by natural selection.

When speculating as to the evolutionary origins of any psychological or behavioral trait, it is important to exercise considerable caution, given that much work in sociobiology and evolutionary psychology has been charged with concocting superficially plausible stories on the basis of inadequate evidence. This failing was famously satirized by Stephen Jay Gould and Richard Lewontin (1979), who branded adaptationist accounts concerning the evolved functions of various traits just so stories, no more respectable than Rudyard Kipling's account of how the elephant got his trunk, which involved a crocodile attached to the elephant's nose and a python pulling in the opposite direction, resulting in considerable elongation of the appendage. Similar accusations continue to be made against various hypotheses proposed by evolutionary psychologists.[5] Are they fair? For present purposes, I remain agnostic with respect to the charge leveled against evolutionary psychology in general. However, I will suggest that the label "just so story" is quite appropriate for certain evolutionary explanations of a capacity for religious experience. I will focus on the claim that belief in God has the function of lessening the fear of death, which would otherwise detrimentally affect the psychological well-being of thoughtful creatures like us, impairing our ability to survive and reproduce. An account along these lines has been proposed by Persinger (2002a), among others:

> A biological capacity for the God experience was critical for the survival of the species. Without some experiences that could balance the terror of personal extinction, the existence of the human phenomenon called the "self" could not be maintained. (p. 274)

Persinger claims that by associating oneself with the infinite or with a greater whole, one manages to escape the unpleasant burden of one's finitude and impending death. What can be said for this hypothesis? Well, even leaving aside the concern that there may be no such thing as a species-universal God experience, it is still beset with problems. First of all, correlation is not cause. The experience may have arisen for some other role and only by happy coincidence have the effect of making unavoidable death more bearable. Association of a capacity with a beneficial effect does not entail that the capacity arose because it produced that effect. Second, there is a difference between religious belief and religious experience. Religious belief could, presumably, have arisen without religious experience. Thus, it is not clear why the death avoidance adaptation should involve a capacity for experience rather than belief by some other means. And, if there are many different routes to religious belief, then a single adaptationist account is unlikely to encompass all of them. Third, there is a failure to consider the possibility that all sorts of other mechanisms could have evolved to block out thoughts of one's inevitable demise or cope with such thoughts. A death thought prevention system would do the job nicely. Another solution would be to wire death thoughts into the sex drive, so that as soon as you start having them, you procreate instead. The question of whether or not we *do* have such mechanisms, which, for the most part, satisfactorily perform the function ascribed to religion, is not even addressed. By analogy, one would not hypothesize that the nose is a propulsion system without first having given due consideration to the role played by limbs. Fourth, and perhaps most problematic, is the assumption that an understanding of death really did pose a threat to our ancestors' survival. Last week, I had a pub conversation with a lecturer from the English Department at Durham University, who informed me at length that inevitable death without hope of an afterlife did not bother him in the slightest. Despite my own protestations that death was horrific and somehow metaphysically unacceptable, he would not concede. Now I don't know how many people are indeed troubled by the prospect of death, in what ways, and to what extent. And I don't know whether religious people are less preoccupied with it than others or, alternatively, equally preoccupied by it but not as horrified by it. Even if death did pose less of a problem for them, the direction of causation would be unclear. Do people become religious because they are *already* unable to grasp the possibility that death really is the end, or do they have fewer problems with death because of their religious dispositions?

Such questions need to be carefully addressed before one starts positing death-avoidance functions. Furthermore, even if current humans, atheists in particular, are often troubled by death, it by no mean follows that our ancestors were. I tend to think about death rather more when I'm not concentrating on other, more immediate things. An urgent piece of work or a particular threat to my well-being tends to shift my attention somewhat. Furthermore, as an academic philosopher, I have far more time to think about death than many people, including, I suspect, our Pleistocene ancestors. They may well have had so much else to contend with that the prospect of eventual death was the last thing on their minds. So it is unclear that death thoughts amounted to a problem in the first place, and it is also unclear why religious experience should have emerged as a solution. It might also be argued that unwavering religious belief could have a similarly detrimental effect to behavioral paralysis in the face of death. If you know you have eternal life in a better place, why worry about this world? The resultant apathy would surely not have conferred a survival advantage. So this all looks suspiciously like a just so story. To make things worse, Persinger (2002b) just assumes that religious experience has some function:

> From a Darwinian perspective, we might appreciate the maintenance of the temporal lobe experiences that promote the God belief. If there had not been survival value associated with both the experience and the belief in gods, these behaviors should have been selected against long ago. They should have been deleted from our genetic expressions. (p. 290)

The argument is that for any current human trait X, X would not now exist unless X conferred some past survival advantage. Presumably this must apply to traits such as a disposition toward heart attacks, brain hemorrhages, unpleasant skin growths, constipation, and lung cancer. In response, it could be argued that such things are not normal, healthy everyday features of organisms, whereas a capacity for religious experience, like eyes, ears, and lungs, is. However, even if one were to accept the highly questionable view that the capacity for religious experience is a healthy trait that many of us exercise frequently, the argument still fails. Tooth decay, bad breath, and occasional instances of very poor reasoning are pretty much universal throughout the species but don't merit functional explanations. The same applies to countless other bodily characteristics, capacities and behavioral traits. So the argument doesn't even get off the ground.[6]

Now perhaps other such stories have more going for them. However, this case study does bring to light a more general question; that of how any such account could be supported by adequate evidence. What evidence could possibly arbitrate between a host of rival stories, given that most of the historical facts may not just be currently unavailable but irrevocably unavailable? As Robert Richardson (2001) has argued, in the case of many evolutionary stories concerning human cognition, the relevant evidence may be impossible, in practice, to obtain and "without history, evolutionary explanation is empty" (p. 334).

But let us suppose that the conceptual and evidential problems are eventually overcome and that a plausible functional account of religious experience is formulated. The question I want to look at now is that of whether such an account could constitute evidence for or against the view that religious experiences incorporate genuine communication with the Divine, apprehension of the true nature of Being, or something along similar lines. Ramachandran and Blakeslee (1998) explicitly adopt a stance of principled agnosticism concerning this question. Newberg, d'Aquili and Rause (2001), however, suggest that mystical experiences do indeed comprise grounds for belief in a higher reality:

> [We] saw evidence of a neurological process that has evolved to allow humans to transcend material existence and acknowledge and connect

with a deeper, more spiritual part of ourselves perceived of as an absolute, universal reality that connects us to all others. (p. 9)

However, what is clear from their discussion is that this view has no empirical basis. None of the studies cited provide any evidence whatsoever for or against a "universal reality that connects us to all others." It is just unsubstantiated speculation, unconnected with the science (Pigliucci, 2002).

Nevertheless, I want to suggest that a *comprehensive* account of the neurobiology of religious experience would *inevitably* have considerable repercussions for the view that such experiences involve contact with something real, be it God or a higher reality. Thus, it would also have repercussions for the question of whether religious beliefs are well grounded, in so far as such beliefs are based on religious experiences. This is something that I argued in a 2003 article. I will summarize the argument here and elaborate it in certain respects.

Why should a biological account of religious experience have any implications for the epistemological question of whether one should believe in the reality of what one experiences? Well, consider, first of all, the possibility that religious experience is the result of a malfunction. Massimo Pigliucci (2002) succinctly states the implications of such a hypothesis:

if we realize that mystical experiences originate from the same neurological mechanisms that underlie hallucinations from sensorial deprivation and drug-induced "visions," I bet dollar to donut that the reality experienced by meditating Buddhists and praying nuns is entirely contained in their mind and is not a glimpse of a "higher realm," as tantalizing as that idea may be. (p. 270)

The bottom line is that incredulity is the best bet when an experience arises from malfunction and, if that is so with religious experience, it is best explained without reference to the supernatural. Cheyne (2001) advocates a similar position with regard to certain sensed presence experiences, which he explains in terms of malfunctional activation of vigilance systems in the brain. Given that these experiences can be traced to specific brain processes *going wrong*, rather than the intervention of an external source, Cheyne maintains that they call for a "straightforward naturalistic explanation" (p. 136).

The tension between a malfunction explanation and the claim that the resultant experiences are veridical becomes unavoidable if one accepts a noncontingent connection between function and well-formed belief. Certain theists and atheists alike have argued that well-formed beliefs just are those that are generated by properly functioning cognitive apparatus operating in normal environmental conditions.[7] If this is the case, then any belief arising as a result of malfunction is, by implication, not to be trusted.

Of course, malfunction is only one possibility. Another is that religious experience is an unavoidable by-product or side-effect of some other functional cognitive process. An analogous example would be the human chin, which, it has been argued, emerged as an inevitable side-effect of building a functional human-type jaw (Gould & Lewontin, 1979). Again, this would seriously threaten the case for veridicality. If the historical emergence of something can be fully accounted for in terms of some other wholly non-mysterious phenomenon, then there is no need to resort to an additional supernatural element to explain its presence.

However, what about an account that assigns a *function* to religious experience? Again, no such account will be neutral with respect to the question of veridicality. If a *comprehensive* functional account made no reference to the causal role of the supernatural in producing the experience, this would imply that the supernatural had no role to play in the genesis of the experience. Otherwise the account would be incomplete. If the function of religious experience were, say, to communicate with God, then any functional account that did not make reference to God would be either false or highly impoverished.

Thus, it would seem that any *complete* functional account will constitute evidence either for or against veridical religious experience and, consequently, for or against the credibility of any religious beliefs that are founded in the experience. However, things are not so simple. Investigation of the function of religious experience cannot be a wholly empirical affair, meaning that one cannot simply read functions off the natural world without first making significant assumptions. For example, if one were to examine a fish and attempt to explain the function of its fins, one could only do so if one entertained, at some point in one's examination, the possibility that water were a feature of the fish's environment. To venture a more vivid example, in *The Country of the Blind*, a short story by H. G. Wells (2004), the protagonist, Nunez, finds himself in the valley of the blind, where all the inhabitants lost their sight hundreds of years ago and passed on the trait to future generations. This valley has cut off from the rest of the world for hundreds of years and so the whole population has been deprived of any experience of sighted people until the arrival of Nunez. Indeed, they have even lost the concept of sight. Nunez tries repeatedly to convince them that he can see. However, they refuse to admit the possibility of sight and instead interpret his various assertions as reports of delusional experiences. They hypothesize that these delusions have their source in the enlarged, rapidly moving globes on either side of Nunez's nose and thus propose to cure his delusions by removing them.

The point of the example is that biological structures are interpreted and assigned functions only on the basis of prior assumptions about possible constituents of the environment, such as the ambient optic array in the case of sight. If such things are denied, the biology will be interpreted differently, albeit wrongly in the case of Nunez's eyes. The same applies to the function of brain areas, which will be interpreted through a backdrop of presuppositions concerning what the world is like. Now this is not a problem in the majority of cases, where everyone agrees as to what the relevant features of the environment are. However, it is extremely problematic when it comes to religious experience, a case where some people take God to be a very real part of the world that it is possible to commune with, while others begin with the assumption of a Godless world. To pursue the analogy with Wells' story, we don't know who is blind and who is not.

Neuroscience cannot provide decisive evidence for or against the existence of cats, coriander, kestrels, or curtains solely by monitoring the brain processes that occur when such entities are perceived, given that the processes in question would only be interpreted as relating to those entities if their existence and presence were already presupposed or at least regarded as likely. And I suggest that a similar lesson applies to so-called religious experiences. Regardless of whether or not one believes in a higher being or greater reality beyond the mundane world, one can interpret the data so as to accord with one's prior beliefs. The science itself will not, in this case, be able to arbitrate between conflicting presuppositions.

What I am *not* suggesting here is that naturalism and various religious belief systems amount to utterly rigid standpoints that cannot be arbitrated between. So the result is not endorsement of a species of relativism, according to which two radically divergent worldviews can assimilate all the information they like, in such a way as to cohere with their own basic assumptions. I am making the more modest suggestion that neuroscience just does not have enough of an empirical kick to do the job. Something far less subtle and easy to absorb into one's prior worldview would be required to break the deadlock and challenge entrenched patterns of interpretation. Why should we expect neuroscience to come up with the goods when much more dramatic evidence pertaining to the grounds for religious conviction is available to us in the form of famines, plagues, tsunamis, genocidal maniacs, acts of self sacrifice, visions of futility, feelings of meaningfulness, the beauty of nature and the brutality of nature, the combined impact of which has failed to settle the issue?

FEELING IS BELIEVING?

I will conclude these rather skeptical musings on a more positive note. Despite the various empirical and conceptual problems associated with research on religion and the brain, I do think that neuroscience can cast at least some light on the nature of religious experience and belief. In this section, I will provide a brief sketch of what I take to be an interesting avenue of research.

Subjective reports and neurobiological studies generally emphasize the central role of *emotion* in religious experience, and I suspect that research into the nature of emotion can contribute to an understanding of religion. The research in question is not specific to religion. However, it is something that can be applied to the topic of religious belief and experience. Hence, the outcome would be an interdisciplinary study of certain aspects of religion, rather than a new science of neurotheology. There are insufficient grounds for positing religion-specific brain processes, and many, if not all, of the emotions involved will not turn out to be religion-specific. So I don't think talk of God spots or a bold new science of religious experience is defensible. But it is still possible to understand certain aspects of religious belief and experience by exploring the role of emotion.

Believing in the existence of God is not like believing that the Eiffel Tower is in Paris. For many believers, it is a very different *kind* of commitment; it is imbued with feeling rather than being a proposition that one can indifferently assert from a standpoint of neutral detachment. The emotional element is not just something that accompanies religious experience and commitment but is integral to it.

Philosophical discussion of religious belief is littered with attempts to prove the existence of God or at least provide good grounds for religious belief on the basis of reason and evidence. Accompanying these, there are various arguments aimed at showing religious belief to be unwarranted. For example, there are many arguments starting from the well known problem of evil, which attempt to show that the world contains too much evil for it to be the product of an all good, all knowing, all loving God.[8] Although many such arguments and counter-arguments are extremely sophisticated, I, like many others, have always had the feeling that they somehow fail to connect with the realities of religious belief. Belief in God is not, ordinarily at least, a proposition that one asserts on the basis of reason or evidence. Rather, it is something that is *felt*. And the same can be said for other spiritual and mystical convictions that do not incorporate a monotheistic God. That heightened emotions play a role in religious experiences and temperaments is indicated by recent work on God and the brain, which emphasizes the role of affect in religious experience (Newberg et al. 2001) and the emotional nature of many people's responses to religious language and imagery (Ramachandran & Blakeslee, 1998). As Ramachandran and Blakeslee (1998) say:

> I find it ironic that this sense of enlightenment, this absolute conviction that Truth is revealed at last, should derive from limbic structures concerned with emotions rather than from the thinking, rational parts of the brain that take so much pride in their ability to discern truth and falsehood. (p. 179)

Such a view does not depend on more specific hypotheses concerning religion-specific brain structures or religion-specific experiences. All it requires is that the various experiences that we term mystical, religious, or spiritual often incorporate heightened emotion. And the neuroscience does at least indicate that much. Even so, it should be noted that this is hardly a new discovery, given that the role of emotion in religious experience was recognized long before neuroscience came along. Nevertheless, neuroscience does perhaps provide further corroboration for it and also has the potential to cast new light on the nature and role of the relevant emotions.

But surely, one might object, the claim that emotion plays a pivotal role runs the risk of trivializing religious conviction, by reducing it to mere feeling. However, this is not the case at all. Recent work on emotion increasingly recognizes that emotions and feelings are not just bodily twinges; they are ways of experiencing the world that contribute to our deepest commitments, our sense of how things are.[9] One experiences the world and thinks about things through a framework of commitment, which does not take the form of a set of deeply entrenched propositions but, rather, a background feeling of what is and should be the case. This is beautifully articulated in numerous works by William James and applied specifically to religion in his *Varieties of Religious Experience*.[10]

According to James, one believes as a whole person, as an active, feeling agent rather than a cold, calculating mind that could, for all events and purposes, be disembodied. Our most fundamental sense of "what is" is not something we acquire by prowling around and looking for evidence. It is felt with a form and degree of conviction that is much deeper. As James (1902) puts it:

> Individuality is founded in feeling; and the recesses of feeling, the darker, blinder strata of character, are the only places in the world in which we catch real fact in the making, and directly perceive how events happen, and how work is actually done. Compared with this world of living individualized feelings, the world of generalized objects which the intellect contemplates is without solidity or life. (pp. 501–502)

Religious belief, he says, is something had at the level of these "living individualized feelings." To believe in God is not simply to place a tick next to the sentence "God exists." Such utterances are superficial and imperfect articulations of the underlying conviction. The convictions that comprise one's deepest sense of how the world is are constituted by feeling, and it is only upon these unarticulated core convictions that reason goes to work:

> in the metaphysical and religious sphere, articulate reasons are cogent for us only when our inarticulate feelings of reality have already been

impressed in favor of the same conclusion. . . . The unreasoned and immediate assurance is the deep thing in us, the reasoned argument is but a
surface exhibition. (p. 74)

Both having a sense of "the more" and having a sense that "this is all there
is" are, for James, forms of responsiveness to the world that come pre-
formed before reason even gets a look in. Whether one is an atheist, a
theist, or something else is not usually an outcome of deliberation. It is a
presupposed receptivity to things, a background sense of how things are
with the world. Any understanding that fails to recognize this element of
our lives and takes a belief in God to be the explicit positing of some entity,
analogous to positing the existence of Paris, will thus lead to a distorted
conception of religious conviction. One can draw on such insights without
committing to James's individualism, which I criticized in the first section
of this chapter.

Is there any way of arbitrating between different background convictions,
of deeming some well-formed and others not? This question is complicated
by James's claim that certain truths can only be recognized by one who is
already committed in some way, just as a true friendship can only reveal
itself as what it is if one first adopts a background of trust and commitment.
As James (1956) puts it, "there are . . . cases where a fact cannot come at all
unless a preliminary faith exists in its coming" (p. 24). Thus, it is not enough
to simply look and judge.

All sorts of tricky questions then arise as to whether some feelings
are better guides than others, whether some are intrinsically religious,
mystical, or spiritual, and how one might go about demarcating healthy,
truth-disclosing backgrounds of commitment from pathological experiential forms and dead ends. Further questions arise concerning the relationships between believing, feeling, emoting, and experiencing. Answering
these questions will not be an easy task and applying the answers so as to
cast light on the nature of religion will require a level of understanding,
caution, and careful interdisciplinary engagement between philosophy,
theology, and various scientific disciplines that is absent from so-called
neurotheology.

NOTES

I am grateful to Beth Hannon and Benedict Smith for helpful comments on an
earlier draft of this chapter.

1. See, for example, the article "This is your brain on God" in *Wired Magazine*
7, no.11 (November 1999).

2. As Emmons and Paloutzian (2003, p. 381) observe, "how religion and spirituality are conceived and measured vary from study to study."

3. I will alternate between the terms "religious," "mystical," and "spiritual," as I address different authors and arguments. I will sometimes use them interchangeably, with "religious" as my default term. This will not have any repercussions for my overall argument.

4. Galvanic skin response is an indirect way of measuring emotional arousal. When one is emotionally aroused, even slightly, the palms sweat and moisture content increases. This can be detected through increased electrical conductance.

5. For several such criticisms, see the essays edited by Rose and Rose (2000).

6. This kind of argument structure is sadly not restricted to Persinger's work. For example, Alper (2002) claims that "every trait we possess, from stereoscopic vision to our opposable thumbs, must have a specific reason for having emerged in us. Since the driving force underlying all evolutionary processes is the preservation of a species, every trait must somehow serve to increase our species' chances of survival" (2002, p. 293). Even leaving aside the fact that natural selection seldom, if ever, acts upon species, this kind of assertion is clearly misguided. Alper, like Persinger, assumes it as a premise for a death-avoidance account of religious experience.

7. See, for example, Plantinga (1993) for a theistic version of this view and Papineau (1993) for a naturalistic account.

8. See Mackie (1982) for one of many excellent discussions of such arguments.

9. See, for example, Damasio (1995, 2000). For several recent philosophical accounts of emotion, see Solomon (2004).

10. See Ratcliffe (2005a) for a detailed discussion of William James's view of emotion.

REFERENCES

Alper, M. (2002). The evolutionary origins of spiritual consciousness. In R. Joseph (Ed.), *Neurotheology: Brain, science, spirituality, religious experience* (pp. 293–303). San Jose: University Press.

Cheyne, J. A. (2001). The ominous numinous: sensed presence and 'other' hallucinations. *Journal of Consciousness Studies, 8*(5–7), 133–150.

Damasio, A. (1995). *Descartes' error: Emotion, reason and the human brain.* London: Picador.

Damasio, A. (2000). *The feeling of what happens: Body, emotion and the making of consciousness.* London: Vintage.

Davis, C. F. (1989). *The evidential force of religious experience.* Oxford: Oxford University Press.

Emmons, R. A., & Paloutzian, R. F. (2003). The psychology of religion. *Annual Review of Psychology, 54,* 377–402.

Gould, S. J., & Lewontin, R. C. (1979). The spandrels of San Marco and the Panglossian Paradigm: A critique of the Adaptationist Programme. *Proceedings of the Royal Society of London, series B, 20,* 581–598.

Hitt, J. (1999). This is your brain on God. *Wired Magazine,* 7, no. 11 (November).

James, W. (1902). *The varieties of religious experience.* London: Longmans, Green.

James, W. (1956). *The will to believe and other essays in popular psychology.* New York: Dover Publications.

Mackie, J. L. (1982). *The miracle of theism: Arguments for and against the existence of God.* Oxford: Oxford University Press.

Newberg, A., & d'Aquili, G. (2000). The neuropsychology of religious and spiritual experience. *Journal of Consciousness Studies, 7*(11–12), 251–266.

Newberg, A., d'Aquili, E., & Rause, V. (2001). *Why God won't go away: Brain science and the biology of belief.* New York: Ballentine Books.

Papineau, D. (1993). *Philosophical naturalism.* Oxford: Blackwell.

Persinger, M. (2002a). The temporal lobe: The biological basis of the God experience. In R. Joseph (Ed.), *Neuroethology: Brain, science, spirituality, religious experience* (pp. 273–278). San Jose: University Press.

Persinger, M. (2002b). Experimental simulation of the God experience: Implications for religious beliefs and the future of the human species. In R. Joseph (Ed.), *Neuroethology: Brain, science, spirituality, religious experience* (pp. 279–292). San Jose: University Press.

Phillips, D. Z. (1986). *Belief, change and forms of life.* London: MacMillan.

Pigliucci, M. (2002). Neuro-theology: A rather skeptical perspective. In R. Joseph (Ed.), *Neuroethology: Brain, science, spirituality, religious experience* (pp. 269–271). San Jose: University Press.

Plantinga, A. (1993). *Warrant and proper function.* Oxford: Oxford University Press.

Ramachandran, V. S., & Blakeslee, S. (1998). *Phantoms in the brain.* London: Fourth Estate.

Ratcliffe, M. (2005a). William James on emotion and intentionality. *International Journal of Philosophical Studies, 13,* 179–202.

Ratcliffe, M. (2005b). The feeling of being. *Journal of Consciousness Studies, 12*(8–10), 45–63.

Richardson, R. (2001). Evolution without history: Critical reflections on evolutionary psychology. In H. R. Holcomb III (Ed.), *Conceptual challenges in evolutionary psychology: Innovative research strategies.* Dordrecht: Kluwer.

Rose, H., & Rose, S. (2000). *Alas, poor Darwin: Arguments against evolutionary psychology.* London: Jonathan Cape.

Solomon, R. C. (Ed.). (2004). *Thinking about feeling: Contemporary philosophers on emotions.* Oxford: Oxford University Press.

Taylor, C. (2002). *Varieties of religion today: William James revisited.* Cambridge: Harvard University Press.

Wells, H. G. (2004). *The country of the blind.* London: Penguin.

CHAPTER 6

Religion as a By-Product of Evolved Psychology: The Case of Attachment and Implications for Brain and Religion Research

Pehr Granqvist

Whether in human infants or monkey infants, whenever the "natural" object of attachment behaviour is unavailable, the behaviour can become directed towards some substitute object. Even though it is inanimate, such an object frequently appears capable of filling the role of an important, though subsidiary, attachment-"figure." Like the principal attachment figure, the inanimate substitute is sought especially when a child is tired, ill, or distressed. (Bowlby, 1982, p. 313)

This chapter follows a line of reasoning in which religion is viewed as a by-product of evolution, and not as a biological adaptation, or set of adaptations, in its own right (see e.g., Atran & Norenzayan, 2004; Hinde, 1999; Kirkpatrick, 2005; Kirkpatrick, this volume). Rather, religion is held to emerge indirectly from the operation of evolved psychological mechanisms that did, in turn, fill an adaptive function in the environments in which the human species evolved. The chapter focuses on one, among other, evolved mechanisms, namely the attachment behavioral system and its relation to religiousness. The first sections of the chapter outline attachment theory, followed by a review of the evidence showing that the attachment system is typically highly activated in believers' perceived God relations and particularly during full-blown religious experiences such as sudden religious conversions. Also reviewed are findings indicating that individual differences in experiences of caregiver sensitivity and attachment security underlie different developmental pathways to religion. Moreover, implications of the attachment and religion findings for brain and religion research are discussed. Finally, while the risk of producing an incoherent text seems clear enough,[1] some words of caution and paradigmatic suggestions are offered to the emerging field of brain and religion research and particularly to its "neurotheology" branch. These considerations are based on the multifactorial nature of religious experience, on a failed replication of key neurotheology findings (to be reviewed), and on the position that religion is a by-product of evolution. Most importantly, however, they are based on what is believed to be a proper understanding of the epistemological role of natural science in this area of research, namely, that it is nothing more, nor less, than an ontologically agnostic inquiry into the empirical constituents of religious experience and its physical and psychological causation. Both ontological reduction and embracement are held to reflect logical errors when drawn from neuroscience findings.

OUTLINE OF ATTACHMENT THEORY

Those who are not so familiar with attachment theory may think that the theory represents Neo-Freudianism gone empirical, with its advocates essentially dedicated to classifying infants and caregivers to different patterns of secure and insecure attachment, based on slight revisions of psychoanalytic theory. However, nothing could be more erroneous (see e.g., Granqvist, 2006). As the misconception is not infrequent, especially in the "hard" sciences, the theory will be fairly thoroughly introduced here. (Readers who are very familiar with attachment theory and research may want to move directly to the next sections.)

John Bowlby (1982, 1973, 1980), the founding father of attachment theory, parted company with Freud when Bowlby posited his motivational model underlying the developing organism's behavioral, cognitive, and affective organization. Whereas Freud took a drive theory approach as the "motor" of his theory, understanding individual development as a series of transformations of a few basic, general drives (i.e., the sex drive and the death drive), Bowlby—inspired by the work of ethologists such as Lorenz (Schiller, 1957) and Hinde (1970)—based his motivational model on control systems theory and Darwinian theory of natural selection. According to such a model, the organism possesses a number of domain-specific behavioral systems (e.g., for reproduction, nourishment, exploration, attachment) that have been designed by selection pressures and that result in higher inclusive fitness in the members of a species who display that the behaviors governed by the systems compared to those who did not.

The implications of these differing points of departure are difficult to exaggerate. For example, whereas Freud (1940) thought that the *human* infant's early preference for its caregiver resulted from the caregiver being associated with satisfaction of the infant's oral needs for nourishment (i.e., ultimately a transformation of the sex drive), Bowlby and other ethologists postulated that this preference, which is clearly visible in *all mammals* and even in birds, reflected the operation of a behavioral system that assured infant proximity to protective caregivers. In other words, the systems postulated are psychological mechanisms, closely corresponding to biological adaptations. And whereas some control systems are mechanical and programmed by humans (e.g., thermostats, missiles), mammalian behavioral systems were programmed by selection pressures in the environments in which the species evolved (i.e., the environment of evolutionary adaptedness, EEA; Bowlby, 1982).

The aspects of attachment theory that deal with the evolution of the attachment system, its biological function, its ontogenetic maturation, and its activating and terminating conditions are often referred to as the "normative aspects" of the theory. The reason is that the system is genetically based and present among virtually all members of all mammalian species. That this particular phenotype (i.e., the attachment system) is genetically based should, thus, not be confused with genetic heritability (the proportion of *variance* in a phenotype explained by variance in its genotype). Had there been substantial variance in this phenotype, the case of its biological function would have been somewhat less compelling.

Besides the normative aspects of attachment theory, a huge body of research—some cross-cultural, some even in other species—has documented replicable individual differences in the organization of attachment behaviors and, in the human case, also in representational products (e.g., speech) related to attachment. This initially somewhat surprising (Ainsworth, Blehar, Waters, & Walls, 1978) finding is nowadays often taken as the starting point in empirical research projects relating to attachment theory. However, as this chapter will demonstrate, there is more to attachment than classifications of individual differences. Here, we will first consider the normative aspects in more detail, before describing the individual differences and their developmental implications. Finally, the study of attachment later in development is introduced.

Normative Aspects of Attachment Theory

A core set of observations behind the formulation of attachment theory was that in particular situations, such as physical separation, illness, pain, fear, distress, and predator approach, mammalian offspring tend to behave in certain ways (Bowlby, 1982). While it is common among offspring in other species to flee to a burrow or den, primate offspring have a strong tendency to flee to its primary caregiver in such situations (Bowlby, cited in Hesse & Main, 2000). It was based on observations such as these that Bowlby (1973, 1980, 1982) argued that mammalian offspring possess an attachment behavioral system, originally designed by selection pressures in the EEA and henceforth activated by situations (external as well as internal to the offspring) that give a natural clue to danger.

Yet, the attachment system is not fully mature at birth, particularly not in higher mammalian species such as humans and other primates, whose periods of brain and behavioral immaturity is disproportionately large compared to other species. The ontogenetic development of the system follows a clear pattern in humans and other primates, from early lack of discrimination and seemingly reflexive signal behaviors, such as crying and smiling, to a more refined, coordinated, and flexible organization of behaviors, where the child comes to take a more active part in maintaining proximity (Bowlby, 1982).

Not until the second half of human infants' first years of life do they show a marked behavioral preference for their primary caregivers (i.e., attachment figures) to others. From having cried whenever on its own in the first few months of life, the infant now cries whenever its attachment figures depart. Not coincidentally, at about the same time, the infant typically becomes more mobile through developing the capacity to crawl off on its own and also develops stranger anxiety. At this point, infants restrict their proximity-directed behaviors (i.e., approaching), which now includes following their attachment figures, whereas they typically withdraw from others. When infants learn to walk on their own a few months later, their capacity to increase the distance from, as well as to actively follow, their attachment figures is further enhanced. Also, at this age, children normally develop a great deal of potentially hazardous curiosity in their surroundings (i.e., in the service of the developing exploratory system).

It is clear by this age that the attachment system is the primary mechanism within children that is responsible for maintaining them in safe levels of proximity to protective caregivers. This is seen, for example, in how most infants and small children monitor the whereabouts of their "secure bases" when engaged in exploration. Should a natural clue to danger occur, children typically immediately withdraw to their attachment figure as a "haven of safety."

With increased cognitive maturation in the preschool years (e.g., temporal understanding, the "theory of mind," ability to attribute goals and intentions to others), children are able to withstand longer separations from their attachment figures. Although present already in infancy, the consequences of attachment behaviors, specifically the responses of the attachment figure, become increasingly stored in cognitive representations (internal working models, IWMs) of self and others in interaction. Although the IWM construct may seem fancy to die-hard behaviorists, even rats and other "lower" organisms develop elementary cognitive representations (e.g., maps) of their surroundings (e.g., Tolman, 1948), which allow them to navigate more efficiently than in the absence of such representations. Through the operation of IWMs, the success of children's forecasts regarding the self's likelihood to manage any given challenge, as well as the attachment figure's likely response in case of alarm, is greatly enhanced. Bowlby (1973, 1980) thus held IWMs as a reasonably accurate representation of the organism's surrounding, especially such aspects of the surrounding that have been related to selection pressures in the EEA. There should be no doubt that signs of the attachment figure's availability when the offspring's attachment system has been highly activated represent core candidates for aspects of the latter kind. Importantly, as IWMs develop prior to the development of explicit memories, their experiential origins will be unbeknownst to their host, and they will operate largely outside their consciousness as a set of implicit memory sequences.

So far, proximity to (usually) protective caregivers has been portrayed as the "set-goal" of the attachment system. Regarding biological functionality, that is more or less the end of the story. However, and as for *psychological functionality*, an important consequence of proximity to protective caregivers in situations giving natural clues to danger is a psychological state of "felt security" (Sroufe & Waters, 1977a). This psychological state, which early on corresponds very closely with physical proximity, becomes ever the more important with maturation. Later in life, from middle childhood to old age, the attachment system is considerably less easily activated, and when it is activated at lower levels, a telephone call, a letter, even the mere knowledge that an attachment figure would be available if the situation got worse, may suffice to give the individual a sense of felt security. However, when the attachment system is highly activated also later in life (e.g., following divorce or the death of a loved one), physical proximity with an attachment figure is, without comparison, the most effective mean of bringing that outcome about.

Relatedly, Bowlby (1979, 1982) repeatedly emphasized that the attachment system is active from the cradle to the grave, even if less easily activated after early childhood. Here, again, we see a notable difference to Freud's theory, which viewed adult behaviors, such as those expressing attachment, as regressive, a sign of dependency (see Granqvist, 2006). One might wonder then what the biological function of attachment, if any at all, has been later in development? A major proposal has been the co-option of this system for the maintenance of adult pair-bonds (e.g., Hazan & Zeifman, 1999), but some controversy has surrounded that proposal (e.g., Kirkpatrick, 1998a). Be that as it may, once a system has established itself within the gene pool due to its promotion of inclusive fitness, it may well continue to operate within animals throughout their life-span as long as its operation in later life periods was not detrimental to fitness in the EEA. Prepubertal sexuality is a case in point, post-menopause sexuality another, and sexual "perversions" a third;

all expressions of the reproductive system operating without leading to its biological function of reproduction.

Finally, as attachment is a genetically based system that is present in all mammals, and as all behaviors, cognitions, and affects are presumably mediated by brain activity, the attachment system is ultimately considered a neural system (see also Bowlby, 1982). However, already early in life, the attachment system draws on diverse neural processes associated with different neural structures, including regulation of attention (prefrontal cortex), sensory feedback (the sensory areas, cortical association area), memory structures (hippocampus, cortical association area), emotional processing (the limbic system, particularly the amygdalae), and motor outputs (motoric region). Consequently, the attachment system should not be confused with any concrete neurological *structure*. It seems wiser to consider it a *function* of the central nervous system.

Individual Differences in Early Attachment Organization

The behaviors resulting from attachment activation are modulated by the dyadic organization of the offspring-caregiver relationship (Ainsworth et al., 1978), which is, in turn, mediated by IWMs of self and others. As noted, such IWMs are thought to be constructed from previous experiences of caregiver availability and sensitivity to the individual's needs in attachment activating situations. In human infants, the behavioral manifestations of the infant's developing IWMs are often inferred from observations made in the Ainsworth strange situation (Ainsworth et al., 1978), a semi-structured laboratory procedure consisting of repeated sequences of play (i.e., exploration), separation from the caregiver (i.e., attachment activation), and reunion with the caregiver (i.e., attachment termination). Through a move to the representational level (Main, Kaplan, & Cassidy, 1985), the manifestations of IWMs are now also inferred from speech and other representational products later in development. Although attachment procedures to study individual differences have been developed on humans, they have more recently been adapted, imported, and shown useful as applied also to other mammals (e.g., Suomi, 1999; Weaver & de Waal, 2002).

Regardless of the age and mode of measuring the organization of attachment in humans, *secure* attachment implies certainty of the caregiver's availability and the self's worthiness of care during attachment activation and of ease in exploring other aspects of the surrounding when the attachment system is less active. Consequently, Main (e.g., Main et al., 1985) has suggested that the attentional focus of secure children shifts flexibly between attachment and exploration depending on whether the attachment system is activated.

In contrast, insecure attachment organization implies certainty of the caregiver's unavailability (insecure/*avoidant* attachment) or uncertainty of the caregiver's availability (insecure/*ambivalent* attachment). Likewise, the self's worthiness of care in attachment activating situations is unclear in these children. Main (e.g., Main et al., 1985) has described the strategy of avoidant children as one of minimizing attention to attachment. Due to certainty of the caregiver's unavailability, the avoidant child defensively shifts attention to other aspects of the surroundings also in situations that should typically activate the attachment system and instead engages in defensive exploration. As evidence for the defensive quality of avoidant behavior, studies have documented psychophysiological reactions (e.g., heart-rate and skin conductance recordings) indicative of stress in these children during the strange situation (e.g., Sroufe & Waters, 1977b), in spite of their seeming behavioral "independence."

The strategy of ambivalent children has been described, in contrast, as one of maximizing attention to attachment (e.g., Main et al., 1985). Due to uncertainty of the caregiver's availability, the child keeps close track of and often clings to the caregiver even in situations that do not typically give clues to danger. The child's exploration of other aspects of the surrounding consequently suffers. While the minimizing and maximizing strategies give rise to very different behavioral and linguistic "outputs," they share an underlying rigid organization of attention and information processing with regard to attachment. Importantly, both also make the offspring less fine-tuned to differentiate between attachment activating and more neutral, normally exploration-facilitating conditions than the attentional organization of secure offspring, which is more flexible (see Suomi, 1999, for a similar description of infant rhesus monkeys).

Finally, a fourth, insecure/*disorganized* quality of attachment has been described (Main & Solomon, 1990). The disorganized child's attentional strategy is thought to break-down during stress (e.g., Hesse & Main, 2000) as manifest in disorganized behaviors, for example, behavioral freezing, prolonged stilling with a trance-like facial expression, simultaneous displays of contradictory behaviors. The disorganized behaviors show striking resemblances to what Hinde (1970) characterized as conflict behaviors in other mammals. The inference that the behavioral break-down results from stress is supported by elevated concentrations of a stress-related hormone (i.e., cortisol) in these infants during the strange situation (e.g., Spangler & Grossmann, 1993).

Numerous studies have shown that the best predictor of the infant's response to the strange situation is caregiver sensitivity to the infant during the infant's first year of life (e.g., Ainsworth et al., 1978; De Wolff & van Ijzendoorn, 1997). While there was some controversy between attachment and temperament theorists on this matter in the past, a large-scale behavioral genetic study of twins and adoptees has now documented a high proportion of explained variance from shared environment whereas the influence of genetic heritability even failed to make it into the statistical model (Bokhorst, Bakermans-Kranenburg, van Ijzendoorn, Fonagy, & Schuengel 2003). Needless to say, both of these findings are highly unusual in psychology.

Sensitivity is implied when a caregiver *usually* notices the infant's signals, interprets them correctly, and responds to them promptly and adequately (Ainsworth et al., 1978). Not surprisingly, based on caregiver observations, caregivers of secure infants are independently judged higher in sensitivity than caregivers of insecure infants. Caregivers of avoidant babies are more rejecting (i.e., turn down the infant's bids for attachment, subtly avoid physical closeness) and caregivers of ambivalent infants are more inconsistent (e.g., oftentimes being neglecting, sometimes behaving sensitively) (see De Wolff & van Ijzendoorn, 1997, for a meta-analysis). These observations are helpful in understanding why the infants organize themselves around the caregiver in their own particular ways so as to escape danger, that is, why secure infants turn to their caregivers when distressed, are effectively consoled, and quickly return to exploration; why avoidant babies minimize their attention to attachment (i.e., avoid further rejection and the prospect of abandonment, while maintaining a safe level of proximity); and why ambivalent infants maximize their attention to attachment (i.e., activating the caregiver's attentiveness).

Caregivers of disorganized babies are not necessarily lower in general sensitivity. However, they have been found, in several studies, to be more often abusive and to display subtle behaviors that are frightening (e.g., quasi-predatory movements) and/or that indicate that the caregiver is frightened (e.g., sudden increase in distance from the infant, suggesting that the infant is experienced as alarming; see Hesse & Main, 2000). In other words, rather than being the solution to fear, these caregivers are actually part of the source of it. Yet, being in possession of an attachment system, infants are programmed to maintain safe levels of proximity to their caregivers, especially when alarmed. It is easy to see how this could create an irresolvable dilemma for the infant, hence, presumably, the behavioral break-down seen in conflict behaviors during attachment activation (Hesse & Main, 2000).

Cassidy (1994) has suggested that different strategies of affect regulation characterize individual differences in attachment organization. By drawing on the definition of Thompson (1994), as well as on Bowlby's postulated set-goal of the attachment system, affect regulation is defined as an adaptive process that drives the organism toward achieving its goals (i.e., to obtain proximity, in the case of attachment). Affect regulation not only refers to the inhibition of affective states, but sometimes also to a heightening of them. The responsibility for regulating affect is implicitly shared in secure dyads in that the infants freely and flexibly signal negative affect when distressed and positive affect when content and in that they are willing to let caregivers help them resolve it would the scenario be of the former kind. This free display of affect is presumably a result of caregiver sensitivity in relation to previous displays. As a consequence of adequate caregiver responses, the child will subsequently achieve control over the affect states and their displays while still being able to turn to others for support when needed. When viewed this way, avoidant behavior may be seen as a strategy of minimizing negative affect (e.g., avoid crying during separation), whereas ambivalence reflects its maximization (e.g., complain when picked up, complain when let down), and disorganization reflects its confusion or, again, its break-down (e.g., hitting the parent when in an apparently good mood).

Due to the theoretical foundation in control systems theory and Darwinian theory, in conjunction with the solid measurement procedures developed to tap individual differences in attachment, attachment theory has now established itself as one of the major research paradigms in developmental psychology. Yet, unless it had been successful in predicting relevant aspects of development, it would have been of limited usefulness. However, attachment security, from infancy onward, has been found an important predictor of socioemotional development, even in long-term longitudinal studies following participants from infancy to adulthood. For example, attachment security predicts absence of behavioral problems (of both internalizing and externalizing kinds), higher empathic responses, higher social competence, higher peer popularity, earlier maturation of theory of mind, and higher resiliency to stress (see Weinfield, Sroufe, Egeland, & Carlson, 1999, for a review). Naturally, insecurity of attachment, and particularly disorganized attachment, has the opposite correlates (van Ijzendoorn, Schuengel, & Bakermans-Kranenburg, 1999; Weinfield et al., 1999). These predictive relations are often held to be explained by the temporal continuity and the self-verifying and generalizing nature of the child's IWMs, although other processes as well as environmental stability are likely involved as well (e.g., Weinfield et al., 1999).

Three correlates of attachment security are of particular relevance here. First, secure attachment is linked to a more successful internalization of parental standards and values (Ainsworth, Bell, & Stayton, 1974; Richters & Waters, 1991). For example, from an early age, secure children behaviorally adopt the conduct "recommended" by their sensitive attachment figures to a larger extent than do insecure children, whose attachment figures are also less sensitive (Londerville & Main, 1981). Second, as in the opening quote from Bowlby, Ainsworth (1985) made the intriguing suggestion that in the absence of a sensitive caregiver, insecure children may eventually turn instead to attachment "surrogates." This hypothesis has been supported with respect to insecurely attached children's reliance on peers, teachers, and relatives outside of the immediate family context (e.g., Booth, Rubin, & Krasnor, 1998; Elicker, Englund, & Sroufe, 1992).

Finally, aspects of infant disorganization (e.g., freezing, stilling) have been suggested to represent proto-dissociative states that may psychologically guard the infant from the behaviorally irresolvable dilemma described above (Hesse & Main, 2000). If that becomes a habitual response mode when faced with stress, disorganized attachment would make the individual prone to later experiences of dissociative mental states (e.g., experiences of de-personalization, out-of-the-body experiences). Confirmatory evidence comes from studies linking infant disorganization to dissociative states throughout childhood and adolescence (Carlson, 1998; van Ijzendoorn, Schuengel, & Bakermans-Kranenburg, 1999).

Attachment Later in Development

Although attachment theory and research initially concerned early childhood, interest eventually was directed to attachment processes later in development. As noted, Bowlby (1973, 1980, 1982), and also Ainsworth (1985), had stated that the attachment system is active throughout life, and both had considered long-term adult love relationships as exemplifying later attachment relationships. However, other researchers, working in two different traditions, developed the empirical study of attachment later in development.

Attachment at the representational level. The first of these traditions was pioneered by Main and colleagues in developmental psychology (Main et al., 1985) and emphasized the representational level of attachment later in development as manifested not only in behaviors, but also in speech and other representational products. For example, through the use of a structured interview about visually represented fictional child-parent dyads in different separation situations (the adapted Separation Anxiety Test, SAT; Kaplan, 1987), 6-year-old children varying in attachment classifications as infants were found to speak very differently about what pictured children would feel and do while separated. Whereas children who had been independently judged secure as infants acknowledged feelings of vulnerability and imagined constructive means of coping with the separations, children judged insecure as infants did not. For instance, the responses of previously disorganized children indicated fearfulness (e.g., the killing of self, invisible agents of action). In another task of this project, Main (1991) reported that some previously ambivalent infants had difficulties understanding the privacy of thought (cf. telepathy) and attributed psychical powers to themselves as well as their parents.

However, the truly pioneering work of Main and colleagues (1985) consisted in the construction of a semi-structured interview about adults' attachment biographies, the Adult Attachment Interview (AAI; Main, Goldwyn, & Hesse, 2003). Through the use of this method, adult attachment classifications of parents were found highly and specifically predictive of infants' ways of organizing themselves around the parent in the strange situation (e.g., disorganized mothers had disorganized infants, secure mothers secure infants), a finding that has now been replicated in at least 20 independent samples (see van Ijzendoorn, 1995, for a meta-analysis of the first 14). Moreover, as infant classifications are not genetically heritable, the transmission of attachment is environmental in origin and partly mediated by the parent's sensitivity to the infant (see Fleming et al., 2002 and Suomi, 1999 for identical conclusions from experimental studies of rodents and rhesus monkeys, respectively). The vital role behind these predictive relations in humans is that when coding AAIs, the coder judges the *form* of current attachment discourse rather than only the *content* of discourse.

Secure (or "autonomous") discourse is characterized by coherence (e.g., internal consistency between global/semantic and specific/episodic memories). Importantly, such discourse can be present among individuals who are judged to have had largely negative experiences with parents, in which case "earned security" is the sub-classification used in demarcation to "continuous security." While an exception in and of itself, earned security is may be facilitated by therapy and reparative experiences with other attachment figures (Bowlby, 1988; Main et al., 2003). Earned security is, moreover, associated with similar levels of sensitivity to the offspring as is continuous security (Pearson, Cohn, Cowan, & Cowan, 1994).

Insecure discourse is, in contrast, characterized by incoherence. For example, ambivalent (or "preoccupied") discourse is marked by vagueness of speech and confused, detailed ranting about the failure of parents in providing for the speaker (i.e., preoccupying anger). Disorganized ("unresolved" or "cannot classify") discourse is found in one of two ways, firstly, in lapses of reasoning (e.g., dead, not-dead) and discourse (e.g., sudden intrusions of traumatic memories) specifically in relation to a significant event of abuse or loss through death (i.e., trauma), and secondly, in a more global incompatibility of discourse strategy (e.g., highly positive description of parent in the absence of episodic support in one part of the transcript, combined with highly preoccupying anger against the same parent in a different part of the transcript). Like disorganized infant attachment, disorganized AAI classifications have been found related, as expected, to dissociative states (Hesse & van Ijzendoorn, 1999). Also, AAI classifications have now been successfully predicted from the same individuals' infant strange situation classifications in several independent samples (see Fraley, 2002, for a meta-analysis; see Hesse, 1999, for additional aspects of convergent and discriminant validity of the AAI).

Romantic attachment. The second adult attachment tradition, developed by Hazan and Shaver (1987) in social psychology, concerns itself with adult pair bond relationships, particularly romantic love relationships, as the primary attachment relationships in adulthood. Taking Bowlby's (1973, 1980, 1982) reasoning as the point of departure, the attachment system, the caregiving system, and the reproductive system are supposedly integrated in romantic love relationships; that is, both partners serve as attached, as caregivers, and as the primary persons in whom issues related to reproduction are invested (see Shaver & Mikulincer, 2002).

Also, a wide variety of self-report questionnaire methods have been developed, and the one mostly used currently (Brennan, Clark, & Shaver, 1998) yields two continuous dimensions of romantic attachment: *Avoidance* (of intimacy and dependency) and *Anxiety* (about insufficient love and the prospect of abandonment). While there are no latent taxa underlying these dimensions (Fraley & Waller, 1998), the dimensions can be used to form the four now well-familiar groups (see Shaver & Mikulincer, 2002, for a review). Concerning the origin of individual differences in romantic attachment, childhood attachment is thought to be an important determinant, as mediated by generalizing IWMs derived from the parental attachment relationships, but no data has hitherto been reported that addresses this issue.

A special topic of interest in the literature on romantic attachment is that of attachment processes in adolescence and early adulthood. The reason is that these are attachment transitional periods, where attachment components (i.e., the proximity seeking, safe haven, and secure base phenomena) are gradually transferred from parents to peers, most often love partners (e.g., Friedlmeier & Granqvist, 2006; Hazan & Zeifman, 1999). This attachment transition implies increasing autonomy vis-à-vis parents, as well as a relocation of attachment figures in the individual's attachment hierarchy, where long-term love partners gradually come to possess the principal position. Favorable experiences with parents are likely for the benefit of the smoothness with which the adolescent/young adult will make this transition, for example, finding a secure romantic partner while maintaining an affectional bond with sensitive parents, whereas unfavorable experiences with parents are detrimental, leaving the latter adolescents in a situation wherein felt security cannot be obtained either through parents or through a love partner (e.g., Allen & Land, 1999).

INVOLVEMENT OF THE ATTACHMENT SYSTEM IN RELIGIOUS EXPERIENCE

For hundreds of years, believers have likened their first experienced personal encounter with God to falling in love. Similarly, it has been known for at least 100 years that those experiences do not happen at random, but are associated with a precipitating period of emotional turmoil (e.g., James, 1902). Moreover, although likely surprising to those who associate religiousness primarily with a particular set of cognitive-intellectual and value-oriented positions, it is well-established that when asked to describe the most important aspect of their religion, most believers pick their personal relationship with God (Gallup & Jones, 1989). Scholars of diverse theoretical persuasions in psychology have naturally struggled to explain such findings (see e.g., Spilka, Hood, Hunsberger, & Gorsuch, 2003). It was not until Lee Kirkpatrick (1992, 1999, 2005) applied attachment theory to religion that these pieces, along with others to be reviewed, came to fit in a solid theoretical framework that was also empirically testable and that in fact came to be empirically corroborated in future research, as will be described. In this section, focus will be on the normative aspects of attachment and believers' perceived God relations. First, believers' perceived relationships with God are briefly discussed in relation to the defining characteristics of attachment, and some terminological words of caution are offered. This is followed by a consideration of maturational aspects of attachment and the developing God relation.

Believers' Perceived God Relations vis-à-vis Attachment Relationship Criteria

The most obvious point of departure for the attachment theoretical application to religion was the centrality of the believer's personal relationship with a personal, caring God (see Kirkpatrick, 1999, 2005). However, the term "attachment relationship" does not refer to all types of close relationships, but exclusively to relationships that meet three distinct criteria: proximity maintenance, safe haven, and secure base (e.g., Ainsworth, 1985). Bowlby (1973) added a fourth criterion concerning characteristics of the attachment figure in relation to the attached person, namely that the former is perceived as stronger and wiser during stress.

Regarding proximity maintenance, God is thought by believers to be omnipresent, by definition always near. There are several means available to make this a more personal and concrete experience, such as religious symbols and rituals, for example, visits to the Temple. The most salient mean of obtaining closeness to God, however, is probably accomplished in prayer (Kirkpatrick, 1999). Maintaining proximity also means resisting separations. Accordingly, in two recent attachment experiments, theistic believers showed an increase in their wish to be close to God when primed with subliminal separation stimuli targeting either their relationship with God ("God has abandoned me") or their mothers ("Mommy is gone") versus participants in attachment neutral control conditions (Birgegard & Granqvist, 2004).

Regarding the safe haven aspect of attachment, individuals turn to God in situations of distress, and the more distressing the situation, the more likely they are to do so (Pargament, 1997). In highly distressing situations, the most likely religious/spiritual response is to pray to God (Argyle & Beit-Hallahmi, 1975), suggesting that private prayer may function as a religious analogue to attachment behaviors (see Kirkpatrick, 1999, 2005). Further, and as noted above, in highly distressing life situations, religious experiences, significant religious changes, and conversions occur at a disproportionately high rate (Spilka et al., 2003; Ullman, 1982). Also, experiments using subliminal exposures of threat-related words, such as failure or death, have supported the notion of God as a safe haven in a Jewish sample of Israeli college students, who showed an increase in the psychological accessibility of God following the exposures (Gewirtz, 2004).

While the safe haven aspects of religious experience described are clearly embedded in the religious individual's relationship with an anthropomorphically shaped and institutionally sanctioned deity, this need not be the case. On the contrary, many seemingly spontaneous occurrences of "paranormal" experiences that are not sanctioned by institutionalized religion, such as out-of-the body experiences, are also generally precipitated by significant turmoil (Irwin, 1993). As such experiences may well occur in the absence of the individual's attributions to a divine power or any other form of sanctified, comforting presence, their occurrence does not require perceptions of the availability of any anthropomorphic safe haven. Later, we will consider the possibility that such experiences occurring in relation to perceptions of an available safe haven may have very different psychological correlates than the other experiences.

Concerning the secure base phenomenon, there is typically a notable increase in well-being following the conversion experience (Ullman, 1982), which, in attachment terms, may suggest that the individual obtains felt security from his or her perceived encounter with God. It is notable also that God is perceived to possess sensitivity-related attributes that are supposedly ideal for a secure base. For example, factor analytic studies show factors of "availability" (e.g., "gives comfort," "a warm-hearted refuge," "who will take loving care of me"; Tamayo & Desjardins, 1976) and "benevolence" (e.g., "comforting," "loving," "protecting"; Gorsuch, 1968) to account for most variance in God image. Moreover, correlates of religiosity suggest that possessing an image of and relating to God as a sensitive secure base is associated with positive outcomes, over and above the effects of virtually every conceivable covariate (e.g., George, Ellison & Larson, 2002). In the event that a person with such a perceived God relation would nevertheless become sick or depressed, their remissions are typically faster than the remissions of individuals without them (e.g., Koenig, George, & Peterson, 1998).

Finally, regarding relative strength and wisdom, and in being described as omnipotent and omniscient, God is perceived as both stronger and wiser than the believers themselves. While these descriptions as well as the omnipresence description of God may well express the "official dogma" more than the believers' own perceptions, it is still of interest to note that official dogma sanctions the idea of an attachment figure that is flawless in sensitivity.

Moreover, the fact that people *do* turn to God in distress, which in turn helps them to feel better, clearly indicates that they do in fact view God as stronger and wiser than themselves.

To summarize, in serving the function of obtaining/maintaining a state of felt security, aspects of attachment presumably function in a similar way for believers in relation to God as they do for children in relation to their parents. Hence, on the basis of the above considerations, it seems reasonable to conclude that God is used *like* an attachment figure by some adults and that the attachment system is typically highly operative in their perceived God relations. Whether God *is* an attachment figure, however, is another matter and not an easy one to settle. First, while an open issue at present, and as illustrated by the opening quote from Bowlby, it is far from inconceivable that many of the findings reported above could hold also for an individual's relation to other attachment "surrogates" that are not typically thought of as attachment figures (e.g., a child's "relation" to his/her blanket). As we will see later, however, the psychological significance of other attachment surrogates wane with maturation, whereas—if anything—the opposite is the case with God. Second, if one were to consider verifiable (i.e., through ordinary sensory channels) existence as well as observable behaviors in relation to the attached person as necessary conditions for inclusion in the class of "attachment figures," then God would not pass. This is not a declaration of atheism, but simply a testimony of the difficulties inherent in observing God's behaviors. On the other hand, and to the best of the author's knowledge, no one in the field of attachment has suggested in print that those should be considered necessary conditions, but it may be taken for granted. In either case, due to these ambiguities, and to prevent semantic dilution of the attachment concept, God will be referred to as an attachment-"like" figure, and the believer's perceived God relation as an attachment-"like" relationship.[2]

A final terminological note, of immediate relevance, on the use of the attachment concept in this context is that whereas the attachment system has a clear biological function within its usual sphere of operation (i.e., promotion of inclusive fitness through caregivers' protection of the offspring), the same cannot be said for its operation within the perceived God relation. In other words, it is highly unlikely that the latter relation promoted inclusive fitness by systematically protecting the individuals who had it from danger in the EEA. If most Neanderthals kneeled down to pray when chased by predators, for example, this chapter would likely not have been written. Although some theorists would suggest that the God relation promoted inclusive fitness in some other ways than protection from danger, such as through sexual selection or group selection mechanisms, there are other compelling arguments against such proposals (see Kirkpatrick, this volume).

However, and as noted, once a mechanism has established itself within the gene pool, it may well continue to operate within individuals and in contexts that were not associated with its biological function. Hence, the question of biological functionality is more or less isomorphic to the question of whether the believer-God relation involves the attachment system and is an attachment relationship. In fact, corporations, cultures, religions, and societal institutions may well capitalize on any system's operation outside the sphere of its biological functionality, whether knowingly or not. For example, pornography capitalizes on the reproductive system but is certainly not the biological set-goal of that system; hence, pornography is one of its by-products. No other resemblances with pornography implied, it is in this sense that the term "religion as a by-product" is used. In essence, religion is presumably a free-rider on evolved mechanisms and clearly riding the attachment system.

The Developing God Relation vis-à-vis Maturation of Attachment

So far, we have considered adult expressions of religious experience in relation to normative attachment considerations. The story really starts in childhood, though, and it should not be surprising by now that the perceived God relation develops in temporal conjunction with the maturation of the attachment system and the cognitive developments associated with its maturation. Moreover, already in childhood, situational experiences associated with heightened attachment activation are linked to an increased significance of the God relation (see Granqvist & Dickie, 2006, for a more detailed overview).

Although some scholars have theorized about the "spirituality" of infancy, characterized by the "sanctified" presence of the nurturing mother (e.g., Erikson, 1963; Fowler, 1981), it makes no sense to attribute such adult concepts to infants, unless the spirituality concept is stretched well beyond its, admittedly fuzzy, limits. Far from being cognitively able to grasp symbolic thought, the infant is busy enough to display a series of more or less reflexive behaviors, such as rooting, sucking, crying—and later on smiling and following—that are necessary to obtain the biological set-goals of nourishment and proximity to its protective caregiver. Naturally, the infants whose set-goals are frequently and regularly met are more content and well-organized than other infants, but this is no basis from which spirituality may be attributed.

However, as attachment to primary caregivers increasingly moves toward goal-corrected partnerships in preschool, and children have developed elementary capacity for symbolic thought (Bowlby, 1982), they are able to withstand longer separations, presumably due to the emerging capacity to represent their attachment figures symbolically. Already at this age, children develop a concept of God that they describe or draw as a person (Heller, 1986). Besides the development of symbolic thought, children start to elaborate a theory of mind; others have intentions and goals that motivate their behaviors. It is easy to see how these two aspects of cognitive development pave the way for an emerging understanding of God, particularly when adults provide feedback consonant with the existence, or at least concept, of God. Hence, just as children experience themselves and imagine concrete others to have intentions, followed by certain behaviors, these attributes may now be cognitively generalized to abstract, symbolic others. Such abstractions are highly charming for adults to listen to because, although abstractions, they tend to be comparatively concrete and anthropomorphic in the view of adults (cf. the Piagetian concepts of preoperational egocentrism and animism). A child at this age may, for example, explain the rain as a result of God's need to pee.

Once these cognitive developments have occurred, when the attachment system is highly active, such as during separation, children might start to draw on this abstract (yet anthropomorphic) attachment surrogate and to do so more in such situations than in situations not involving attachment activation. Relatedly, Rizzuto (1979) has suggested that it is at this age that children develop a "living" God representation.

In middle childhood, as children enter school and move even farther from parents' immediate care, their God concepts become somewhat less anthropomorphic, although at the same time God is typically viewed as *personally* closer than in early childhood (Eshleman, Dickie, Merasco, Shepard, & Johnson, 1999; Tamminen, 1994). From early childhood on, empirical data clearly indicates that God is, indeed, perceived as available to serve a safe haven and secure base function in times of stress. For example, Tamminen (1994) found that 7- to 12-year-old Finnish children reported feeling close to God particularly during emergencies (e.g., escaping or avoiding danger, encounter with death or sorrow) and loneliness. Moreover, among the Finnish children, the category of situations in which God's guidance had been most frequently experienced consisted of external danger and difficulties, embraced by approximately 40 percent of the participating children. Additionally, Eshleman, Dickie, Merasco, Shepard, and Johnson (1999) found that American pre- and elementary school children placed a God symbol closer to a fictional child when the fictional child was in attachment activating situations (e.g., sick and in hospital, had fallen from a bike, the child's dog had died) than when the fictional child was in situations that were less clear-cut in terms of attachment activation (e.g., fictional child had stolen an apple, stolen a ball, and hurt another child).

These latter findings have now been conceptually replicated in two studies, one conducted in Sweden with 5- to 7-year-old children from religious and nonreligious homes (Granqvist, Ljungdahl, & Dickie, 2005), and one conducted in the United States with children of the same ages, most parents of whom were highly religious (Dickie, Charland, & Poll, 2005). The results of these two studies were conceptual, rather than direct, replications because they were based on a theoretically more clear-cut distinction between attachment activation and nonactivation. More specifically, the attachment neutral stories included the fictional child in good-mood, bad-mood, and neutral-mood situations. Even with that more stringent control, children thus placed God closer to the fictional child in the attachment activating situations.

Adolescence and early adulthood, the most clearly visible attachment transitional periods in most individuals' lives, have also been long-known as major religious transitional periods (e.g., Granqvist, 2003; James, 1902). These are the life-periods most intimately associated with sudden religious conversions and other significant changes during which the God relation gains increased significance. As noted above, sudden religious conversions and other major religious changes are, not unexpectedly, typically precipitated by significant emotional turmoil, such as relationship problems with parents, with love partners, and other kinds of distress that are highly likely to keep the attachment system hyperactive at this sensitive period of attachment transition (Granqvist, 1998; Kirkpatrick & Shaver, 1990).

Compared to the preceding periods, mid-adulthood is, normatively speaking, less associated both with attachment transitions and religious drama as well as, in the latter case, more associated with maintenance and socialization of the religious habit (James, 1902) to the next generation. However, there are notable exceptions, the most pronounced being spousal break-up in separation and divorce. Not surprisingly, then, such attachment transitions have been found associated with increased significance of the God relation (e.g., Granqvist & Hagekull, 2000; Kirkpatrick, 2005).

Finally, in old age, the private God relation often re-gains importance, particularly when people suffer such a major attachment loss as the loss of their spouse through death. In an elegant study, which employed a prospective longitudinal design and a population-based sample of elders—some of whom were to suffer prospective bereavement and some of whom were not—Brown, Nesse, House, and Utz (2004) found not only a prospective increase in the importance of the God relation for the bereaved compared to the nonbereaved, but also that grief over the loss prospectively decreased as a function of the increased significance of the bereaved spouses' God relation. None of these effects were obtained for increases in church attendance, indicating that it may be specifically the attachment component of the individual's religiousness that is activated in such situations, and that its activation is what is needed to bring favorable psychological outcomes about in the context of attachment-related loss.

INDIVIDUAL DIFFERENCES IN ATTACHMENT AND DIFFERENTIAL DEVELOPMENTAL PATHWAYS TO RELIGION

Just as individual differences in attachment security moderate the behavioral and linguistic output of attachment activation in general, so do they moderate the effects of attachment activation in the context of believers' perceived

God relations. However, the matter is not as straightforward as one might guess. From the outset, Kirkpatrick (1992; Kirkpatrick & Shaver, 1990) noted that two partly opposing hypotheses could naturally be deduced from attachment theory concerning relations between religion and security—insecurity of attachment.

The first hypothesis has already more or less been spelled out; in the absence of a secure attachment relationship, the individual may turn to attachment surrogates to regulate distress (Ainsworth, 1985; Bowlby, 1982). As applied to religion, God and other entities, such as spirits or angels, would represent such surrogates for insecurely attached individuals (the *compensation hypothesis*). This idea had been supported, for example, by findings showing that religious converts, whose conversions were often preceded by emotional turmoil, reported more unfavorable childhood relationships with parents than a matched comparison-group of nonconverts (Ullman, 1982).

In contrast, through the operation of generalizing IWMs, securely attached individuals readily perceive others as available when needed (model of other), as well as exploit this availability due to an implicit valuing of themselves as worthy of care (model of self; Bowlby, 1973). Perhaps, then, this inclination can be further generalized to their perceived God relations, in which case secure, rather than insecure, attachment would be the foundation of a corresponding relationship with God (the *IWM/correspondence* hypothesis). This idea had been supported, for example, in cross-cultural research showing that God is construed as more loving in cultures where parenting is warm/accepting and more distant in cultures marked by rejecting parenting (Lambert, Triandis, & Wolf, 1959; Rohner, 1986).

A socially based aspect of religiosity has been added to Kirkpatrick's correspondence hypothesis (Granqvist, 2002; Granqvist & Hagekull, 1999). Hence, besides IWM correspondence, it has been suggested that religious beliefs and behaviors in the case of secure attachment partly reflect the adoption of a sensitive attachment figure's religious standards, whereas insecure offspring are hypothesized to be relatively less likely to adopt their more insensitive attachment figure's religious standards (*social correspondence*; Granqvist, 2002). This addition had been supported by numerous studies showing that the religiosity of offspring with more favorable parental relationships is highly similar to their parent's religiosity, whereas the religiosity of offspring with less favorable relationships is more or less orthogonal to parental religiosity (e.g., Spilka et al., 2003). Such results also converge with the findings in the attachment literature noted above, indicating that securely attached offspring are more inclined to adopt parental standards in general. Another reason for the addition of a principle of social correspondence was that *some* theoretical moderator was needed to avoid making attachment predictions irrefutable (cf. Popper, 1959), as the same outcome would otherwise have been predicted from opposing directions (i.e., secure and insecure attachment). Moreover, parental religiousness consistently *did* act as such a moderator in the empirical studies (Granqvist, 1998, 2002, 2005; Granqvist & Hagekull, 1999; Granqvist, Ivarsson, Broberg, & Hagekull, 2005; Kirkpatrick & Shaver, 1990). Thus, securely attached individuals are expected to become actively religious insofar as their parents were, in line with social correspondence, and in which case their perceived God relations are expected to have attributes of security through IWM correspondence.

The correspondence and compensation hypotheses may be seen, then, as delineating distinct developmental pathways to religion, as well as to different religious profiles (i.e., modes of being religious). One of these paths is suggested via experiences with sensitive, religious caregivers (correspondence), and one is via regulation of distress following experiences with insensitive caregivers (compensation; Granqvist, in press; Kirkpatrick, 2005). It is in this developmental pathway sense that the compensation and correspondence hypotheses are used henceforth.

Below, findings supporting each of these pathways in relation to naturally occurring instances of religious beliefs and behaviors are reviewed. This is followed by a brief section on laboratory studies, in which attachment manipulations have been performed and their effects, as well as the moderating effects of security–insecurity, on religious outcomes have been studied. Finally, findings are reviewed on attachment security–insecurity in relation to a less orthodox domain of spirituality and associated paranormal experiences, namely the New Age movement. It should be cautioned that none of the studies to be reported followed study participants from infancy onward, although more short-term longitudinal studies are included.[3]

The Compensation Pathway

Many of the findings reported in the normative attachment-and-religion section have in fact now been found true specifically for individuals who have experienced parental insensitivity while growing up, whether using self-reports (e.g., Granqvist, 1998, 2002, 2005; Granqvist & Hagekull, 1999, 2003; Kirkpatrick & Shaver, 1990) or more indirect AAI-based assessments (Granqvist, Ivarsson et al., 2005) as attachment history criteria. For example, sudden religious conversions, the peaks of religious drama, are associated with parental insensitivity. This was originally reported in the pioneering study of Kirkpatrick and Shaver (1990) and has since been shown to hold in a meta-analysis of all studies conducted, including almost 1,500 participants (Granqvist & Kirkpatrick, 2004). Moreover, several studies have shown that other significant increases of religiousness reported by individuals whose parents have been judged low in sensitivity are typically relatively intense and precipitated by significant emotional turmoil, which is most typically relationship-derived (Granqvist & Hagekull, 1999;

Granqvist, Ivarsson et al., 2005). While the cited studies tapped religious changes retrospectively, Granqvist and Hagekull (2003) showed that the conclusion was warranted also prospectively. More specifically, reports of parental insensitivity predicted prospectively increased religiousness, particularly increased importance of the perceived God relation, following romantic relationship break-up.

Similarly, insecure romantic attachment has been found predictive of essentially the same kinds of religious changes. For example, Kirkpatrick (1997) found over a two-year period that women with insecure, particularly ambivalent, attachments prospectively established a new relationship with God (including religious experiences, such as being "born again" and speaking in tongues) to a larger extent than securely attached women. Findings of prospective increases in religiousness were replicated in a second study by Kirkpatrick (1998b) that spanned a shorter time period (e.g., four months) and included men and women. Again, such increases were tied to ambivalent romantic attachment. In both of these studies, the magnitude of the effects was modest. However, when the contextual condition of romantic relationship break-up was considered in yet another independent sample, insecure romantic attachment more strongly predicted prospective increases in religiousness (Granqvist & Hagekull, 2003).

Although these findings might seem to suggest that individuals with insecure attachment characteristics would become more and more religious over time, recall that this is expected primarily in the context of a need to regulate distress. Accordingly, religiousness may also decrease for such individuals (Granqvist, 2002). As expected, this happens following contextual conditions where the need to regulate distress is comparatively low, such as after establishing a new intimate relationship (Granqvist & Hagekull, 2003).

In summary, the developmental pathway to religion in the case of insecure attachment is one marked by attachment system (hyper-)activation, where the perceived God relation serves a distress regulatory function for the believer, whose other attachment figures are insufficient or unavailable. This conclusion is supported regardless of whether attachment insecurity refers to current romantic attachment or estimates of past experiences with parents. Also, the conclusion corresponds well with the more general speculations on the use of attachment surrogates offered by Bowlby (1982) and Ainsworth (1985). The opportunistic, surrogate use of religion is further strengthened in findings showing the God relation to wane when the need to regulate distress is low.

However, whereas AAI judges' estimates of parental insensitivity as the interviewees grew up did predict the interviewees' history of using religion to regulate distress, classifications of the interviewees' *current* attachment organization were generally unrelated to such compensatory aspects of religiosity in the only AAI study conducted (Granqvist, Ivarsson, et al., 2005).

An intriguing suggestion offered by these findings is that some individuals who have suffered attachment-related adversities in the past may in fact have "earned" a certain degree of attachment security from their surrogate God relation. While speculative at this point due to ambiguities of process direction, if confirmed in future studies, this would indicate that the God-relation is potentially reparative and that compensation may be psychologically functional, not just reactive.

The Correspondence Pathway

Believers' God relations are far from fully represented by the characteristics described in the above section. On the contrary, most religious individuals would shun away from these descriptions as unrepresentative of themselves and most members of their religious community. While Freudians might suspect a defensive maneuver here, empirical data supports it. In line with the correspondence hypothesis, participants reporting experiences of being sensitively cared for by parents have been shown to score higher in religiousness, but only insofar as their parents also displayed high levels of religiosity (Granqvist, 1998, 2002; Granqvist & Hagekull, 1999; Kirkpatrick & Shaver, 1990). In addition, they have been shown to score higher on a scale created to assess religiosity as socially based in the parental relationship (Granqvist, 2002; Granqvist & Hagekull, 1999). Moreover, both sets of findings have been supported in the AAI study when independent estimates of parental sensitivity were used (Granqvist, Ivarsson, et al., 2005).

Evidence for IWM correspondence has also accrued in relation to attachment history. Most notably, the AAI study showed independent estimates of parental sensitivity to be associated with participant reports of a loving, as opposed to a distant, God image (Granqvist, Ivarsson, et al., 2005). In addition, although religious changes are less frequent for individuals who have experienced sensitive caregiving, they sometimes do occur. When they do, the life-context and the constituents of the change are very different from those reported above. For example, prospective increases in religiousness occurred for participants reporting sensitive parenting following the establishment of a new intimate relationship (Granqvist & Hagekull, 2003).

Similarly, in the case of romantic attachment, positive relations have been obtained between secure romantic attachment and scores on the scale used to assess religiosity as socially based in the parental relationship (Granqvist, 2002). Regarding IWM-aspects of correspondence, such aspects have typically been supported in contemporaneous relations between religiosity and romantic attachment security. For example, Kirkpatrick and Shaver (1992) found that people with a secure romantic attachment displayed a higher degree of a personal belief in and relationship with God, as well as perceptions of God as loving. These findings have since been conceptually replicated in a number of studies (Byrd & Boe, 2000; Granqvist & Hagekull, 2000, 2003; Kirkpatrick, 1998b; TenElshof & Furrow, 2000). For example, Byrd and Boe found that participants reporting secure romantic attachments engaged more in prayers that served to maintain closeness to God. However, even in prospective analyses, IWM-correspondence between romantic attachment security and religious change is supported in expected contexts, for example, following the formation of a close romantic relationship in between religiosity assessments (Granqvist & Hagekull, 2003).

In sum, substantial empirical support has been obtained for the idea that the developmental pathway to religion for individuals with secure attachments begins with sensitive, religious caregivers and leads to the development of a perceived God-relation with security-related attributes, such as a loving God image.

God in the Lab

Recently, two sets of attachment and religion studies, using direct attempts to activate attachment, have been performed (Birgegard & Granqvist, 2004; Granqvist, Ljungdahl, et al., 2005). In both, the effects of attachment activation were compared with attachment nonactivation on religious outcomes, and the potentially moderating effects of attachment security were studied. The normative attachment activation effects of these studies were described above. In both sets, however, security moderated the normative effects.

The first set of experiments employed subliminal priming methodology with separation cues to activate adult theistic believers' attachment systems (see Shaver & Mikulincer [2002] for a review of attachment studies using priming methodology). Although, as we have seen, individuals who have experienced insensitive care are the ones who typically regulate distress through their perceived God relation (i.e., a compensation effect), across the three experiments conducted within the first set of studies, an increase in the use of God to regulate distress was observed following the separation primes among adult believers who had reported sensitive experiences with parents, thus supporting IWM correspondence instead. As indirect assessments of religiosity (i.e., regression residuals from pre- to post priming) were used in the context of subliminal priming, participants were unconscious of attachment activation, which may have undermined the possibility of a "higher-order" compensatory use of religion in individuals who had experienced parental insensitivity, thus resulting in their withdrawal from God or, put differently, their defensive shift of attention away from attachment. Conversely, individuals with more sensitive experiences drew on God in this situation, presumably via automatic activation of IWMs, or turned their attention to attachment. They typically rely on other means to regulate distress in the context of conscious attachment activation.

Similarly, in the Swedish study of 5- to 7-year-old children's placements of a God symbol in relation to a fictional child who was in situations of attachment activation versus nonactivation, secure children placed God closer to the fictional child when the fictional child was in attachment-activating conditions, whereas the pattern was actually reversed when the fictional child was in attachment-neutral situations (i.e., insecure children placed God closer). Another way of describing this interaction pattern is that secure children's attention was on proximity to God specifically during attachment activation, whereas insecure children did not make a distinction between the two kinds of situations in their God figure placements. Importantly, this study used the adapted SAT (Kaplan, 1987), an indirect (semi-projective) method, to classify security, and the God placement procedure was similarly semi-projective (i.e., the fictional child, not the participating child, was in different situations with regard to attachment activation). As in the adult subliminal experiments, this may have undermined the higher-order compensatory use of religion in insecure children and instead yielded automatic activation of IWMs and thus support of the correspondence hypothesis.

Based on the foregoing review, we may predict that when attachment activation is consciously connected to its source, and its effects cause considerable subjective distress, individuals with insecure attachment will regulate distress by drawing on God (cf. "contrast" effects in priming studies; Wheeler & Pettey, 2001). However, when attachment activation is not consciously connected to its source, and God is the only attachment-like figure available in the situation, automatic activation of IWMs will lead individuals with secure attachments to experience God as psychologically accessible (cf. "assimilation" effects in priming studies; Wheeler & Petty, 2001).

Compensation and Unorthodox Spirituality within the New Age

A large body of the attachment and religion research has been conducted in Sweden, a country marked by the continuous decline of traditional Western religion (Stark, Hamberg, & Miller, 2005). At the same time, a notable increase in more private, unorthodox, and less institutionalized forms of religion-like spirituality, most notably in the New Age movement, have co-occurred (for similar developments in another part of Western Europe, see Houtman & Mascini, 2002) . Therefore, it was asked whether the New Age "religions" would attract some of the individuals who left more traditional forms of religion (Granqvist & Hagekull, 2001; Granqvist, Ivarsson, et al., 2005; see also Farias & Granqvist, in press, for a review of the psychology of the New Age).

Whereas traditional Western religion has an attachment-like figure (i.e., a theistic God) at the center from which all else is supposedly derived, the New Age movement typically does not. Instead, the New Age has been thought to represent the "celebration of the self" (Heelas, 1996), where the individual takes pride in many of the attributes traditionally ascribed to the deity. As we shall see, however, it may be more adequate to characterize the New Age as a failed attempt of reparation of the self. In either case, predictions from attachment theory were clear enough.

First, the within-generational increase in New Age endorsement could not be accounted for as socially based in the early parental relationship with religious parents, nor could it be characterized in terms of IWM correspondence, as "New Agers" typically do not perceive of a personal relationship with a loving God (see also Kirkpatrick, 2005). Hence, parental sensitivity and security of attachment could be ruled out as predictors of New Age endorsement.

Secondly, insecure attachment had been found to have correlates very similar to those implied in New Age endorsement in previous studies. More specifically, disorganized and ambivalent attachment were thought to be the prime candidates for later involvement in the New Age. For example, and as noted in the introduction, disorganized attachment predicts dissociative mental states, many of which are not only present but even sanctioned within the New Age (e.g., out-of-body experiences, trance states, hypnotic suggestion). Likewise, just as disorganized attachment is linked to experiences of abuse, so are many of the paranormal experiences associated with the New Age (e.g., Irwin, 1993). Also, disorganized (unresolved) attachment within the AAI system has as one of its central features difficulties of maintaining coherent and rational discourse surrounding loss through death. Moreover, Main and colleagues had found that disorganized AAI discourse correlates with many of the central features of the New Age (e.g., belief in astrology, contact with the dead; Main & Morgan, 1996).

Similarly, ambivalent attachment had been associated with difficulties in understanding the privacy of thought—a cardinal feature of the belief in telepathy—as well as with the attribution of psychic powers to some humans, most notably the self and the attachment figure. Needless to say, both sets of beliefs are well-represented within the New Age. Finally, ambivalent (preoccupied) attachment within the AAI is often expressed as preoccupying anger, wherein angry ranting against the attachment figure may occur in the presence of "authoritative" psychological statements, marked by overused phrases and psychological jargon ("psychobabble"). This naturally brings some of the popular psychology literature of the New Age movement to mind (e.g., on "toxic," "dysfunctional" families and encounter groups). As a first step to test these predictions, a continuous questionnaire scale was created to measure a New Age lifestyle orientation, labeled the New Age Orientation Scale

(NAOS; Granqvist & Hagekull, 2001). This scale has now been tested in diverse populations, drawn both from New Age settings (e.g., "alternative" book stores and cafés) and the general population. Although serious attempts were made to tap the theoretical heterogeneity of New Age–related beliefs and activities, all studies conducted to date indicate that scale scores form one homogenous factor that is highly internally consistent (average inter-item r = ca .45; α = ca .95; Farias, Claridge, & Lalljee, 2005; Granqvist & Hagekull, 2001; Granqvist, Fredrikson et al., 2005; Granqvist, Ivarsson et al., 2005).

In other words, although New Agers often take pride in formulating their own philosophies of life, that pride rests on a fallacious assumption, as other New Agers form "their own" philosophies of life in essentially the same manner.

Next, New Age endorsement was studied in relation to parental sensitivity and security of attachment. All findings obtained to date supports the compensation hypothesis. First, regarding parental sensitivity, participants drawn from New Age settings reported lower parental sensitivity than those drawn from the general population (Granqvist & Hagekull, 2001). Also, NAOS scores have been found to be positively related both to self-reports of parental insensitivity (Granqvist & Hagekull, 2001) and AAI judges' independent estimates of parental insensitivity (Granqvist, Ivarsson, et al., 2005). Second, regarding romantic attachment, positive correlations have been found between romantic attachment disorganization (i.e., fearful avoidance) and NAOS scores (Granqvist & Hagekull, 2001), as well as between ambivalence and the inclination to be interested in spirituality and esoteric books (Saroglou, Kempeneers, & Seynhaeve, 2003). Finally, concerning attachment organization within the AAI, higher NAOS scores have been associated, as expected, with independent judges' assignments of ambivalent (preoccupied) as well as disorganized attachment states (both trauma specific unresolved states and more globally disorganized "cannot classify" states; Granqvist, Ivarsson, et al., 2005).

These latter findings are particularly noteworthy when considering that AAI classifications are often unrelated to self-reports of external phenomena, although strongly related to behavioral observations and more indirect assessments of theoretically relevant constructs (see Hesse, 1999). In addition, the findings from the AAI study (Granqvist, Ivarsson, et al., 2005) show that whereas some individuals who have experienced parental insensitivity while growing up, and who have used God as a surrogate to regulate distress, *may* have earned a certain degree of attachment security from doing so, the same cannot be said for individuals drawn to the New Age. In contrast, the most serious forms of *current* attachment insecurity lingers within these individuals. A speculative theoretical interpretation of these discrepancies between traditional religion and the New Age in relation to insecurity within the AAI system is that traditional religion may promote earned security through offering perceptions of a reparative attachment surrogate, conceived of as the perfect attachment figure, whereas such a figure is absent within the New Age. Of course, it is also possible that only the most seriously insecure individuals, who have suffered more serious forms of parental insensitivity (potentially including abuse), are drawn to the New Age, whereas the insecure attachment history of some individuals who come to use God as a surrogate may have been somewhat less serious. If that is the case, it is also readily understandable why the former individuals shun any attachment-like figure (e.g., it may be perceived as frightening), whereas the latter are less inclined to do so and instead make use of it. In any event, we are cautioned not to generalize without further study across spiritual domains if we want to understand the psychology of individuals drawn to the supernatural.

We have thus seen that the attachment system is operating within believers' perceived God relations, although very differently depending on individual differences in attachment security. Before closing this section on attachment and religion, a few additional issues have to be addressed. First, in much of what was said above, a distinction was not made between different patterns of insecurity in relation to religious outcomes, partly due to inconsistencies in results. However, a tentative conclusion that can be derived is that "charismatic" experiences (e.g., glossolalia), as well as an emphasis on alternative spirituality, as in the New Age, are associated with ambivalent attachment, marked by maximization of attachment and a general deficit in the regulation of distress. Spiritual experiences charac-terized by dissociative alterations in consciousness can be hypothesized to be linked to disorganization. Of course, such experiences are often present in the New Age but may also occur within nonorthodox expressions of traditional religion, for example, in spontaneously occurring mystical and trance states (though not necessarily their volitional production in media-tion and prayer following a long period of exercise). The religious picture of avoidant attachment has been less clearly decipherable. For example, romantic attachment avoidance has been linked to contemporaneous athe-ism and agnosticism (Kirkpatrick & Shaver, 1992) on the one hand and to prospectively increased religiousness following romantic relationship dissolution (Granqvist & Hagekull, 2003) on the other. A topic currently under investigation is whether avoidant attachment is linked to a socially facile expression of religion (e.g., God is loving), which is, fundamen-tally, internally inconsistent (e.g., God sends sinners to hell; cf. idealiza-tion within the AAI). To fully tap such inconsistencies, a semi-structured interview focusing on the *form* of religious discourse is being used (Granqvist & Main, 2003).

Secondly, most of the research reviewed has concerned religion and spiri-tuality within the Western world (for an exception, see Gewirtz, 2004, using a Jewish sample in Israel). Clearly, cross-cultural research is badly needed here, especially in other (theistic) traditions that express the belief in a meta-physical attachment-like figure. Third, as high scores on any religious variable has low religiousness as their opposite, it should be understood that this chapter has also dealt with the negation of religion, although that requires from the reader a mental reversal of the findings presented.

Finally, although the attachment system is active within the individual's God relation, this does not mean that attachment theory may be considered a comprehensive psychology of religion. On the contrary, if there is a multi-dimensional phenomenon, religion is likely one of the first that comes to mind. As argued elsewhere, attachment theory is primarily relevant for understanding the relational dimensions of religion (Granqvist, 2006; Kirkpatrick, 2005), and although important, religion is larger than that. Relatedly, the attachment system is not the sole evolutionary adaptation on which religion rides piggy-back. There are clearly other mechanisms—associated with other systems—involved, such as kin-selection, reciprocal altruism, alliance tactics, naïve physics, naïve biology, and folk psychology (see Atran & Norenzayan, 2004; Kirkpatrick, 2005). More generally, it is obvious that besides mechanisms such as the attachment system, a complex operator (i.e., the human brain) is required to produce religious outcomes.[4] For example, the human brain's capacity to comprehend abstractions is likely a prerequisite for what we normally think of as religious beliefs and interpretations, and it also explains why other animals are likely incapable of these same things. Combined with the more visibly domain-specific adaptations, however, it is easy to see how this general capacity to use abstractions may have produced a set of outcomes (i.e., religion) that represent, functionally speaking, output that the operator was not designed to produce.

IMPLICATIONS, CONCERNS, AND RECOMMENDATIONS FOR BRAIN AND RELIGION RESEARCH: WILL NEUROTHEOLOGY PLEASE RISE?

In terms of implications, it is clear from the above sections that tools that activate the attachment system may be useful in facilitating the occurrence of religious experience. As it runs the risk of being unethical to activate the system at higher levels, researchers are advised to attempt activation with caution (e.g., separation primes, mild fear inductions). In any event, this represents one of the potential uses of attachment theory that may help researchers studying religious experience in the lab, including its neurophysiological, biological, and chemical correlates.

As is also implied above, however, simply activating the brain's attachment function is likely to prove an inefficient means of producing religious experience. The reason is that religious experiences are multifactorial; that is, they often do involve the operation of the attachment system, but their occurrences depend on other factors as well. Results from research in the psychology of religion, spanning over several decades, have—again and again—attested to the validity of this conclusion (see Spilka et al., 2003). For example, although psychedelic drugs have tremendous effects on the likelihood that people enter altered states of consciousness, as mediated by the effects of the drugs on the release of neurotransmitters in the brain, religious and mystical experiences (with religious interpretations) do not typically result unless the *setting* is religious (e.g., a divine service; Spilka et al., 2003). The same applies to the well-known effects of sensory deprivation on religious experience. Although a very well-established conclusion in the psychology of religion, in their fascination over brain activity—and what particular brain regions that light up in the religious experience versus baseline conditions—"neurotheologists"[5] have often overlooked the multifactorial nature of religious experience.

This last remark serves to shift the focus of this chapter to a scrutiny of neurotheology as a developing field of brain and religion research. As it turns out, neurotheologists have often times also failed to distinguish between very different kinds of religious and paranormal experiences. Moreover, some of the key neurotheology findings have failed to replicate under double-blind conditions. Finally, the ontological and evolutionary conclusions occasionally drawn by neurotheologists on the basis of the few findings produced are baffling to the analytically minded, often reflecting very simple errors of logic. Each of these issues will be discussed in their own right, while the "theology" part of the "neuro-theology" equation is largely left for others to evaluate. The chapter will end with a few recommendations for the future development of brain and religion research.

The Multifactorial Nature of Religious Experience

The neurotheological literature has neglected consideration of sensory input conditions that makes the brain produce religious outcomes. This is akin to cognitively modeling spider phobia without including visual sensation of the spider as input to the brain in the cognitive model. Although, for example, the visual sensation of God certainly cannot be regarded as objective input to the brain in a scientific model, the visual sensation of a Crucifix or the auditory sensation of a Baroque organ could, and indeed do increase the brain's production of religious experience. These remarks are not directed at neurotheologists studying neural *correlates* of religious experience but are of upmost relevance to those who claim to trigger the experience in the lab through manipulating just one variable.

For example, Michael Persinger (2002) has claimed in a large number of reports to produce religious experience through the application of a particular magnetic-field device to peoples' temporal lobes. Persinger claims that approximately 80 percent[6] of all individuals from the normal population can be made to experience what he calls a "sensed presence" of a sentient being, believed by Persinger to represent the core of religious experience (i.e., the experience of God). This would be accomplished by electrical discharge in the limbic structures, essentially resulting in a micro epileptic-like seizure. As is well-known, temporal lobe epilepsy has long been thought to play a significant role in religious experience (see Saver & Rabin, 1997 and the chapter by Schachfer, this volume). Persinger has not advocated as strongly, though, that sensory deprivation is a necessary condition for the experience. Nor has he adequately addressed the moderating influence of personality factors (but see Persinger & Koren, 2005). What these examples illustrate is that Persinger's findings may not reflect (simply) the causal operation of the magnetic fields in discharging limbic structure activity but presumably (also) the causal effect of sensory deprivation and a moderating influence of personality. Yet, the influence of these latter parameters has been notably overlooked in his interpretations of the results.

There Are Different Kinds of Religious and Paranormal Experiences

Concerning the failure to distinguish between different kinds of religious/ paranormal experiences, Persinger's research is a case in point. It departs from an empirically unsubstantiated assumption that the sensed presence experience represents the core of religious experience. Anecdotal reports from a few selected participants have been cited as support for this assumption (Persinger, 1997), yet other participants viewed the experience in purely secular terms, without that being used as a qualifier in the assumption or in the interpretation of results. In addition, the most frequently used dependent variable in Persinger's studies over the years (the "Exit scale"; Persinger, Tiller, & Koren, 2000) was constructed inductively and specifically for the task at hand but with unknown reliability and construct validity. Besides the one sensed presence item included in the scale, many of the experiences listed are somewhat vague ("tingling sensations," "felt odd," "the same idea kept occurring"), and their relations to the paranormal, mystical, and religious experiences, to which the findings are generalized, remain disputable.

Moreover, as we saw in the above sections on attachment, the psychological correlates of traditional religion and more unorthodox spirituality, such as in the New Age, are very different. This might well have implications also for the correlates of different religious/spiritual experiences. In other words, experiencing a subjective sense of closeness to God, for example, is likely to be something very different than out-of-body experiences, haunt-experiences, perceived UFO-abductions, and so forth, although Persinger (1997, 2002) does not view these experiences as conceptually different from one other in any important way. All of them are simply held to result from limbic discharge gone awry.

Although faring much better in comparison, correlational SPECT and PET studies have focused on limited aspects of religious experience, for example, repetitive recital of religious texts (Azari et al., 2001) and meditation (e.g., Newberg & Iversen, 2003). While these were good and practically feasible starting points, they do not represent all forms of religious experience, and likely not full-blown mystical experiences. (Empirically, we have no way of knowing whether participants did reach, for example, mystical states, as the measurements of religious experience/meditational peak were "home-built," constructed specifically for the individual studies.) Consequently, these investigations indicated the involvement of higher cortical regions, suggesting that focused attention, concentration, and other higher-order cognitive functions would be implicated rather than the basal affective components associated with limbic firing, as suggested by Persinger and others (e.g., Ramachandran & Blakeslee, 1999). While difficult to study in the lab, full-blown mystical experiences, such as those often involved in sudden religious conversion, may well involve massive limbic discharge.

Neurotheology Findings that Fail to Replicate

It is generally a problem in science that theories are under-determined by data (Quine, 1992) but almost in no other area does that seem truer than in neurotheology research. Although the "theory" part of the "theory-data" equation also requires a lot of tidying up in this discipline (see below), it is notable that what may have seemed the most well-replicated empirical findings—those of Persinger and the magnetic field device, replicated by Persinger himself in a long list of studies (see 1997)—in fact cannot be replicated under double-blind conditions by other researchers (Granqvist, Fredrikson, et al., 2005). These researchers sought to replicate the findings prior to performing a costly follow-up brain-imaging study that was planned to investigate the neural correlates of lab-triggered sensed presence and mystical experience. The failed replication had a number of design improvements compared to the original experiments, while still sticking in detail to the inductively based lessons allegedly learned by Persinger over the years. In fact, the magnetic field device and the computer software utilized was sent to the researchers by Persinger, and the experimental set-up, including

sensory deprivation, as well as the administration of the fields (time of exposure, particular wave pattern, strength, calibration, etc.) followed Persinger's
instructions in detail. Moreover, effective magnetic field deliverance was
verified pre- and post-experiment. (See Larsson, Larhammar, Fredrikson, &
Granqvist, 2005, for their response to Persinger & Koren's, 2005, attempted
rebuttal of the failed replication.)

However, from reading Persinger's studies (e.g., 1997), it was clear that
they were not properly double-blinded (i.e., neither participants, nor experimenters should be aware of experimental group assignment). Hence, one
important design improvement was to make the set-up double-blind, which
was accomplished by having two experimenters, one who made experimental
group assignments (and never interacted with the participants), and one who
was unaware of group assignment (the one who interacted with the participants). While this may seem a somewhat finicky design requirement, it was
considered important due to the described vagueness of some of the experiences used in the dependent variable (i.e., the EXIT scale) in Persinger's
(1997) studies as well as the study under description. Considering humans'
general suggestibility to induction (i.e., placebo effects), selective experi-
menter interaction across conditions could otherwise easily lead participants in the experimental condition to have some of the vague experiences,
whereas those in the control condition (no magnetic field activated) would
be less inclined to have them. If that were the case, a main-effect of experimental condition would result, just as Persinger's studies had demonstrated,
although in his case allegedly as an effect of the magnetic fields. In addition,
certain easily suggestible individuals in the experimental condition would be
particularly inclined to report the experiences, in which case a moderating
influence of personality would be obtained (i.e., a statistical interaction effect
with experimental condition). As we have seen, a moderating influence of
"temporal lobe signs" has also repeatedly been observed by Persinger (1997,
see also Cook & Persinger, 2001).

It may not be so surprising to find, then, that the items used to tap temporal lobe signs (Makarec & Persinger, 1990) are in fact almost identical to the
items of standard suggestibility questionnaires, such as Tellegen's absorption scale (Tellegen & Atkinson, 1974), validated against suggestibility to
hypnotic induction. Indeed, these two scales are so similar that they are tapping the same construct, with a correlation of .72, almost identical to the
internal consistency reliability ($\alpha = .73$) of the Temporal Lobe Signs questionnaire (Granqvist, Fredrikson, et al., 2005; r not reported). To conclude,
an alternative suggestibility interpretation to the interpretation of magnetic
field effects could certainly not be ruled out *a priori* and therefore needed to
be addressed more thoroughly.

Another methodological improvement of the study under description is
that it did not presume generalizability of the sensed presence experience

to religious experiences in general but used an adapted (i.e., to state-format) version of the most well-validated mystical experience scale (Hood, 1975) to empirically address that issue. Also, to make possible an investigation of whether religiousness moderated the experimental effects, both religious and nonreligious participants were included. Finally, although Cook and Persinger (2001) had indicated that the effect was so strong that only 16 participants were required to obtain significant results, to be on the safe side in terms of statistical power, the study under description included as many as 89 participants.

As noted, the study results failed to replicate those of Persinger (Granqvist, Fredrikson, et al., 2005). Instead, a pattern of findings was obtained that strongly favored the alternative suggestibility interpretation. First, neither main effects nor any interaction effects with experimental condition were obtained on any outcome variable, whether the EXIT scale and the mysticism scale in their entirety or the critical sensed presence item were used. Second, the suggestibility variables (i.e., the absorption and temporal lobe signs) displayed positive main effects on the outcomes. Third, religiousness was not associated with higher scores on any of the outcome variables. In follow-up analyses, however, religiousness specifically predicted mystical experiences *with religious interpretations* but not mystical experiences in the absence of such interpretations (Granqvist & Larsson, in press). This, again, contrasts with the less orthodox spirituality of the New Age. Like the suggestibility variables, scores on the New Age scale (Granqvist & Hagekull, 2001) were namely associated both with higher EXIT and overall mystical scale scores (see Farias & Granqvist [in press] for other indications of elevated suggestibility specifically in New Agers and not in traditionally religious individuals).

However disappointing it was that application of the magnetic fields failed to yield the predicted experiences, it was notable in this study that such experiences occurred seemingly spontaneously in a minority of study participants. On closer examination, however, this is not surprising. First, as in Persinger's (e.g., 1997) studies, when participants filled out the pre-experimental questionnaires (e.g., the Temporal Lobe Signs Inventory), they were asked about all kinds of anomalous experiences, spirituality, and religiousness, which may have acted as a prime for unusual experiences. Secondly, the magnetic field device was attached to participants' temporal lobes, potentially enhancing suggestibility further. Thirdly, they were then placed in a sensory deprivation context, which is, as noted, a well-known facilitator of religious and other anomalous experiences. For the highly suggestible, it is easy to see how these conditions may result in at least low levels of anomalous experiences. And for the less easily suggestible, it may at least activate relevant cognitive schemas; hence, religious individuals were more inclined to *interpret* any low-level mystical experience that did occur in religious terms.

Although these findings and interpretations might seem less relevant to other neurotheologists who may not have believed in Persinger's findings to begin with, they do imply that priming, cognitive schemas, sensory conditions, and personality dispositions are relevant for the production, and hence understanding, of religious and related experiences. Many of these constructs cannot be equated with, or studied as, neural states, nor do they seem likely to be possible to translate to neural states in the near future. Hence, the prospect for neuroscience to become a *comprehensive* paradigm for the study of religious experience does not seem promising (relatedly, see Paloutzian, Fikes, & Hutsebaut, 1992), although it will hopefully make important contributions for an understanding of the *neural* mechanisms and correlates associated with these experiences.

Evolutionary and Ontological Considerations in Neurotheology

From the few findings produced in the field, the wildest ontological and evolutionary conclusions have been drawn, and popular media has of course gone along for the ride. In fact, whereas only a handful to a dozen empirical studies have been published on brain and religion associations, hundreds of theoretical papers and books have been produced. Notably, the theoretical papers have most often been published in an "interdisciplinary" journal aiming for integration of science and religion (*Zygon*; impact rate 2004: 0.15). Although the question of the ontology of God is, in principle, independent of the question of the evolutionary function of religion, there are strong reasons to suspect that, in practice, they have not always been viewed this way by writers in neurotheology. In fact, the questions of God-ontology and evolutionary function often coincide with the neurotheologist's position on whether or not the brain is "hard-wired" for religion (the brain has a "God spot," "God module," etc.).

Regarding evolutionary considerations, a diverse set of opinions have been proposed by neurotheologists, but the most frequent are religion-as-an adaptation, or a special case of adaptation (exaptation), and evolution as driven by "intelligent design." While it is not within the scope of this chapter to address which of these alternatives is likely to be true (see Kirkpatrick, this volume, for a discussion), expressed opinions of neurotheologists are relevant for a diagnosis of their failure to distinguish between evolutionary considerations/religious modularity of the brain and God-ontology, and where in this picture neuroscience findings become relevant.

First, Persinger (e.g., 2002) might seem to have adopted a religion-as-by-product position in his argument that the God experience is an epiphenomenon of limbic discharge gone awry. In reference to the first believer studied who had the God experience under the influence of magnetic fields,

Persinger states (2002): "I never had the heart to tell that person about the electrical recordings. In fact, the realization that the God Experience could be an *artefact* of the human brain was intellectually paralyzing. But since then, like hundreds of other brain scientists who have been determined to separate semantics from science, I have observed the *symptoms* again and again" (p. 276, italics added). However, his position is adaptationist: "A biological capacity for the God experience was critical for the survival of the species" (2002, p. 274). While Persinger may then be complemented for his ability to distinguish between biological functionality and the ontology of God, his use of the words "artefact" and "symptoms" makes it fairly clear that he reaches a conclusion of God's nonexistence partly based on the alleged lab-triggering of religious experience. When drawn from neuroscience findings, and even if the God experience could have been replicably triggered in the lab by independent researchers, this ontological reduction is nothing more than a pure example of the genetic fallacy. First, the question of the God experience is not equivalent to the question of God's actual presence; the first is an issue of experiences that people have, the second a question of ontology that may well be independent of peoples' experiences. More importantly, however— and as believers are often quick to point out— perhaps the triggering of limbic discharge is a reinvention of the wheel God has been using all along to get to people (i.e., a "God mediator"). This latter conclusion would, of course, be equally erroneous when drawn from neuroscience findings.

Second, Newberg, d'Aquili, and Rause (2002), in their oft-cited bestseller *Why God won't go away*, explicitly state that they do not adopt a position on religion as an adaptation (e.g., "the evolutionary process suggests that the mind's ability to enter unitary states did not evolve specifically for the purpose of spiritual transcendence," pp. 123–124), and they then go on to do exactly that, although a special case of that. They draw a direct parallel between the "neurological machinery of transcendence [which] may have arisen from the neural circuitry that evolved for mating and sexual experience" (p. 125, brackets added) to birds' wings, the foundation of which evolved to regulate temperature (i.e., their "original" adaptive function), only to be co-opted for flying (i.e., an exaptation). Note here that an exaptation merely represents a new adaptive function; unless a bird would have wings that allowed it to fly, it would likely fail to survive or reproduce in the new environment where most other birds had wings. A few pages later, Newberg and colleagues express the adaptation conclusion they initially rejected ever more forcefully: "we believe that evolution has adopted this machinery, and has favored the religious capabilities of the religious brain because religious beliefs and behaviors turn out to be good for us in profound and pragmatic ways" (p. 129), and "the strong survival advantages of religious belief make it very likely that evolution would enhance the neurological wiring that makes transcendence possible" (p. 139). In other words, the neurological machinery of transcendence is seen as a domain-general adaptation, albeit a special case of it (see Alper, 2002, for an even more explicit religion-as-adaptation example).

Not coincidentally, the ontological conclusion follows just a few lines later: "our research has left us no choice but to conclude that the mystics may be on to something, that the mind's machinery may in fact be a window through which we can glimpse the ultimate realness of something that is truly divine" (pp. 140–141). Whether Newberg and colleagues' research did not leave them any choice but to engage in ontological embracement, as stated, or was simply taken as an opportunity to play with rhetorics and promote their ontological beliefs, could be discussed, but in either case the conclusion is erroneous, reflecting the confusion of biological functionality/religious modularity of the brain with ultimate ontology. Were they atheists, they might have suspected their mystics of hallucinating on grounds of low inter-rater agreement between the mystics' reports of what was going on and the likely reports of the examiners in the room, had the perceptions of the latter regarding the presence of the divine been subjected to simultaneous research. It would be interesting to know if Newberg and colleagues would have derived a similar conclusion from doing brain-imaging research on dedicated fantasizers while fantasizing (i.e., do their fantasies exist outside of their brains?). Again, whether some brain areas are activated or some neurotransmitters released during meditative experience is orthogonal to the question of the ontological existence of the external referent imagined in the meditative state. Moreover, as discussed by Kirkpatrick (this volume), activation of brain areas during religious experience is far from convincing evidence that the brain is hard-wired for religion; particular areas of children's brains will be activated when they imagine Santa Clause in anticipation of Christmas, but their brains were not hard-wired for that same effect.

Finally, although neurotheology is set out to be interdisciplinary, to integrate science and religion, and so forth, it may be surprising to find that some of the scholars in the field have gone so far as to suggest intelligent design as the basis for evolution, while still working within an alleged scientific discipline (see Hamilton III, 2002; Joseph, 2002). Although this could easily be dismissed as not worthy of serious consideration among many scientists, it should probably be taken very seriously and dealt with primarily as an epistemological issue in the practice of science. While advocating intelligent design is, by definition, a declaration of faith, to reject the same idea from the practice of science is not necessarily an outcome of atheism, but may simply be an expression of concern for the integrity of scientific explanation. Unless we aim for a resurge of medieval scholasticism, when immaterial metaphysics and teleological causation had their hey-days, while scientific progress was modest at best, the idea of intelligent design will continue to be foreign to the practice of all natural sciences, based as they are on materialist metaphysics and physical principles of causation. This should be the case whether or not any individual engaged in science is personally religious (i.e., ultimately *believes* in intelligent design). If they so happen to be, they must practice to resist the temptation of evoking teleological explanations when dealing with scientific thought with the same dedication that they practice meditation and prayer to experience a sense of personal closeness with God.

Recommendations for the Future: Will "-Theology" Please be Left Out?

It seems as though one has no choice but to conclude from the above scrutiny that the field of neurotheology does not seem to have much scientific potential for the future. With that being said, brain and religion research may well prove to be one of the most exciting and fruitful areas in the future science of religion. In this concluding section, a few recommendations will be offered to make the field reach its full potential.

First, theology—narrowly defined as anything dealing with the ontology of God—should be clearly demarcated from the practice of brain and religion science. In other words, attempts at integrating science and religion should probably be abandoned in the first step, as it seems to be doing both disciplines more harm than good. This is not to reject either one as a legitimate intellectual enterprise, but to express a conviction that they, if any two paradigms, are truly incommensurable (Kuhn, 1962). Among other things, natural science is based on materialist metaphysics and physical causation, engaging in explanation, description, and taxonomies, while applying Occam's razor. In contrast, religion (again, among other things) is based on immaterialist metaphysics and teleological causation, engaging in values and existential props, while applying Occam's shaving foam. Bridging these incompatible principles requires bigger leaps than bridging, say, quantum mechanics as a natural science with normative political ideology, although it would hardly be surprising if someone had tried just that, or will try.

Secondly, brain and religion research should give attention to the multidimensional and multifactorial nature of religious experience. Concerning different kinds of religious experience, those that involve profound dissociative alterations in consciousness may, for example, have very different correlates, neural and otherwise, than those that do not (e.g., meditative states, peace and tranquility). Regarding multiple causes, future attempts at triggering religious experience in the lab to study their neural correlates may be considerably enhanced in efficiency if they:

- activate relevant motivational systems/neural functions (e.g., attachment);
- facilitate/counteract neurochemical release (e.g., dopamine-enhancers, serotonin-blockers);

- utilize sensory priming (e.g., a visually presented Crucifix, the auditory presentation of a Baroque organ, the olfactory presentation of incense); and

- use a facilitating setting (e.g., sensory deprivation).

Even under these conditions, however, it may be necessary to screen for participants high in suggestibility who possess cognitive schemas of relevance to a particular interpretation of the experience under study. Admittedly, this will be complex, but so are the determinants of religious experience. Also, even if, for example, full-blown mystical experiences will be difficult/impossible to trigger in the lab while maintaining ethical standards of scientific conduct, future imaging investigators should capitalize on the psychometric developments made in the psychology of religion and investigate whether variance in the experience studied correlates with variance in neural firing.

Finally, if the religion-as-by-product position adopted here is correct, links between neural activity and religious experience are likely to be indirect and mediated by the (sum-total) operation of the evolved psychological mechanisms thought to underlie religious experience, one of which is the attachment system.

NOTES

1. It is hoped that through this linguistic licensing, the reader will turn the other cheek to, or at least be indulgent with, the author's violation of relevance (Grice, 1989).

2. It is far from clear that the most realistic approach toward category membership placements is in terms of necessary and sufficient conditions, as implied in the above sections. A very different approach is suggested in Wittgenstein's (1953) notion of family resemblances. As applied to the family" of attachment relationships, the infant-caregiver relationship constitutes the prototype of the category. For inclusion of a new "family member," it should bear some convincing resemblances to this prototype, just as we have seen that the believer-God relationship does.

3. All of the attachment data requiring coding that is reported in this chapter was, of course, coded blind with regard to participant religiousness and spirituality. For example, the two certified coders used to code the AAIs were blind to other individual data and to the other coder's codings. Nevertheless, each coder's results reproduced, in detail, the results of the other coder.

4. The complexity of the brain likely evolved gradually, due to the hominids' increased ability to provide effective solutions to *specific* survival- and reproductive-related tasks. Hence, although the brain now has the appearance of being a high-efficiency, domain-*general* operator, selection pressures likely still acted domain-specifically, which is expressed also at present in our superiority at solving fitness-related tasks (e.g., detecting others' cheating in social exchange) compared to other tasks (e.g., Cosmides & Tooby, 1992).

5. The term neurotheologist is used in reference to scholars who have adopted that label themselves or published in neurotheology-titled books without making reservations as to the appropriateness of mixing theology—narrowly conceived as ontological considerations regarding God—and neuroscience. To label Persinger a neurotheologist may seem a stretch at first, but as will be seen, he engages in ontological considerations, or reductions to be more specific, based on neuroscience findings. Hence, on closer examination, the label is appropriate, as atheism is a position on theology.

6. Persinger's meta-analysis (1997), however, indicated that not fully 50 percent of participants receiving magnetic field application had such experiences, and it is unclear whether these represented all participants exposed or a subgroup of particularly "temporal-lobe-labile" participants. In other words, it is beyond this author's knowledge from where the figure 80 percent derived.

REFERENCES

Ainsworth, M. D .S. (1985). Attachments across the life-span. *Bulletin of the New York Academy of Medicine, 61*, 792–812.

Ainsworth, M. D. S., Bell, S. M., & Stayton, D. J. (1974). Infant-mother attachment and social development: "Socialisation" as a product of reciprocal responsiveness to signals. In M.P.M. Richards (Ed.), *The integration of a child into a social world* (pp. 99–137). Cambridge: Cambridge University Press.

Ainsworth, M. D. S., Blehar, M. C. Waters, E., & Wall, S. (1978). *Patterns of attachment: A psychological study of the strange situation.* Hillsdale, NJ: Lawrence Erlbaum.

Allen, J. P., & Land, D. (1999). Attachment in adolescence. In J. Cassidy & P.R. Shaver (Eds.), *Handbook of attachment theory and research* (pp. 319–335). New York: Guilford.

Alper, M. (2002). The evolutionary origins of spiritual consciousness. In R. Joseph (Ed.), *Neurotheology* (pp. 267–284). San Jose: California University Press.

Argyle, M., & Beit-Hallahmi, B. (1975). *The social psychology of religion.* London: Routledge and Kegan Paul.

Atran, S., & Norenzayan, A. (2004). Religion's evolutionary landscape: Counterintuition, commitment, compassion, communion. *Behavioral and Brain Sciences, 27*, 713–770.

Azari, N. P., Nickel., J., Wunderlich, G., Niedeggen, M., Hefter, H., Tellmann, L., et al. (2001). Neural correlates of religious experiences. *European Journal of Neuroscience, 13*, 1649–1652.

Birgegard, A., & Granqvist, P. (2004). The correspondence between attachment to parents and God: Three experiments using subliminal separation cues. *Personality and Social Psychology Bulletin, 30*, 1122–1135.

Bokhorst, C. L., Bakermans-Kranenburg, M.J.P., van Ijzendoorn, M. H., Fonagy, P., & Schuengel, C. (2003). The importance of shared environment in mother-infant attachment security: A behavioral genetic study. *Child Development, 74*, 1769–1782.

Booth, C. L., Rubin, K. H., & Krasnor, L. R. (1998). Perceptions of emotional support from mother and friend in middle childhood: Links with social-emotional adaptation and preschool attachment security. *Child Development, 69*, 427–442.

Bowlby, J. (1973). *Separation anxiety and anger.* Vol. 2 of 3 in Attachment and loss series. New York: Basic Books.

Bowlby, J. (1980). *Loss*. Vol. 3 of 3 in Attachment and loss series. New York: Basic Books.

Bowlby, J. (1982). *Attachment* (2nd ed.). Vol. 1 of 3 in Attachment and loss series. New York: Basic Books.

Bowlby, J. (1988). *A secure base: Parent-child attachment and healthy human development.* New York: Basic Books.

Brennan, K. A., Clark, C. A., & Shaver, P. R. (1998). Self-report measurement of adult attachment: An integrative overview. In J. A. Simpson & W. S. Rholes (Eds.), *Attachment theory and close relationships* (pp. 46–76). New York: Guilford.

Brown, S. L., Nesse, R. M., House, J. S., & Utz, R. L. (2004). Religion and emotional compensation: Results from a prospective study of widowhood. *Personality and Social Psychology Bulletin, 30,* 1165–1174.

Byrd, K. R., & Boe, A. D. (2000). The correspondence between attachment dimensions and prayer in college students. *The International Journal for the Psychology of Religion, 11,* 9–24.

Carlson, E. A. (1998). A prospective longitudinal study of attachment disorganization/disorientation. *Child Development, 69,* 1107–1128.

Cassidy, J. (1994). Emotion regulation. Influences of attachment relationships. In N. A. Fox (Ed.), *The development of emotion regulation: Biological and behavioral consideration* (pp. 228–249). New York: Cambridge University Press. *Monographs of the Society for Research in Child Development, 59*(2–3).

Cook, C. M., & Persinger, M. A. (2001). Geophysical variables and behavior: XCII. Experimental elicitation of the experience of a sentient being by right hemispheric, weak magnetic fields: Interaction with temporal lobe sensitivity. *Perceptual and Motor Skills, 92,* 447–448.

Cosmides, L., & Tooby, J. (1992). Cognitive adaptations for social exchange. In J. Barkow, L. Cosmides, & J. Tooby (Eds.), *The adapted mind* (pp. 163–228). New York: Oxford University Press.

De Wolff, M S., & van Ijzendoorn, M. H. (1997). Sensitivity and attachment: A meta-analysis on parental antecedents of infant attachment. *Child Development, 68,* 571–591.

Dickie, J. R., Charland, K., & Poll, E. (2005). *Attachment and children's concepts of God.* Unpublished manuscript, Department of Psychology, Hope College, MI.

Elicker, J., Englund, M., & Sroufe, L. A. (1992). Predicting peer competence and peer relationships from early parent-child interactions. In R. D. Parke & G. W. Ladd (Eds.) *Family-peer relationships: Modes of linkage* (pp. 77–106). Hillsdale, NJ: Lawrence Erlbaum.

Erikson, E. H. (1963). *Childhood and society* (2nd ed.). New York: Norton.

Eshleman, A. K., Dickie, J. R., Merasco, D. M., Shepard, A., & Johnson, M. (1999). Mother God, father God: Children's perceptions of God's distance. *The International Journal for the Psychology of Religion, 9,* 139–146.

Farias, M., Claridge, G., & Lalljee, M. (2005). Personality and cognitive predictors of New Age practices and beliefs. *Personality and Individual Differences, 39,* 979–989.

Farias, M, & Granqvist, P. (in press). The psychology of the new age. In D. Kemp (Ed.), *Handbook of the new age.* London: Brills.

Fleming, A. S., Kraemer, G. W., Gonzalez, A., Lovic, V., Rees, S. & Melo, A. (2002). Mothering begets mothering: The transmission of behavior and its neurobiology across generations. *Pharmacology, Biochemistry and Behavior, 73,* 61–75.

Fowler, J. W. (1981). *Stages of faith: The psychology of human development and the quest for meaning.* San Francisco: Harper & Row.

Fraley, R. C. (2002). Attachment stability from infancy to adulthood: Meta-analysis and dynamic modeling of developmental mechanisms. *Personality and Social Psychology Review, 6,* 123–151.

Fraley, R. C., & Waller, N. G. (1998). Adult attachment patterns: A test of the typological model. In J. A. Simpson & W. S. Rholes (Eds.), *Attachment theory and close relationships* (pp. 77–114). New York: Guilford.

Freud, S. (1940). *An outline of psychoanalysis.* New York: Norton.

Friedlmeier, W., & Granqvist, P. (2006). Attachment transfer among German and Swedish adolescents: A prospective longitudinal study. *Personal Relationships, 13*(3).

Gallup, G. H., Jr., & Jones, S. (1989). *One hundred questions and answers: Religion in America.* Princeton, NJ: Princeton Religion Research Center.

George, L. K., Ellison, C. G., & Larson, D. B. (2002). Explaining the relationships between religious involvement and health. *Psychological Inquiry, 13,* 190–200.

Gewirtz, V. (2004). *The relation to God from an attachment theory perspective: Internal models of God and their accessibility in states of distress.* Unpublished Ph.D. dissertation, Bar-Ilan University, Ramat Gan, Israel.

Gorsuch, R. L. (1968). The conceptualization of God as seen in adjective ratings. *Journal for the Scientific Study of Religion, 7,* 56–64.

Granqvist, P. (1998). Religiousness and perceived childhood attachment: On the question of compensation or correspondence. *Journal for the Scientific Study of Religion, 37,* 350–367.

Granqvist, P. (2002). Attachment and religiosity in adolescence: Cross-sectional and longitudinal evaluations. *Personality and Social Psychology Bulletin, 28,* 260–270.

Granqvist, P. (2003). Attachment theory and religious conversions: A review and a resolution of the classic and contemporary paradigm chasm. *Review of Religious Research, 45,* 172–187.

Granqvist, P. (2005). Building a bridge between attachment and religious coping: Tests of moderators and mediators. *Mental Health, Religion, and Culture, 8,* 35–47.

Granqvist, P. (2006). On the relation between secular and divine relationships: An emerging attachment perspective and a critique of the depth approaches. *The International Journal for the Psychology of Religion, 16,* 1–18.

Granqvist, P. (in press). The study of attachment in the psychology of religion. In D. Wulff (Ed.), *Handbook for the psychology of religion.* New York: Oxford University Press.

Granqvist, P., & Dickie, J. R. (2006). Attachment theory and spiritual development in childhood and adolescence. In P. L. Benson, E. C. Roehlkepartain, P. E. King, & L. Wagener (Eds.), *The handbook of spiritual development in childhood and adolescence* (pp. 197–210). Thousand Oaks, CA: Sage Publications.

Granqvist, P., Fredrikson, M., Unge, P., Hagenfeldt, A, Valind, S, Larhammar, D., et al. (2005). Sensed presence and mystical experiences are predicted by suggestibility, not by the application of weak complex transcranial magnetic fields. *Neuroscience Letters, 379,* 1–6.

Granqvist, P., & Hagekull, B. (1999). Religiousness and perceived childhood attachment: Profiling socialized correspondence and emotional compensation. *Journal for the Scientific Study of Religion, 38,* 254–273.

Granqvist, P., & Hagekull, B. (2000). Religiosity, adult attachment, and why "singles" are more religious. *The International Journal for the Psychology of Religion, 10,* 111–123.

Granqvist, P., & Hagekull, B. (2001). Seeking security in the new age: On attachment and emotional compensation. *Journal for the Scientific Study of Religion, 40,* 529–547.

Granqvist, P., & Hagekull, B. (2003). Longitudinal predictions of religious change in adolescence: Contributions from the interaction of attachment and relationship status. *Journal of Social and Personal Relationships, 20,* 793–817.

Granqvist, P., Ivarsson, T., Broberg, A.G., & Hagekull, B. (2006). Examining relations between attachment, religiosity, and New Age spirituality using the Adult Attachment Interview. *Developmental Psychology.*

Granqvist, P., & Kirkpatrick, L.A. (2004). Religious conversion and perceived childhood attachment: A meta-analysis. *The International Journal for the Psychology of Religion, 14,* 223–250.

Granqvist, P., & Larsson, M. (in press). Contribution of religiousness in the prediction and interpretation of mystical experiences—activation of religious schemas. *Journal of Psychology.*

Granqvist, P., Ljungdahl, C., & Dickie, J.R. (2005). God is nowhere, God is now here: Attachment activation, security of attachment, and perceived closeness to God among 5–7 year-old children from religious and non-religious homes. *Attachment and Human Development.*

Granqvist, P., & Main, M. (2003). *The Attachment to God Interview.* Unpublished manuscript, Department of Psychology, Uppsala University, Sweden.

Grice, H. P. (1989). *Studies in the way of words.* Cambridge, MA: Harvard University Press.

Hamilton, W. F., III. (2002). Theogenesis: The intelligent universe. In R. Joseph (Ed.), *Neurotheology* (pp. 267–284). San Jose: California University Press.

Hazan, C., & Shaver, P. R. (1987). Romantic love conceptualized as an attachment process. *Journal of Personality and Social Psychology, 52,* 511–524.

Hazan, C., & Zeifman, D. (1999). Pair bonds as attachments: Evaluating the evidence. In J. Cassidy & P. R. Shaver (Eds.), *Handbook of attachment: Theory, research, and clinical applications* (pp. 336–355). New York: Guilford.

Heelas, P. (1996). *The New Age movement: The celebration of the self and the sacralization of modernity.* Oxford, UK: Blackwell.

Heller, D. (1986). *The children's God.* Chicago: University of Chicago Press.

Hesse, E. (1999). The Adult Attachment Interview: Historical and current perspectives. In J. Cassidy & P.R. Shaver, *Handbook of attachment: Theory, research, and clinical applications* (pp. 395–433). New York: Guilford.

Hesse, E., & Main, M. (2000). Disorganized infant, child, and adult attachment: Collapse in behavioral and attentional strategy. *Journal of the American Psychoanalytic Association, 48,* 1097–1127.

Hesse, E., & van Ijzendoorn, M. H. (1999). Propensities towards absorption are related to lapses in the monitoring of reasoning or discourse during the Adult Attachment Interview: A preliminary investigation. *Attachment and Human Development, 1,* 67–91.

Hinde, R. A. (1970). *Animal behavior: A synthesis of ethology and comparative psychology* (2nd ed.). New York: McGraw-Hill.

Hinde, R. A. (1999). *Why gods persist: A scientific approach to religion.* London: Routledge.

Hood, R. W., Jr. (1975). The construction and preliminary validation of a measure of reported mystical experience. *Journal for the Scientific Study of Religion, 21,* 29–41.

Houtman, D., & Mascini, P. (2002). Why do churches become empty, while New Age grows? Secularization and religious change in the Netherlands. *Journal for the Scientific Study of Religion, 41,* 455–473.

Irwin, H. J. (1993). Belief in the paranormal: A review of the empirical literature. *Journal of the American Society for Psychical Research, 87,* 1–39.

James, W. (1902). *Varieties of religious experience.* New York: Longmans, Green.

Joseph, R. (2002). The death of Darwinism. In R. Joseph (Ed.), *Neurotheology* (pp. 69–110). San Jose: California University Press.

Kaplan, N. (1987). *Individual differences in 6-years-olds' thoughts about separation: Predicted from attachment to mother at age 1.* Unpublished doctoral dissertation, Department of Psychology, University of California, Berkeley.

Kirkpatrick, L. A. (1992). An attachment-theory approach to the psychology of religion. *The International Journal for the Psychology of Religion, 2,* 3–28.

Kirkpatrick, L. A. (1997). A longitudinal study of changes in religious belief and behavior as a function of individual differences in adult attachment style. *Journal for the Scientific Study of Religion, 36,* 207–217.

Kirkpatrick, L. A. (1998a). Evolution, pair-bonding, and reproductive strategies: A reconceptualization of adult attachment. In J. A. Simpson & W. S. Rholes (Eds.), *Attachment theory and close relationships* (pp. 353–393). New York: Guilford.

Kirkpatrick, L. A. (1998b). God as a substitute attachment figure: A longitudinal study of adult attachment style and religious change in college students. *Personality and Social Psychology Bulletin, 24,* 961–973.

Kirkpatrick, L. A. (1999). Attachment and religious representations and behavior. In J. Cassidy & P. R. Shaver (Eds.), *Handbook of attachment theory and research* (pp.803–822). New York: Guilford.

Kirkpatrick, L. A. (2005). *Attachment, evolution, and the psychology of religion.* New York: Guilford.

Kirkpatrick, L. A., & Shaver, P. R. (1990). Attachment theory and religion: Childhood attachments, religious beliefs and conversions. *Journal for the Scientific Study of Religion, 29,* 315–334.

Kirkpatrick, L. A., & Shaver, P. R. (1992). An attachment-theoretical approach to romantic love and religious belief. *Personality and Social Psychology Bulletin, 18,* 266–275.

Koenig, H. G., George, L. K., & Peterson, B. L. (1998). Religiosity and remission of depression in medically ill older patients. *American Journal of Psychiatry, 155,* 536–542.

Kuhn, T. (1962). *The structure of scientific revolutions.* Chicago: University of Chicago Press.

Lambert, W. W., Triandis, L. M., & Wolf, M. (1959). Some correlates of beliefs in the malevolence and benevolence of supernatural beings: A cross-societal study. *Journal of Abnormal and Social Psychology, 58,* 162–169.

Larsson, M., Larhammar, D., Fredrikson, M., & Granqvist, P. (2005). Reply to M. A. Persinger and S. A. Koren's response to Granqvist et al. "Sensed presence and mystical experiences are predicted by suggestibility, not by the application of transcranial weak magnetic fields." *Neuroscience Letters, 380,* 348–350.

Londerville, S., & Main, M. (1981). Security of attachment, compliance, and maternal training in the second year of life. *Developmental Psychology, 17,* 289–299.

Main, M. (1991). Metacognitive knowledge, metacognitive monitoring, and singular (coherent) vs. multiple (incoherent) models of attachment: Findings and directions for future research. In C. M. Parkes & J. Stevenson-Hinde (Eds.), *Attachment across the life cycle* (pp. 127–159). London: Tavistock/Routledge.

Main, M., Goldwyn, R., & Hesse, E. (2003). *Adult attachment scoring and classification systems.* Unpublished manuscript, University of California, Berkeley, Department of Psychology.

Main, M., Kaplan, N., & Cassidy, J. (1985). Security in infancy, childhood and adulthood: A move to the level of representation. In I. Bretherton & E. Waters (Eds.), *Growing points of attachment theory and research* (pp. 66–104). Chicago: University of Chicago Press.

Main, M., & Morgan, H. (1996). Disorganization and disorientation in infant Strange Situation behavior: Phenotypic resemblance to dissociative states. In L. Michelson & W. Ray (Eds.), *Handbook of dissociation: Theoretical, empirical, and clinical perspectives* (pp. 107–138). New York: Plenum.

Main, M., & Solomon, J. (1990). Procedures for identifying infants as disorganized/disoriented during the Ainsworth Strange Situation. In M. T. Greenberg, D. Cicchetti, & E. M. Cummings (Eds.), *Attachment in preschool years: Theory, research, and intervention* (pp. 121–160). Chicago: University of Chicago.

Makarec, K., & Persinger, M. A. (1990). Electroencephalographic validation of a temporal lobe signs inventory. *Journal of Research in Personality, 24,* 323–337.

Newberg, A., d'Aquili, E., & Rause, V. (2002). *Why God won't go away. Brain science and the biology of belief.* New York: Ballantine.

Newberg, A. B., & Iversen, J. (2003). The neural basis of the complex mental task of meditation: Neurotransmitters and neurochemical considerations. *Medical Hypotheses, 61,* 282–291.

Paloutzian, R. F., Fikes, T. G., & Hutsebaut, D. (2002). A social cognition interpretation of neurotheological events. In R. Joseph (Ed.), *Neurotheology* (pp. 189–194). San Jose: California University Press.

Pargament, K. (1997). *The psychology of religion and coping.* New York: Guilford Press.

Pearson, J. L., Cohn, D. A., Cowan, P. A., & Cowan, C. P. (1994). Earned- and continuous security in adult attachment: Relation to depressive symptomatology and parenting style. *Development and Psychopathology, 6,* 359–373.

Persinger, M. A. (1997). Keynote Address, International Symposium, Magnetic Fields: Recent Advances in Diagnosis and Therapy. Lawson Research Institute Conference, London, Ontario, Canada.

Persinger, M. A. (2002). Experimental simulation of the God experience: Implications for religious beliefs and the future of the human species. In R. Joseph (Ed.), *Neurotheology* (pp. 267–284). San Jose: California University Press.

Persinger, M. A., & Koren, S.A. (2005). A response to Granqvist et al. "Sensed presence and mystical experiences are predicted by suggestibility, not by the application of transcranial weak magnetic fields." *Neuroscience Letters, 379,* 346–347.

Persinger, M. A., Tiller, S. G., & Koren, S. A. (2000). Experimental simulation of a haunt experience and elicitation of paroxysmal electroencephalographic activity by transcerebral complex magnetic fields: Induction of a synthetic "ghost"? *Perceptual and Motor Skills, 90,* 659–674.

Popper, K. (1959). *The logic of scientific discovery.* London: Routledge & Kegan Paul.

Quine, V. W. (1992). *Pursuit of truth.* Cambridge, MA: Harvard University Press.

Ramachandran, V. S., & Blakeslee, S. (1999). *Phantoms in the brain.* New York: William Morrow.

Richters, J. E., & Waters, E. (1991). Attachment and socialization: The positive side of social influence. In M. Lewis & S. Feinman (Eds.), *Social influences and socialization in infancy: Genesis of behavior series* (Vol. 6, pp. 185–213). New York: Plenum.

Rizzuto, A. M. (1979). *The birth of the living God: A psychoanalytical study.* Chicago: Chicago University Press.

Rohner, R. P. (1986). *The warmth dimension: Foundations of parental acceptance-rejection theory.* Thousand Oaks, CA: Sage.

Saroglou, V., Kempeneers, A., & Seynhaeve, I. (2003). Need for closure and adult attachment dimensions as predictors of religion and reading interests. In P. Roelofsma, J. Corveleyn, & J. van Saane (Eds.), *One hundred years of psychology and religion* (pp. 139–154). Amsterdam: VU University Press.

Saver, J. L., & Rabin, J. (1997). The neural substrates of religious experience. *The Journal of Neuropsychiatry and Clinical Neurosciences, 9,* 498–510.

Schiller, C. H. (Ed.) (1957). *Instinctive behavior: The development of a modern concept.* New York: International Universities Press.

Shaver, P. R., & Mikulincer, M. (2002). Attachment-related psychodynamics. *Attachment and Human Development, 4,* 133–161.

Spangler, G., & Grossmann, K. E. (1993). Biobehavioral organization in securely and insecurely attached infants. *Child Development, 64,* 1439–1450.

Spilka, B., Hood, Jr., R. W., Hunsberger, B., & Gorsuch, R. (2003). *The psychology of religion: An empirical approach* (3rd ed.). New York: Guilford.

Sroufe, L. A., & Waters, E. (1977a). Attachment as an organizational construct. *Child Development, 48,* 1184–1199.

Sroufe, L. A., & Waters, E. (1977b). Heart rate as a convergent measure in clinical and developmental research. *Merrill-Palmer Quarterly, 23,* 3–27.

Stark, R., Hamberg, E. M., & Miller, A. (2005). Exploring spirituality and unchurched religions in America, Sweden, and Japan. *Journal of Contemporary Religion, 20,* 3–23.

Suomi, S. J. (1999). Attachment in rhesus monkeys. In J. Cassidy & P. R. Shaver (Eds.), *Handbook of attachment: Theory, research, and clinical applications* (pp. 181–197). New York: Guilford Press.

Tamayo, A., & Desjardins, L. (1976). Belief systems and conceptual images of parents and God. *Journal of Psychology, 92*, 131–140.

Tamminen, K. (1994). Religious experiences in childhood and adolescence: A viewpoint of religious development between the ages of 7 and 20. *The International Journal for the Psychology of Religion, 4*, 61–85.

Tellegen, A., & Atkinson, G. (1974). Openness to absorbing and self-altering experiences ("absorption"), a trait related to hypnotic susceptibility. *Journal of Abnormal Psychology, 83*(3), 268–277.

TenElshof, J. K., & Furrow, J. L. (2000). The role of secure attachment in predicting spiritual maturity of students at a conservative seminary. *Journal of Psychology and Theology, 28*, 99–108.

Thompson, R. A. (1994). Emotion regulation: A theme in search of definition. In N. A. Fox (Ed.), *The development of emotion regulation: Biological and behavioral consideration* (pp. 25–52). Cambridge, New York: Cambridge University Press. *Monographs of the Society for Research in Child Development, 59*(2–3).

Tolman, E. (1948). Cognitive maps in rats and men. *Psychological Review, 55*, 189–208.

Ullman, C. (1982). Cognitive and emotional antecedents of religious conversion. *Journal of Personality and Social Psychology, 43*, 183–192.

van Ijzendoorn, M. H. (1995). Adult attachment representations, parental responsiveness, and infant attachment: A meta-analysis on the predictive validity of the Adult Attachment Interview. *Psychological Bulletin, 117*, 387–403.

van Ijzendoorn, M. H., Schuengel, C., & Bakermans-Kranenburg, M. J. (1999). Disorganized attachment in early childhood: Meta-analysis of precursors, concomitants, and sequelae. *Development and Psychopathology, 11*, 225–249.

Weaver, A., & de Waal, F.B.M. (2002). An index of relationship quality based on attachment theory. *Journal of Comparative Psychology, 116*, 93–106.

Weinfield, N. S., Sroufe, L. A., Egeland, B., & Carlson, E. A. (1999). The nature of individual differences in infant-caregiver attachment. In J. Cassidy & P.R. Shaver (Eds.), *Handbook of attachment: Theory, research, and clinical applications* (pp. 68–88). New York: Guilford.

Wheeler, S. C., & Petty, R. E. (2001). The effects of stereotype activation on behavior: A review of possible mechanisms. *Psychological Bulletin, 127*, 797–826.

Wittgenstein, L. (1953). *Philosophical investigations.* Oxford: Basil Blackwell.

CHAPTER 7

RELIGIOUS CONVERSION, SPIRITUAL TRANSFORMATION, AND THE NEUROCOGNITION OF MEANING MAKING

Raymond F. Paloutzian, Erica L. Swenson, and Patrick McNamara

As scientists discover laws of the universe that are congruent with mind, artists discover visual images of the world that are harmonious with mind. Both explore the truth and beauty of the mind; at an abstract cognitive level, they are identical. (Robert L. Solso, 2003)

We have often wondered why art history and religious history are almost completely dependent upon each other. They overlay one another so much that it is practically impossible to learn one without being immersed in the other. Why did human beings express their creative abilities and their religious needs, strivings, and commitments in such an interlocking way? This is no mere coincidence. Solso (2003) argued that the mental abilities needed for the evolution of art are inherent in the capabilities that came with the development of the human brain. In particular, humans' creation of visual art corresponds to the development of visual perception involving neural structures and processes that enabled organisms to see both near and distant or peripheral objects. Extending this idea, the human capacity for religion may be a product of the same factors that enabled humans to develop art. In other words, the neural and psychological processes that made it possible for people to create artistic expression may be the same ones that made it possible for people to search for and find religion. At an individual level, artistic insight and religious conversion may be neurologically similar and may reflect the same psychological process of meaning-making.

Common psychological functions seem to be expressed through religion and art, embodied in perfect unity in religious art. Let us explore some neurological and psychological processes fundamentally routed in the human brain that may suggest that when humans became able to perceive, abstract, and conceptualize sufficiently enough for artistic insight, they were able to experience the revelation necessary for religious conversion. We are not trying to give a definitive explanation of how religious conversion or spiritual transformation happens in the brain—the research is too premature for that. At this point, we are using neurological research to suggest how phenomena might occur and to explore how that might correspond with the meaning system model. Let us begin by looking at religious conversion and spiritual transformation at a psychological level.

RELIGIOUS CONVERSION AND SPIRITUAL TRANSFORMATION

Conversions remain as interesting, controversial, and potentially powerful in human affairs today as they were when Paul heard a voice and was blinded on the road to Damascus, Augustine found peace in the garden in Milan, and when the early followers of Muhammad submitted to follow the Five Pillars of Islam. Since then, millions of conversions have altered the lives of ordinary people worldwide. In addition to adopting one of the world's three great missionary religions (Christianity, Buddhism, Islam), people adopt New Religions Movements (NRMs) and a variety of spiritualities not representative of traditional religious institutions (Paloutzian, Richardson, & Rambo, 1999). Thus, religious conversion and spiritual transformation can be regarded as identifiable, prominent ways that people change in the vast majority of human cultures. Given its pervasiveness and that a basic goal of psychology is to gain knowledge of the processes by which people change, understanding religious conversion is part of the heart and soul of our effort to synthesize neurological and psychological knowledge (Paloutzian, 2005).

To grapple with the ideas of religious conversion and spiritual transformation, it is necessary to distinguish between the concepts of religion and spirituality. This is because (a) the technicalities of what each concept means differ in the research literature (Zinnbauer & Pargament, 2005), and (b) they have overlapping connotations when translated into a meaning system model of change (Paloutzian, 2005). Whether there are common neurological processes that mediate religious conversion and spiritual transformation is a matter for future discussion. Let us examine the first two of these issues.

Religion, Spirituality, and Change

Zinnbauer and Pargament (2005) summarize the research on the distinction between religion and spirituality and clarify how the two concepts do and do not correspond. Briefly, people tend to associate both religion and spirituality with frequent prayer and church attendance and intrinsic religious orientation (Allport & Ross, 1967; see Hill & Hood, 1999, for review). Both terms convey the idea of connecting with that which is perceived to be sacred (Hill et al., 2000). Spirituality is more associated with mystical experience and concern about personal growth and existential issues. In contrast, religion tends to connote participation in institutionalized religious practices and belief in church or denominational teachings (Zinnbauer et al., 1997). These distinctions can be seen by examining the wording on the instruments to measure each construct (see Hill & Hood, 1999, for examples). Measures of religiousness ask about things such as belief in certain teachings, participating in religious services, and supporting institutional religious programs. Measures of spirituality ask about things such as connecting with whatever is of the highest meaning to oneself, a sense of striving for oneness, and transcending one's own limitedness.

The (at minimum) four-fold ways that people claim or do not claim to be *religious* and/or *spiritual* are explained elsewhere (Paloutzian & Park, 2005; Paloutzian, 2006); suffice it to say that their meanings overlap but are not synonymous. Moreover, there is disagreement about which is the larger category. Religion is sometimes seen as one type of spirituality among many, and spirituality is sometimes seen as a subset of a larger category of phenomena called "religion" (Zinnbauer & Pargament, 2005). Although this distinction is interesting and important to keep in mind, it seems less crucial when we superimpose the model of meaning systems (Park, 2005; Park & Folkman, 1997; Silberman, 2005) on the literature on religion and spirituality, specifically when applied to religious conversion and spiritual transformation (Paloutzian, 2005). This is because for the purpose of understanding the psychological processes that mediate a change in a person's fundamental commitments, orientations, and beliefs, the particular label we use for it matters less than knowledge of the change process itself. Because of this, at an abstract cognitive and functional level, there may be little difference between religious conversion and spiritual transformation (Paloutzian & Park, 2005; Paloutzian, 2005). The language of the meaning system model ought to be powerful enough to incorporate research on these and closely related concepts.

From Religious Conversion to Meaning System Change

Although research on religious conversion is one of the earliest topics studied by scientific psychology (James, 1902; Starbuck, 1899), and although it has been empirically examined from a psychodynamic (Ullman, 1982, 1989), social-cognitive (Paloutzian, 1981), sociological (Richardson, 1985, 1995), and attachment theory (Granqvist & Kirkpatrick, 2004; Kirkpatrick, 2005a;

Oksanen, 1994) framework, psychologists of religion have longed for an idea capable of integrating the disparate lines of research. We think that the model of religion as a meaning system (Park, 2005; Park & Folkman, 1997; Silberman, 2005) is capable of doing this. This is because whatever else religion is about and regardless of theoretical ideas guiding research on it, religion is fundamentally about meaning. Humans apparently are built with a tendency to represent one thing with another; to assess information relative to a larger, more global idea; to use that idea to shape the interpretation of incoming information to guide behavior and establish a sense of consistency in their mental representation of life and their position in it. The implication is that religious conversion is about change in a person's spiritual meaning system (Paloutzian, 2005).

Although a meaning system involves emotions, actions, beliefs, expectations, and contingencies, it can be best conceptualized as a cognitive structure whose elements include an idea of global meaning, plus processes of appraisal and evaluation of new information in comparison to it (Park, 2005; Park & Folkman, 1997; Silberman, 2005). When pushed beyond some threshold, these processes would result in doubts—the reflection of a discrepancy between the *ought* and the *is* in a person's life (Hill, 2002; Paloutzian, 2005). A great deal of research has focused on what prompts religious conversion, such as family stressors or a need for meaning. These are well documented elsewhere (Beit-Hallahmi & Argyle, 1997; Paloutzian, Richardson, & Rambo, 1999; Rambo, 1993; Spilka, Hood, Hunsberger, & Gorsuch, 2003), so we will not go into these studies. As seen with a meaning system model, the greater the discrepancies, the more likely it is that a transformation of one or more elements of the meaning system will occur (Paloutzian, 2005).

Toward a Neurology of Spiritual Transformation

Given the evidence that the human brain developed in a way that gave it ample ability to symbolize and perform other relationship operations that are part of meaning systems (Deacon, 1998) and given evidence that religious activity seems to involve identifiable brain areas (Azari, Vol. 3, chap. 3; Azari, in press; Azari, Missimer, & Seitz, 2005; Azari et al., 2001a, 2001b), the question rises about the possible correspondences between psychological knowledge of religious conversion as seen through a meaning system model and possible neurological correlates or mediators of these processes. It would seem that there are two general ways that this issue can be examined. First, we can search for whatever knowledge can be gained through an examination of the dramatic special cases of conversion and assume that the inferences about brain processes that might have been involved based on the historical records are accurate. Second, we can apply the knowledge from current research in brain science to the understanding of the psychological processes involved in conversion and extrapolate it to the neurological level. It will be helpful to examine the literature of each type. Many of the historical exemplars of conversion showed behaviors that suggest distinct neurological involvement.

THE NEUROLOGY OF EXEMPLARS OF CONVERSION

It is now almost proverbial to link temporal lobe epilepsy with religious experience and with conversion experiences in particular. Saver and Rabin (1997) trace the first recorded scientific observation of heightened religiosity in epileptics to Esquirol in 1838. William James (1902) may have been the first scientific psychologist to suggest that St. Paul's dramatic conversion experience on the road to Damascus may have been a "psychological nerve storm" like that of epilepsy. Like some epileptics, St. Paul experienced what neurologists would call auditory "command hallucinations" (a voice that gave him commands to follow), visual hallucinations, and then an apparently hysterical form of blindness, as well as an intense emotional upheaval (Saver & Rabin, 1997). We know that the Russian novelist Dostoyevsky, who focused on religious themes in his later novels, had some form of epilepsy with seizures he often described as ecstatic religious experiences. A perusal of the lives and experiences of many of the great religious leaders and saints down through the ages will reveal many signs of temporal lobe epilepsy such as intense emotionality, visions, transient ictal phenomena like smell and taste illusions, absence seizures or spells resembling a lapse of attention or a trance-like state, out of body experiences, auditory and visual hallucinations, changes in sexual desire and so forth. Saver and Rabin (1997) provide a table of at least 15 religious founders and mystics who may have had some form of epilepsy.

When temporal lobe epilepsy is associated with psychotic episodes, it certainly also increases the chances that the patient will experience unusually intense religious experiences and conversion experiences (Beard, 1963; Dewhurst & Beard, 1970; Geschwind, 1983). Dewhurst and Beard (1970) provide instructive examples of six cases of sudden religious conversions in six temporal lobe epileptics. In all cases the conversion occurred during the hours or days following increased seizure activity. Unlike the Dewhurst and Beard cases where the religious experienced occurred after the onset of seizure activity, Waxman and Geschwind (1975) claimed that heightened religiosity can also occur during the inter-ictal period when no seizure activity was obvious. They claimed that this "inter-ictal behavior syndrome" consisted of hyper-religiosity, intense emotionality, circumstantiality, aggressive irritability and hypergraphia. Bear and Fedio (1977) later reported higher religiosity scores in patients with temporal lobe epilepsy relative to other patient groups with chronic neurologic disorder, and Bear (1979) attempted to provide a neuroanatomical explanation for the association by invoking a possible hyperconnectivity between the limbic and temporal lobes. But other authors failed to confirm a relationship between temporal lobe epilepsy and religiosity (Roberts & Guberman, 1989; Tucker, Novelly, & Walker, 1987).

The consistent association of religious phenomena with temporal lobe epilepsy has led some authors to claim that the temporal lobes constitute the neural substrate of religious conversion experiences (e.g. Persinger, 2002; Ramachandran & Blakeslee, 1999). This conclusion is open to question, however. First, religious saints, mystics, and founders of new religious or spiritual movements often do not follow a pattern of mental impairment that is typically associated with temporal lobe epilepsy. Instead, they often lead lives of extraordinary accomplishment. Second, electrical spikes in the temporal lobes often have effects on other parts of the brain that could also contribute to the clinical symptomology of temporal lobe epilepsy (Devinsky, 2004; Leung & Wu, 2006). Third, many temporal lobe epilepsy patients with religious symptoms also have electrical foci in other parts of the brain in addition to the temporal lobes. For example, at least half of Dewhurst and Beard's (1970) original patients also evidenced loci in the frontal lobes. Fourth, overactivity of the temporal lobes is known to elicit compensatory responses (e.g., increased activity of the frontal lobes) elsewhere in the brain, in particular in the orbitofrontal cortex. Thus, one needs to be careful when assigning the neural substrate for religious conversion to a single part of the brain—given the connectivity patterns between the frontal lobes and the temporal lobes.

The frontal lobes are in mutual inhibitory balance with posterior cortical sites including the temporal lobes and structures deep to the temporal lobes including the hippocampus, amygdala, and the limbic system (Goldberg, 1987; Lhermitte, 1986). If electrical spikes are occurring in the temporal lobes, it seems likely that a compensatory inhibitory response would be elicited in the frontal lobes and thus the neurologic network that is producing enhanced religiosity might be frontal-temporal, not just temporal.

Certainly, the neuroanatomy supports the latter supposition. The portion of the frontal lobes that directly modulate temporal and limbic cortex is the orbitofrontal cortex (OFC). The hallmark of OFC damage is social and emotional disinhibition, which demonstrates that one function of the OFC is to inhibit impulses arising from limbic and temporal lobes (Chow & Cummings, 1999; Schnider & Gutbrod, 1999). The OFC is densely interconnected with structures of the limbic system and the temporal lobes. The superior temporal lobes sends afferents to the OFC, and the medial OFC both receives and sends projections to the temporal limbic and limbic regions (Chow & Cummings, 1999; Nauta, 1979; Van Hoesen, Pandya, & Butters, 1975; Zald & Kim, 1996). The OFC sends direct inhibitory fibers onto the amygdala, including a dense set of fibers from the caudal OFC onto the central nucleus of the amygdala. Because the amygdala is the major source of efferents to the brainstem and hypothalamus, the medial OFC indirectly controls a range of endocrine and autonomic behavioral responses. A clear example of OFC inhibitory control of a limbic system behavior is that of reactive aggression. A specialized OFC-amygdala circuit mediates dis-inhibition of aggressive responses (Blair, 2004). This latter circuit is controlled by efferents from the medial OFC and runs from the medial portion of the amygdala through the stria terminalis and the medial hypothalamus to the peri-aqueductal gray. In short, the anatomy supports the contention that one needs to speak of densely interconnected and functional neural networks when examining behaviors linked to the limbic temporal lobes and therefore also when talking about conversion and spiritual transformation.

Given the above functional neuroanatomy and the clinical evidence from temporal lobe epilepsy, one could just as easily argue that religious conversion and spiritual transformation may be mediated by OFC because OFC is the site that controls limbic and related responses. Instead, it seems more reasonable to say that the complex psychological process called "religious conversion" *may* be related to a series of neural networks housed in limbic and OFC sites because they normally mediate emotional states (limbic), language comprehension (medial temporal lobe), hippocampus (memory), and personality (OFC). Thus, the confluence of all of these higher order brain/ mind functions orchestrate a transformation process that is best explained at the level of social psychology until we have better data on neurological correlates of conversion and spiritual transformation—when our knowledge at these different levels of analysis can be integrated.

The evidence summarized above suggests that the processes that mediate religious conversion and spiritual transformation cannot be localized in a particular brain area. The temporal lobe epilepsy model is too simple to accommodate the full range of conversion and transformation phenomena and may not be an area that is uniquely involved in conversion. It may profit our understanding, therefore, to invoke other levels of analysis and realize that religious conversion and spiritual transformation involve meaning system processes broadly construed, in addition to a broad range of neural processes. We need to consider how social, psychological, and neurological factors work in combination to create sufficient force within someone's global meaning system so that it would change from a nonconverted brain state at time T to a transformed brain state at time T+1. In light of this, it may be that the knowledge gained from the exemplars of dramatic conversion is suggestive but nevertheless insufficient to account for the neurological involvements in the more ordinary cases of conversion.

The ideal research design would of course include empirical studies of brain activity before and after conversion in the same people. Rarely does the real world allow scientists to collect (ideally) definitive data of this sort. But perhaps we can move toward more accurate knowledge of conversion and transformative processes broadly construed by applying knowledge from neuroimaging and other brain research to the understanding of conversion processes. Paloutzian and Swenson (in press) and Park and McNamara (Vol. 3. chap. 3) recently examined possible areas of correspondence between neurological findings and an analysis of meaning systems to take one step toward a multilevel interdisciplinary (Emmons & Paloutzian, 2003) understanding of spiritual experiences. They suggest that it may be fruitful to synthesize these two levels of knowledge. By extrapolation, it may be fruitful to attempt an elementary synthesis of knowledge gained from multiple levels of analysis (including neurological, hormonal, and psychological) around the question of how religious conversions and spiritual transformations occur in the broad band of ordinary cases.

POSSIBLE NEUROLOGICAL CORRELATES OF SPIRITUAL TRANSFORMATION

Although still speculative at this point, we hope to evaluate the processes involved in spiritual transformation by looking at the results of brain imaging studies. Several techniques are used to monitor brain activity during various kinds of mental behavior. Functional magnetic resonance imaging (fMRI), positron emission tomography (PET), and electroencephalography (EEG) can measure activity in various neurotransmitter systems (Raichle, 1998). Single photon emission computed tomography (SPECT) images help scientists identify which areas of the brain are active because the injected tracer is carried through the blood stream to the active brain cells, which appear darker on a SPECT image (Newberg, Alavi et al., 2001). As techniques become more advanced, it becomes easier to identify which brain regions and neurotransmitters are active during meditation and other spiritual practices (d'Aquili & Newberg, 1999; Newberg, d'Aquili, & Rause, 2001; Newberg & Newberg, 2005). Although these techniques have not yet been used in research on conversion per se, they have been used to study meditation, prayer, and religious rituals. Extrapolating from these studies, we hope to begin to understand the neurocognitive processes involved in spiritual transformation.

Paloutzian and Swenson (in press) describe possible correspondences between neurological activity and meaning system functions in the context of spiritual experiences. The present chapter extends that analysis by applying it to the understanding of the neurocognitive processes that may be involved in how conversion happens. Using what we know about the general changes that take place in the brain during different mental events may help us draw preliminary connections between neural activity during meditation and possible neuropsychological activity during spiritual transformations, that is, the processes that actually occur between times T and T + 1.

An Experiential/Affective Process

Although not universally true, many sudden conversions are associated with heightened feelings and states of arousal (Paloutzian, 1996). Prior to conversion, a person may pray and meditate. Prayer and meditation have been linked to the following positive physiological and psychological states (Newberg, Alavi et al., 2001; Newberg & Newberg, 2005): (a) The person may feel that his or her stress, worries, and anxiety have dissipated. This relaxed state is indicated by lower levels of the stress hormone cortisol in urine and plasma during meditation (Sudsuang, Chentanez, & Veluvan, 1991). (b) The person is likely to feel less pain and fear than under normal conditions, while breathing slower and having sensations of joy and euphoria (Newberg & Newberg, 2005). These positive feelings are associated with the release of beta-endorphins during meditation (Kiss, Kocsis, Csaki, Gorcs, & Halasz, 1997). Beta-endorphins are opioids produced in the hypothalamus and distributed to the brain's sub-cortical areas. (c) The sensations of happiness and euphoria may be further enhanced by the overall elevation in serotonin during meditation, as shown by the increased breakdown products of serotonin in urine after meditation (Walton, Pugh, Gelderloos, & Macrae, 1995). Higher levels of serotonin provide feelings of happiness and have a modulatory effect on dopamine, which also leads to feelings of euphoria (Newberg & Newberg, 2005). (d) The person may experience the sensation of progressively deeper relaxation. This is linked to the increased parasympathetic nervous system activity during meditation, which leads to lower heart and respiratory rate (Newberg & Newberg, 2005). (e) Sensitivity to pain and activity in the central nervous system may be reduced thanks to the neurohormone melatonin (Shaji & Kulkarni, 1998). Melatonin is produced in increased levels during meditation (Tooley, Armstrong, Norman, & Sali, 2000).

A meaning system analysis says that such experiences are important not merely because of their unusual phenomenology or because they happen to be pleasurable, but because they are interpreted and experienced within the person's meaning system. They are appraised and given new meaning (Park, 2005) and given the right circumstances can produce change in central elements of the person's meaning system sufficient to call it religious conversion or spiritual transformation (Paloutzian, 2005).

These positive effects may be enhanced when the potential convert is in a social context with religious adherents who are also praying and meditating (Paloutzian, Fikes, & Hutesbaut, 2002). It would make sense that experiencing a sense of euphoric happiness through prayer or meditation would make a person more likely to convert, especially when circumstances dictate a new religious or spiritual attribution for the experience (Spilka, Shaver, & Kirkpatrick, 1985; Spilka et al., 2003). We hypothesize that the positive physiological experiences that a person has during meditation will make sudden conversion more likely. It seems, therefore, that neurological evidence may be consistent with well-known principles from social psychology that indicate that a change in belief may be a *consequence* of a change in behavior. In fact, in a classic text on the relation between attitude, belief, and behavior change, it was observed that in the Old Testament (Hebrew Bible), "the rabbis are enjoined not to make their parishioners or converts believe in God *before* they are asked to pray, but to have them pray first so that belief will follow" (Zimbardo & Ebbesen, 1970, p. 13).

A Transformative Experience as Self-Authenticating

Further, there seems to be a self-authenticating aspect to conversion and spiritual transformation such that, although at one level converts do have rationales and can state reasons for their change, at another level they may embrace the change for the experience itself. The change can be its own validation, and its perceived truth does not depend upon independent verification. This would presumably be true for those experiences that were particularly potent or blissful. For example, those who are heavily involved in charismatic expressions of Christianity may be sustained by the very nature of the experience that occurs when they participate in the practice prescribed by their faith, that is, the mental and emotional sensations that the person experiences when speaking in tongues. Participants may regard the experience as proof of its own validity, such that one may claim an awareness of God even though it can be neither sensed nor assessed by another person. When asked for verification of the claim to have connected with God, a person will occasionally respond, "I know it was God because I experienced it." Given such an initial experience and interpretation of it, whatever may follow can be interpreted within a new meaning system that solidifies it in the mind of the person.

Observing what one's body is doing may also be part of this process. Participation in a spiritual or religious activity engages the body in a process that automatically invokes a blend of evaluating, questioning, and confronting a spiritual question even if the person's mind doesn't consciously think so. For example, the mere presence of one's body at a religious ritual in which one does not consciously believe (Spilka, 2005) acknowledges the ritual and religion in question and sets in motion a process of appraisal that could lead to an (unintended or unanticipated) change in the meaning system initially invoked to interpret it. In other words, there may be a discrepancy between what one's body is doing and what one's mind is thinking. According to a meaning system model, this discrepancy would have to be appraised and resolved, and one way to resolve it is to accept the beliefs and practices that one is participating in. Thus, experiencing a state of bliss or peace, as is common during a spiritual experience (Paloutzian & Swenson, in press; Newberg & Newberg, 2005), may involve behaving in a way that begins the process of spiritual transformation.

Ergotropic and Trophotropic Activity

Let us further speculate about brain activity during spiritual transformation by extrapolating from research on a spiritual activity such as meditation. Newberg, Alavi et al. (2001) found that when Buddhists meditate, the hypothalamic ergotropic centers (lateral part) and trophotropic centers (medial part) reach maximum intensity. If some conversion and transformative experiences are similar to meditation, then perhaps ergotropic and trophotropic activity may be at least moderately involved in the process of spiritual transformation.

Newberg and d'Aquili (2000) suggest that during a spiritual experience, one experiences simultaneous activation of the ergotropic and trophotropic systems. During powerful, unusual states of consciousness, which may include spiritual transformations, several changes and subsequent sensations may occur. Trophotropic activity increases, which is associated with feelings of quiescence. Feeling this sense of calmness may be perceived as the divine giving reassurance and peace. This could encourage the person to commit to religion or spirituality. In addition to feeling peace, the person undergoing a transformational experience is likely to have heightened concentration and arousal due to an increase in ergotropic activity. He or she is focused on the perceived meaning of what is occurring. In rare, powerful conversions, the person may experience more exaggerated effects of the trophotropic and ergotropic activity. These experiences would be marked by an energy release, orgasmic-like rush, and trance-like state (Newberg & d'Aquili, 2000), all of which could easily transform someone's meaning system due to the powerful self-authenticating nature of the experience combined with the absence of any need for external or public assessment of its truth value.

Activity in Frontal and Parietal Regions

Neurological images taken during religious experiences show activity in the frontal and parietal brain structures (Azari et al., 2001a, 2001b; Newberg, Alavi et al., 2001). These areas of the brain tend to be involved in cognitive processes such as concentrating or orienting oneself in space. During conversion or spiritual transformation, the person is often concentrating on the beliefs of the religion he or she is joining. As indicated in the term spiritual transformation, the person's self-identity is changing. Whether this occurs in solitude or in a social context, the person is actively orienting him or herself in relation to the perceived spiritual world—God or an Ultimate Concern, the universe, or perhaps spiritual bodies such as angels. Because the process of spiritual transformation, at least in some cases, involves sustained, willful attention, we infer that the prefrontal and cingulated cortex could appear active during such times. The prefrontal and medial frontal cortical areas seem to be active when humans make inferences, plan, reason, and make decisions (Azari et al., 2005; Posner & Petersen, 1990). These mental operations may be involved in conversions that are deliberate, that is, the person willfully decides to change his or her life and follow a new religion. Thus, when a person weighs the options and makes a commitment to a new form of spirituality out of well-reasoned logic, his or her prefrontal and medial frontal cortical areas may be active. This would be consistent with Frith, Friston, Liddle, and Frackowiak's (1991) description of the prefrontal cortex as the seat of the human will. A person who intentionally chooses to redefine him or herself spiritually is engaging his or her will; this would presumably appear on brain imaging as activity in the prefrontal area. Also, however, this same activity might be what is invoking the person's meaning system at the highest known level—the level of self-aware, conscious thought.

An illustrative study using SPECT suggests that the dorsal lateral prefrontal region is involved in spiritual activity. In Newberg, Alavi et al.'s (2001) study of eight Tibetan Buddhist meditators and eight nuns, the brain images of the monks while mediating appeared very similar to the brain images of the nuns while praying. Both show increased activity in the dorsal lateral prefrontal region and decreased activity in the posterior superior parietal region. These areas are involved in cognitive processes such as complex visual perception, concentration, and orientation. Although we can only conjecture, the dorsal lateral prefrontal region may also be active during spiritual transformations that involve vivid images, focused attention, and reorientation. Whether the brain perceives a sense of oneness, as in the case of the Buddhists, or a connection to Christ, as in the case of the nuns, it seems that this brain region is active. It may also be active, therefore, in spiritual transformations that involve cognitive processes such as perceiving visual stimuli (e.g., a cross at the front of the sanctuary), concentrating (e.g., focusing on tenets of a religion), and orientation (e.g., trying to center oneself and become one with the universe).

Unlike the temporal lobe epilepsy theory of conversion, new evidence increasingly suggests that religious experiences (and by implication, perhaps also conversion) are cognitively mediated (Azari, in press). Azari (in press) found that religious subjects in a religious state had higher blood flow in the right dorsolateral prefrontal cortex, as indicated by PET. This brain area did not appear active in the nonreligious subjects. Both Buddhist and Christian religious experience involves the activation of dorsomedial and dorsolateral frontal cortical areas (Seitz, in press). The dorsolateral prefrontal cortex plays an important role in complex cognitive processes, which may include how people infer that God is responsible for their per-ceived "calling" to convert, or how they make meaning out of their past, present, and future. The process of spiritual transformation inherently involves complex cognitive processes such as subjective awareness and belief-thought, and sufficient changes in them may constitute a trans-formed self-identity. Meaning-making , furthermore, is a complex cogni-tive process that involves appraising information in light of global beliefs (Park, 2005; Park & Folkman, 1997; Silberman, 2005). Therefore, based upon Azari et al.'s (2001b) PET findings and the way religion and spiritu-ality seem to be involved with higher order cognition in meaning-making (Paloutzian & Swenson, in press), we think the dorsolateral prefrontal cor-tex may be active during spiritual transformations.

Parietal cortex

Christian spiritual experiences show activation in the parietal midline structure and precuneus (Seitz, in press). These areas are involved in the recall of a memory trace. Although tentative at this point, the parietal areas may also be activated during spiritual transformation. This is because an important factor in the transformative process may be the memory of previ-ous encounters with religion or spirituality. Although the person may not have personally encountered a perceived divine until the time of conversion, he or she may have observed such changes in the lives of other people or learned about conversion through church, movies, articles, or other media. At the time the person initially learned about conversion, he or she may have been uninterested and apathetic. The memory of people's accounts of their own conversions may nevertheless have influenced his or her own con-version even if only at a nonconscious level. Thus, although the present state of knowledge allows us only to tie somewhat loose ends together, we can at least speculate that spiritual transformations involve activity in the parietal cortex, since it plays a role in the recall of previous experiences (Seitz, in press).

Caveat

Although advances in technology have made it possible to begin to under-stand brain activity during religious experiences, we must be careful not to overstate the current state of knowledge. Neuroimaging does not give an exact picture of brain activity. Additionally, it is important to keep in mind that activated brain areas, such as the frontal cortex, are not uniquely spe-cialized for spiritual or religious experiences (Seitz, in press). The brain areas that are likely to be active during spiritual transformation are active in many other mental and behavioral processes.

CONCLUSION

Of the many implications that could be drawn from our attempt to bring neurological and psychological knowledge together around the problem of understanding religious conversion and spiritual transformation, two stand out as particularly interesting and perhaps far-reaching. The first has to do with whether religious commitments are primarily to beliefs or to relationships. The second has to do with the capability of the human mind to conceive of, detect, and keep core ideas that it may see as true and beautiful, but not communicable.

Belief or Relationship?

The findings from two different lines of research seem to indicate that religiousness, and by implication religious conversion, may be heavily relationship-related. For example, research on religious conversion within the framework of attachment theory suggests that the dominant factor in determining whether someone experiences religious conversion during young adulthood is the attachment style of the person's primary caregivers during childhood. People who have insecure attachment relationships with their primary caregivers are more likely to develop an attachment to a loving God who they believe will never leave them (Kirkpatrick, 2005a, 2005b). Similarly, other evidence shows that the brain areas that are most active during certain religious activities such as prayer and meditation are the same areas that play a significant role in perceived social relationships (Azari, in press; Seitz, in press). Putting these two lines of evidence together, it is tempting to imagine that these same areas may also be involved in religious conversion. This ought especially to be so to the degree that, consistent with Kirkpatrick's findings, religious conversion is fundamentally a relational process. The possibility of this correspondence awaits more definitive evidence.

Art and Religion as Self-Authenticating

One way to appreciate what religious conversion is about is to liken it to creative insight in art. We can pose that both religion and art are ways that people try to tell a "truth that cannot be told" (Solso, 2003). During a conversion a person may know life's most direct meaning while at the same time it is the most difficult to grasp. To be "at one" with whatever is ultimate would seem to be an experience that fits universal properties of the mind. Such a process that would occur in the case of religious or other spiritual transformation would seem to involve the same global cerebral functions that came with the development of art as the human species knows it (Solso, 2003). This would have to include meaning-making functions.

Change evidenced by meaning made or remade is a central feature of how the human mind works. Across the vast sweep of human history, people have searched for and found religious meaning and more than once have proclaimed that what they found was the formerly untold Truth and have defended this (self-authenticating) claim to the death of themselves and, unfortunately, others. In particular, the finding of new religious meaning by either insight or revelation, usually initially in the mind and heart of only one person, has triggered the forces that would lead to the development of the world's great religions and, in companion form, most of the world's greatest works of art. This too cannot be mere coincidence but instead suggests common neurobiological and psychological processes that mediate art and religion, artistic creativity and religious insight, and construction of meaning in art and meaning found in religious conversion. In fact, both meaning construction in art and meaning found in religious conversion can be understood as meaning making in spiritual transformation. Like science and art, whose timeless aspects are held to be both true and beautiful because they match the mind's capability to hold and appreciate them (Solso, 2003), it may be that at the most abstract cognitive level the meanings of artistic insight and religious conversion are identical. It may also be that for the same neurological reasons Truth, psychologically speaking, is in the meaning system of the beholder (Paloutzian, 2006).

REFERENCES

The authors wish to thank the Catlin Foundation whose grant supported Erica Swenson's research assistantship and contribution to this chapter. Correspondence concerning this chapter can be addressed to Raymond F. Paloutzian, Department of Psychology, Westmont College, Santa Barbara, CA 93108-1099 (email: paloutz@westmont.edu).

Allport, G. W., & Ross, J. M. (1967). Personal religious orientation and prejudice. *Journal of Personality and Social Psychology, 5,* 432–443.

Azari, N. P. (in press). The cognitivity of religious experience and emotion: Evidence from neuroscience. In C. Jäger (Ed.), *Brain—religion—experience: Multidiscipline encounters.* New York: Springer Publisher.

Azari, N. P., Missimer, J., & Seitz, R. J. (2005). Religious experience and emotion: Evidence for distinctive cognitive neural patterns. *The International Journal for the Psychology of Religion, 15*(4), 263–280.

Azari, N. P., Nickel, J., Wunderlich, G., Niedeggen, M., Hefter, H., Tellmann, L., et al. (2001a). Neural circuitry of religious experience. In Proceedings of the *31st Annual Meeting of the Society for Neuroscience* (Vol. 1, p. 382). San Diego: Society for Neuroscience.

Azari, N. P., Nickel, J., Wunderlich, G., Niedeggen, M., Hefter, H., Tellmann, L., et al. (2001b). Neural correlates of religious experience. *European Journal of Neuroscience, 13,* 1649–1652.

Bear, D. M. (1979). Temporal lobe epilepsy: A syndrome of sensory-limbic hypercon-nection. *Cortex*, *15*, 357–384.

Bear, D. M., & Fedio, P. (1977). Quantitative analysis of interictal behavior in temporal lobe epilepsy. *Archives of Neurology*, *34*, 454–467.

Beard, A. (1963). The schizophrenia like psychoses of epilepsy. II: Physical aspects. *British Journal of Psychiatry*, *109*, 113–129.

Beit-Hallahmi, B., & Argyle, M. (1997). *The psychology of religious behaviour, belief and experience.* London: Routledge.

Blair, R. J. R. (2004). The roles of the orbitofrontal cortex in the modulation of anti-social behavior. *Brain and Cognition*, *55*, 198–208.

Chow, T. W., & Cummings, J. L. (1999). Frontal-subcortical circuits. In B. L. Miller & J. L. Cummings (Eds.), *The human frontal lobes: Functions and disorders* (pp. 3–26). New York: Guilford Press.

d'Aquili, E. G., & Newberg, A. B. (1999). *The mystical mind: Probing the biology of reli-gious experience.* Minneapolis: Fortress Press.

Deacon, T. W. (1998). *The symbolic species: The co-evolution of language and the brain.* New York: Norton.

Devinsky, O. (2004). Diagnosis and treatment of temporal lobe epilepsy. *Review of Neurologic Disorders*, *1*(1), 2–9.

Dewhurst, K., & Beard, A. W. (1970). Sudden religious conversions in temporal lobe epilepsy. *Journal of Psychiatry*, *117*, 497–507.

Emmons, R. A., & Paloutzian, R. F. (2003). The psychology of religion. *Annual Review of Psychology*, *54*, 377–402.

Frith, C. D., Friston, K., Liddle, P. F., & Frackowiak, R. S. (1991). Willed action and the prefrontal cortex in man: A study with PET. *Proceedings of the Royal Society of London*, *244*, 241–246.

Geschwind, N. (1983). Interictal behavioral changes in epilepsy. *Epilepsia Supplement*, *24*(1), S23–S30.

Goldberg, G. (1987). From intent to action. Evolution and function of the premotor systems of the frontal lobe. In E. Perceman (Ed.), *The frontal lobes revisited.* (pp. 273–306). New York: IRBN Press.

Granqvist, P., & Kirkpatrick, L. A. (2004). Religious conversion and perceived child-hood attachment: a meta-analysis. *The International Journal for the Psychology of Religion*, *14*(4), 223–250.

Hill, P. C. (2002). Spiritual transformation: Forming the habitual center of personal energy. *Research in the Social Scientific Study of Religion*, *13*, 87–108.

Hill, P. C., & Hood, R. W., Jr. (1999). *Measures of religiosity.* Birmingham: Religious Education Press.

Hill, P. C., Pargament, K. I., Hood, R. W., McCullough, M. E., Swyers, J. P., Larson, D. B., et al. (2000). Conceptualizing religion and spirituality: Points of common-ality, points of departure. *Journal for the Theory of Social Behavior*, *30*, 51–77.

James, W. (1902). *The varieties of religious experience.* New York: Longmans.

Kirkpatrick, L. A. (2005a). *Attachment, evolution, and the psychology of religion.* New York: Guilford Press.

Kirkpatrick, L. A. (2005b). Evolutionary psychology: An emerging new foundation for the psychology of religion. In R. F. Paloutzian & C. L. Park (Eds.), *Handbook of the psychology of religion and spirituality* (pp. 101–119). New York: Guilford Press.

Kiss, J., Kocsis, K., Csaki, A., Gorcs, T. J., & Halasz, B. (1997). Metabotropic glutamate receptor in GHRH and beta-endorphin neurons of the hypothalamic arcuate nucleus. *Neuroreport, 8*, 3703–3707.

Leung L. S., & Wu, K. (2006). Epilepsy-based changes in hippocampal excitability: causes and effects. *Advances in Neurology, 97*, 63–68.

Lhermitte, F. (1986). Human autonomy and the frontal lobes. Part II: Patient behavior in complex and social situations: The "environmental dependency syndrome". *Annals of Neurology, 19*(4), 335–343.

Nauta, W. (1979). A proposed conceptual reorganization of the basal ganglia and telencephalon. *Neuroscience, 4*(12), 1875–1881.

Newberg, A. B., Alavi, A., Baime, M., Pourdehnad, M., Santanna, J., & d'Aquili, E. G. (2001). The measurement of regional cerebral blood flow during the complex cognitive task of meditation: A preliminary SPECT study. *Psychiatry Research: Neuroimaging, 106*, 113–122.

Newberg, A. B., & d'Aquili, E. G. (2000). The neuropsychology of religious and spiritual experience. *Journal of Consciousness Studies, 7*(11–12), 251–266.

Newberg, A. B., d'Aquili, E. G., & Rause, R. (2001). *Why God won't go away: Brain science and the biology of belief.* New York: Ballantine Books.

Newberg, A. B., & Newberg, S. K. (2005). The neuropsychology of religious and spiritual experience. In R.F. Paloutzian & C.L. Park (Eds.), *Handbook of the psychology of religion and spirituality* (pp. 199–215). New York: Guilford Press.

Oksanen, A. (1994). *Religious conversion: A meta-analytical study.* Lund, Sweden: Lund University Press.

Paloutzian, R. F. (1981). Purpose in life and value changes following conversion. *Journal of Personality and Social Psychology, 41*, 1153–1160.

Paloutzian, R. F. (1996). *Invitation to the psychology of religion* (2nd ed.). Boston: Allyn and Bacon.

Paloutzian, R. F. (2005). Religious conversion and spiritual transformation: A meaning-system analysis. In R. F. Paloutzian & C. L. Park (Eds.), *Handbook of the psychology of religion and spirituality* (pp. 331–347). New York: Guilford Press.

Paloutzian, R. F. (2006). Psychology of religion, the human sciences, and the golden ring: Constructing the meaning of religion. In P. Clayton (Ed.), *Oxford handbook of religion and science.* Oxford, UK: Oxford University Press.

Paloutzian, R. F., Fikes, T. F., & Hutsebaut, D. (2002). A social cognition interpretation of neurotheological events. In R. Joseph (Ed.), *Neurotheology: Brian, science, spirituality, religious experience* (pp. 215–222). San Jose: University Press.

Paloutzian, R. F., & Park, C. L. (2005). Integrative themes in the current science of the psychology of religion. In R. F. Paloutzian & C. L. Park (Eds.), *Handbook of the psychology of religion and spirituality* (pp. 3–20). New York: Guilford Press.

Paloutzian, R. F., Richardson, J. R., & Rambo, L. R. (1999). Religious conversion and personality change. *Journal of Personality, 67*, 1047–1079.

Paloutzian, R. F., & Swenson, E. L. (in press). Spiritual experiences, neurology, and the making of meaning. In C. Jäger (Ed.), *Brain—religion—experience: Multidiscipline encounters.* New York: Springer Publisher.

Park, C. L. (2005). Religion and meaning. In R. F. Paloutzian & C. L. Park (Eds.), *Handbook of the psychology of religion and spirituality* (pp. 295–314). New York: Guilford Press.

Park, C. L., & Folkman, S. (1997). Meaning in the context of stress and coping. *Review of General Psychology, 1*(2), 115–144.

Persinger, M. A. (2002). Experimental simulation of the God experience: Implications for religious beliefs and the future of the human species. In R. Joseph (Ed.), *Neurotheology* (pp. 267–284). San Jose, CA: University Press.

Posner, M. I., & Petersen, S. E. (1990). The attention system of the human brain. *Annual Review of Neuroscience, 13*, 25–42.

Raichle, M. E. (1998). Behind the scenes of functional brain imaging: A historical and physiological perspective. *Proceedings of the National Academy of Sciences, 95*, 765–772.

Rambo, L. R. (1993). *Understanding religious conversions.* New Haven: Yale University Press.

Ramachandran, V. S., & Blakeslee, S. (1999). *Phantoms in the brain.* New York: William Morrow.

Richardson, J. T. (1985). The active vs. passive convert: Paradigm, conflict in conversion/recruitment research. *Journal for the Scientific Study of Religion, 24*(2), 119–236.

Richardson, J. T. (1995). Clinical and personality assessment of participants in new religions. *The International Journal for the Psychology of Religion, 5*(3), 145–170.

Roberts, J. K. A., & Guberman, A. (1989). Religion and epilepsy. *Psychiatric Journal of the University of Ottawa, 14*, 282–286.

Saver, J. L., & Rabin, J. (1997). The neural substrates of religious experience. *The Journal of Neuropsychiatry and Clinical Neurosciences, 9*(3), 498–510.

Schnider, A., & Gutbrod, K. (1999). Traumatic brain injury. In B. L. Miller & J. L. Cummings (Eds.), *The human frontal lobes: Functions and disorders* (pp. 487–508). New York: Guilford Press.

Seitz, R. J. (in press). The neurophysiological basis of religious experience. In C. Jäger (Ed.), *Brain—religion—experience: Multidiscipline encounters.* New York: Springer.

Shaji, A. V., & Kulkarni, S. K. (1998). Central nervous system depressant activities of melatonin in rats and mice. *Indian Journal of Experimental Biology, 36*(3), 257–263.

Silberman, I. (2005). Religion as a meaning-system: Implications for the new millennium. *Journal of Social Issues, 61*(4), 641–664.

Solso, R. L. (2003). *The psychology of art and the evolution of the conscious brain.* Cambridge, MA: MIT Press.

Spilka, B. (2005). Religious practice, ritual, and prayer. In R.F. Paloutzian & C. L. Park (Eds.), *Handbook of the psychology of religion and spirituality* (pp. 365–377). New York: Guilford Press.

Spilka, B., Hood, R. W., Jr., Hunsberger, B., & Gorsuch, R. (2003). *The psychology of religion. An empirical approach* (3rd ed.). New York: Guilford Press.

Spilka, B., Shaver, P., & Kirkpatrick, L. A. (1985). A general attribution theory for the psychology of religion. *Journal for the Scientific Study of Religion, 24*, 1–20.

Starbuck, E. D. (1899). *The psychology of religion.* London: Walter Scott.

Sudsuang, R., Chentanez, V., & Veluvan, K. (1991). Effects of Buddhist meditation on serum cortisol and total protein levels, blood pressure, pulse rate, lung volume and reaction time. *Physiology and Behavior, 50*, 543–548.

Tooley, G. A., Armstrong, S. M., Norman, T. R. & Sali, A. (2000). Acute increases in night-time plasma melatonin levels following a period of meditation. *Biological Psychology, 53*(1), 69–78.

Tucker, D. M., Novelly, R. A., & Walker, P. J. (1987). Hyperreligiosity in temporal lobe epilepsy: Redefining the relationship. *Journal of Nerve-Related Mental Disorders, 175*, 181–184.

Ullman, C. (1982). Cognitive and emotional antecedents of religious conversion. *Journal of Personality and Social Psychology, 43*, 183–192.

Ullman, C. (1989). *The transformed self: The psychology of religious conversion.* New York: Plenum Press.

Van Hoesen, G. W., Pandya, D., & Butters, N. (1975). Some connections of the entorhinal (area 28) and perirhinal (area 35) cortices of the rehesus monkey. II: Frontal lobe afferents. *Brain Research, 95*, 25–38.

Walton, K. G., Pugh, N. D., Gelderloos, P., & Macrae, P. (1995). Stress reduction and preventing hypertension: Preliminary support for a psychoneuroendocrine mechanism. *Journal of Alternative Complementary Medicine, 1*, 263–283.

Waxman, S. G., & Geschwind, N. (1975). The interictal behavior syndrome of temporal lobe epilepsy. *Archives of General Psychiatry, 32*, 1580–1586.

Zald, D. H., & Kim, S. W. (1996). Anatomy and function of the orbitofrontal cortex: Anatomy, neurocircuitry and obsessive compulsive disorder. *Journal of Neuropsychiatry and Clinical Neurosciences, 8*(2), 125–138.

Zimbardo, P., & Ebbesen, E. B. (1970). *Influencing attitudes and changing behavior.* Menlo Park, CA: Addison-Wesley.

Zinnbauer, B. J., & Pargament, K. I. (2005). Religiousness and spirituality. In R. F. Paloutzian & C. L. Park (Eds.), *Handbook of the Psychology of Religion and Spirituality,* (pp. 21–42). New York: Guilford Press.

Zinnbauer, B. J., Pargament, K. I., Cole, B., Rye, M. S., Butter, E. M., Belavich, T. G., et al. (1997). Religion and spirituality: Unfuzzying the fuzzy. *Journal for the Scientific Study of Religion, 36*, 549–564.

CHAPTER 8

RELIGION AND THE BRAIN: EVIDENCE FROM TEMPORAL LOBE EPILEPSY

Steven C. Schachter

As succinctly stated by Saver and Rabin, "All human experience is brain-based, including scientific reasoning, mathematical deduction, moral judgment, and artistic creation, as well as religious states of mind," and that the challenge for behavioral neuroscientists "is to delineate the distinctive neural substrates of religious experience and their alteration in brain disorders" (Saver & Rabin, 1997). In this regard, investigations of the relationships between religiosity and brain function have often converged on the temporal lobes, including studies of people with epileptic seizures thought to originate in the temporal lobes, which is the subject of this review.

Epilepsy will first be briefly reviewed to provide a context for the studies of religiosity in patients with Temporal Lobe Epilepsy (TLE). Problems associated with the definition and measurement of religiosity and spirituality, as well as methodological issues in studies of religiosity, have been described elsewhere and are beyond the scope of this review (Berry, 2005; Stefanek, McDonald, & Hess, 2005).

OVERVIEW OF EPILEPSY

Epilepsy is a common neurological disorder that affects up to 4 million people in the United States (Hauser & Hesdorffer, 1990). A variety of medical conditions cause epilepsy, including congenital brain malformations, inborn errors of metabolism, brain trauma, brain tumors, stroke, intracranial infection, malformations of cerebral blood vessels, and disorders that cause cerebral degeneration such as Alzheimer's disease. Yet up to 50 percent of patients with epilepsy have no identifiable cause.

Consequently, epilepsy is a syndrome, not a single disease, resulting from many different medical conditions, some yet to be discovered, which all have in common one or more symptoms that are clinically recognized as epileptic seizures. An epileptic seizure results when an abnormal and excessive synchronization of brain neurons causes a sudden and temporary change in behavior, the nature of which is determined by the specific networks of brain cells that discharge abnormally during the seizure. Seizures, therefore, usually lead to episodes in which consciousness is altered, or in which there are motor, sensory, autonomic, or psychic experiences with retained consciousness. While the behavioral symptoms of seizures experienced by any single patient tend to be similar and stereotyped, seizure manifestations vary from patient to patient, because the involved neuronal networks may be different from one patient to another.

Seizures are classified based on the symptoms they cause and the area(s) of the brain affected. The current seizure classification scheme divides epileptic seizures into partial seizures and generalized seizures.

Partial seizures originate in a discrete, or focal, region of the brain's outer layer, the cortex, and can be subdivided into those partial seizures that impair consciousness (called "complex partial seizures") and those that do not (called "simple partial seizures"). Both types of partial seizures, once underway, can spread rapidly via neuronal networks to other cortical regions, resulting in further behavioral alterations, including a convulsion (also called a "secondarily generalized tonic-clonic seizure").

Simple Partial Seizures

The symptoms of simple partial seizures depend on where the abnormally synchronized electrical discharges occur in the brain and at what point in this process the symptoms enter consciousness. For example, simple partial seizures affecting the part of the brain that controls muscle movements may cause rhythmic movements of the face, arm, or leg. Likewise, simple partial seizures affecting cortical regions that bring sensations into consciousness or those regions responsible for emotions and memory may produce symptoms such as olfactory, visual, or auditory hallucinations; feelings of déjà vu or jamais vu; and fear, panic, or euphoria.

Because, by definition, simple partial seizures do not affect consciousness, patients remember the symptoms caused by simple partial seizures. Since one or more discrete regions of cortex are involved in all conscious experiences that can occur under normal, everyday conditions or in altered states in which someone is nonetheless still conscious, and because seizures can arise from virtually any cortical region in any given patient, then virtually any conscious experience can also occur as the primary symptom of a simple partial seizure in some patient with epilepsy. Hence, it would not be unexpected that brief spiritual or religious experiences could occur during simple partial seizures, if one assumes that such feelings have fixed cortical representations. Accordingly, simple partial seizures that result in transient religious experiences are of particular interest. Called "ecstatic auras," and described by Fyodor Dostoevsky in *The Idiot*, possibly based on his own experiences (Hughes, 2005), these manifestations of simple partial seizures are described, albeit rarely, in case reports. For example, Cirignotta et al. evaluated a 30-year-old man with a 17-year history of episodes of "psychomotor arrest, slight lapse of consciousness, and above all, an ineffable sensation of 'joy'" (Cirignotta, Todesco, & Lugaresi, 1980). The joy he felt was "so intense that he cannot find its match in reality . . . His mind, his whole being is pervaded by a sense of total bliss." At the conclusion of a 24-hour electroencephalographic (EEG) recording, the patient had one of his typical episodes, and the EEG showed typical changes of a partial seizure over the right temporal lobe region.

Another patient, reported by Naito and Matsui, was a 62-year-old woman with no prior psychiatric history, but who was described as pious and possessing "a strong faith in the god of a new religion in Japan" (Naito & Matsui, 1988). At the age of 54, she suffered a head injury associated with unconsciousness and five years later had the first of several ecstatic episodes, for which she was occasionally, but not always, amnesic. For example, she would suddenly cry out, "I saw my god! I saw my god!" or "A halo appeared around god. Thank my god! Oh! Thank my god!" Another type of episode occurred once while she watched the rising sun, which she described as follows: "Triple haloes appeared around the sun. Suddenly the sunlight became intense. I experienced a revelation of god and all creation glittering under the sun. The sun became bigger and engulfed me. My mind, my whole being was pervaded by a feeling of delight." An EEG, done in between these experiences, showed an abnormality arising from the left temporal lobe region during sleep, and she was diagnosed with and treated for TLE, after which the ecstatic episodes apparently stopped.

Complex Partial Seizures

Complex partial seizures are the most common seizure type in adults and the most difficult of all the seizure types to fully control with treatment. The hallmark of complex partial seizures is loss of awareness or consciousness, even though the individual appears to be awake. There may be a warning, called an "aura," immediately preceding loss or reduction of awareness/consciousness, which may be the only aspect of the seizure that patients later remember. The warning is actually a simple partial seizure. Typical auras are a rising sensation in the abdomen or chest, or emotional symptoms such as fear or panic, but auras may consist of complicated delusions, hallucinations, or the perception of smells or tastes.

Complex partial seizures typically last less than three minutes. During that time, patients may appear awake, but lose contact with their environment and do not respond normally to instructions or questions. Thus patients often say that they "black out." During this part of the seizure, they usually stare and either remain motionless or display repetitive semi-purposeful behaviors, called "automatisms," which may include facial grimacing, chewing, lip smacking, snapping fingers, gesturing, repeating words or phrases, walking, running, or even undressing. Patients do not recall these behaviors. After complex partial seizures, patients are often sleepy and confused and complain of headaches. These symptoms, called the "postictal state," can last minutes to hours and may also include a disturbance of language or psychotic ideation, as described below.

The most common part of the brain giving rise to complex partial seizures is the mesial (inner) aspect of the temporal lobe, known also as part of the limbic lobe, including the amygdala and the hippocampus. This is especially true of patients whose seizures are not fully controlled by medications. Such patients, who are said to have TLE, usually have their first seizure before puberty, and often have a history of convulsive seizures in early childhood with high fevers.

Generalized seizures, by contrast, involve widespread regions of cortex and subcortical networks on both sides of the brain at the outset. The most familiar subtype of generalized seizures is the tonic-clonic seizure (sometimes called "grand mal," or convulsion), which is often preceded by a cry, followed by sudden falling to the ground and convulsive movements, sometimes with tongue or mouth biting and loss of bladder control.

Diagnostic Tests

The two most important diagnostic tests for epilepsy are the electroencephalogram (EEG; also called a brainwave test) and neuroimaging studies. EEGs record brain electrical activity and are generally performed when the patient is not experiencing seizure-related symptoms (interictal); even so, patients with epilepsy often, but not always, have characteristic EEG abnormalities, especially during sleep. EEGs that are obtained during seizures (ictal recordings) are helpful to confirm that behaviors suspected of being seizures actually are caused by epileptic seizures; that is, ictal recordings offer the best possible proof that sudden onset, transient behaviors are seizures. The primary exception to this principle is that simple partial seizures may show no specific change in simultaneous EEG recordings. Recent technological advances have made it possible to record brainwaves over several days, increasing the likelihood of recording the EEG during a seizure in patients with frequent seizures. Such testing is required to determine the site of cortical onset of seizures for patients undergoing evaluation for brain surgery and would constitute the best available evidence that a particular behavior was directly caused by a seizure.

Neuroimaging studies, such as magnetic resonance imaging (MRI) and computed tomography (CT), are performed to look for structural brain abnormalities, especially in patients with partial seizures. MRIs in children may reveal congenital abnormalities, whereas scans of young adults presenting with partial seizures may show mesial temporal volume loss or sclerosis (a common cause of TLE), changes associated with previous head trauma, congenital abnormalities, brain tumors, and abnormal blood vessels. In mid-life and beyond, scans may reveal strokes, tumors, and cerebral degeneration.

Functional neuroimaging studies can identify discrete areas of abnormal cortical functioning, even in patients with normal CT or MRI scans. Two common tests are single photon emission computerized tomography (SPECT) and positron emission tomography (PET), which can demonstrate characteristic discrete cortical changes in physiology during and between seizures. Functional imaging studies are generally reserved for patients undergoing evaluation for epilepsy surgery but like ictal EEG recordings can provide concrete evidence of alterations in brain function in association with specific seizure-related behaviors.

Treatment

Antiepileptic drugs (AEDs) are the mainstay of epilepsy therapy and are selected based on the patient's seizure type (generalized or partial), age, gender, and concomitant medical/psychiatric conditions as well as other factors. The primary goal of treatment is to completely suppress seizures without causing troublesome side effects. Nearly all AEDs have potential side effects, including headache, dizziness, drowsiness, ataxia, double vision, slurred speech, and confusion. They can also affect cognition and behavior. AEDs are generally taken by patients for years, especially when epilepsy begins in puberty or later.

Initial treatment prevents further seizures without side effects in up to 70 percent of patients. The prognosis for complete seizure control in the other 30 percent of patients is less favorable, even with the introduction of many new AEDs in the past 15 years. This is particularly true for patients with seizures that originate in the mesial temporal lobes. These patients often require numerous trials of AEDs, either alone or in combination, and they are often evaluated to determine if removing a portion of brain tissue would reduce their seizures without producing permanent neurological or behavioral dysfunction. Nearly four in five such patients with TLE who are candidates for surgery may become seizure-free by removal of the anterior portion of the temporal lobe.

Associated Mood Disorders

Nearly one in three patients with epilepsy report significant concern about their mood, and patients with TLE are particularly likely to experience concomitant mood disorders. The three most common associated psychiatric disorders in this population are depression, anxiety, and psychosis.

Depression occurs in 10 percent to 20 percent of patients with controlled seizures and up to 60 percent of patients whose seizures do not respond to treatment (Mendez, Cummings, & Benson, 1986; O'Donoghue, Goodridge, Redhead, Sander, & Duncan, 1999). Depression in patients with epilepsy is generally a long-lasting, waxing and waning disorder, usually associated with variable levels of irritability and emotionality. Some patients experience depression during a simple partial seizure (ictal depression) or during the postictal state. The suicide rate in depressed patients with epilepsy is up to 10 times higher than in the general population and as much as 25 times higher in patients with complex partial seizures of temporal lobe origin (Harden & Goldstein, 2002).

Depression may arise from brain dysfunction, as well as a response to the social and vocational disabilities associated with having epilepsy (Gilliam & Kanner, 2002). Interestingly, depression may also be a risk factor for the development of epilepsy (Kanner & Barry, 2003).

Anxiety is nearly as common as depression in patients with epilepsy and, like depression, markedly compromises the quality of life and psychosocial functioning. Possible risk factors and neurobiological mechanisms have been reviewed elsewhere (Beyenburg, Mitchell, Schmidt, Elger, & Reuber, 2005). Anxiety occurring as a symptom of simple partial seizures is often mistaken for a panic disorder. Anxiety most commonly occurs between seizures and may be disabling, even in patients with infrequent or well-controlled seizures, such as patients who become seizure free following brain surgery (Wilson, Bladin, & Saling, 2004).

The incidence of psychosis varies from about 3 percent in patients with generalized epilepsy to 14 percent in patients with TLE, and from 0.6 percent to 7 percent of patients with epilepsy in the community to 19 percent to 27 percent of epilepsy patients requiring hospitalization.

Psychotic symptoms can occur as simple partial seizures, manifesting as hallucinations or delusions. Like other seizure-related symptoms, they are usually transient. Psychosis may also occur in some patients during the postictal period; generally, this begins years after the onset of epilepsy. Patients at particularly high risk for postictal psychosis are those who have seizures that begin independently from both temporal lobes (bilateral seizure foci), or bilateral mesial temporal or limbic lobe lesions, or clusters of complex partial seizures. The typical pattern in such patients is a cluster of complex partial seizures of mesial temporal lobe origin, followed by affective symptoms together with grandiose and religious delusions, as well as simple auditory hallucinations. Psychosis may also occur between seizures (interictally), characterized as delusions and hallucinations with full alertness and ability to concentrate, though disorganized behavior and thought disorders may also occur. Religious ideation occurring in the context of delusions and hallucinations as the manifestations of an interictal psychosis is well described.

Psychosocial Aspects of Epilepsy

There are very few if any aspects of everyday living that are not affected by having a diagnosis of epilepsy. Fear of having a seizure is common among people with epilepsy and is "the worst thing about having epilepsy" according to nearly half of a sample of community-based people with epilepsy responding to a survey (Fisher et al., 2000a, 2000b). Specific fears include fear of dying from a seizure, fear that others would witness a seizure, fear of embarrassment in public, fear of losing employment, and fear of being involved in an automobile accident. Seizure worry can impact quality of life as profoundly as depression (Loring, Meador, & Lee, 2004).

Because seizures by their nature are unpredictable events, patients with epilepsy often struggle with regaining control over their lives. Au et al. describe self-mastery, which is generally measured by locus of control and self-efficacy, as the belief that a patient can control the course of his or her life despite having epilepsy (Au et al., 2002). They hypothesized that increasing coping skills of patients with epilepsy would result in better self-management and that psychosocial interventions that increase self-efficacy and social support would enhance quality of life. Consistent with this hypothesis, learning coping skills and stress management techniques can be beneficial (Gramstad, Iversen, & Engelsen, 2001; Sabaz et al., 2003), whereas believing that one's health condition was significantly a matter of chance is detrimental to quality of life (Au et al., 2002). The roles of religion or spirituality in improving self-mastery, reducing fear and uncertainty, and coping with stress for patients with epilepsy have not been systematically explored as in other disorders (Harrison et al., 2005; Koenig, McCullough, & Larsson, 2001; Stefanek, McDonald, & Hess, 2005).

EPILEPSY AND RELIGIOSITY

Epilepsy and religion have been intertwined for centuries, despite the attempts of ancient Greek physicians to explain epilepsy—then known as "The Sacred Disease"—as a natural disorder, no more divine than any other disease (Hippocrates, 1846; Riggs & Riggs, 2005). Indeed, seizures, and in particular generalized tonic-clonic seizures, have been viewed in many cultures from antiquity to the present day as resulting from supernatural influences, whether divine, demonic or both (Carrazana et al., 1999; Glaser, 1978; Ismail, Wright, Rhodes, & Small, 2005; Jilek-Aall, 1999; Kottek, 1988; Murphy, 1959). Religious figures, consequently, have often been called on to heal people with epilepsy. As recounted in the New Testament gospels of Matthew (17:14–20), Mark (9:14–29), and Luke (9:37–43), who was a physician, Jesus cast out the evil spirit from a boy with epilepsy who had just had a seizure, thereby curing him (DeToledo & Lowe, 2003).

Based on the recognition that partial seizures can cause a variety of symptoms, and an understanding of the relationship between epilepsy and psychosis, some modern scholars have suggested that temporal lobe seizures, or a related postictal or interictal psychosis, were the possible cause of prophetic visions and spiritually significant life-changing events of historical figures such as Muhammad (Freemon, 1976), Emanuel Swedenborg (Bradford, 1999), St. Birgitta of Vadstena (Landtblom, 2004), Joan of Arc (Foote-Smith & Bayne, 1991), Teresa de Ahumada (Garcia, 2003) and the apostle Paul (Saul of Tarsus) (Landsborough, 1987). Much controversy surrounds these assertions (Brorson & Brewer, 1988; Freemon, 1976; Johnson, 1994), in large part because of the hearsay nature of the facts and the lack of confirmatory medical and neurophysiological evidence.

In the 1800s, physicians and psychiatrists noted increased expressions of religiosity in patients with epilepsy who were confined to asylums (Devinsky, 2003), and, according to modern authors, this religiosity was interpreted as a "craving for sympathy by the desperate, helpless, socially isolated, intellectually deteriorating epileptic" (Devinsky, 2003) or as the result of "disability, social isolation and . . . [an] enhanced need for the consolation of religion" (Dewhurst & Beard, 1970).

In the 1970s, several landmark reports by Dewhurst and Beard (Dewhurst & Beard, 1970), Waxman and Geschwind (Waxman & Geschwind, 1975), Bear and Fedio (Bear & Fedio, 1977), and Geschwind (Geschwind, 1979) brought renewed attention to religiosity experienced during seizures or in association with a postictal or interictal psychosis and advanced the assertion that heightened interest in religious matters could develop as a personality trait, that is, as part of a nonpsychotic interictal behavioral syndrome in patients with TLE.

A publication by Beard described 26 epileptic patients (out of 69 studied) who showed symptoms of religiosity (Beard, 1963). Dewhurst and Beard subsequently presented the detailed case histories of six patients from the same cohort, all with a diagnosis of TLE, who underwent sudden religious conversions (Dewhurst & Beard, 1970). In the opinion of Devinsky (Devinsky,

2003), this "classic paper provided some of the early support for the modern concept of the temporal lobe as the seat of religious cognitive-emotional experiences." Four of the six patients had a strong religious upbringing. The initial religious conversion was temporally related to preceding seizures in three patients; a second religious conversion in a fourth patient followed a cluster of seizures. In all patients, the manifestations of the conversion persisted indefinitely, even though seizure frequency or severity improved in most of the cases. Religious ideation was often accompanied by visual, auditory, and olfactory hallucinations, as well as paranoia. The following case illustrates these points:

> When he was a boy, the patient was taken to church by his father, who was very concerned that his son should live a religious life. This was the more so when the father was converted from Methodism to Christian Science. At the age of 9 the boy decided to become a minister, and at that time he used to get up at 6 a.m. to sing hymns. However, his interest in religion ebbed as the years passed and had become minimal by the time he was 21.
>
> A fortnight after [his first minor seizure, which was an epigastric flush], while walking alone, he suddenly felt God's reality and his own insignificance. As a result of this revelation, he recovered his faith and determined to live in a Christian manner. However, this conversion experience gradually lost its impact and he once again ceased concerning himself with religion. Then [12 years later] he had two of his rare grand mal attacks in one day. Within twenty-four hours of the second seizure he had another conversion experience as part of a florid religious psychosis that lasted a week—he had a sudden dream-like feeling, saw a flash of light, and exclaimed "I have seen the light." He suddenly knew that God was behind the sun and that this knowledge meant power; he could have power from God if he would only ask for it. He had a series of visions in which he felt that his past life was being judged; a book appeared before him, a world atlas with a torn page; a pendulum was swinging and when it stopped, the world would end.
>
> [Five months after a left temporal lobectomy], the patient was still so involved in his psychotic experience that he had no interest in other topics. He completely believed in the validity of everything he had seen and heard during the acute phase . . . He considered that he had received a message from God to mend his ways and help others, and the fact the he had been singled out in this way meant that he was God's chosen instrument. Twelve months after operation . . . his religious beliefs remained strong and he was attending church regularly. The patient had since remained fit-free.

Thus the cases of Dewhurst and Beard are consistent with religiosity associated with postictal and interictal psychoses in patients with TLE. This assessment, of course, is speculative and limited by the absence of confirmatory neurophysiological testing.

Similarly, Waxman and Geschwind reported three patients with TLE who had religious conversions, as well as changes in sexual behavior and tendencies toward compulsive drawing and writing, which was often "concerned with moral, ethical, or religious issues" (Waxman & Geschwind, 1975). The authors postulated that this cluster of behavioral traits, which they called "interictal personality changes," constituted a syndrome associated with TLE, which "may provide a useful model for the major psychoses because of its association with dysfunction at specific loci in the central nervous system," specifically "temporal lobe foci."

Whereas Waxman and Geschwind initially viewed interictal personality changes as a useful model for understanding psychosis, Geschwind subsequently differentiated the interictal behavioral syndrome from the psychoses associated with TLE described earlier, stating that only a "small number of patients with this syndrome are psychotic, although even in these cases one usually observes the same fundamental personality pattern" (Geschwind, 1979). Thus, he suggested that heightened interest in religious matters could occur interictally in the absence of psychosis in patients with TLE, often in association with "hypergraphia (a tendency to highly detailed writing often of a religious or philosophical nature), hyposexuality (diminished sex drive sometimes associated with changes in sexual taste), and irritability of varying degree." He posed the question: "If this syndrome is so common, why has it not been observed by others more frequently?" and went on to answer his own question: "I have repeatedly had the experience of demonstrating these personality features in patients whose records made no mention of personality change or indeed denied its presence. Most physicians do not enquire about a tendency to write poetry or keep a diary, or about religious conversions. Studies which do not look for this syndrome of course cannot find it."

ADDITIONAL PROSPECTIVE STUDIES

The papers just summarized and other contemporaneous observations set forth the hypotheses that religious conversions and ecstatic auras originated in the temporal lobes and that longer lasting changes in religious behavior could be influenced by more chronic pathological and functional disturbances of the same structures.

Thus, the stage was set for further studies to support or refute these hypotheses. These additional case reports and prospective studies, whether in healthy persons or in groups of patients diagnosed with TLE, either typically took a cognitive approach to defining religiosity, which, as described by Caird, "attempts to scale responses to questionnaires about attitudes or beliefs," or a behavioral approach, which "assesses the frequency of practices such as church attendance or private prayer" (Caird, 1987).

Studies in Non-epileptic Persons

Persinger has published extensively on the correlations between religiosity and a history of symptoms reminiscent of those experienced by persons with TLE during simple partial seizures. For example, nearly 20 years ago, he administered a self-report inventory that included 140 temporal lobe symptoms to healthy college students and found that subjects who reported religious experiences, whether or not they regularly attended church, reported significantly more temporal lobe symptoms than subjects who did not report religious experiences. He concluded that religious experiences are "normal consequences of temporal-lobe function" (Persinger, 1984). Several years later, Persinger extended these results in a study of 868 college students enrolled in first-year psychology courses over a 10-year period (Persinger, 1991). He found a relationship between a religious experience as a preadolescent and "temporal lobe" symptoms as adults, such as feeling the presence of a Cosmic Consciousness, episodes in which their souls left their bodies, experiencing visions, depersonalization, intense smells, widened affect, and feeling the presence of another Being late at night. To the author, these results suggested that "the earlier the onset of limbic lability, the more subjective experiences are infused with affect and meaningfulness," reflecting temporal lobe activity. This concept is similar to the "sensory-limbic hyperconnection" explanation of Bear and Fedio for the interictal behavior syndrome (see below). In a similar population, Persinger found that self-reported complex partial seizure-like symptoms correlated with paranormal and religious beliefs (Persinger, 1993), which he postulated were related to anatomically different temporo-limbic circuits.

In a similar study in nonepileptic subjects, MacDonald and Holland correlated self-reported complex partial seizure-like symptoms and a five-dimensional model of spirituality (Expressions of Spirituality Inventory; ESI) in 262 healthy undergraduates (MacDonald & Holland, 2002). Scores from the ESI subscales Paranormal Beliefs and Experiential/Phenomenological Dimension positively correlated with these symptoms, whereas neither ESI Cognitive Orientation Toward Spirituality nor ESI Religiousness predicted complex partial seizure-like symptoms in the regression analysis. The correlations persisted when age, sex, and reported religious involvement were controlled.

Studies in Patients with Temporal Lobe Epilepsy

Bear and Fedio (Bear & Fedio, 1977) administered questionnaires to patients with TLE who had unilateral temporal EEG abnormalities, as well as to healthy subjects, patients with neuromuscular disorders, and observers.

They found that a high percentage of the patients with TLE had features of the interictal behavior syndrome and, further, that there were differences in the behavioral profile between patients with TLE according to whether the EEG abnormalities occurred on the left or right. Thus, religiosity was associated with TLE lateralized to the left side. To explain their observations, Bear and Fedio postulated that "sensory-limbic hyperconnection," resulting from TLE, accounted for the characteristic deepening of emotions in patients with TLE.

By contrast, Tucker and colleagues evaluated 76 patients with TLE of unilateral onset for hyper-religiosity, as measured by the Wiggins Religiosity Scale (Tucker, Novelly, & Walker, 1987; Wiggins, 1969). Two control groups consisted of patients with primary generalized seizures and patients with nonepileptic seizures. Overall religiosity scores in each cohort were consistent with the normative sample, and there were no significant group differences in religiosity between the left versus the right TLE groups, nor between patients with TLE and either control group, therefore refuting the notion that hyper-religiosity was an interictal behavioral trait in patients with TLE. As the authors noted, though, a different tool was used in their study to measure religiosity than the one employed by Bear and Fedio, and, perhaps more significantly, that one-third of the patients studied by Bear and Fedio had significant psychiatric histories, often requiring hospitalization, unlike the sample of Tucker et al. The implication here is that the population studied by Bear and Fedio may have been enriched with patients with psychosis and that therefore their finding of increased religiosity was possibly directly related to psychosis and only indirectly related to epilepsy.

However, Roberts and Guberman administered a questionnaire to 57 consecutive patients with epilepsy seen at a general hospital (Roberts & Guberman, 1989). The instrument consisted of 45 questions, including 23 items regarding current interest in religion, three items pertaining to an event such as a religious conversion ("My religious beliefs have undergone major change. There was a period in my life when I suddenly found religion. I have had some very unusual religious experiences.") and three questions regarding paranormal interests, defined in this study as "abnormal interests." The results showed that nearly 60 percent of the subjects had "abnormal interests," and 51 percent indicated a past event such as a religious conversion. There was a significant association between "abnormal" interests, psychopathology, and religious conversion. The significance of these results are somewhat unclear because seizure types were not provided, and there was no control group.

Ogata and Miyakawa interviewed 234 Japanese patients with various forms of epilepsy, including 137 patients with TLE (Ogata & Miyakawa, 1998). Only three patients acknowledged religious experiences during the interviews. Each of these patients had TLE, comprising 2.2 percent of all TLE patients in this series, and each experienced hyper-religiosity interictally and as part of a postictal psychosis, representing 27 percent of patients with postictal psychosis in the overall sample. One patient also had simple partial seizures with symptoms suggestive of a religious experience: "auditory hallucinations of the voice of deities telling her to 'kneel and pray before the gods and Buddha.'" Interestingly, none of the religious experiences of these patients was typical for the Japanese culture.

In a particularly intriguing study, Wuerful and colleagues evaluated 33 patients with refractory partial-onset epilepsy and correlated amygdala and hippocampal volumes on quantitative MRI scans with scores on the religiosity, writing, and sexuality sub-scales of the Neurobehavioral Inventory (Blumer, 1995), an expanded and revised version of the Bear & Fedio scale (Bear, 1979; Wuerfel et al., 2004). They found that hyper-religiosity significantly correlated with reduced right hippocampal volumes. As the authors point out, some patients had frontal lobe epilepsy whereas others had TLE, and yet hyper-religiosity was found in patients with both groups, suggesting that some of the subjects with reduced right hippocampal volume had frontal lobe onset seizures.

CONCLUSION AND DIRECTIONS FOR FURTHER RESEARCH

Do the experiences of patients with TLE suggest that the temporal lobes are responsible for religious experiences and associated behavior? The medical evidence needed to answer this question affirmatively is surprisingly scanty given the sophistication of modern clinical epilepsy research, and, therefore, caution should be exercised in reaching conclusions that are not fully warranted. Descriptions and investigations of ecstatic auras are extremely rare in the literature, and there are no available EEG studies of religious conversions. Further, to the author's knowledge, there are no functional imaging studies (such as PET or SPECT scans) of these transient phenomena. Clearly, additional neurophysological and neuroimaging studies are needed.

It appears to be well established that hyper-religiosity can occur in association with psychosis in patients with epilepsy. But what this means with respect to the temporal lobes is unclear. It would be of interest to determine whether hyper-religiosity is more often seen in patients with TLE and psychosis than in patients with nontemporal lobe onset seizures and psychosis and in nonepileptic patients with psychosis.

Yet the religious experiences described above in association with simple partial seizures or an epilepsy-related psychosis are remarkably similar, suggesting some common underlying neuroanatomical basis and include many of the features of mystical experiences as summarized by Linn (Linn, 1967) and quoted by Runions (Runions, 1979):

1. *Inevitability*. The subject often insists that his experience is inexpressible and indescribable, that it is impossible to convey what it is like to one who has never experienced it.

2. *Noesis*. The subject has the feeling that the mystery of the universe has been plumbed, than an immense illumination or revelation has occurred . . . It seems to consist of layer upon layer of truth that, as it unfolds, may find expression in some familiar or even common-place thought that suddenly seems pregnant with new meaning . . .

3. *Transiency*. The actual mystical state may last only a moment or it may go on for an hour or two . . . It is as unforgettable as it is highly treasured, and it colors all subsequent activity.

4. *Passivity* . . . there is an abeyance of the will, as if the subject were in the grip of a superior power . . .

5. *Unio Mystica*. There is a sense of mystic unity with an infinite power, and oceanic feeling in which opposites are reconciled, in which there are "darknesses that dazzle" and "voices of silence." There is a quality of timelessness, in which minutes and centuries are one and in which the past and the present are one.

However, even if one assumes that ecstatic auras and religious conversions are manifestations of pathologic dysfunction in the temporal lobes of rare patients with epilepsy, it is unclear whether these findings can be generalized to other patients with TLE given the apparent rarity of these findings, or even nonepileptic individuals—both because such experiences may require pathologic activation of neuronal substrates and because functional localization in the epileptic brain is often different than in the nonepileptic brain.

Likewise, hyper-religiosity, as part of an interictal behavioral syndrome in nonpsychotic patients with epilepsy, has not been found in all studies and has not be convincingly localized within the brain. The evidence from studies in nonepileptic subjects is suggestive but not conclusive.

The study of Wuerfel, just described, suggests a structural underpinning of religiosity in the right hippocampus but raises the question of whether epilepsy per se is related or an epiphenomenon. Would nonepileptic subjects with small right hippocampi be hyper-religious?

Finally, it remains to be determined whether a change in religious practices or interests is related to other associated mood disorders or psychosocial aspects of epilepsy. For example, a cognitive model would predict that patients might look for a Higher Power when confronted with an unpredictable problem such as seizures. Qualitative studies of hyper-religious patients with epilepsy would be helpful to explore each individual's perspectives of the determinants of their religiousness and the interrelationships of their religious beliefs and their epilepsy (Ismail, 2005 #9386).

REFERENCES

Au, A., Li, P., Chan, J., Lui, C., Ng, P., Kwok, A., et al. (2002). Predicting the quality of life in Hong Kong Chinese adults with epilepsy. *Epilepsy and Behavior*, *3*(4), 350–357.

Bear, D. M. (1979). Temporal lobe epilepsy—A syndrome of sensory-limbic hyper-connection. *Cortex*, *15*(3), 357–384.

Bear, D. M., & Fedio, P. (1977). Quantitative analysis of interictal behavior in temporal lobe epilepsy. *Archives of Neurology*, *34*(8), 454–467.

Beard, A. W. (1963). The schizophrenia-like psychoses of epilepsy. II: Physical aspects. *The British Journal of Psychiatry: The Journal of Mental Science*, *109*, 113–129.

Berry, D. (2005). Methodological pitfalls in the study of religiosity and spirituality. *Western Journal of Nursing Research*, *27*(5), 628–647.

Beyenburg, S., Mitchell, A. J., Schmidt, D., Elger, C. E., & Reuber, M. (2005). Anxiety in patients with epilepsy: Systematic review and suggestions for clinical management. *Epilepsy and Behavior*, *7*, 161–171.

Blumer, D. (1995). The neurobehavioral inventory: Personality disorders in epilepsy. In J. J. Ratey (Ed.), *Neuropsychiatry of personality disorders* (pp. 230–263). Boston: Blackwell Science.

Bradford, D. T. (1999). Neuropsychology of Swedenborg's visions. *Perceptual and Motor Skills*, *88*(2), 377–383.

Brorson, J. R., & Brewer, K. (1988). St. Paul and TLE. *Journal of Neurology, Neurosurgery, and Psychiatry*, *51*, 886–887.

Caird, D. (1987). Religiosity and personality: Are mystics introverted, neurotic, or psychotic? *The British Journal of Social Psychology*, *26*, 345–346.

Carrazana, E., DeToledo, J., Tatum, W., Rivas-Vasquez, R., Rey, G., & Wheeler, S. (1999). Epilepsy and religious experiences: Voodoo possession. *Epilepsia*, *40*(2), 239–241.

Cirignotta, F., Todesco, C. V., & Lugaresi, E. (1980). Temporal lobe epilepsy with ecstatic seizures (so-called Dostoevsky epilepsy). *Epilepsia*, *21*, 705–710.

DeToledo, J. C., & Lowe, M. R. (2003). Epilepsy, demonic possessions, and fasting: Another look at translations of Mark 9:16. *Epilepsy and Behavior*, *4*, 338–339.

Devinsky, O. (2003). Religious experiences and epilepsy. *Epilepsy and Behavior*, *4*, 76–77.

Dewhurst, K., & Beard, A. W. (1970). Sudden religious conversions in temporal lobe epilepsy. *The British Journal of Psychiatry: The Journal of Mental Science*, *117*, 497–507.

Fisher, R. S., Vickrey, B. G., Gibson, P., Hermann, B., Penovich, P., Scherer, A., et al. (2000a). The impact of epilepsy from the patient's perspective I. Descriptions and subjective perceptions. *Epilepsy Research*, *41*(1), 39–51.

Fisher, R. S., Vickrey, B. G., Gibson, P., Hermann, B., Penovich, P., Scherer, A., et al. (2000b). The impact of epilepsy from the patient's perspective II: views about therapy and health care. *Epilepsy Research*, *41*(1), 53–61.

Foote-Smith, E., & Bayne, L. (1991). Joan of Arc. *Epilepsia, 32*(6), 810–815.

Freemon, F. R. (1976). A differential diagnosis of the inspirational spells of Muhammad the Prophet of Islam. *Epilepsia, 17,* 423–427.

Garcia, A. E. (2003). La epilepsia extatica de Teresa de Jesus [The ecstatic epilepsy of Teresa of Jesus]. *Revue Neurologique, 37*(9), 879–887.

Geschwind, N. (1979). Behavioural changes in temporal lobe epilepsy. *Psychological Medicine, 9,* 217–219.

Gilliam, F., & Kanner, A. M. (2002). Treatment of depressive disorders in epilepsy patients. *Epilepsy and Behavior, 3*(5 Supplement 1), 2–9.

Glaser, G. H. (1978). Epilepsy, hysteria, and "possession." *The Journal of Nervous and Mental Disease, 166*(4), 268–274.

Gramstad, A., Iversen, E., & Engelsen, B. A. (2001). The impact of affectivity dispositions, self-efficacy and locus of control on psychosocial adjustment in patients with epilepsy. *Epilepsy Research, 46*(1), 53–61.

Harden, C. L., & Goldstein, M. A. (2002). Mood disorders in patients with epilepsy: Epidemiology and management. *CNS Drugs, 16*(5), 291–302.

Harrison, M. O., Edwards, C. L., Koenig, H. G., Bosworth, H. B., Decastro, L., & Wood, M. (2005). Religiosity/spirituality and pain in patients with sickle cell disease. *The Journal of Nervous and Mental Disease, 193,* 250–257.

Hauser, W. A., & Hesdorffer, D. C. (1990). *Epilepsy: Frequency, causes and consequences.* New York: Demos.

Hippocrates. (1846). The sacred disease. In *The genuine works of Hippocrates* (pp. 843–858). London: Sydenham Society.

Hughes, J. R. (2005). The idiosyncratic aspects of the epilepsy of Fyodor Dostoevsky. *Epilepsy and Behavior, 7*(3), 531–538.

Ismail, H., Wright, J., Rhodes, P., & Small, N. (2005). Religious beliefs about causes and treatment of epilepsy. *The British Journal of General Practice: The Journal of Royal College of General Practitioners, 55,* 26–31.

Jilek-Aall, L. (1999). Morbus sacer in Africa: Some religious aspects of epilepsy in traditional cultures. *Epilepsia, 40*(3), 382–386.

Johnson, J. (1994). Henry Maudsley on Swedenborg's messianic psychosis. *The British Journal of Psychiatry: The Journal of Mental Science, 165,* 690–691.

Kanner, A. M., & Barry, J. J. (2003). The impact of mood disorders in neurological diseases: Should neurologists be concerned? *Epilepsy and Behavior, 4*(Supplement 3), 3–13.

Koenig, H. G., McCullough, M. E., & Larsson, D. B. (2001). *Handbook of religion and health.* Oxford: Oxford University Press.

Kottek, S. S. (1988). From the history of medicine: Epilepsy in ancient Jewish sources. *The Israel Journal of Psychiatry and Related Sciences, 25*(1), 3–11.

Landsborough, D. (1987). St. Paul and temporal lobe epilepsy. *Journal of Neurology, Neurosurgery, and Psychiatry, 50,* 659–664.

Landtblom, A. (2004). Did St. Birgitta suffer from epilepsy? A neuropathography. *Seizure, 13,* 161–167.

Linn, L. (1967). Clinical manifestations of psychiatric disorders. In A. M. Freedman & H. I. Kaplan (Eds.), *Comprehensive textbook of psychiatry* (pp. 572). Baltimore: Williams and Wilkins.

Loring, D. W., Meador, K. J., & Lee, G. P. (2004). Determinants of quality of life in epilepsy. *Epilepsy and Behavior, 5*(6), 976–980.

MacDonald, D. A., & Holland, D. (2002). Spirituality and complex partial epileptic signs. *Psychoogical Reports, 91*, 785–792.

Mendez, M. F., Cummings, J. L., & Benson, D. F. (1986). Depression in epilepsy. Significance and phenomenology. *Archives of Neurology, 43*(8), 766–770.

Murphy, E. L. (1959). The saints of epilepsy. *Medical History, 3*, 303–311.

Naito, H., & Matsui, N. (1988). Temporal lobe epilepsy with ictal ecstatic state and interictal behavior of hypergraphia. *The Journal of Nervous and Mental Disease, 176*(2), 123–124.

O'Donoghue, M. F., Goodridge, D. M., Redhead, K., Sander, J. W., & Duncan, J. S. (1999). Assessing the psychosocial consequences of epilepsy: A community-based study. *The British Journal of General Practice: The Journal of Royal College of General Practitioners, 49*(440), 211–214.

Ogata, A., & Miyakawa, T. (1998). Religious experiences in epileptic patients with a focus on ictus-related episodes. *Psychiatry and Clinical Neurosciences, 52*, 321–325.

Persinger, M. A. (1984). People who report religious experiences may also display enhanced temporal lobe signs. *Perceptual and Motor Skills, 58*, 963–975.

Persinger, M. A. (1991). Preadolescent religious experience enhances temporal lobe signs in normal young adults. *Perceptual and Motor Skills, 72*, 453–454.

Persinger, M. A. (1993). Paranormal and religious beliefs may be mediated differentially by subcortical and cortical phenomenological processes of the temporal (limbic) lobes. *Perceptual and Motor Skills, 76*, 247–251.

Riggs, A. J., & Riggs, J. E. (2005). Epilepsy's role in the historical differentiation of religion, magic, and science. *Epilepsia, 46*(3), 452–453.

Roberts, J. K. A., & Guberman, A. (1989). Religion and epilepsy. *Psychiatric Journal of the University of Ottawa: Revue de psychiatrie de l'Universitie d'Ottawa, 14*(1), 282–286.

Runions, J. E. (1979). The mystic experience. A psychic reflection. *Canadian Journal of Psychiatry, 24*, 147–151.

Sabaz, M., Lawson, J. A., Cairns, D. R., Duchowny, M. S., Resnick, T. J., Dean, P. M., et al. (2003). Validation of the Quality of Life in Childhood Epilepsy Questionnaire in American epilepsy patients. *Epilepsy and Behavior, 4*(6), 680–691.

Saver, J. L., & Rabin, J. (1997). The neural substrates of religious experience. *The Journal of Neuropsychiatry and Clinical Neurosciences, 9*, 498–510.

Stefanek, M., McDonald, P. G., & Hess, S. A. (2005). Religion, spirituality and cancer: Current status and methodological challenges. *Psycho-Oncology, 14*, 450–463.

Tucker, D. M., Novelly, R. A., & Walker, P. J. (1987). Hyperreligiosity in temporal lobe epilepsy: Redefining the relationship. *The Journal of Nervous and Mental Disease, 175*(3), 181–184.

Waxman, S. G., & Geschwind, N. (1975). The interictal behavior syndrome of temporal lobe epilepsy. *Archives of General Psychiatry, 32*(12), 1580–1586.

Wiggins, J. S. (1969). Content dimensions in the MMPI. In J. N. Butcher (Ed.), *MMPI: Research developments and clinical applications.* New York: McGraw-Hill.

Wilson, S. J., Bladin, P. F., & Saling, M. M. (2004). Paradoxical results in the cure of chronic illness: The "burden of normality" as exemplified following seizure surgery. *Epilepsy and Behavior, 5*(1), 13–21.

Wuerfel, J., Krishnamoorthy, E. S., Brown, R. C., Lemieux, L., Koepp, M., Tebartz van Elst, L., et al. (2004). Religiousity is associated with hippocampal but not amygdala volumes in patients with refractory epilepsy. *Journal of Neurology, Neurosurgery, and Psychiatry, 75,* 640–642.

CHAPTER 9

The Frontal Lobes and the Evolution of Cooperation and Religion

Patrick McNamara

INTRODUCTION

The prefrontal cortex (PFC) constitutes approximately one-third of human cortex and is the last part of the human brain to become fully myelineated in ontogeny, with maturation occurring in late childhood/early adolescence (Huttenlocher & Dabholkar, 1997). The PFC receives projections from the mediodorsal nucleus and gives rise to primary motor cortex, as well as premotor, supplementary motor, and the dorsal and orbital sectors of the prefrontal (proper) lobes. All of these PFC areas send inhibitory efferents onto their sites of termination in other areas of the brain and spinal cord, thus suggesting a supervisory or regulative role for the PFC.

Impairment in prefrontal cortical function in humans is functionally implicated in virtually every major neuropsychiatric disorder including depression (Starkstein & Robinson, 1991), schizophrenia (Lewis, Crus, Eggan, & Erickson, 2004), obsessive-compulsive disorder (Tek & Ulug, 2001), bipolar disorder (Haznedar et al., 2005), Parkinson's disease (Starkstein & Merello, 2002), Huntington's disease (Troster & Woods, 2003), the dis-inhibitory impulsivity syndromes (Berlin, Rolls, & Iversen, 2005), the addictions (Winstanley, Theobald, Dalley, Cardinal, & Robbins, 2006), and several others besides (e.g., memory retrieval dysfunction and the dementias (Cummings & Mega, 2003). The frontal lobes mediate what are believed to be distinctively human mental capacities such as language generativity (Miller & Cummings, 1999), autobiographical memory retrieval (Wheeler, Stuss, & Tulving, 1997), theory of mind (Baron-Cohen, 2004) empathy (Adolphs, Baron-Cohen, & Tranel, 2002), working memory (Goldman-Rakic, 1987), executive functions (Goldberg & Bougakov, 2005), impulse control

(Berlin, Rolls, & Iverson, 2005), volition (Passingham, 1995) and possibly even the sense of self (Northoff & Bermpohl, 2004).

To the extent that religion draws on these putatively distinctly human capacities the frontal lobes likely mediate important aspects of religiosity. We will see that the neurochemistry of the frontal lobes plays a crucial role in support of religious experience.

Neurochemistry of Frontal Lobes

The frontal lobes are densely innervated by dopaminergic (DA) fibers originating in the Ventral Tegmental Area (VTA) and the Substantia Nigra (SN). The nigrostriatal system indirectly influences the frontal lobes through the basal ganglia. The mesocortical system originates in the VTA and termi-nates in the ventral striatum, amygdala, nucleus accumbens, and the frontal lobes. This latter mesocortical system is crucially important for understand-ing human behavior as its stimulation appears to be intrinsically rewarding. All drugs/substances of addiction, for example, appear to derive their addict-ing properties by their abilities to potently stimulate this frontal dopaminer-gic system. Dopamine neurons of the VTA and SN have long been associated with the reward and pleasure systems of the brain. Virtually all of the known addictions (including, cocaine, heroin, amphetamines, alcohol, food, and sex) exert their addictive actions, in part, by prolonging the influence of dopamine on target neurons (Wise, 2005). VTA DA neuron responses appear to be necessary to facilitate formation of associations between stimuli that predict reward and behavioral responses that obtain reward (Schultz et al., 1995). The orbital frontal cortex integrates the most complex level of associations of reinforcement with both stimuli and responses (Rolls, 2004). In summary, stimulation of dopaminergic terminals in the meso-limbic-frontal systems constitutes the substrate for a most potent reward/reinforcing system.

The neurochemistry of the dopaminergic systems of the frontal lobes is shaped by a number of genes and genetic polymorphisms distinct to human beings.

Genetics of PFC

Prefrontal information processing is strongly influenced, though, of course, not determined by, specific genetic factors. Swan and Carmelli (2002) studied 78 dizygotic and 80 monozygotic twin pairs using a test battery of "executive func-tions" linked to the frontal lobes including Digit Symbol Substitution, color–word interference (Stroop), Trail Making B, and verbal fluency. Performance on all measures was adjusted for age and education. Significant genetic influ-ences on performance were observed on each measure (range of heritability: 34–68%). The shared executive factor had a heritability of 79 percent, which is similar to what has been reported by others (Fan, Wu, Fossella, & Posner, 2001) and accounted for 10–56 percent of the genetic variance in performance on each of the four tests. Schoenemann, Budinger, Sarich, and Wang (2000) studied links between brain volumes and cognitive abilities in sibling pairs. The only significant effect described a genetic correlation between frontal lobe volume and performance on the Stroop test. With respect to the issue of heritability of the frontal lobe volumes, one should expect strong effects as whole brain as well as gray and white matter volumes heritabilities are, in general, substantial (Winterer & Goldman, 2003). Pearson and intra-class correlations on frontal brain volumes between monozygotic twins range from 0.6 to 0.9. Geschwind, Miller, DeCarli, and Carmelli (2002) investigated heritability of frontal lobe volumes in 72 monozygotic and 67 dizygotic twins and reported that they ranged from 0.5–0.7 (at least in the left hemisphere).

With respect to specific genes that influence PFC function, the gene that codes for the enzyme *catechol-O-methyltransferase* (COMT), which is involved in cortical dopamine catabolism, is particularly interesting. Statistically significant associations of COMT genotype variations with prefrontal cognitive function have been confirmed (Egan et al., 2001; Joober et al., 2002; Malhotra et al., 2002). The postsynaptic COMT enzyme methylates released dopamine as part of its metabolism to homovanillic acid. Studies in rats, knockout mice, and monkeys suggest that COMT is of particular importance with respect to intrasynaptic dopamine regulation in the prefrontal cortex, where an alternative route of dopamine-removal (i.e., dopamine transporter reuptake as in the striatum) is largely nonexistent. In humans, the COMT gene contains a highly functional and common variation in its coding sequence, at position 472 (guanine-to-adenine substitution), which translates into a valine-to-methionine (Val/Met) change in the peptide sequence. This single amino acid substitution dramatically affects the temperature lability of the enzyme, such that at body temperature the met allele has one-fourth the enzyme activity of the val allele. The met allele, furthermore, appears to be a unique human mutation because it has not been found in great apes, suggesting that it may be a factor in the evolution of the human prefrontal cortex and thereby of human consciousness more generally.

Prefrontal Neurochemistry and Religiosity

There is evidence that dopaminergic systems of the PFC contribute to religiosity:

1. A polymorphism on the dopamine receptor gene, DRD4, has been found to be significantly associated with measures of spirituality and "self-transcendence" on a personality scale (Comings, Gonzales, Saucier, Johnson, & MacMurry, 2000).

2. Disorders of excessive dopaminergic functioning, such as schizophrenia and obsessive compulsive disorder, are often associated with increases in religiosity (Brewerton, 1994; Saver & Rabin, 1997; Siddle, Haddock, Tarrier, & Faragher, 2002; Tek & Uleg, 2001; White, Joseph, & Neil, 1995). Anti-psychotic agents that block dopaminergic actions at the level of the limbic system result in changes (typically diminishment) in religious behaviors and religious delusions in these patients.

3. Hallucinatory agents that purportedly enhance religious or mystical experiences may also enhance dopamine transmission. 5-HT, however, is known to exert tonic inhibitory effects on dopaminergic, particularly in the limbic system, and thus removal of the inhibitory 5-HT influence enhances DA activity resulting in religious and hallucinatory experiences (Borg, Andree, Soderstrom, & Farde, 2003; Iqbal & van Praag, 1995; Robert, Aubin-Brunet, & Darcourt, 1999).

4. Many religious behaviors and basic religious cognitive processes depend on the prefrontal lobes (see McNamara, 2002, for review), and prefrontal system functioning, in turn, is strongly influenced by dopaminergic activity (Goldman-Rakic, 1987).

5. Dopaminergic activity, particularly limbic-prefrontal activity, functions to signal "significant" or salient stimuli (Schultz, Dayan, & Montague, 1997), thus if DA activity is increased due to treatment with dopamine enhancing drugs or to other factors, incoming information will more likely be tagged as overly significant, and a greater number of experiences will be experienced as "highly significant"—a hallmark of religious experiences.

6. Changes in prefrontal function can be associated with changes in religious behaviors (Miller et al., 2001).

Religiosity has traditionally been linked to the temporal lobes (e.g., Dewhurst & Beard, 1970; Bear & Fedio, 1977; Geschwind, 1983; Persinger, 1987). While the temporal lobes undoubtedly play a role in the religious experience, McNamara (2001, 2002) and McNamara, Andresen, and Gellard (2003) have prevented several lines of experimental and clinical evidence implicating the frontal lobes in mediation of a number of religious and ritual practices. The frontal lobes, as mentioned above, are critical for inhibition of impulsive behaviors and likely mediate high level executive functions (Stuss & Benson, 1984), voluntary actions (Passingham, 1995), the sense of self (Edwards-Lee & Saul, 1999; McNamara, Durso, & Harris, 2006) and theory of mind (Brune & Brune-Cohrs, 2006) capacities as well. All of the foregoing mental capacities are fundamental to both religious practices (e.g., prayer) and to cooperative behaviors. It is therefore reasonable to consider a role of the frontal lobes in religiosity. Newberg et al. (2001), using SPECT imaging techniques, have recently documented strong prefrontal activation during meditative states. Similarly, Azari et al. (2001) using neuroimaging techniques, reported greater dorsolateral frontal, dorsomedial frontal, and medial parietal cortex activation during religious recitation in self-described "religious" patients. A more recent study (McNamara, Durso, & Brown, 2006) has demonstrated uncommonly low levels of religiosity in patients with moderate to severe Parkinson's disease—a disease involving loss of striatal and prefrontal dopamine. Dopamine, in fact, has also been shown to be released during meditative practices (Kjaer et al., 2002) and hence may also relate to the ability of religious practices to affect these systems.

Some of the other chapters (e.g., those by Sosis, Bulbulia, Alcorta, McNamara and Emmons, and others) in these volumes argue that religious ritual facilitates cooperation within human groups. In the rest of this chapter, I will argue that one way that religion performs this adaptive function is by tapping the neurochemistry of the prefrontal lobes to support moral, filiative, and prosocial behaviors.

Costly Signaling Theory: The Evolution of Cooperation and Religion's Solution to the Free-rider Problem

The recent application of costly signaling theory (CST) to evolutionary models of religion provides a theoretical model and offers a plausible mechanism for understanding how religion facilitates cooperative interchanges (Sosis, 2003; Sosis & Alcorta, 2003). Costly signals are those behaviors that involve strategic costs to the individual displaying them, costs that extend beyond the baseline costs that all behavioral actions entail, and are therefore hard to fake by individuals not able to bear the relevant costs (Sosis & Alcorta, 2003). Costly signaling theorists have argued that religious behaviors are costly-to-fake signals that advertise an individual's level of commitment to a group, and they view religion's ability to promote cooperation as its primary adaptive function (Irons, 1996, 2001; Sosis, 2003, 2004).

For cooperation to evolve, the problem of the free rider must be overcome. A free rider is someone who takes the benefits of cooperation without paying any of the costs associated with cooperation. They are cheats and exploiters. One way to handle this problem of the free rider is to impose stringent membership conditions for participation in the cooperative group. These membership requirements can serve as hard-to-fake tests (and ultimately signals when the individual adopts them) of an individual's willingness and ability to cooperate with others. What kinds of signals could serve such a role? CST theorists (Irons, 1996, 2001; Sosis, 2003, 2004) have pointed out that a number of religious behaviors, like restrictive diets, participation in rituals and rites, ascetical practices, and altruistic giving might be such signals as these behaviors are both costly and hard-to-fake. It is precisely the costliness of these behaviors or traits that render them effective since individuals incapable of bearing such costs could not maintain the behavior or trait. Free riders would find it too expensive to *consistently* pay the costs of religious behavior and thus could be winnowed out over time of the cooperative group. Most people (even free riders) can sustain a restrictive diet or attendance at ritual services for a short period of time, but few free riders would be willing to engage in such costly behaviors over long periods of time. Thus, for someone who is willing to cooperate, that is, who is willing to pay the costs involved in cooperation, they will need a way to inhibit over a long period of time the kinds of free-rider behavioral strategies that would exclude them from participation in the cooperative group. The frontal lobes provide such strong inhibitory capacities.

Since group members cannot measure directly a person's frontal lobe capacity or the person's willingness to inhibit free-rider behavioral strategies, they will need a different measure of willingness to inhibit free-rider tendencies. Willingness to perform costly religious behaviors for relatively long periods of time can function as reliable signals of willingness to inhibit free-rider strategies and ability to commit to cooperation within the group. Included in such costly religious behavioral patterns are the hard-to-fake *virtues and character strengths*, as free riders would not be willing to incur the costs in developing and practicing such virtues. Sustaining virtuous behavior is, to say the least, difficult. That is why character and virtue cannot be faked, at least not over the long term. Just as ritual and religious practices, *when practiced consistently over time*, help winnow out free riders from the group, so too will development of hard-to- fake character strengths. To act generously and altruistically consistently over time is a convincing indicator of character as it requires the ability to consistently inhibit short-term gratification of selfish impulses.

Religiosity, in short, promotes development of character strengths by facilitating inhibition of free-rider behavioral strategies via the requirement of the adoption of costly programs of behavior. Costly religious behaviors that are practiced consistently over long periods of time and that are associated with inhibition of free rider and exploitative behavioral impulses function as costly and reliable signals of quality and commitment. What could be more effortful or costly than to consistently inhibit appetitive drives around short-time rewards in hopes that such postponement of immediate gratification will pay off sometime down the road? It is a good bet that cooperation with such an individual, an individual who consistently displays virtuous behaviors, would be productive since he or she has, in effect, demonstrated that they could reliably inhibit free-rider appetitive drives/strategies.

Throughout history, religious practices have been the primary, although not exclusive, way that individuals and communities develop and foster these character strengths. Such religious practices, when they are associated with development of character strengths, enhance successful dyadic and group cooperation by signaling the trustworthiness of the individuals involved and their willingness to subordinate individual interests to group goals. Once again free riders would be winnowed out via development of character strengths because free riders would be unwilling or unable to inhibit selfish exploitative impulses in favor of cooperative exchanges. *CST, therefore, predicts that human beings needed to develop the ability to facultatively inhibit powerful impulsive and related free-rider behavioral strategies when seeking to cooperate with, or become a member of, a particular cooperative group.* It follows that the human mind/brain had to develop powerful inhibitory capacities around the suite of impulsive appetitive behaviors that motivate the free-rider behavioral strategy. This inhibitory capacity is precisely one of the best-established and major functions of the frontal lobes (Banyas, 1999; Barkley, 1997; Damasio & Anderson, 2005; Fuster, 1989; McNamara, 2001).

Role of the Frontal Lobes in Development of Cooperative Behavioral Strategies

Studies of potential neural correlates of the individual disposition to cooperate were reviewed recently by Fehr and Rockenbach (2004). Various independent studies show that the frontal lobes are the neural systems most consistently activated in association with decision-making around cooperative dilemmas. Much of this work has involved use of the public goods game. In this game an arbitrary number of players are given tokens that they can either contribute to a project that is beneficial for the entire group (the public good) or keep for themselves. A dilemma of cooperation arises from the fact that all group members profit equally from the public good, whether they contribute or not, and that each player receives a lower profit from tokens contributed to the public good than from tokens retained. A noncooperative player (a free rider) contributes nothing to the public good but benefits nonetheless. Interestingly, in one shot interactions between players of this "public goods" game between 40 percent and 60 percent of the players actually contribute to the "public good," evidencing a considerable amount of cooperation. Consistent, however, with CST predictions regarding the role of time in cooperative group dynamics, cooperation diminishes over time when interactions are repeated beyond one-shot interactions (reflecting perhaps the inability or unwillingness of free riders to sustain cooperative strategies over time). Fehr and Gachter

(2002) showed that cooperation could be restored in these circumstances if free-riding could be inhibited by punishing noncontributors. Interestingly, when participant's brains were scanned during punishment decisions, the striatal-prefrontal dopaminergic system evidenced differentially high levels of activation. This association between the decision to cooperate and prefrontal dopaminergic activity has now been confirmed in several other studies (Blakemore, Winston, & Frith, 2004; de Quervain et al., 2004; Fehr & Rockenbach, 2004). It may be that those individuals who manifest the most consistent disposition to cooperate also evidence high (relative to noncooperators) prefrontal dopaminergic activity.

Prefrontal Cognitive Functions and Prosocial Behavior

As everyone knows, positive emotion toward, or liking potential collaborators can facilitate cooperation. Traditional neuropsychology placed the filiative emotions in the limbic system, but we now know that the limbic system itself is regulated by orbital frontal cortex and the frontal lobes participate directly in emotional processes. Data from clinical lesion studies, electrophysiologic studies, and PET activation studies suggest that the left frontal lobe normally mediates positive emotions and the right frontal cortex mediates negative emotions (see reviews in Bear, 1983; Borod, 1993; Davidson, 1995; Gainotti, Caltagirone, & Zocolotti, 1993; Starkstein & Robinson, 1991; Tucker & Williamson, 1984). Left frontal damage, for example, is far more likely to cause depression than are similar lesions to the right frontal cortex (Royall, 1999; Starkstein & Robinson, 1991). Conversely, lesions in right orbitofrontal cortex are more likely to lead to mania and unconcern than are similar lesions on the left (Bear, 1983; Borod, 1993; Damasio, 1996). Electrophysiologic studies consistently demonstrate right anterior activation during aversive emotional states in both animals and humans (Davidson, 1995). Patients with primary depression perform poorly on tests of left frontal function (indicating release of right frontal function) (see Royall, 1999 for review).

As mentioned above, dopamine neurons of the ventral tegmental area (VTA) and the substantia nigra (SN) that project in the meso-cortical tracts to the frontal lobes have long been associated with the reward and pleasure systems of the brain. Virtually all of the known addictions (including, cocaine, heroin, amphetamines, alcohol, food, and sex) exert their addictive actions, in part by prolonging the influence of dopamine on target neurons (Randolph-Schwartz, 1999; Schultz et al., 1995). VTA DA neuron responses appear to be necessary to facilitate formation of associations between stimuli that predict reward and behavioral responses that obtain reward (Schultz et al., 1995). The optimal stimuli for activating DA neurons are unexpected appetitive rewards, whereas fully predicted stimuli are ineffective. DA activity appears to link stimuli predicting reward to the response-facilitation mechanisms in the nucleus accumbens and basal ganglia.

Inhibition of Anti-social Impulses

All religions claim to promote prosocial behavior, and it must be said that improved empathy and moral insight can be acquired via religious practices. Fundamental to the ability to engage in moral choice, empathy, and prosocial behaviors in general is the ability to delay gratification of one's own impulses. Freud argued that the ability to inhibit sexual and aggressive impulses is a prerequisite for social and civilized behavior. I have argued above that the evolution of cooperation likely depended to some extent on the ability to inhibit short-term appetitive drives associated with free-rider behavioral strategies. If individuals can derive real benefits (e.g., a larger return later) by learning to inhibit current appetitive or consumatory responses, then natural selection would favor those individuals with the ability to delay gratification of impulses. The child's acquisition of the ability to delay gratification of impulses develops in tandem with maturation of the frontal lobes (Samango-Sprouse, 1999). In adults prefrontal lesions are often associated with ECF deficits and disinhibition of drives and aggression (Benson & Blumer, 1975; Fuster, 1989; Pincus, 1999; Schnider & Gutbrod, 1999). One of the most disabling impairments associated with traumatic brain injury (which impacts primarily prefrontal cortex) is loss of the ability to delay gratification of prepotent or previously rewarded responses (Schnider & Gutbroad, 1999). Relaxed inhibitory control over appetitive and sexual drives leads to inappropriate social behaviors that prevent the patient from returning to full functional independence. Early evidence for a role of the frontal lobes in supporting the ability to inhibit impulsivity came from the 1868 report of the physician Harlow on his patient Phineas Gage. Gage, a railway workman, survived an explosion that blasted an iron bar (about 4 feet long and 1 inch wide) through his frontal lobes. After recovering from the accident, Gage's personality changed. He became irascible, impatient, impulsive, unruly, and inappropriate (Benson & Blumer, 1975). The damage had mostly been in the orbitalfrontal region of Gage's frontal lobes.

One way to investigate the role of the frontal lobes in supporting inhibition of the free-rider strategy is to investigate neuropsychological correlates of anti-social behavior. "Sociopaths" are by definition anti-social individuals, and the evidence for prefrontal dysfunction in these individuals is accumulating rapidly (Damasio, Tranel, & Damasio, 1991). Sociopaths typically exhibit an inability to empathize with others, egocentrism, an inability to form lasting personal commitments, and a marked degree of impulsivity. While they may appear to be charming, they evidence serious deficits in expression of the social emotions (love, shame, guilt, empathy, and remorse). On the other hand, they are not intellectually handicapped and are skillful manipulators of others (Davison & Neale, 1994; Spinella, 2005). What little evidence exists suggests that sociopathy is associated with orbitalfrontal dysfunction (Damasio et al., 1991; Smith, Arnett, & Newman, 1992). Dorsolateral function, however, is preserved and would explain the lack of intellectual deficit in these individuals.

The more violent forms of anti-social behavior are also associated with frontal deficits. In their review of the literature on neuroimaging in violent offenders, Mills and Raine (1994) concluded that frontal lobe dysfunction is associated with violent offending. Raine, Buchsbaum, Stanley, and Lottenberg (1994), for example, found that violent offenders (22 subjects accused of murder) evidenced significantly lower glucose metabolic activation levels in medial and lateral prefrontal cortex relative to controls. High sensation seekers, criminals, and other individuals scoring high on measures of impulsivity and aggression also show prefrontal and frontal dysfunction, as well as significantly lower levels than others of the serotonin metabolite, 5-HIAA (see review in Raine, 1993). Serotonin exhibits important modulatory effects on dopaminergic activity in the frontal lobes (Robert et al., 1999). Individuals with psychiatric disorders characterized by disinhibited and aggressive behaviors such as anti-social personality disorder (Deckel, Hesselbrock, & Bauer, 1996), sociopaths (Damasio et al., 1991; Smith et al., 1992), substance use disorders (Tarter, Jacob, & Bremer, 1989), conduct disorder (Moffitt, 1993), and attention deficit hyperactivity disorder (Barkley, 1997; Swanson et al., 1998), have all been shown to perform poorly on frontal lobe tests. McAllister and Price (1987) found that 60 percent of psychiatric patients with prefrontal cortical pathology displayed disinhibited social behaviors, and 10 percent displayed violent outbursts. Heinrichs (1989) showed that the best predictor of violent behavior in a sample of 45 neuropsychiatric patients was a prefrontal lesion.

The Evolution of the Neurochemistry of the Frontal Lobes, Cooperation, and Religion

It may be that in the distant evolutionary past when the mutation that led to the COMT polymorphism regulating aminergic, particularly dopaminergic activity in the frontal lobes, our ancestors began to find that it was unusually easy to feel inclined to affiliate and cooperate with others. What is more, they themselves were better able to inhibit the powerful urge to attempt to take advantage of the cooperative fruits (e.g., killing of large game) of others . . . even over the long term. Thus, these new frontal capacities made long-term cooperative enterprises more feasible by supporting inhibition of the free-rider behavioral strategy and by supporting the building of hard to fake character strengths and the birth of ritual practices more generally.

REFERENCES

Adolphs, R., Baron-Cohen, S., & Tranel, D. (2002). Impaired recognition of social emotions following amygdala damage. *Journal of Cognitive Neuroscience, 14*(8), 1264–1274.

Azari, N. P., Nickel, J., Wunderlich, G., Niedeggen, M., Hefter, H., Tellmann, L., et al. (2001). Neural correlates of religious experience. *European Journal of Neuroscience, 13*(8), 1649–1652.

Banyas, C. A. (1999). Evolution and phylogenetic history of the frontal lobes. In B. L. Miller & J. L. Cummings (Eds.), *The human frontal lobes: Functions and disorders* (pp. 83–106). New York: Guilford Press.

Barkley, R. A. (1997). Behavioral inhibition, sustained attention, and executive functions: Constructing a unifying theory of ADHD. *Psychological Bulletin, 121*(1), 65–94.

Baron-Cohen, S. (2004). The cognitive neuroscience of autism. *Journal of Neurology, Neurosurgery, and Psychiatry, 75*(7), 945–948.

Bear, D. M. (1983). Hemispheric specialization and the neurology of emotion. *Archives of Neurology, 40*, 195–202.

Bear, D. M., & Fedio, P. (1977). Quantitative analysis of interictal behavior in temporal lobe epilepsy. *Archives of Neurology, 34*, 454–467.

Benson, D. F., & Blumer, D. (1975). *Psychiatric aspects of neurological disease.* New York: Grune and Stratton.

Berlin, H. A., Rolls, E. T., & Iversen, S. D. (2005). Borderline personality disorder, impulsivity, and the orbitofrontal cortex. *American Journal of Psychiatry, 162*(12), 2360–2373.

Blakemore, S. J., Winston, J., & Frith, U. (2004). Social cognitive neuroscience: Where are we heading? *Trends in Cognitive Science, 8*(5), 216–222.

Borg, J., Andree, B., Soderstrom, H., & Farde, L. (2003). The serotonin system and spiritual experiences. *American Journal of Psychiatry, 160*, 1965–1969.

Borod, J. C. (1993). Cerebral mechanisms underlying facial, prosodic, and lexical emotional expression: A review of neuropsychological studies and methodological issues. *Neuropsychology, 7*, 445–463.

Brewerton, T. D. (1994). Hyperreligiosity in psychotic disorders. *Journal of Nervous and Mental Disease, 182*, 302–304.

Brune, M., & Brune-Cohrs, U. (2006). Theory of mind-evolution, ontogeny, brain mechanisms and psychopathology. *Neuroscience and Biobehavioral Reviews, 30*(4), 437–455.

Comings, D. E., Gonzales, N., Saucier, G., Johnson, J. P., & MacMurray, J. P. (2000). The DRD4 gene and the spiritual transcendence scale of the character temperament index. *Psychiatrica Genetics, 10*(4), 185–189.

Cummings, J. L., & Mega, M. S. (2003). Neuropsychiatry and behavioral neuroscience (2nd ed., revised). New York: Oxford University Press.

de Quervain, D. J., Fischbacher, U., Treyer, V., Schellhammer, M., Schnyder, U., Buck, A., et al. (2004). The neural basis of altruistic punishment. *Science, 305*(5688), 1254–1258.

Damasio, A. (1996). *Descartes' error: Emotion, reason, and the human brain.* London: Papermac.

Damasio, A., & Anderson, S. W. (2005). The frontal lobes. In K. Heilman & E. Valenstein (Eds.), *Clinical neuropsychology* (4th ed., pp. 404–446). New York: Oxford University Press.

Damasio, A. R., Tranel, D., & Damasio, H. (1991). Individuals with sociopathic behavior caused by frontal damage fail to respond autonomically to social stimuli. *Behavioral Brain Research, 41,* 81–94.

Davidson, R. J. (1995). Cerebral asymmetry, emotion and affective style. In R. J. Davidson & K. Hugdahl (Eds.), *Brain asymmetry* (pp. 361–383). Cambridge: MIT Press.

Davison, G. C., & Neale, J. M. (1994). *Abnormal psychology* (6th ed.). New York: Wiley.

Deckel, A. W., Hesselbrock, V., & Bauer, L. (1996). Antisocial personality disorder, childhood delinquency and frontal brain functioning: EEG and neuropsychological findings. *Journal of Clinical Psychology, 52,* 639–650.

Dewhurst, K., & Beard, A. W. (1970). Sudden religious conversions in temporal lobe epilepsy. *British Journal of Psychiatry, 117,* 497–507.

Durkheim, E. (1995). *The elementary forms of the religious life.* New York: Free Press. (Original manuscript published in 1915)

Edwards-Lee, T. A., & Saul, R. (1999). Neuropsychiatry of the right frontal lobe. In B. L. Miller & J. L. Cummings (Eds.), *The human frontal lobes: Functions and disorders* (pp. 304–320). New York: Guilford Press.

Egan, M. F., Goldberg, T. E., Kolachana, B. S., Callicott, J. H., Mazzanti, C. M., Straub, R. E., et al. (2001). Effect of COMT Val108/158 Met genotype on frontal lobe function and risk for schizophrenia. *Proceedings of the National Academy of Science of the United States of America, 98,* 6917–6922.

Fan, J., Wu, Y., Fossella, J. A., & Posner, M. I. (2001). Assessing the heritability of attentional networks. *BMC Neuroscience, 2,* 14.

Fehr, E., & Gachter, S. (2002). Altruistic punishment in humans. *Nature, 415,* 137–140.

Fehr, E., & Rockenbach, B. (2004). Human altruism: Economic, neural and evolutionary perspectives. *Current Opinion in Neurobiology, 14,* 784–790.

Fuster, J. M. (1989). *The prefrontal cortex. Anatomy, physiology and neuropsychology of the frontal lobe* (2nd ed.). New York: Raven Press.

Gainotti, G., Caltagirone, C., & Zocolotti, P. (1993). Left/right and cortical/subcortical dichotomies in the neuropsychological study of human emotions. *Cognition and Emotion, 7,* 71–93.

Geschwind, N. (1983). Interictal behavioral changes in epilepsy. *Epilepsy, 24*(Suppl 1), 523–530.

Geschwind, D. H., Miller, B. L., DeCarli, C., & Carmelli, D. (2002). Heritability of lobar brain volumes in twins supports genetic models of cerebral laterality and handedness. *Proceedings of the National Academy of Sciences, 99,* 3176–3181.

Goldberg, E., & Bougakov, D. (2005). Neuropsychologic assessment of frontal lobe dysfunction. *Psychiatric Clinics of North America, 28*(3), 567–580.

Goldman-Rakic, P. (1987). Circuitry of primate prefrontal cortex and regulation of behavior by representational memory. In V. Mountcastle & F. Plum (Eds.), *Higher cortical function: Handbook of physiology* (pp. 373–417). New York: American Physiological Society.

Haznedar, M. M., Roversi, F., Pallanti, S., Baldini-Rossi, N., Schnur, D. B., Licalzi, E. M., et al. (2005). Fronto-thalamo-striatal gray and white matter volumes and anisotropy of their connections in bipolar spectrum illnesses. *Biological Psychiatry*, *57*(7), 733–742.

Heinrichs, R. (1989). Frontal cerebral lesions and violent incidents in chronic neuropsychiatric patients. *Biological Psychiatry*, *25*, 174–178.

Huttenlocher, P. R., & Dabholkar, A. S. (1997). Regional differences in synaptogenesis in human cerebral cortex. *Journal of Comparative Neurology*, *387*(2), 167–178.

Iqbal, N., & van Praag, H. M. (1995). The role of serotonin in schizophrenia. *European Neuropsychopharmacology*, *5 Suppl*, 11–23.

Irons, W. (1996). Morality, religion, and human nature. In W. Richardson & W. Wildman (Eds.), *Religion and science: History, method, and dialogue* (pp. 375–399). New York: Rutledge.

Irons, W. (2001). Religion as a hard-to-fake sign of commitment. In R. Neese (Ed.), *Evolution and the capacity for commitment* (pp. 292–309). New York: Russell Sage Foundation.

Joober, R., Gauthier, J., Lal, S., Bloom, D., Lalonde, P., Rouleau, G., et al. (2002). Catechol-O-methyltransferase Val 108/158-Met gene variants associated with performance on the Wisconsin Card Sorting Test. *Archives of General Psychiatry*, *59*, 662–663.

Kjaer, T. W., Bertelsen, C., Piccini, P., Brooks, D., Alving, J., & Lou, H. C. (2002). Increased dopamine tone during meditation-induced change of consciousness. *Cognitive Brain Research*, *13*, 255–259.

Lewis, D. A., Cruz, D., Eggan, S., & Erickson, S. (2004). Postnatal development of prefrontal inhibitory circuits and the pathophysiology of cognitive dysfunction in schizophrenia. *Annals of the New York Academy of Sciences*, *1021*, 64–76.

Malhotra, A. K., Kestler, L. J., Mazzanti, C., Bates, J. A., Goldberg, T., & Goldman, D. (2002). A functional polymorphism in the COMT gene and performance on a test of prefrontal function. *American Journal of Psychiatry*, *159*, 652–654.

McAllister, T., & Price, T. (1987). Aspects of the behavior of psychiatric inpatients with frontal lobe damage: Some implications for diagnosis and treatment. *Comprehensive Psychiatry*, *28*, 14–21.

McNamara, P. (2001). Frontal lobes and religion. In J. Andresen (Ed.), *Religion in mind* (pp. 237–256). Cambridge: Cambridge University Press.

McNamara, P. (2002). The motivational origins of religious practices. *Zygon*, *37*(1), 143–160.

McNamara, P., Andresen, J., & Gellard, J. (2003). Relation of religiosity and scores on verbal and non-verbal fluency tests to subjective reports of health in the elderly. *The International Journal for the Psychology of Religion*, *13*(4), 259–271.

McNamara, P., Durso, R., & Brown, A. (2006). Religiosity in patients with Parkinson's disease. *Journal of Neuropsychiatric Diseases and Treatment*.

McNamara, P., Durso, R., & Harris, E. (2006). Frontal lobe mediation of the sense of self: Evidence from the studies of patients with Parkinson's disease. In A.P. Prescott (Ed.), *The concept of self in medicine and health care.* Hauppauge, NY: Nova Science.

Miller, B.L., & Cummings, J.L. (1999). *The human frontal lobes: Functions and disorders.* New York: The Guilford Press.

Miller, B., Seeley, W. W., Mychack, P., Rosen, H. J., Mena, I., & Boone, K. (2001). Neuroanatomy of the self: Evidence from patients with frontotemporal dementia. *Neurology, 57*(1), 817–821.

Mills, S., & Raine, A. (1994). Neuroimaging and aggression. *Journal of Offender Rehabilitation, 21,* 145–158.

Moffitt, T. E. (1993). The neuropsychology of conduct disorder. *Developmental Psychopathology, 5,* 135–151.

Newberg, A., Alavi, A., Baime, M., Pourdehnad, M., Santanna, J., & d'Aquilli, E. (2001). The measurement of regional cerebral blood flow during the complex cognitive task of meditation: A preliminary SPECT study. *Psychiatry Research, 106*(2), 113–122.

Northoff, G., & Bermpohl, F. (2004). Cortical midline structures and the self. *Trends in Cognitive Science, 8*(3), 102–107.

Passingham, R. E. (1995). *The frontal lobes and voluntary action.* New York: Oxford University Press.

Persinger, M. A. (1987). *Neuropsychological bases of God beliefs.* New York: Praeger.

Pincus, J. H. (1999). Aggression, criminality and the frontal lobes. In B. L. Miller & J. L. Cummings (Eds.), *The human frontal lobes: functions and disorders* (pp. 547–556). New York: Guilford Press.

Raine, A. (1993). *The psychopathology of crime: Criminal behavior as a clinical disorder.* San Diego: Academic Press.

Raine, A., Buchsbaum, M. S., Stanley, J., & Lottenberg, S. (1994). Selective reductions in prefrontal glucose metabolism in murderers. *Biological Psychiatry, 36,* 365–373.

Randolph-Schwartz, J. (1999). Dopamine projections and frontal systems function. In B. L. Miller & J. L. Cummings (Eds.), *The human frontal lobes: Functions and disorders* (pp. 159–173). New York: Guilford Press.

Rappaport, R. A. (1979). *Ecology, meaning and religion.* Berkeley: North Atlantic Books.

Robert, P. H., Aubin-Brunet, V., & Darcourt, G. 1999. Serotonin and the frontal lobes. In B. L. Miller & J. L. Cummings (Eds.), *The human frontal lobes: Functions and disorders* (pp. 125–138). New York: Guilford Press.

Rolls, E. T. (2004). The functions of the orbitofrontal cortex. *Brain and Cognition, 55*(1), 11–29.

Royall, D. R. (1999). Frontal systems impairment in major depression. *Seminars in Clinical Neuropsychiatry, 4*(1), 13–23.

Samango-Sprouse, C. (1999). Frontal lobe development in childhood. In B. L. Miller & J. L. Cummings (Eds.), *The human frontal lobes: Functions and disorders* (pp. 584–604). New York: Guilford Press.

Saver, J. L., & Rabin, J. (1997). The neural substrates of religious experience. *Journal of Neuropsychiatry and Clinical Neurosciences, 9,* 498–510.

Schnider, A., & Gutbrod, K. (1999). Traumatic brain injury. In B. L. Miller & J. L. Cummings (Eds.), *The human frontal lobes: Functions and disorders* (pp. 487–508). New York: Guilford Press.

Schoenemann, P. T, Budinger, T. F., Sarich, V. M., & Wang, W. S. (2000). Brain size does not predict general cognitive ability within families. *Proceedings of the National Academy of the Sciences, 97,* 4932–4937.

Schultz, W., Dayan, P., & Montague, R. (1997). A neural substrate of prediction and reward. *Science, 275*, 1593–1599.

Schultz, W., Romo, R., Ljungberg, T., Mirenowicz , J., Hollerman, J., & Dickinson, A. (1995). Reward-related signals carried by dopamine neurons. In J. Houk, J. Davis, & D. Beiser (Eds.), *Models of information processing in the basal ganglia* (pp. 118–130). Cambridge: MIT Press.

Siddle, R., Haddock, G., Tarrier, N., & Faragher, E. B. (2002). Religious delusions in patients admitted to hospital with schizophrenia. *Social Psychiatry and Psychiatric Epidemiology, 37*(3), 130–138.

Smith, S., Arnett, P., & Newman, J. (1992). Neuropsychological differentiation of psychopathic and nonpsychopathic criminal offenders. *Personality and Individual Differences, 13*, 1233–1243.

Sosis, R. (2003). Why aren't we all Hutterites? Costly signaling theory and religious behavior. *Human Nature, 14*, 91–127.

Sosis, R. (2004). The adaptive value of religious ritual. *American Scientist, 92*, 166–172.

Sosis, R., & Alcorta, C. S. (2003). Signaling, solidarity and the sacred: The evolution of religious behavior. *Evolutionary Anthropology, 12*, 264–274.

Spinella, M. (2005). Prefrontal substrates of empathy: Psychometric evidence in a community sample. *Biological Psychology, 70*(3), 175–181.

Starkstein, S. E., & Merello, M. (2002). *Psychiatric and cognitive disorders in Parkinson's disease.* Cambridge: Cambridge University Press.

Starkstein, S. E., & Robinson, R. G. (1991). The role of the frontal lobes in affective disorder following stroke. In H. S. Levin, H. M. Eisenberg, & A. L. Benton (Eds.), *Frontal lobe function and dysfunction* (pp. 288–303). New York: Oxford University Press.

Stuss, D. T., & Benson, D. F. (1984). Neuropsychological studies of the frontal lobes. *Psychological Bulletin, 95*, 3–28.

Swan, G. E., & Carmelli, D. (2002). Evidence for genetic mediation of executive control: A study of aging male twins. *Journals of Gerontology Series B: Psychological Sciences and Social Sciences, 57*, 133–143.

Swanson, J. M., Sergeant, J. A., Taylor, E., Sonuga-Barke, E. J. S., Jensen, P. S., & Cantwell, D. P. (1998). Attention-deficit disorder and hyperkinetic disorder. *Lancet, 351*, 429–433.

Tarter, R. E., Jacob, T., & Bremer, D. A. (1989). Cognitive status of sons of alcoholic men. *Alcoholism: Clinical and Experimental Research, 13*, 232–235.

Tek, C., & Ulug, B. (2001). Religiosity and religious obsessions in obsessive-compulsive disorder. *Psychiatry Research, 104*, 99–108.

Troster, A. I., & Woods, S. P. (2003). Neuropsychological aspects of Parkinson's disease and parkinsonian syndromes. In R. Pahwa, K. E. Lyons, & W. C. Koller (Eds.), *Handbook of Parkinson's disease* (pp. 127–157). New York: Dekker.

Tucker, D. M., & Williamson, P. A. (1984). Asymmetric neural control systems in human self-regulation. *Psychological Review, 91*(2), 185–215.

Wheeler, M. A., Stuss, D. T., & Tulving, E. (1997). Toward a theory of episodic memory: The frontal lobes and autonoetic consciousness. *Psychological Bulletin, 121*, 331–354.

White, J., Joseph, S., & Neil, A. (1995). Religiosity, psychoticism, and schizotypal traits. *Personality and Individual Differences, 19,* 847–851.

Winstanley, C. A., Theobald, D. E., Dalley, J. W., Cardinal, R. N., & Robbins, T. W. (2006). Double dissociation between seroternergic and dopaminergic modulation of medial prefrontal and orbitofrontal cortex during a test of impulsive choice. *Cerebral Cortex, 16*(1), 106–114.

Winterer, G., & Goldman, D. (2003). Genetics of human prefrontal function. *Brain Research: Brain Research Reviews, 43*(1), 134–163.

Wise, R. A. (2005). Forebrain substrates of reward and motivation. *Journal of Comparative Neurology, 493*(1), 115–121.

CHAPTER 10

Mind Design and the Capacity
for Ritual Performance

Carl Seaquist

Every fall a majority of the population of ancient Athens (including some women and slaves) walked over 18 miles to Eleusis in order to participate in "secret" rites. The festival was among the best known in Greece and is mentioned or discussed by many classical authors, including Pindar, Sophocles, and Aristotle; the earliest written source is the nearly 500-line hymn to Demeter attributed by some of the ancients to Homer. Yet despite or perhaps because of this notoriety, many basic details of the rites remain unclear to modern scholars. Given how widespread attendance was at this festival, the basic elements of performance were well-known to the ancients, but since this was technically a "mystery cult," everyone who attended had to be initiated when they first participated, and with few exceptions the most crucial parts of the performance were only alluded to but never directly discussed in public.

The interpretation of the Eleusinian mysteries would appear, at first sight, straightforward. A cut ear of grain was probably displayed at a key part of the festival, and one of the main plot lines of the *Homeric Hymn to Demeter* tells of the rape of Persephone by Hades and her eventual recovery by her mother Demeter, on the compromise that Persephone spend a part of each year in the underworld during the winter when no plants grow. Most interpreters would therefore say that Demeter and her daughter are vegetation divinities, and that key elements of the ritual[1] were symbolic of the natural course of the year, with plants appearing to die in the winter, only to come back to life in the spring—just like Persephone, who goes to the underworld in the same way as dead mortals, only to rise (unlike mortals) later in the year and return to life.

One may further argue that the myths that went along with this ritual served as a sort of native interpretation of the ritual: after all, the story told in the *Hymn* may be classified as an "aetiological myth," in that it tells the story of the origins of the festival and concludes by telling how Demeter went to the "law-administering kings" and taught them the secrets of her worship (lines 473–485). There are similarly close connections between myths and rituals in many cultures, and scholars have variously conjectured both that rituals are symbolic (they contain coded messages about the world) and that myths are symbolic (they contain messages about rituals or about the world).

If rituals and myths are designed to communicate hidden meanings, then it should not be surprising that their interpretations may not be immediately clear. Showing an ear of grain in silence is a somewhat ambiguous symbol, since the officiant could be pointing to the corn itself, its annual lifecycle, the fact that it has been cut by human hands, an implicit contrast between the rural area in which it was grown and the urban area in which most participants lived, and so forth. Similarly, the myth that went along with the ritual was itself somewhat hard to interpret (it was, after all, narrative rather than expository, and open to the same methods of interpretation as any story), but at least it could help to direct an observer's interpretation of the ritual.

Let us assume that Demeter represents the spring; and Persephone, the plants that grow during the spring but lie as though dead during the winter. Then the story of the rape of Persephone could be viewed as an allegorical narrative, an indirect statement of the fact that plants grow in the spring but not in the winter. Isn't this fact about the seasons rather obvious? Why write a 500-line poem to tell a story that everyone, even little children, know without being told? And why focus on this fact when there are so many other obvious but important facts that don't have long, allegorical poems written about them? If we ask these questions about the myth told in the *Hymn*, we could also ask similar questions about the festival itself. If the goal is simply to instruct people about the seasons, why take a week to do so, to require them to buy and sacrifice a pig, to walk 60 kilometers? The symbolic approach to myth and ritual may seem intuitively obvious, because it has such a strong tradition in both scholarly and popular literature, from antiquity to the present, but there are good reasons to be skeptical of it.

We might think the ritual serves other purposes than the myth. For example, by performing rites in the temple of the goddess, perhaps the ritual serves to thank the goddess for bringing the spring each year, or by praising her to help ensure that she will bring the spring again next year. Such an operative dynamic is what scholars know as *do ut des:* it is as if the worshippers are saying "we give you worship so that you might give us crops next year." We might conclude that the myth is symbolic, but the ritual is practical: the myth only tells a story (maybe a fact about the seasons, maybe the origin of the ritual), but the ritual actually does something useful. Once the spring comes, there are practical means of bringing the crops in, and before the spring comes, there are practical ways of ensuring that it will come. According to this view, ritual should fall under the same category as harvesting. Both would be viewed as skills requiring specialized knowledge, which bring about a specific aim.

There is another way in which rituals tend to be associated with the sacred; consider again the Eleusinian mysteries. The playwright Sophocles said of initiates in the mysteries "three-times happy are those among mortals who have seen these rites and thus enter into Hades: for them alone there is life, whereas for the others all things are bad" (fragment 837, Radt 1985, my translation). It would appear that wealth in this life, in the form of bounteous crops, is one result of participating in the mysteries, and another is a better state in the afterlife. Greek conceptions of life after death were rarely discussed at much length, but if we take Odysseus' journey to the underworld in book 11 of the *Odyssey* as representative, the Greeks imagined that the shades of the dead live a very impoverished life, unable to speak unless sated on blood of the living, just flitting about as shadows of their former selves. If the mysteries guaranteed a better state in the eternity of the afterlife, then the efforts to be initiated in them would seem quite reasonable. No wonder thousands participated every year. Thus, we could theorize that rituals differ from pragmatic actions either because we do not see a connection between their means of attainment and the ends to which they aim, or because their ends seem (regardless of their means) *otherworldly* in their orientation.

I have presented two views of rituals: that they encode information about the world that particular societies find especially important, or that they are practical means of attaining useful ends, like a better harvest or life after death. How should we choose between these options? Is it possible to combine them? This chapter will consider these questions with reference to several theories of ritual, which have been developed in the last 30 years, that apply methods from the cognitive sciences to the study of rituals. In what follows, I briefly summarize[2] the major cognitive theories of ritual, and then try to look for a larger trajectory in this research, by considering some continuities and discontinuities between what may at first appear to be rather disparate theories. My interest is the general terrain rather than each little feature of each theory, so sometimes for convenience of exposition I simplify arguments and glide over terminological distinctions.

SPERBER ON SYMBOLISM

Dan Sperber (1975) proposes that symbolism is best understood not in terms of abstract signs and their meanings that form a system of thought all their own but, rather, as part of our normal patterns of thought about the world. The view that Persephone is a symbol for the plants that die and are reborn is an example of the former view, the one that Sperber rejects. Although this approach to symbolism has been, and continues to be, the most common one among anthropologists, historians, and scholars of literature, my initial remarks should be sufficient to demonstrate that it is far from clear that it is a sensible approach to symbolic materials.

Consider what happened when an ancient Athenian saw grain being harvested. He saw the ear of grain lifted in the air, then dropped into a basket. He would understand what was happening, even if he was from the city and had never observed a harvest before, because he could understand from his previous experience what was happening. He had eaten bread and seen it prepared from raw grain. He knew grain was grown in the fields, and he had in fact seen it growing. When he observed the harvest, he had a context to place it in: he knew how he got there, why he was there, etc. So nothing in the experience seemed deeply surprising to him, though some details of the act of harvesting no doubt differed from what he would have expected. In short, his background knowledge, knowledge of the context of this particular harvest, and general inferential abilities allowed him to understand what he was seeing. Nothing happened to make him think that he was missing something important.

Now, contrast this to the situation where an ear of grain was shown in the mysteries. Here the observer had less context to interpret the action. The grain seemed less likely to be destined for the dinner table, and in fact the whole context (the fact that the ritual was taking place in a temple, the march from the city, the indications that something was *meant* by showing the grain) indicated that something special was going on. But it was not clear what that something special was. So the observer would have searched his memory, trying to identify some fact that would make sense of the action. He would try to reason from previous knowledge, for example, thinking back to times he had observed ritual sacrifices and libations in Athens to develop a context for the current situation.

So Sperber encourages us to think of symbolism as a method, or stage, of reasoning. More precisely, he would have us think of it as the action of the component of the mind that is used in understanding objects and actions that cannot be properly accounted for by normal inferential processes. We can think of normal inferential processes as resulting from the interaction between memory and something we will call the "rational device," that is, the part of the mind that applies logical operations and intuitive psychological understandings of the world to data presented by the senses. When such "rational" thought is not sufficient to interpret a given datum, then another part of the mind comes into play. We can call this the "symbolic device" because it processes what we may call "symbolic" data. We could hypothesize a number of differences between the rational and symbolic devices: perhaps the symbolic device is less constrained in producing output; or it is more likely to reprocess its own output, even with little or no additional inputs; or it can produce multiple outputs simultaneously while marking these outputs as in some way provisional, in other words ready for reprocessing at a later time. In any case, symbolism would be understood as a means of processing data, rather than as a separate type of data.

Sperber argues for a particular theory of mental architecture (i.e., a theory of how the mind is put together and how its various parts interact) much more detailed than my brief characterization can do justice to. Curiously, there has been relatively little substantive criticism of Sperber's theory, with the exception of Toren (1983). It is not my place to present a detailed study here. What I wish to emphasize is that Sperber presents a radically new way of thinking about symbolism. He views symbolism as a mental process rather than a relation between something out in the world and its meaning. Meaning (the meaning of a ritual, or a myth, or a symbol) would count as an output of the symbolic device, but the connection between a sensory input and any semantic output could be highly contingent under such a theory. Two people may need to have similar cultural knowledge and similar means of interpreting symbolic data to reach the same interpretation of a symbol. So the connection between a symbol and its meaning, understanding these in the traditional sense, should not be understood as a fixed fact within a culture but, rather, as, at best, a statistical fact about the likely outcomes of symbolic processing by people within that culture.

I am inclined to date the beginning of cognitive studies of ritual to Sperber's book. After all, every tradition needs its history, even if it is somewhat factitious, and this seems the best place to begin. Of course, the history of processing models of cultural facts goes much farther back, so we could choose to begin with Freud, or even with Anaxagoras. But I would be inclined to consider these as part of the prehistory of cognitive studies of ritual, because of their reliance on dated and inadequate theories of mind. In any case, Sperber's book proposed a general theory of symbolism and devoted little attention to ritual. But the theory is particularly relevant to ritual study, since rituals are nonpropositional in a way that myths or other narratives (since they are expressed in language) are not, and thus they are particularly open to symbolic interpretation. So let us consider Sperber's theory as a first example of a processing model of ritual knowledge, and as a contribution to the study of cognitive architecture. And let us consider the theories I am about to discuss in the context of Sperber's theory of symbolism.

LAWSON AND MCCAULEY'S LINGUISTIC ANALOGY

Though Sperber and Frits Staal[3] presented cognitive theories of religion in the 1970s, it was only after the 1990 publication of E. Thomas Lawson and Robert McCauley's *Rethinking Religion* that scholars first began to consider the cognitive study of religion as a distinct subject in its own right. Their book remains the best-known work in this area, and the subsequent growth of the field owes a great deal to their efforts. Like Sperber, they present a theory of cognitive architecture and focus on the part of the mind that deals with symbolic/religious conceptions. But whereas Sperber feels that mistaken analogies between symbolism and language have kept people from realizing that symbolism derives from a cognitive mechanism, they favor an approach that models religion (in particular ritual) using formal methods from linguistics.

Let us begin with two key elements of Lawson and McCauley's theory: they propose that any proper theory of ritual is a theory of ritual *action*, and that the proper formal analogue of the ritual is the sentence. Furthermore, they think that any ritual, no matter how complex, is ultimately just a single action—perhaps a very complex action, but a single action none the less. Consequently, any ritual could in principle be described by a single sentence (maybe a complex one); let us call such a sentence an "action sentence." They call the part of the mind that generates such action sentences the "action representation system."

Just as a sentence is composed of both words and rules governing their combination in sentences, so the components of the action representation system are word-like elements (which they call "constituents") and rules of combination (or "formation rules") that determine how those elements can be put together to generate a viable action. By analogy to the sentence, Lawson and McCauley propose that ultimately any religious ritual is composed of three parts: two key participants united by an "action complex," which is analogous to a verb (this may govern an optional third participant, the instrument). One participant is an agent (who performs the key action of ritual), and the other is the patient (who has the action performed on him). These correspond roughly to linguistic subject and object. Just as nouns in English can be modified by adjectives and verbs by adverbs, so in Lawson and McCauley's model agents can have properties, as can actions. Whereas any action representation must have an agent, action complex, and object, properties are optional. Call this the "sentential theory of action": actions are like sentences, and the components of actions are like the components of sentences.

The sentential theory of action gets more complicated when Lawson and McCauley propose that any proper mental representation of a ritual contains (in some way) a representation of all the rituals (they call these "enabling actions") that are presupposed by that ritual. Consider the following example (Lawson and McCauley 1990, p. 96): a Christian enters a church and blesses himself with water. The best sentence to describe this ritual is "the parishioner blesses himself by means of water." But this statement doesn't fully communicate the structure of the ritual action. It is only because the water has already been purified that we can use it for this purpose. Any mental representation of the ritual must indicate the full representation of the ritual, including all the enabling actions that lie behind it. So the full action sentence might be something like "the parishioner blesses himself by means of water that has previously been purified by a priest, who was ordained by God." It is this embedding that makes some ritual actions complex: any ritual that presupposes enabling actions can only be described by an action sentence with subordinate, relative clauses.

Now, linguistics not only presents rules that tell us how words get put together to form sentences, it also tells us how those sentences get meanings; this part of linguistics is called "semantics." In Lawson and McCauley's theory, the part of the mind that assigns meanings to rituals is called the "religious conceptual scheme." The mind has another, similar component that assigns meanings to nonritual actions, which we can call the "profane conceptual scheme." These two "conceptual schemes" contain representations of cultural content, in other words, they provide the meanings that we find in rituals and other actions. The action representation system just gives us the form of a ritual; the conceptual schemes provide content to those forms. Think of the action representation system as generating molds: we can add copper or iron to a mold, and the result differs depending on the input metal. But the mold is the same regardless. It is a form devoid of contents.

Interestingly, Lawson and McCauley don't give any reasons for any of the formal apparatus they develop, or the assumptions they make in the initial development of their theory. They hold that cognitive theories of religion have empirical content; in other words, their theory makes predictions that can be verified by evidence from real religions. Thus, they assume that the best current theory will be the one that agrees best with the evidence from actual rituals. So they simply present their theory, in all its complexity, and trust that it will win out over competitors.

Lawson and McCauley make it clear that their ritual theory is inspired by linguistic theory, and the notions of agent, patient, etc. seem clearly linguistic. But it may be that the notion of agent, at least, has other motivations. In McCauley and Lawson (2002), a recurrent subject is "theory of mind," a property that humans but few other animals seem to possess. Theory of mind is the name for the belief that beings other than oneself possess minds. Thus, if I say that Smith has a theory of mind, it means that Smith can recognize Jones as having a mind just like Smith does. Many animals, it would seem, view other animals as little more than automata: they learn to predict their actions but don't think too much about why they behave as they do. An animal with theory of mind may hypothesize that another animal is pushing the fallen tree trunk over because it believes that there might be grubs under it and that the other animal feels hungry. Belief and hunger are properties we feel in ourselves, and the projection of these onto others implies that we believe other creatures have minds similar to ours. A key concept here is agency: when we attribute minds like ours to others, we believe that those creatures can be agents, that they can determine their own goals and work to achieve them. A compass needle may spin around, but we attribute this motion not to a belief that the compass has but, rather, to earth's electromagnetic field. But when a dog spins around, we don't attribute this to an electromagnetic field: we assume it wants to chase its own tail. If Lawson and McCauley's interest in agency is driven by their interest in theory of mind, it is possible that their use of a linguistic analogy is not intended to tell us much about the underlying sentential structure of the mind (in other words, maybe the part of the mind that lets us use language is fairly distinct from the part that lets us use ritual) but, rather, is merely a useful analogy.

RELIGIOUS NATURALISM AND THE CENTRALITY OF RITUALS

To tackle the next part of Lawson and McCauley's theory, I should explain what it means to naturalize religious cognition. Briefly, naturalizing something means understanding it in the context of our broader understanding of how the world operates. Empirical psychology is based on the assumption that all our thoughts and actions are the result of physical processes in the body in reaction to interactions with the outside world that are (in principle, if not always in practice) observable; and that our internal, physical states are the result of genetic blueprints that played themselves out in the process of ontogenetic development. There might be psychological phenomena that cannot be identified with particular physical phenomena, but in some way the physical and the psychological depend on each other, and psychological events result from merely physical processes. Thus psychology is naturalized: it is seen as deriving from natural (in this case, physical) processes. Now, one common approach to religion is known as the "phenomenology of religion." According to this view, religion is something *sui generis;* it is entirely unlike anything else and operates according to its own rules. Thus, while events in the physical world can be explained, the theory goes, there is no way to explain religious phenomena like (for example) conversion: our understanding of the natural world simply doesn't account for religious phenomena. So religious phenomena aren't natural (they might, of course, be *supernatural*). A phenomenological psychology of religion, then, would not be naturalistic. It would operate according to different rules than the rest of psychology. A naturalistic psychology of religion, in contrast, would explain religious cognition in the same way that it explains other types of cognition. And everyone who works in the cognitive study of religion is a naturalist.

Lawson and McCauley want a naturalized psychology of religion, so they want to be able to explain how people conceptualize ritual actions in the same way they would any other type of (merely profane) action. They thus propose that, once we have a formal analysis of some ritual, we should look at where the supernatural being occurs in the ritual's action sentence. It may be in the agent slot, or the patient slot, of the main clause in the sentence, or it may be agent or patient in one of the relative clauses representing embedded actions. Note that we can expect a supernatural being[4] to be somewhere in the representation of the action precisely because the action is a ritual: rituals draw their content from the religious conceptual scheme, and this is the scheme that allows us to conceive of supernatural beings. If all the agents and objects were profane, then the action could be represented without using the religious conceptual scheme, and the action would not be a ritual. Other than the fact that a supernatural being occurs someplace in the action sentence, their analysis of ritual structure is basically the same as their analysis of action structure. This is how their theory is naturalistic: rituals are represented like any other actions, but for the one small difference that some of their participants are held to be supernatural beings.

Lawson and McCauley go on to argue that a number of properties of rituals can be predicted by looking at where the supernatural being occurs in the action sentence.

First, they present a hypothesis regarding how central a ritual is a to religious tradition. Through interviewing religious people, it is possible to determine how central a ritual is to the overall framework of a particular religion. It might not be possible to communicate the notion of centrality to interviewees, but it should be possible for scholars to identify the relative centrality of particular rituals by talking to people who practice the religion in question. Lawson and McCauley then claim that centrality will correspond to how deeply the clause containing the supernatural being is embedded in the action sentence. In the example given above ("the parishioner blesses himself by means of water that has previously been purified by a priest, who was ordained by God"), there were three clauses: in the first the main action was blessing; in the second, purification; in the third, ordination. The embedding of clauses stopped then because a god figured in the third clause. This ritual is more central than one that requires four clauses, but less central than one that requires two. This aspect of the theory constitutes a hypothesis because the relative centrality of a given ritual can be anticipated, before informants are consulted, by looking at the level of clausal embedding of the relevant supernatural being in the action sentence for that ritual.

Second, they argue that "special agent rituals" (those in which the relevant supernatural being is the agent of the action) have certain properties. They are reversible but nonrepeatable: there are rituals that can reverse the results of these rituals (for a marriage ceremony there is, in principle, a divorce ceremony), but in general there is no need to repeat these rituals, since once they have effected a result, that result is fairly permanent. Special patient rituals, in contrast, are repeatable but nonreversible. Similarly, special agent rituals tend to be performed less often than special patient rituals, because they need not be repeated, and they tend to be associated with greater sensory stimulation. A tedium effect comes into play with frequently repeated rituals, so over time they tend to be performed with less sensory stimulation.

THE DEFINITION OF RELIGION

Let me pause briefly to summarize the overall structure of Lawson and McCauley's theory. Rituals are actions, and their overall form is analogous to a sentence. What differentiates them from profane actions is the role that supernatural agents play; supernatural beings are represented in the religious conceptual scheme, and when meaning is added to the bare form of the action sentence, some of that meaning comes from the religious conceptual scheme. This theory naturalizes rituals because the basic framework can be used to explain profane actions as easily as ritual actions. So the only thing that makes rituals special (makes them a clear subset of actions generally) is the role of supernatural beings.

As it happens, the argument that what is unique and special about religions is belief in supernatural beings is gaining traction[5] in the cognitive study of religion, in part due to Lawson and McCauley's efforts. This separates it from a dominant strain of thought in religious studies more broadly, where many people would argue that there are religions that don't require belief in supernatural beings. Classical Buddhism is a common example. If everything is, in a deep and mystical sense, one rather than many, then there really isn't a distinction between morals and immortals. Distinctions of any kind aren't real, this one included. But Lawson et al. argue that no real Buddhists believe this, or at least none that really count. In practice, Buddhists worship gods in much the same way that Hindus do, and in fact "real" Buddhism, that is, Buddhism on the street rather than in theological treatises, is heavily involved in the worship of all manner of gods. So Lawson and McCauley hold that supernatural conceptions are the defining quality of religions, and they feel that the goal of a naturalistic theory of ritual is to explain how the cognitive processes that are used for profane purposes also allow people to form conceptions of supernatural beings.

But I will propose that it is possible to naturalize religious cognition without defining religious cognition as thought about supernatural beings. People who subscribe to a wide range of definitions of religion can still agree on what phenomena count as religious, and thus it is reasonable to hope that we can make progress understanding (and naturalizing) religious cognition without subscribing to some particular definition of religion. Lawson and McCauley want to naturalize religion but still make a firm divide between religious and profane beliefs. I am proposing that we need not presume such a firm divide. Maybe religions can be set on a continuum, with some (like Classical Buddhism) looking rather unlike what we think of as prototypical religion, and maybe other traditions that we don't consider to constitute religions (like Marxism) nevertheless share many features with religions. We can similarly assume that mental representations of religious phenomena are on a continuum, with prototypical cases being clearly dependent on belief in supernatural beings.

I will leave it for the reader to determine whether this points to a problem for Lawson and McCauley's theory. I think it does present significant problems, but I won't lay my case out in detail here. Let me just say this. Perhaps the joining of the religious conceptual scheme to the action representation system is jerry-rigged: maybe they try to join two models that don't fit together particularly well. If the religious conceptual scheme accounts for all of the religious content of rituals, and the action representation scheme accounts for all of the structural features of rituals, then there is nothing particularly religious about ritual actions (in other words, all the religious features are exogenous to them as actions).

McCauley and Lawson (2002) is largely focused on contrasting their theory with Whitehouse's, so let me now turn to Whitehouse, and return to Lawson and McCauley later.

WHITEHOUSE'S MODES OF RELIGIOSITY

Harvey Whitehouse is an anthropologist whose field research was carried out on New Britain, an island off the coast of New Guinea. The village in which he worked was a center of a type of religion known as a "cargo cult," and around the time of his arrival, it was being swept up by a charismatic heterodoxy. Thus, he was faced with mapping the interrelationship between two different types of religion, the "traditional" cargo cult (called the Pomio Kivung) and the innovative new religion that was evolving under his very eyes. The general theory of ritual that he proposed to account for his observations thus relied on an opposition between two poles corresponding to these two types of religion. But he makes it clear that the two poles are not distinct types of religion. The new religion he found in the village of Dadul had much in common with the cargo cult from which it evolved, but with significant differences. When Whitehouse speaks of the two poles, he calls them "modes," and he argues that all religions are somewhere on a continuum, often exhibiting aspects of both modes but tending to emphasize one at the expense of the other. The "imagistic mode" is the older of the two, he argues, and paleolithic religions were purely imagistic, but most contemporary religions exhibit aspects of the "doctrinal mode," sometimes to the near exclusion of the imagistic.

Toward the end of his ethnographic monograph *Inside the Cult*, Whitehouse (1995)[6] presents a table intended to highlight the key differences between these modes (p. 197), and by examining this, we get an idea of what he means by the term "mode" (he never really defines the word, and to some extent it appears to be pretheoretical, as if no further clarification of what it means is necessary). Thus, for example, religions in the doctrinal mode rely on verbal expression; are highly repetitive; spread by proselytization; and can occur over wide areas. Religions in the imagistic mode tend toward iconic imagery (i.e., their symbols lend themselves naturally to particular kinds of interpretation) without the need for verbal explanation; can have rituals that are performed very infrequently; and are hard to spread because they tend to occur only locally.

If these modes were types of religions, we could in principle demonstrate that known religions fall into one category or the other, and not into other categories that we could define (e.g., religions that rely on iconic imagery but occur widely). Then we could say that we had naturalized the modes of religiosity by demonstrating that naturally occurring religions belong to a discrete set of types. But Whitehouse makes it clear that the modes are not types of religions, and that most contemporary religions exhibit elements of both modes. Then it is not clear why he believes there are precisely two modes or what explanatory function the modes of religiosity serve. Why not identify a third mode, characterized by iconic imagery and wide distribution, or a fourth, or a fifth? Or why not identify a certain number of axes (Whitehouse proposes 13 "variables" in his characterization of the modes) and plot any given religion in a complex space defined by these 13 axes?

Part of the answer can be found when Whitehouse compares his imagistic/doctrinal distinction to similar distinctions that are well established in the anthropological literature, for example, Lewis' contrast between central and peripheral cults or Turner's between fertility rituals and political rituals. He argues that his distinction picks up on many of the same intuitions and makes sense of much of the data that motivated these other distinctions but that it is superior precisely because it is founded on a more sophisticated and scientific psychology. Clearly, he thinks the agreement among scholars that rituals can be divided into two categories lends credence to the belief that some natural distinction underlies all these various theories. And he believes that his theory best accounts for that distinction.

It is perhaps useful to consider next Whitehouse's discussion of the field-work that Frederik Barth conducted among the Baktaman of New Guinea. The Baktaman perform complex and highly secretive rites of passage (rituals used to advance a group of people to the next stage in their life course), and because they are a small society, these rituals may only be performed once every 10 or 20 years. A student of ritual may reasonably ask how it is that the Baktaman remember how to perform these rites, since they have so little practice in performing them, and there is a prohibition on speaking of their details in public. In seeking to answer this problem, Whitehouse points to a line of research examining "flashbulb memory," a type of memory used to store details of highly unusual experiences that an individual takes to be of great importance.

Most memories, it is now widely acknowledged, make use of "scripts," or typical sequences of events that tend to recur. We usually think of memories as being like movies, which we can run through our heads when we want to recall some detail from the past. But in fact it takes a great deal of space to store digitized movies on a computer, and similarly it would take a great deal of capacity to store our memories as movies in our brains. For most events, we may recall salient details, but in general we remember details not of particular events but, rather, of typical events (this Whitehouse calls "semantic memory"). If asked what I had for dinner last week, I may respond meatloaf, white potatoes, and green beans, when in fact I had lima beans instead: that is, if I generally have green beans with meatloaf, then I may have a "meatloaf script" that entails eating green beans along with meatloaf. I may only remember that the store was out of green beans, so I bought limas instead, if this event was sufficiently significant to me to justify my maintaining a specific memory of the event. Otherwise, I may simply rely on my generic meatloaf script and remember, erroneously, that I had green beans that night.

We remember lots of details about an event, the theory goes, only in unusual situations, when the details really matter, or when our senses are heightened by great emotional stimulation, for example, fear. Many people remember where they were when they heard that President Kennedy was killed, or when they saw the first footage of the Challenger disaster, or learned that the Twin Towers had been destroyed. These would be examples of flashbulb memories. Whitehouse argues that the emotions and intense sensory stimulation of Baktaman initiation rites, which are in great contrast to the rather mundane daily life of these people, would seem adequate for the formation of flashbulb memories. The cargo cult from which the new religion derived, however, is at the doctrinal end of the spectrum. Its methods of worship, and the means by which it is taught, rely heavily on missionary Christianity and thus place great emphasis on enforcing uniformity in ritual practice as a means of maintaining doctrinal orthodoxy. Correct ritual practice in such a religion could be expected to rely on semantic memory.

In short, the contrast between imagistic and doctrinal modes is paralleled, and underwritten, by the contrast between flashbulb and semantic memory. This reliance on distinct types of memory in turn serves to naturalize Whitehouse's theory. After all, the two types of memory are used for remembering all kinds of facts, not just religious facts, and they account for the contrast between religions. But it would seem unusual if a particular religion made use of only one type of memory to the exclusion of the other, since both types of memory are used in day-to-day cognition. This is consistent with Whitehouse's position that religions need not adhere only to one or the other of his modes. Just as people in all contemporary societies use both types of memory, so their religions can have elements of both modes.

WHITEHOUSE VERSUS MCCAULEY AND LAWSON

Recently the small field of cognitive studies in religion has started to coalesce around two dominant paradigms, those of McCauley and Lawson and that of Whitehouse. This is in part a result of their own efforts: McCauley and Lawson (2002) in their latest book, *Bringing Ritual to Mind*, present their theory explicitly as an alternative to Whitehouse's. They argue that their theory and Whitehouse's differ primarily in the empirical predictions that they entail, and consequently that carefully designed studies of contemporary and historical religions can select between the two theories. Whitehouse, meanwhile, has gained the funding to establish a research center at Queen's University in Belfast and is working to assemble an interdisciplinary team to consider a wide range of religions in the context of the modes of religiosity theory. Both sides, in other words, believe that the difference between their theories can be determined by demonstrating which agrees better with actual evidence.

There are a number of elements to this dispute. McCauley (1999) had argued that Whitehouse's treatment of flashbulb memories was somewhat naive and not supported by more recent research; this challenge recurs at some length in McCauley and Lawson (2002). Whitehouse (2000) responded to some of this criticism but without substantially changing his theory. Similarly, Whitehouse (2004) held up particular rituals as counterexamples to Lawson and McCauley's theory. This is not the place to resolve these disputes. Other, and perhaps more critical, issues have received less attention thus far, and it is to some of these that I turn.

Lawson and McCauley presented their original thesis as a whole, without giving any motivation for its various parts. As I read them, they believe that the best theory of ritual cognition will agree best with the facts about particular rituals. But it isn't clear that what they present is really an empirical theory: it is not clear, in other words, that counterexamples to their theory are even possible. It isn't clear that there is any way of measuring the degree of sensory stimulation in a ritual,[7] and the idea of centrality of a ritual is still rather murky (Lawson and McCauley's theory predicts how central a ritual should be, based on its form, but it is not clear that these predictions could be verified). In this context, it is interesting and perhaps significant that one of the most penetrating criticisms of the Whitehouse-Lawson-McCauley debate is given by Scott Atran (2002, pp. 290–292) only in a (rather long) footnote. Among other observations, he points out that "there are really no clear cases for trying to choose between the two models because there are no reliable methods for evaluating cases."

And the theory does not appear to be very rich. It purports to be a general theory of how rituals are represented in the mind, but in practice it appears to serve mostly as the motivation for several "hypotheses," for example that more frequently performed rituals will display less sensory stimulation. This seems a rather obvious generalization, one that hardly requires an elaborate theory to justify it. If an explanation is necessary, we might want to look to economics rather than cognitive science: elaborate rituals with great amounts of sensory stimulation require a lot of time and (often) material resources to stage, so there is a practical limit to how often they can be performed. Curiously, Whitehouse argues that among the Pomio Kivung rituals he observed, the most frequent ones were also the most "complex and elaborate" (Whitehouse 1995, p. 66): since this is somewhat contrary to our expectations, such a fact would appear in greater need of explanation than its opposite.

Another odd feature of Lawson and McCauley's theory: we might imagine a budding priest learning first one ritual, then another, but this would be, strictly speaking, impossible according to the theory, unless the priest began at the beginning, with Jesus instituting the Christian church—a real example, according to Lawson and McCauley (1990, p. 114). Their theory implies that a Christian cannot bless himself with water, in other words he cannot know to[8] perform the actions such that they constitute that ritual, unless he knows that Jesus founded the church. It would appear that it is impossible to know how to correctly perform rituals unless one knows the correct, orthodox theology that underlies those rituals. A person can, curiously, correctly perform rituals without a knowledge of theology, but he would not know that he was performing that ritual, even if he knew he was doing the same actions as other people, and even if he knew the name and purpose of the ritual. Lawson and McCauley's theory really seems to be about understanding the orthodox theology behind rituals, rather than about knowing how to perform them.

Yet Whitehouse criticizes them for "restricting themselves to the problem of explaining how ritual *procedures* are transmitted, rather than how *ritual meanings* are reproduced and transformed" (Whitehouse 2004, p. 145). When he draws attention to the doctrinal aspect of ritual, Whitehouse is emphasizing the fact that rituals often are learned and transmitted as vessels for doctrine, that is, for theology. I began this chapter by considering the *Homeric Hymn to Demeter* to emphasize that often myths are viewed as means of understanding rituals; there is a significant quantity of scholarship that sees the relation between action and word (ritual and myth) in this way.

But Whitehouse picks up on another trend in scholarship, which sees ritual as a handmaiden for doctrine. His point may be valid. Some rituals could be preserved precisely because they are vehicles for doctrine. Unfortunately, it isn't clear that his theory is the best way of pursuing this claim. The theory draws attention elsewhere, for example, to memory and cognition, when really this claim depends more on the social context of ritual.

It would appear, then, that the theories of both Whitehouse and Lawson and McCauley focus our attention on the meanings that people attribute to rituals. Whitehouse does so explicitly, whereas Lawson and McCauley claim to focus on the structure of ritual representations, though these structures tell us more about theology than about "ritual procedures." We find a radically different take on the question of meaning in the work of Frits Staal, to which we turn now.

STAAL AND RITUAL COMPLEXITY

The ritual theory of Frits Staal[9] shares some similarities to the last two theories I have considered. It is like Lawson and McCauley's in that it takes the analogy between ritual and language seriously, and it is like Whitehouse's in that it focuses attention primarily on memory. Staal's theory originates in fieldwork, like Whitehouse's. In the 1960s, he studied the recitation of Vedic mantras (hymns) among a small group of Brahmans in South India, and in the 1970s he came back and observed the performance of a highly complex ritual, which took 12 days and 17 priests (plus numerous helpers) to perform, called the Agnicayana. At the time, the ritual had only been performed 17 times in the previous century, in part because of the expense involved in staging it. The results of this research are contained in Staal (1983), a massive, two-volume study of the ritual as it was performed in 1975 and in comparison to its canonical form as presented in a series of ancient Indian ritual texts. These texts describe every ritually significant action that must be performed over the course of 12 days, and Staal's need to compare the actual ritual, as it was performed, with these ritual texts led him to study the sequencing of the ritual, act by act, in a way that is very rarely done by scholars.

I recently had the opportunity to discuss Staal's theory before a seminar composed of computational linguists, and they were surprised to learn that very few ritual scholars study in detail the actions that are performed in the course of carrying out rituals. "What do ritual scholars study, if not ritual?" was a sensible question that I had no good answer for. Ritual scholars usually study the social context of ritual, and they try to discover the explicit and hidden meanings of rituals, but they rarely describe the rituals they have observed in great detail. Staal's empirical researches are important not only because the complexity of the Agnicayana is far greater than that found in most rituals, but also because of the detail with which the performance was described. And the uniqueness of his general theory of ritual stems largely from the uniqueness of his field and textual research.

Like Lawson and McCauley, Staal tries to provide a formal analysis of the structure of religious ritual, and like them he takes the formal apparatus for his analysis from modern linguistic theory. But whereas Lawson and McCauley begin with an a priori analysis (they assume that the structure of ritual is the structure of the sentence), Staal begins with actual, observational facts. And while Lawson and McCauley assume at the outset that they know the exact rules governing ritual structure (see Lawson and McCauley, 1990, p. 100), Staal merely argues for the general form of such rules, leaving the details to be determined by further, empirical study. He describes some simple patterns found in the Agnicayana and other Vedic rituals and attempts to demonstrate that even the most complex rituals in the Vedic tradition are composed of relatively simple actions, by means of two types of rules: phrase structure rules, which generate action sequences from individual (atomic) actions, and transformation rules, which act on the resulting sequences and change them into different sequences. Whereas Lawson and McCauley begin by assuming that each ritual, no matter how complicated, is represented in the minds of participants as a single action (it achieves a single purpose), they never explain how it is that a ritualist knows what to do next, at any given moment in the performance of a complex ritual. What they present is not really a theory of ritual structure, but of the structure of ritual interpretations, in other words, an account of what rituals mean. Staal, in contrast, begins with the sequencing of actions and shows how ritualists can remember extremely complex sequences of actions, sequences so long and detailed that they may seem to present human memory with insuperable challenges. The Agnicayana, after all, lasts for 12 days, and one of the priests is responsible for knowing the entire ritual and being able to catch and correct errors that may be performed by the other priests. How does he remember how the ritual should go, especially when the ritual is performed so seldom?

Staal's answer[10] is that priests don't remember these indefinitely long sequences of actions, because that would indeed be too difficult. Rather, they remember how to perform individual actions, such as pouring liquid out of a vessel, placing small offerings in a fire, or laying a brick on an altar, and they have a general representation in their minds of the overall structure of the ritual. Then they know how to sequence particular actions by applying a small set of rules recursively, and this is sufficient to successfully guide their actions throughout even the most complex rituals.

The key here is recursion. In the early 1950s, in the process of trying to find the most general principles that govern the human ability to use language, Noam Chomsky discovered that it is possible to order all possible languages (not just natural languages like English or Japanese, but also artificial languages like programming languages or mathematical languages) in a sequence from most complex to least complex. A rough sorting of languages into four categories is today known as the "Chomsky hierarchy," and this is the locus classicus for discussions of the complexity of languages. The general theory of language complexity has proved to have significant practical applications, particularly in computer science, and has been important to the design of computer compilers. The reason is clear: more complex languages require greater computing power to "parse" (or, roughly speaking, to understand) than a simpler language would, and it is crucial for computer scientists to design programs that can deal successfully with the inputs they receive. Otherwise, programs will crash, or run indefinitely without producing output, or produce the wrong output, and then they are at best useless.

If we think of the human brain as a type of computer, then we see how this problem applies to human cognition. By studying the complexity of natural languages, we learn the minimum processing capabilities of the human brain, since we have plenty of evidence that humans can use natural languages. Your ability to read this book is proof enough of that. And Staal's key argument, in a nutshell, is that the "language" of Vedic ritual is of the same level of complexity as natural languages like English or Japanese.

Staal draws two conclusions from this observation. First, he argues that rituals are per se meaningless. People can, and do, attribute all sorts of meanings to rituals, and we have seen that the identification of ritual meanings is one of the main research projects in ritual studies, but those meanings may tell us more about the people attributing them to rituals than they do about the rituals themselves. Staal argues that to perform a ritual, a ritualist need not have a mental representation of the meaning of the ritual, but he does need to have a representation of the actions to be performed and their sequencing. In fact, many of the ritualists he spoke to did not seem to attribute any meanings to their rituals, and some ancient philosophers and ritualists writing in Sanskrit had argued that rituals are in fact meaningless. So Staal believed he had empirical and theoretical support for this view, though it is very much contrary to the standard position among modern ritual studies scholars.[11] This brings us back to my observations at the beginning of this chapter. Maybe, as Sperber argued, three decades ago rituals are not primarily devices for communicating hidden meanings. Maybe they are simply practical activities, which tend to get meanings attributed to them, perhaps because their purposes deal with hidden matters that are not easily observed (like a good life after death) or because the connection between their means and their ends is not always obvious.

In any case, if rituals are meaningless, then the goal of ritual studies should not be to identify the meanings of rituals, since that would clearly be pointless. Rather, we should focus attention on how rituals are performed, and similarly the cognitive study of ritual should focus on how people know how to perform rituals. It isn't necessary to assume that rituals are meaningless, however, to realize that it should matter to ritual studies how rituals are performed (and how ritualists learn and remember how to perform rituals). The interaction of form and meaning may well be the next big question for the cognitive study of ritual, and the study of how rituals are performed[12] definitely should be included.

In Seaquist (2004) I argue that Staal's claim that rituals are meaningless is not as radical as some people might believe. He allows that rituals can be meaningful in all sorts of ways (e.g., people can attribute meanings to rituals, and rituals can serve social functions like enhancing group solidarity), but not in the one way that is most important in the context of his comparison of ritual to language. Linguistic meaning is compositional; in other words, the meaning of an entire utterance is a function of the meanings of each component. "The boy hit the ball" does not have the same meaning as "the boy hit the television" because the two sentences do not contain exactly the same words, and the difference between those sentences lies just in the difference between their component words. If rituals have the same structure as linguistic utterances, and given that utterances can be meaningful due to compositional semantics (their parts individually contributing to and collectively constituting their meanings), we would expect that ritual meanings would also be compositional. But this doesn't seem to the case. Whenever someone proposes the meaning for a given ritual, that meaning doesn't seem to be a compositional function of the parts of the ritual. Therefore whatever meanings rituals have, they are imposed on them from the outside: they don't derive from the ritual itself. Thus, when Staal argues that rituals are meaningless, he is not arguing that we can't find meanings in rituals but, rather, that, in some rather important sense, the meanings that we find aren't really in the ritual at all.

Second, Staal concluded that the capacity to perform rituals is just the capacity to use language (in the sense that both types of performance are exercises of the same underlying ability, though in different arenas) and that ritual is older than language. His arguments here are rather rudimentary: for example, his claim that animals have ritual but not language may best be viewed as a simplification of the work of early ethologists like Konrad Lorenz. But the other chapters in this book give ample indication that the intuition behind the theory is worthy of further investigation, and curiously the trend in recent scholarship is to support Staal's basic intuition, which seemed bizarre to most readers when it was first presented in the late 1970s.

CONCLUSION

It may benefit ritual studies to borrow observations, methods, or theories from the cognitive sciences, but this by itself does not make for a cognitive

224224224224224224224224224224224224224224224224224224224224224224224224224224224224224224224224224224224ффф224244ффф

theory of ritual: A true cognitive theory of ritual will have to contribute to our understanding of the structure of the human mind. I therefore have tried to indicate ways in which ritual studies scholars have attempted to increase our understanding of mental architecture. Sperber made a good start at this in the mid-1970s, but there has been very little attempt to build on this foundation. In fact, the continued obsession in the scholarly literature with trying to find the real meanings of rituals has obscured the message that we ought to take from Sperber's work. Staal makes a serious claim about the structure of the ritual faculty, and his theory is indeed a contribution to cognitive science. Yet the near-universal misunderstanding of his theory has prevented people[13] from building on his work.

Lawson and McCauley claim to present a theory of cognitive architecture, but the formal side of their theory really just models the interrelationships that they see between rituals and sheds little or no light on the way rituals themselves are represented in the mind. Besides their claim that rituals are represented as actions, their formal analysis only serves to show how rituals can be represented as depending on previous rituals for their efficacy. A quick look at any of the tree diagrams in Lawson and McCauley (1990) shows that deep and surface structures of rituals are basically the same, except that one ritual is embedded in another in the sense that a later ritual cannot be performed unless another ritual was performed (or rather, is believed to have been performed) sometime in the past. An example would be the Christian mass, which requires that at some time in the past the officiating priest was ordained. Contrast this with the sense in which Staal speaks of embedding: namely, when the performance of one ritual includes the performance of another as a proper part, as when a mass requires the performance of the Eucharist as a part of its performance.

Whitehouse's theory seems to be more clearly a case of using cognitive theory to explain rituals, rather than a contribution to cognitive science in its own right. But inasmuch as representations in an individual's mind might depend on larger social processes, his theory might contribute to the cognitive sciences, in particular, to discussions of the "extended mind." This phrase comes from an article by David Chalmers and Andy Clark (1998) and refers to the theory that cognition extends beyond the skull and the software that it contains, with the result that in some sense it contains objects that aren't even part of a person's physical body.

I have tried throughout this chapter to introduce topics that cut across all the theories that I have considered, such as the role of naturalism in cognitive theories and the relative importance of studying ritual structure and meaning. Another interesting problem, which I have addressed perhaps less directly, is the curious fact that the people who have contributed most to the field have generally misrepresented the significance of their theories. Staal focused so much on his claims about the meaninglessness of ritual that he has devoted almost no attention to the broader implications of his observation that ritual cognition is as complex as linguistic cognition. Whitehouse has focused so much on defending his theory against Lawson and McCauley that he has not emphasized the fact that his theory naturalizes ritual cognition by showing how it makes use of general-purpose memory processes. These scholars may object to my claim, of course, but I do believe that the cognitive study of religion now runs the risk of turning into so many ghettos, with each author trying to defend his theory[14] against competitors. To the extent that this happens, we run the risk of losing an understanding of the larger problems, and we lose the ability, so important to the sciences, of letting theories build on each other. Rather than viewing the field as composed of competing theories, only one of which can be true, we should focus instead on how the theories interact. I have attempted to focus in this chapter on those larger problems and glide over details of particular theories when they did not contribute to a better understanding of those problems.

NOTES

1. Note that I sometimes call the festival, which lasted about a week and was performed partly in and around Athens and partly in Eleusis, a "ritual" and sometimes a "performance." I do not intend these three words to have different senses, and I use them interchangeably in this paper.

2. Due to the scope of my argument in this chapter, I omit discussion of two theories that are very important for the cognitive study of religion and ritual: Sperber's work on the "epidemiology of representations" and Pascal Boyer's on the representation of religious agents; see Sperber (1996) and Boyer (1994).

3. See below for a discussion of Staal.

4. Note that Lawson and McCauley's terminology is unfortunate. The concept of the supernatural presupposes the concept of the natural, and the latter is far from being a cultural universal. Nature, or *physis*, played a major role in the Greek tradition of philosophy, as well as in nonphilosophical speculations about the world, and the notion of nature is consequently quite understandable in modern Western conceptual schemes. But a good case can be made that, in many other traditions, the natural/supernatural distinction makes no sense. The Fang believe in witches. We think of witches as beings possessing supernatural powers. But witches are part of the normal furniture of the world for the Fang. For Lawson and McCauley's theory to work, they need ritualists to actually contemplate the natural/supernatural distinction as part of their thinking about ritual, and there is no way to assume that ritualists do this in societies that don't recognize that very distinction.

5. It appears that Whitehouse does not agree with McCauley and Lawson on this; see Whitehouse (2004, p. 142).

6. I believe that this monograph presents the clearest and most successful exposition of Whitehouse's views. Whitehouse (2000) is intended as a more general work, a synthesis of the position first laid out in detail in *Inside the Cult*.

7. This is actually acknowledged in McCauley and Lawson (2002, pp. 118–119), though the problem is then ignored in favor a long discussion about how to measure frequency (a less significant problem, I suspect).

8. I must add the words "know to" because Lawson and McCauley repeatedly emphasize that their theory is a theory not of ritual but, rather, of ritual knowledge.

9. Staal's theory has been widely misunderstood, and much of the reason for this, I believe, has to do with the way he has presented his argument. My presentation will, therefore, differ rather significantly from that found in, for example, Staal (1990). Since I have laid out the evidence for my interpretation of his argument at great length in Seaquist (2004), I will not do so again here.

10. Staal's theory is pretty thoroughly expressed in two early papers, Staal, 1979a and Staal, 1979b. These, along with a lot of other material, are collected and loosely rewritten in Staal, 1993. Also to be recommended is the first half of Staal, 1993, which clearly defends Staal's view that rituals are per se meaningless.

11. This is now beginning to change, as many of the chapters in this series demonstrate, thanks to the recent interest in the evolutionary origins of ritual. It is worthwhile to point out, however, that Staal's theory does differ significantly from other evolutionary arguments, much like it differs from Lawson and McCauley's. The signalling theories discussed by Sosis in the present volume, for example, focus (like much of traditional ritual studies) on social relations more than on internal mental processes.

12. Another important work in this context is Humphrey and Laidlaw (1994). I have not addressed this book in the present chapter because it does not present itself as being a contribution to the cognitive study of religion. But in fact Humphrey and Laidlaw make a good case for studying ritual practice (looking at the actions that constitute ritual performance) while setting aside questions of ritual meaning.

13. Scholars who have made attempts to build on Staal's work on ritual include Roy Edwin Gane, Richard Payne, and Kristofer Schipper (see Seaquist 2004, pp. 118–128, for details).

14. This may reflect a style of scholarship common in the social sciences. In some social science disciplines, everyone develops their own theory and christens it with a name. The cognitive study of religion would do well to rely more on styles of scholarship common in the natural sciences, in other words, to let distinct theories emerge as an indirect result of debates over evidence, mechanisms, and causal processes, rather than treating theories as ends in their own right.

REFERENCES

Atran, S. (2002). *In Gods we trust: The evolutionary landscape of religion.* New York: Oxford University Press.

Boyer, P. (1994). *The naturalness of religious ideas.* Berkeley: University of California Press.

Chalmers, D., & Clark, A. (1998). The extended mind. *Analysis, 58,* 10–23.

Humphrey, C., & Laidlaw, J. (1994). *The archetypal actions of ritual: A theory of ritual illustrated by the Jain Rite of Worship.* Oxford, UK: Clarendon Press.

Lawson, E. T., & McCauley, R. (1990). *Rethinking religion: Connecting cognition and culture.* Cambridge, UK: Cambridge University Press.

McCauley, R. (1999). Bringing ritual to mind. In E. Winograd, R. Fivush, & W. Hirst (Eds.), *Ecological approaches to cognition: Essays in honor of Eric Neisser.* Hillsdale, NJ: Erlaum.

McCauley, R., & Lawson, E. T. (2002). *Bringing ritual to mind: Psychological foundations of cultural forms.* Cambridge, UK: Cambridge University Press.

Radt, S. (Ed.). (1985). *Tragicorum graecorum fragmenta* (Vol. 4). Göttingen: Vandenhoeck & Ruprecht.

Seaquist, C. (2004). *Ritual syntax.* Unpublished doctoral dissertation, University of Pennsylvania, Department of Religious Studies.

Sperber, D. (1975). *Rethinking symbolism.* Cambridge, UK: Cambridge University Press.

Sperber, D. (1996). *Explaining culture: A naturalistic approach.* Oxford, UK: Blackwell.

Staal, F. (1979a). The meaninglessness of ritual. *Numen, 26,* 2–22.

Staal, F. (1979b). Ritual syntax. In M. Nagatomi, B. Matilal, & J. M. Masson (Eds.), *Sanskrit and Indian studies: Essays in honor of Daniel H. Ingalls* (pp. 119–142). Ingalls and Dordrecht: Reidel.

Staal, F. (Ed.). (1983). *Agni: The Vedic ritual of the fire altar.* Berkeley, CA: Asian Humanities Press.

Staal, F. (1990). *Rules without meaning: Ritual, mantras, and the human sciences.* New York: Peter Lang.

Staal, F. (1993). From meanings to trees. *Journal of Ritual Studies, 7,* 11–32.

Toren, C. (1983). Thinking symbols. *Man* (NS), *18,* 260–268.

Whitehouse, H. (1995). *Inside the cult: Religious innovation and transmission in Papua New Guinea.* Oxford, UK: Oxford University Press.

Whitehouse, H. (2000). *Arguments and icons: Divergent modes of religiosity.* Oxford, UK: Oxford University Press.

Whitehouse, H. (2004). *Modes of religiosity: A cognitive theory of religious transmission.* Walnut Creek, CA: Altamira.

CHAPTER 11

THE BRAIN, RELIGION, AND BASEBALL: COMMENTS ON THE POTENTIAL FOR A NEUROLOGY OF RELIGION AND RELIGIOUS EXPERIENCE

Warren S. Brown

SETTING THE STAGE

The neurological study of religion, religiousness, and religious experience described in this volume is a new and developing field. While religious symptoms manifested by particular patients with neurological disorders have been described in the neurological literature over the last century, in the past decade there has been a significant increase in experimental research in this area. Thirty years ago an entire volume on the neurology of religious experience scarcely would have been possible. The development of a significant body of experimental research on neural correlates of religious behavior and experiences has even led some to designate this a unique field of study, variously called "neurotheology" or "theobiology" (Rayburn & Richmond, 2002).

This field of study, like the neuroscience study of other important high-level human capacities, has been notably accelerated by the development of techniques of relatively nonintrusive forms of functional imaging of brain activity (e.g., functional MRI, PET, SPECT, multichannel EEG, MEG, etc.). These techniques have allowed investigators to study brain function *in vivo* during many forms of cognitive, emotional, and psychosocial mental activity.

The chapters of this volume cover a wide variety of perspectives on the neurology, neuroscience, and developmental psychology of religiousness and the religious experiences of persons. However, before we can adequately understand this research, a number of issues regarding the nature of religion and its study need to be resolved. This concluding chapter will discuss the chapters of this volume and, more generally, the field of the neurology of religion and religious experience with respect to several more general questions and issues.

In the second section ("What Sort of Thing Is Religion"), I take up the issue of what sort of thing religion is and what other domains of human thought and behavior religion is most like. In the third section ("Appropriate Levels of Scale and the Scientific Study of Religion"), I consider the neurology of religious experience with respect to levels of scale of scientific study (micro to macro) in attempt to determine if religion and religious experience, as scientific variables, are at a level of scale appropriate for neurological study. The fourth section ("Neurology of Religion and the Cartesian Worldview") describes the effects of a Cartesian worldview on our thinking about religion. The issue of abstract concepts and misplaced concreteness is addressed in the fifth section ("Reductionism versus Emergence"). Finally, in the sixth section ("Guidelines for a Nonreductive Neurology of Religiousness"), I offer my opinion regarding how the neurology of religion and religious experience ought to proceed and what might be accomplished in this area.

WHAT SORT OF THING IS RELIGION?

To have a coherent and meaningful neurology of religion, it is important to have clearly in mind what it is that one wishes to study. Is religion a fundamental and unique form of brain function? Or is it a human capacity reliant on an interactive combination of many basic brain functions—that is, a conglomerate of individual human capacities such as intelligence? Or is religion not a phenomenon of individual persons at all but, rather, a form of human interrelatedness and social activity?

One way to approach this issue is to consider what other domain of human functioning religion is most like. First, let us consider whether religiousness is a human cognitive ability that is like the capacity for language or music and thus can be studied in a manner similar to the neurological study of these capacities. Candace Alcorta (Chapter 4, this volume) argues that religiousness is such a basic human capacity. She says, "Music, language, and religion are all cultural constructions that must be learned through social transmission; however, both the capacity for and constraints on such learning appear to be 'hard wired' in all human brains. . . . [O]ur ability to speak any language, enjoy any musical tradition, or engage in any religious experiences all appear to derive from genetically encoded neural capacities common to all humans" (p. 3). From the point of view of neurology, the critical claims made by Alcorta are that, while the specific expressions of religion are learned, religiousness itself is "hard wired." Such "hard wiring" implies that there exists a unique neurophysiological substrate that is not shared by other neurocognitive processes, and that this substrate is genetically endowed. In favor of this view of religiousness, Alcorta relies primarily on cultural similarities in religions and religiousness, as well as her theory that religion is an "experience expectant" system with a critical period for its development.

Before discussing further the claim that religion is like language or music in its neurological substrates, we must recognize that neither "language" or "music," per se, are capacities specific enough for neurological study. With respect to language, it has become increasingly clear that the neurology of language must be studied with respect to more refined cognitive contributions. In fact, even the division of language into "expressive" versus "receptive" capacities, widely utilized in clinical settings, is not sufficiently fine grain for neuroscience study. To track the neural systems involved one must focus on such subparts of language as syntax, semantics, lexicon, phonology, graphemics, etc. Only by fractionating language into such cognitive subcomponents can one make reasonable sense of the neural systems that participate in the emergent, abstract property we refer to as language (e.g., see Boller, Grafman, & Berndt, 2001).

Music is very similar to language with respect to neurological study. Like language, there is the expression of music and the appreciation of music. Both of these sub-domains are composed of multiple contributing capacities, each of which are more likely to have discrete neural systems that would be amenable to neurological study. For example, musical appreciation requires perception of rhythm, pitch, melody, harmonics, and emotional engagement. Expression of music also engages various motor skills that contribute to vocal or instrumental musical expression. Finally, music involves, in some circumstances, a unique form of written notation. (For a review of the neuropsychological study of music, see Peretz and Zatorre, 2005).

So, to the degree that individual religiousness is like language or music, it is also not itself a thing that can be studied at the level of neurology. One must first fractionate the behaviors and experiences into their cognitive subcomponents and then study the many contributing processes to find relatively unique or specific neural systems.

However, there are some very critical ways in which religiousness is not like either language or music. First, for both language and music there exists an extensive literature suggesting specific syndromes associated with relatively localized areas of damage to the brain. For example, various forms of language disorder (aphasia, alexia, or agraphia) are associated with damage to specific brain areas such as the left superior temporal gyrus, the left angular gyrus, and left inferior frontal lobe (Boller et al., 2001). While neuroimaging has made it clear that language processing always involves a large bihemispheric network, there are nevertheless rather specific symptom complexes associated with localized left hemisphere brain damage. While the syndromes are less clearly described for music, again there are consistent reports of syndromes of musical disability associated with localized brain damage (Peretz, 2002; Peretz & Zatorre, 2005).

In contrast, there are not religion-specific syndromes or disorders that are associated with any particular areas of the brain. The closest candidate is the religious manifestation of temporal lobe epilepsy (TLE), well described by Stephen Schachter (Chapter 4 of this volume). However, the religious symptoms associated with TLE are only a small part of a wider variety of symptoms, and these symptoms can all be fairly well subsumed within more basic problems associated with deepened emotional responses and increased attribution of personal significance. Similarly, the impact of Parkinson's disease on religiousness (as describe by McNamara et al. in Chapter 1 of this volume) is a reflection of a more general outcome related to reduced interest in most daily activities and reduced initiative. Thus, religiousness is clearly not like language and music with respect to specific neuropathology and specific behavioral outcomes.

Behind much of the discussions of a neurology of religiousness is the assumption that genetics has endowed humankind with religious capacities or tendencies. Linden Eaves (2004) has presented evidence suggesting genetic contributions to religious tendencies such as church attendance, self-transcendence, and conservatism. However, these tendencies are hard to distinguish from more general aspects of personality and temperament, and Eaves does not present data that would support distinct genetic contributions to these aspects of religiousness. Alcorta (Chapter 4, this volume) argues in favor of a genetic contribution to religiousness because religious practices can be found in nearly all cultures. However, it would be difficult to identify aspects of religiousness that are sufficiently consistent across cultures to be a candidate for common genetic influence. Despite the fact that we can group the wide variety of cultural manifestations within the single abstract concept "religion," the variety of cultural expressions of religion are arguably much greater than the cultural variations associated with either music or language. Similarly, it would be hard to argue that there has been a sufficient duration of time since the appearance of complex cultures within *homo sapiens* for the genetic evolution of specific brain systems for something as complex as religiousness. Thus, it is more likely that religion is ubiquitous due to cultural evolution and transmission, rather than genetic evolution (Ayala, 1998), and that the genetic factors that have been suggested by Eaves have an influence on the form and degree of participation of specific persons via more general personality factors.

All of this suggests that we must look elsewhere for an appropriate metaphor for understanding the nature of religiousness. Matthew Ratcliffe (Chapter 5 of this volume) suggests the possibility that religion is more like baseball—a cultural and sociological concept that summarizes a wide variety of group and individual activities, events, and experiences. Certainly the concept of "baseball" includes a very complex array of behaviors and experiences. It encompasses group participation as either spectators or players. For participants, baseball represents a particular set of motor skills and a form of group activity. For the dedicated fan, it is a topic of continual interest, conversation, and occasional attendance at games. Baseball can involve moments of intense emotional involvement (e.g., the emotion released by a walk-off home run to end an important game), longer periods of routine (e.g., practice sessions for participants or spring training for the fan), and certain ritual-like practices (e.g., pre-game and between-inning warm-up for players, the seventh-inning stretch, singing the National Anthem, etc.). For some, baseball is a complex entertainment business. Clearly, baseball involves many complex layers of interpersonal and social organization. We should consider the possibility that religion is not itself a basic cognitive process like language or music but, rather, is a more broadly inclusive social phenomenon like baseball.

The one critique of the baseball metaphor is that baseball is culturally not as prevalent as religion. Alcorta (Chapter 4, this volume) believes religion to be a fundamental human capacity because it is culturally ubiquitous. However, it would not be hard to argue that soccer (or "football" for most of the world) is a reasonable analogy since most of the world plays soccer. In addition, a wide variety of other games with the basic structure of soccer (e.g., American football, rugby, and basketball) are played within many different countries and cultures. A game not unlike soccer was played even by the ancient Aztecs and Maya.

If baseball (or soccer) is a better model for religion than either language or music, what would be the implications for neurological study? First, we would not expect to find a specific neurology of baseball—that is, no unique neurological systems that would contribute specifically to baseball and not to other forms of life. Baseball is neither sufficiently unitary as an experience or event, nor sufficiently temporally bound for study at the level of neurology. Second, we would not expect neuropathology specific to baseball, although many forms of neurological disorder might have an impact on different forms of participation in, or appreciation of, baseball. Thirdly, it would be somewhat far-fetched to imagine an evolution of the specific capacity for baseball, or to argue for the survival advantages of baseball to individuals or social groups, or to argue that the specific capacity for baseball is "hard wired."

It is more reasonable to consider baseball a complex social emergent of many more basic sociocultural systems involving a wide variety of activities and experiences that, in turn, piggy-back cognitively, neurologically, and evolutionarily on a large number of more general cognitive capacities and skills. Thus, both religion and baseball are abstract concepts incorporating a wide range of human behaviors and experiences that should not be reified in a way that presumes these abstract concepts point to unitary and fundamental human capacities available for study at the level of the brain. Thus, from the point of view of a naturalist neuroscience (although not from the viewpoint of theology), religion is more accurately understood as a large encompassing social and cultural phenomenon like baseball, rather than a fundamental human capacity like language or music.

To put this same point in a slightly different light, part of the question to be considered prior to engaging in any neurological study of religion is whether religion is essentially individual or corporate—within individuals persons or between persons (or persons and social contexts). If religion is primarily corporate—that is, if it exists in the interpersonal, social, and cultural domains—then any study at the level of neurology cannot be about religion, but must be about the neurology of more general cognitive and psychosocial functions that are engaged by a very particular form of interpersonal and social interactions in particular contexts. There would, therefore, not exist a neurology of religion, per se, nor would there be a neurology of particular forms of religious behavior or experience but, rather, a neurology of contributory neuropsychological systems that interact within the individual and between the individual and the socio-cultural environment, such as to allow for the emergence of religious behaviors and experiences.

APPROPRIATE LEVELS OF SCALE AND THE SCIENTIFIC STUDY OF RELIGION

The nature of an appropriate neuroscientific study of religion and religious experience can also be understood in terms of a hierarchy of the sciences with respect to level of scale of the phenomena being observed—extending from micro levels to more macro views of human functioning. At the most micro level are physics and chemistry. Moving to a slightly more macro level is biochemistry, including study of biological molecules like DNA or neurotransmitter receptors. At a higher level would be the study of the activity of neural cells. At an even higher level, we encounter research on neural interactions in local networks (such as studies of cellular interactions within the spinal cord, hippocampus, or olfactory bulb). Further up the hierarchy is the study of how such local systems interact to allow for properties like visual and auditory sensation, basic motor control, control of vegetative systems, and stereotypic behavior patterns.

At a still higher level, we begin to be able to use low-level psychological terms to describe what is being studied, such as perception, memory, attention, emotion, planning, and so forth. Here it becomes clear that the specifics of the functioning of these neural systems are formed by environmental interactions, mostly during childhood. For example, the specifics of the phonological systems of language are formed during early language experience, although the local circuits for this processing can be found at similar locations within the brains of almost all normal individuals in all cultures. At a more macro level still, we encounter more global attributes such as personality or intelligence. Here we are referring to aspects of whole persons to which many brain areas and brain systems contribute. This micro-to-macro continuum extends on into the social and cultural domains in which higher-level systems emerge from the interaction of individual persons.

One of the important implications of this roughly described micro-to-macro continuum is that appropriate scientific conclusions regarding relationships between phenomena are difficult to draw when skipping over many levels. At the most extreme, it would be hard to conceive of a neurochemistry of baseball, since this would skip over very many levels of human functioning. While a neurochemical change might alter one's experience of baseball, it would do so indirectly by altering neurological and neurocognitive functions at many intervening levels that would have impact on a very wide variety of behaviors and experiences beyond just baseball. It would not be very scientifically meaningful to attempt to establish a direct relationship between a biochemical change and the participation in or experiences of baseball. The appropriate scientific conclusion would be about the effect of the biochemical change on particular forms of brain function, and the impact of these changes on rather generic forms of human behavior or experience that, in turn, might be involved in baseball. Conclusions about baseball, per se (even if baseball provided the context for observing the behavioral impact of the biochemical observation), would be inappropriate without considerable discussion about, and experimental evidence regarding, changes at many levels of intervening human function that are contributors not only to baseball, but also to many other domains of human life.

Let me take as an example of this hierarchy of complexity the relationship between neurochemistry, frontal lobe function, and religiousness described by McNamara (Chapter 9 of this volume). A wide range of neurophysiological, neurological, and behavioral data are surveyed to suggest the important role of dopamine systems and the prefrontal cortex on behavioral inhibition, cooperative social behavior, and religion. One might parse the data that McNamara presents into something like the following micro- to macro-hierarchy of function: First we have genetic contributions to the neurochemistry of dopamine (particularly the enzyme COMT), as well as genetic contributions (most likely less direct) to whatever processes control growth (and size) of the prefrontal cortex. Second, during the very complex interactive biological processes of prenatal development, dopamine neurons extend their axons to innervate the prefrontal cortex, and prefrontal neurons extend their axons "downstream" to innervate and modulate lower-level brain systems. This, then, allows for the emergence of the fundamental neuropsychological processes of executive control and inhibition of action. Capacities for inhibition of action lead, in turn, to the possibility of engaging in cooperative social behavior, including the potential for those behaviors that constitute, in the evolutionary story provided, "costly signaling." This capacity allows, in turn, for the social and cultural emergence of religious rituals, mores, and beliefs, which work recurrently back on the individual to develop virtues and character. Thus, in this quite plausible story, there are many steps between basic brain processes (genetics, neurochemistry, and functional systems) and complex social behaviors such as religiousness. The relevant neurological processes described are not specific to religiousness, but are properties of brain processing that serve the more general neuropsychology capacity of executive function.

A similar view might be taken of the description of religious conversion presented by Paloutzian, Swenson, and McNamara (Chapter 7 of this volume). In their theory, religiousness (and, thus, religious conversion) is a product of a more general cognitive capacity for meaning making (involving "emotions, actions, beliefs, expectations, and contingencies," p. 6). Meaning making is, in turn, the product of interactions of a number of brain systems (involving the frontal, parietal, and medial temporal lobes). I suspect that even this 3-level analysis, while a very useful theory, is nevertheless a simplified summary encompassing a number of additional, discernable, intervening levels of function.

So, with respect to the micro-to-macro hierarchy of increasingly complex systems, we need to be clear where religion lies and whether it is sufficiently "close" to brain function to imagine specifically religious brain systems and to allow the search for correlations that are scientifically meaningful (i.e., correlations that imply direct, or nearly direct, causal relationships). Is religion an immediate cognitive emergent property of brain function involving domain-specific brain systems, or is religion a phenomenon many levels of emergent properties removed from brain functioning? Nobel Laureate Roger Sperry once expressed the problem of the gap between psychological and neurological phenomena in this way: "An objective psychologist, hoping to get at the physiological side of behavior, is apt to plunge immediately into neurology trying to correlate brain activity with modes of experience. The results in many cases only accentuates the gap between the total experience as studied by the psychologist and neuronal activity as analyzed by the neurologist" (Sperry, 1939, p. 295). It would seem to me that religion is not just psychological but, rather, a very high-level property of human sociocultural participation that is dependent on interactive contributions of many psychological (cognitive) systems that themselves emerge from interactions between a number of more basic brain systems. If religion entails social interactions, the gap described by Sperry becomes even greater.

My use of the term "emergent" is not meant to imply that something emerges that is nonmaterial (like a soul or mind in the Cartesian sense). New *properties* can emerge in a complex dynamic system by harnessing the activity of the lowest level physical constituents (atoms, molecules, or neurons) into causally efficacious interactive patterns (see the discussion of complex dynamic systems in the fifth section).

NEUROLOGY OF RELIGION AND THE CARTESIAN WORLDVIEW

Study of the neuroscience of important, high-level human capacities is plagued by the remnants of a Cartesian worldview. Descartes gave Western culture a strong notion of the distinction between body and soul (or body and mind). The body, for Descartes, was a physical machine. However, unable to imagine how rationality could be manifest by a machine, Descartes argued that the soul (or mind) is a distinct nonmaterial entity. As the seat of rationality, the soul was presumed to be hierarchically superior to the body, and more important. In addition, this hierarchically more important soul (or mind) was presumed to reside inside the body.

The discussions of religious experiences and behaviors and brain function within this volume lean strongly toward an embodied (nondualistic) view of human religiousness. However, even within such a nondualist and generally materialist understanding of persons, it is hard to avoid the idea that the most important aspects of being human resides inside the head. The mind is still considered to be an entity that is found entirely inside the head in the form of brain functions that are distinct from the rest of the physical person and also distinct from the social environment. Instead of a body and an inner soul (or mind), we have a body and inner brain function (i.e., a brain-body dualism). This is the view that Daniel Dennett (1991) has referred to as "Cartesian materialism." Consequently, we implicitly assume that all that is important and critical about human life must be identified with functions or properties that are inside individual human persons. This view relegates interpersonal relations and social systems to a secondary status with respect to our understanding of the most unique and important aspects of human nature. Within the Cartesian worldview, everything that is important about humanity must be both *inner* and *individual*.

By definition, a *neurology* of religiousness would deny that religiousness is exclusively about the experiences of a Cartesian nonmaterial mind or soul. However, an implicit assumption of this research is the Cartesian view that any important property of humanness, such as religion, must be resident inside individual human persons (presumably in some unique form of brain functions). Even though the chapters of this volume indicate that it is possible to contemplate religiousness outside of Cartesian body-soul dualism, it does not seem to be the case that we have moved past the Cartesian assumptions regarding innerness and individuality. If religion is a critically important part of what it means to be human, then (in this view) it must be the case that religion resides inside of the person—within neural systems that are uniquely responsible for one's religiousness and religious experiences.

For example, what is the rationale for discussing ritual (Seaquist, Chapter 10 of this volume) or adolescent religious awakening (Alcorta, Chapter 4 of this volume) in a way that presumes that the important determinants of these human events are within individual persons, rather than within the culturally bounded social networks in which persons are embedded? Might not even personal religious conversion (Paloutzian, Swenson, and McNamara, Chapter 7 of this volume) be better understood as a relationship between a whole complex person and a religious community or institution, or between a person and God (as the monotheistic religious traditions would suggest), rather than a primarily an internal event of individual meaning making? The neurochemical perspective on religious experience offered by Newberg (Chapter 2 of this volume) presumes religious experience to be entirely internal, and the existence of these internal mechanisms is "why God won't go away" (Newberg & d'Aquili, 2001b). While Azari's view of religious experience (Chapter 3 of this volume) points primarily to inner brain properties, her theory of religious experience has the merit of also pointing outward in that a religious experience is a form of "relational cognitivity."

An alternative view that gains more distance from the Cartesian view is that, although humans have uniquely developed neural and bodily machinery, what is unique about humankind is the way the machinery is used to interact with the physical and social environment (and, some might believe, interactions with the Divine). The uniqueness of humankind is not about the neural machinery, per se, which, after all, is merely an extension and expansion of biological machinery found also in apes. Rather, human uniqueness resides in the social environment that our machinery allows us to create and to participate in. Thus, when studying uniquely human capacities like religiousness, the critical questions are not about the machinery itself (i.e., about brain systems), but about how, when we are embedded in the social processes of human culture, we are capable of remarkably more complex social interactions and experience notably increased degrees of freedom in thought and behavior compared to the rest of the animal world.

REDUCTIONISM VERSUS EMERGENCE

Reductionism relates to the hierarchy of micro-to-macro levels of scale described earlier in that it presumes that the laws governing lower-level processes (e.g., brain functions) can account for higher-level phenomena (e.g., religious experience) *without residual*. That is, all of the variance at the higher level can be exhaustively explained, in principle, by phenomena at some lower level. *Emergence*, on the other hand, presumes that new properties emerge at higher levels that, while dependent on lower-level functions, cannot be entirely accounted for or explained by lower-level processes. Real *causal* properties emerge as lower-level phenomena form into larger interactive patterns. An account of the lower-level properties cannot do justice to higher-level emergents.

Dynamic systems theory gives the best account of emergence (for a good description of dynamic systems theory with respect to the human brain and behavior, see Juarrero, 1999). The massively and recurrently interconnected neuronal network that is the cerebral cortex is beautifully suited for emergence of the sort of higher-level properties described by the theory of complex dynamic systems. When pushed far from equilibrium by environmental interactions, dynamic systems self-organize into larger *patterns* that are constituted by *relational constraints between elements.* Thus, the elements of the system work together in a coherent or coordinated manner to create the larger-scale functional system. This larger system operates internally by restraining (or entraining) the future possibilities for each constituent element. Once organized into a system, lower-level properties interact (bottom-up) with the relational constraints created by the higher-level patterns (top-down), without implying any exceptions to lawfulness at the microlevel. As Juarrero explains it:

> when parts interact to produce wholes, and the resulting distributed wholes in turn affect the behavior of their parts, interlevel causality is at work. Interactions among certain dynamical processes can create a systems-level organization with new properties that are not the simple sum of the components that create the higher level. In turn, the overall dynamics of the emergent distributed system not only determine which parts will be allowed into the system: the global dynamics also regulate and constrain the behavior of the lower-level components. (Juarrero, 1999, pp. 5–6)

These patterns self-organize (and reorganize) as demanded by the continual give-and-take of interactions with the environment. A new pattern of constraints will manifest new properties of the whole system that were not present prior to this process of self-organization.

In such systems, interactions with novel aspects of the environment cause repeated reorganizations that create increasingly more complex and higher-level forms of system organization. Thus, multiple smaller systems can be organized into even larger systems. Gibbs (2006) explains dynamic self-organization of behavior as follows: "an individual's behavior emerges from interactions of brain, body, and environment. Simple and complex behavioral patterns are higher-order products of self-organization processes. Virtually all living organisms self-assemble, or are self-organizing systems, . . . Self-organized patterns of behavior emerge as stable states from the interaction of many subsystems" (Gibbs, 2006, p. 10). In this way, the dynamics of reorganization result in a nested hierarchy of more and more complex functional systems, reminiscent of the micro-to-macro hierarchy of levels of scale described above.

In addition, *constraints* between individual elements or smaller patterns existing at lower levels result in the emergence of higher-level system properties that manifest substantially *greater freedom*. The system has a substantially greater number of possibilities with respect to its interactions with its surrounding environment than it had prior to each new level of self-reorganization. Again, as Juarrero expresses it, "The higher level of organization, whether thermodynamic, psychological, or social, possesses a qualitatively different repertoire of states and behavior than the earlier level, as well as greater degrees of freedom" (Juarrero, 1999, p. 145).

Thus, dynamic systems theory specifies how truly emergent, nonreductive properties are possible in complex interactive systems, most particularly within the hypercomplex human brain, as well as the social networks in which persons are embedded. Since the emergent properties of a complex dynamic system are interactive patterns that interface with the environment as a whole system, the properties of the patterns themselves cannot be entirely reduced to rules of action specifiable at lower levels. What is implied by emergence and dynamic systems analysis is an ontology of relationships and interactions—that is, *real things* emerge in the form of interactive patterns that are as real (at least in a causal sense) as the physical elements that constitute the patterns.

With respect to the study of neurology of religion and religious experience, one must ask whether the descriptions of the results published thus far have implied an unwarranted reduction of the phenomena of religion to brain systems (i.e., the neural components and sub-systems that are inside single individuals). In the descriptions of research outcomes, is it assumed that the activity of the brain systems that are identified as engaged during the religious experiences can entirely account for the higher-level properties of religious behavior and experiences? Might several levels of emergence of nonreductive causal properties (both individual and social) intervene between neurological descriptors and important aspects of human life such as religion?

GUIDELINES FOR A NONREDUCTIVE NEUROLOGY OF RELIGIOUSNESS

In this concluding chapter I have attempted to formulate a meta-view of the field of the neurological study of religiousness or religious experience—a view from which to both understand the research that has been done thus far, and to consider further research. In so doing, this chapter has been rather negative with respect to what might be learned about religion from neurological study. Nevertheless, a number of the chapters of this volume describe

interesting scientific outcomes that, if properly understood, represent progress in our understanding of the relationship (however distant) between
brain function and religious experiences and behaviors.

How does one go about doing and evaluating studies of brain processes
involved in religious behavior and experience? In what follows, I will venture
some guidelines for both doing such research and evaluating how much has
been learned from existing studies.

1. *We should study a specific, narrowly defined component of religiousness, and
   explicitly recognize the narrowness.* What is meant here is more than simply an explicit operational definition of the religious variable to be studied (although this is always a critically important task). Rather, we must
   choose to study a contributing component of religion that exists at a
   level appropriately narrow and specific for neurological study. Equally
   as important, we must not allow the introduction and discussion of
   the research to extend too far beyond this specificity. For example, if
   the study is about a certain form of meditation (e.g., the research of
   Newberg and colleagues described in Chapter 2 of this volume), the
   discussion of the research should be confined to this particular form of
   meditation and not wander beyond this particularity to a discussion of
   religion or religious experiences in general, as if experiences associated
   with a circumscribed form of meditation could adequately stand in for
   all or most religious experiences.

2. *We must consider all of the intervening cognitive contributions to the specific
   component of religious behavior or experience that we study, and, if possible,
   we should explicitly manipulate or measure in the research the contributions of
   the various intervening cognitive variables.* It is my contention that the religious variables are manifestations of the interaction of many lower-level
   cognitive processes, each with its own neural substrates. Manipulating or measuring intervening cognitive variables would make clear the
   degree to which the neurological correlates of religiousness are secondary manifestations of more general neurocognitive outcomes. A good
   example is the research on religiousness in patients with Parkinson's
   disease reported by McNamara and his colleagues (McNamara, Durso,
   Brown, and Harris, Chapter 1 of this volume). The impact of Parkinson's
   disease on religiousness was found to be primarily manifest in reduced
   participation in the private practices of religion and was paralleled by
   reduced participation in leisure activities and hobbies. To further clarify
   the impact of variables intervening between religious participation and
   brain processes, these authors also administered neuropsychological
   measures of executive function that showed that the outcome in religiousness was secondary to a more general abnormality affecting a wide
   range of behaviors strongly influenced by frontal lobe function.

3. *If possible, we should study the developmental path to the religious behavior
   or experience.* What neural systems must develop before the behavior or

experience can emerge? Are these systems general or specific to religiousness? The developmental timing of the appearance and maturation of the religious behavior or experience in question, when compared to the development of various cognitive capacities and social skills, will give further clues to the intervening neurocognitive skills and abilities manifest in the religious variable. Chapters in this volume by Alcorta (Chapter 4) and Granqvist (Chapter 6) describe the importance of prior social and cognitive development for the emergence of various forms of religiousness in children and adolescents.

4. *Any conclusions implying that a neural system or pattern of neural activation is specific to a religious state or behavior need to be supported by incorporation of many similar but nonreligious control conditions.* Considerable work needs to be done comparing the outcome associated with the religious variable and the possibility of the same outcome when manipulating similar, but nonreligious variables. For example, in the research of Newberg and his colleagues (Newberg et al., 2001a; Newberg, Pourdehnad, Alavi, & d'Aquili, 2003; described by Newberg in Chapter 2 and by Azari in Chapter 3), it would be important to know if any nonreligious practices or experiences would also result in the same pattern of increase in frontal lobe activation and reduction in right parietal lobe activation that was found during religious meditation studied. Without such information, the conclusion that a particular brain state is in any way specific to religious experiences is unwarranted.

5. *We must be clear about the social scaffolding (past and present) necessary for the behavior, experience, or event to be considered religious by the participant.* Religion may well be a contextual variable that controls a person's subjective interpretation of a neural event, not a primary outcome of the neural state itself. The cases of religious experiences associated with temporal lobe epilepsy described by Schachter (Chapter 4 of this volume) are important to consider. Would the experience of temporal lobe epileptic discharge be interpreted as religious by a person with no religious background whatsoever? Does a religious social history predispose a person to interpret a seizure experience as a religious manifestation? Variations in the interactions between the subjective experience resulting from a seizure and a prior religious history, and/or a concurrent religious context, might explain some of the variability in the findings regarding a relationship between temporal lobe epilepsy and religious experiences.

6. *We should avoid reductionist statements in describing research outcomes that imply that functions at one level are "nothing but" the operation of lower levels.* Emergence implies that real, novel, and causal properties emerge in the patterns of interaction of component parts that cannot be reduced to the properties of the parts themselves. So, as important as the brain is to human behavior and experience, no important human psychological property, much less a human sociocultural phenomenon like religiousness, can be reduced to nothing but the activity of a particular neural

system or specific pattern of neural activation. If nothing else, since the operation of neural systems is always embedded in ongoing interactions with the physical or social environment, appropriate interpretation of research findings necessitates specification of the nature of these ongoing interactions.

SUMMARY AND CONCLUSIONS

In these concluding remarks for this volume on *The Neurology of Religious Experience*, I have attempted to take the widest possible view of the field to gain perspective on what can and cannot be accomplished. I have suggested that the property of religion and religiousness might best be placed outside of the individual in characteristics of the sociocultural environment (like baseball), rather than within persons as a unique property of individual neurocognitive functioning (as in language). I have also suggested that attention needs to be paid to levels of scale when attempting to find associations between brain function and religiousness by asking whether the two domains are sufficiently close for study of their relationships, unmediated by many levels of intervening variables. I have also critiqued the basic formulation of the problem of human religiousness from the point of view of a Cartesian worldview, where everything that is important about humanness (like religion) must be both within the person and a property of the individual. Finally, I have used these arguments to make suggestions regarding things to consider in the further development of a neurology of religion and religious experience.

These perspectives and considerations suggest that the designation "neurology of religious experience" should be considered a convenient summary phrase, referring to for what is in reality a neurology of the cognitive contributions to specific behaviors and experiences labeled by the individual as "religious" due to social context (present or past). From my own theological perspective, the concept of "behaviors and experiences labeled by the individual as religious due to social context" would include the possibility that the "social context" includes a detectable presence of a nonmaterial God. However, as Ratcliffe suggests (Chapter 5 of this volume), nothing can be concluded about the reality (or nonreality) of God or his action in the world by a neurological study of religious behaviors and experiences. Existence of a divine being is a theological question, not a neuroscientific question.

REFERENCES

Ayala, F. (1998). Human nature: One evolutionist's view. In W. S. Brown, N. Murphy, & H. N. Malony (Eds.), *Whatever happened to the soul: Scientific and theological portraits of human nature* (pp. 31–48). Minneapolis: Fortress Press.

Boller, F., Grafman, J., & Berndt, R. S. (Eds). (2001). Language and aphasia. In *Handbook of neuropsychology* (2nd ed.). Amsterdam: Elsevier Science.

Dennett, D. (1991). *Consciousness explained.* Boston: Little, Brown.

Eaves, L. (2004). Genetic and social influences on religion and values. In M. A. Jeeves (Ed.), *From cells to souls–and beyond: Changing portraits of human nature* (pp. 102–122). Grand Rapids, MI: Eerdmans Publishing.

Gibbs, R. W. (2006). *Embodiment and cognitive science.* Cambridge, UK: Cambridge University Press.

Juarrero, A. (1999). *Dynamics in action: Intentional behavior as a complex system.* Cambridge, MA: MIT Press.

Newberg, A., Alavi, A., Baime, M., Pourdehnad, M., Santanna, J., & d'Aquili, E. (2001a). The measurement of regional cerebral blood flow during the complex cognitive task of meditation: A preliminary spect study. *Psychiatry Research, 106,* 113–122.

Newberg, A. B., & d'Aquili, E. (2001b). *Why God won't go away: Brain science and the biology of belief.* New York: Ballantine Books.

Newberg, A., Pourdehnad, M., Alavi, A., & d'Aquili, E. G. (2003). Cerebral blood flow during meditative prayer: Preliminary findings and methodological issues. *Perceptual Motor Skills, 97,* 625–630.

Peretz, I. (2002). Brain specialization for music. *Neuroscientist, 8*(4), 372–380.

Peretz, I., & Zatorre, R. J. (2005). Brain organization for music processing. *Annual Review of Psychology, 56,* 89–114.

Rayburn, C. A., & Richmond, L. J. (Eds.). (2002). Introduction. In *Theobiology: Interfacing theology, biology, and other science for deeper understanding. American Behavioral Scientist, 45,* 1785–1788.

Sperry, R. W. (1939). Action current study in movement coordination. *Journal of General Psychology, 20,* 295–313.

INDEX

Action, in ritual, 210
Action representation system, 210–11
Adaptation, religious experiences as, 138–41; Newberg et al. on, 139–40; Persinger on, 138–39; problems with theories of, 94–96
Adolescence, 64–76; cultural definition of, 67–68; emotional intensity in, 68; emotional reactivity in, 71; length of, nutritional and ecological factors on, 68; as life stage, 67–69; reactions to environmental stimuli in, 68; risk taking and novelty seeking in, 68
Adolescence, brain chemistry in: cortisol in, 68; dopaminergic shifts in, 70–71; neurotransmitter systems in, 70
Adolescence, brain growth and development in, 69–71; critical, 67; development in, 69–71; growth in, 58–59; mental processing in, 69; synaptic pruning in, 70; white matter increases in, 70
Adolescence, religion in: on behavior, 72–74; on depression and suicidal ideation, 73–74; emotions and symbols of, 71–72; on life course, 74–75; participation in activities of, 55–57; on social

behaviors, 68; on trust-based social affiliation, 75; on values, 72–73
Adolescence, rites of passage in, 64–67; emotionally valenced social-symbolic networks from, 72; lifelong remembrance of, 67; social and moral bonds from, 66; on social status, 66; universal phases of, 64–66
Affect regulation strategies, in attachment theory, 112–13
Agency: in theory of mind, 212. *See also* Supernatural agents
Agnicayana ritual, 220–21
Ambivalent attachment, 111; New Age spirituality and, 128–29
Amygdala: function and connections of, 69–70; growth of, in adolescents, 69; in spiritual practices, 23
Antiepileptic drugs, 175–76
Anti-social impulses, frontal lobe inhibition of, 197–98
Anxiety, with epilepsy, 176
Arginine vasopressin, 20–21
Art: capacity for, capacity for religion and, 151–52; as self-authenticating, 164–65
Attachment, in children, 120

About the Editor
and Contributors

EDITOR

Patrick McNamara, Ph.D., is director of the Evolutionary Neurobehavior Laboratory in the Department of Neurology at the Boston University School of Medicine and the Veterans Administration New England Health Care System. Upon graduating from the Behavioral euroscience Program at Boston University in 1991, he trained at the Aphasia Research Center at the Boston Veterans Administration Medical Center in neurolinguistics and brain-cognitive correlation techniques. He then began developing an evolutionary approach to problems of brain and behavior and currently is studying the evolution of the frontal lobes, the evolution of the two mammalian sleep states (REM and NREM), and the evolution of religion in human cultures. He has published numerous articles and chapters on these topics pioneering the investigation of the role of the frontal lobes in mediation of religious experience.

CONTRIBUTORS

Candace S. Alcorta is an anthropologist specializing in the evolution and behavioral ecology of religion. She has conducted ethnographic research in Thailand and the United States and is currently completing a study of the relationship between adolescent religious involvement and resilience in fulfillment of doctoral dissertation requirements in the Department of Anthropology at the University of Connecticut.

Nina P. Azari earned her *first* Ph.D. in Human Cognitive Experimental Psychology and completed several years of postdoctoral training and research in human brain imaging at the National Institutes of Health. More recently, she also has completed a *second* Ph.D. in Religious and Theological Studies, the dissertation for which was on philosophical–theological implications of neuroscientific study of religious experience—most specifically her own collaborative work on the subject (a brain imaging study of a Christian religious experience). Consequent to being awarded an Alexander von Humboldt Fellowship, Dr. Azari initiated an international collaboration with the Departments of Neurology and Philosophy at the University of Duesseldorf in Germany, a collaboration that she has maintained and further developed over the past 10 years. Since 2004, Azari has been Assistant Professor of Psychology at the University of Hawaii-Hilo.

Ariel Brown received her B.A. in Psychology from Skidmore College in 2001. She is currently enrolled as a Ph.D. student in Behavioral Neuroscience at the Boston University School of medicine. Her current research interests are in the neuropsychology and functional neuroimaging of higher order cognitive function in neuropsychiatric populations. Past research experience and publications include topics such as implicit learning in amnesics, memory in chronic pain patients, and frontal functioning in Parkinson's Disease.

Warren S. Brown Ph.D., is Professor of Psychology at the Graduate School of Psychology at Fuller Theological Seminary, where he is also Director of the Travis Research Institute. Prior to Fuller, Brown spent 11 years as a research scientist at the UCLA Brain Research Institute, and Department of Psychiatry and Biobehavioral Sciences, where he continues as a BRI member. He is actively involved in research related to human brain processes and cognition, most specifically related to the functions of the corpus callosum. His current research involves cognitive and psychosocial disabilities in individuals born without a corpus callosum. Brown has also done research on neuropsychological changes in aging and dementia; brain processes in language comprehension; attention deficits in schizophrenia; and brain wave changes associated with kidney disease and its treatment. Brown has contributed over seventy-five articles to peer-reviewed scientific journals such as *Neuropsychologia, Psychophysiology, Neurobiology of Aging, Biological Psychiatry, Developmental Neuropsychology, Kidney International,* and *Science.* Brown has also contributed to the understanding of the relationship between religion and neuroscience. He served as editor of two recent books: *Whatever Happened to the Soul: Scientific and Theological Portraits of Human Nature* (with Nancey Murphy and Newton Malony; Fortress Press, 1998) and *Understanding Wisdom: Sources, Science, and Society* (Templeton Press, 2001).

Raymon Durso, M.D., is the Director of the Movement Disorders Clinic at the Veterans Administration New England Healthcare System and the Department of Neurology, Boston University School of Medicine. He is also the Director of the Neuropharmacology Laboratory at the Boston Veterans Administration Medical Center.

Pehr Granqvist is an Associate Professor in Psychology at Uppsala University, Sweden, where he also got his Ph.D. in 2002. He has pursued research in two separate areas of relevance here. First, he has performed several studies examining relations between attachment processes and religion. Secondly, he was one of the principal investigators in the first properly double-blinded study that tested if the application of weak, complex magnetic fields to individuals' temporal lobes resulted in religious experiences, as hypothesized by others. Besides these research areas, he is involved in several projects in developmental psychology, relating attachment measurements and concepts to aspects of social and emotional development.

Erica Harris completed her B.A. from the University of Virginia in January 2001 with a major in Psychology and a concentration in Neuroscience. After graduation, she worked at Duke University Medical Center on studies involving at-risk youths and how they make successful transitions in school. She then obtained her MPH from Boston University in January 2005 with dual concentrations in Epidemiology and Social and Behavioral Sciences. Harris is currently a Research Coordinator in the Department of Neurology at the Boston University Medical Center. She works on a variety of projects including sleep, Parkinson's Disease, dreams, the concept of the self, the frontal lobes, and the relationship between religion and the brain.

Andrew B. Newberg, M.D., is Assistant Professor in the Departments of Radiology and Psychiatry and an Adjunct Assistant Professor in the Department of Religious Studies at the University of Pennsylvania. He graduated from the University of Pennsylvania School of Medicine in 1993. He did his training in Internal Medicine at the Graduate Hospital in Philadelphia and then completed a Fellowship in Nuclear Medicine in the Division of Nuclear Medicine, Department of Radiology, at the University of Pennsylvania. During this time, he has actively pursued a number of neuroimaging research projects, which have included the study of aging and dementia, epilepsy, and other neurological and psychiatric disorders. Dr. Newberg has been particularly involved in the study of mystical and religious experiences, as well as the more general mind/body relationship in both the clinical and research aspects of his career. His research also includes understanding the physiological correlates of acupuncture therapy, meditation, and other types of alternative therapies. He has published numerous articles and chapters on brain function, brain imaging, and the study of religious and mystical experiences. He has also co-authored two books entitled, *Why God Won't Go Away: Brain Science and the Biology of Belief* and *The Mystical Mind: Probing the Biology of Belief*, which explore the relationship between neuroscience and spiritual experience. The latter book received the 2000 award for Outstanding Books in Theology and the Natural Sciences presented by the Center for Theology and the Natural Sciences.

Raymond F. Paloutzian received his Ph.D. degree in 1972 from Claremont Graduate School and has been a Professor of Experimental and Social Psychology at Westmont College, Santa Barbara, California, since 1981. He has been a Visiting Professor, teaching psychology of religion at Stanford University and Guest Professor, Katholieke Universiteit Leuven, Belgium. He is a Fellow of the American Psychological Association (APA; divisions of general, teaching, social issues, psychology of religion, and international), the American Psychological Society, and the Western Psychological Association, and has served as President of APA Division 36 (Psychology of Religion). The Division honored him with the 2005 Virginia Sexton Mentoring Award for contributing to the development of other scholars in the field. He wrote *Invitation to the Psychology of Religion*, 2nd ed. (1996, 3rd ed. forthcoming), and with Crystal Park, edited the *Handbook of the Psychology of Religion and Spirituality* (2005). Dr. Paloutzian is Editor of *The International Journal for the Psychology of Religion*.

Matthew Ratcliffe is a lecturer in philosophy at Durham University. His research interests include philosophy of mind, phenomenology, and philosophy of science. He has published articles on various topics, including intentionality, teleology, subjectivity, intersubjectivity, religious experience, delusions, emotions, and feelings. He is currently working on two monographs, entitled *Rethinking Commonsense Psychology* and *Feelings of Being: Phenomenology, Psychopathology and Taken-for-Granted Reality*.

Steven C. Schachter is Professor of Neurology at Harvard Medical School, Director of Research, Department of Neurology at Beth Israel Deaconess Medical Center in Boston, Massachusetts, and liaison to the Center for the Integration of Medicine and Innovative Technology from Beth Israel Deaconess Medical Center.

Dr. Schachter is past Chair of the Professional Advisory Board of the Epilepsy Foundation and serves on their Board of Directors. He is also past Treasurer of the American Epilepsy Society and served on their Board of Directors. He is the founding Editor-in-Chief of *Epilepsy & Behavior*, which was recognized as the best new science and medical journal of 2000 by the Association of American Publishers, and Editor-in-Chief of the online journal, Epilepsy.com. Dr. Schachter has directed more than 80 research projects involving new treatments for epilepsy and has published 18 books and more than 200 papers.

Carl Seaquist is Visiting Lecturer in Religion at the University of Vermont. He holds a Ph.D. in Religious Studies from the University of Pennsylvania and an M.A. in Philosophy from the University of Wisconsin, Milwaukee.

Erica L. Swenson received her bachelor's degree summa cum laude from Westmont College in 2005. She has been a Research Assistant at the Psychology Department of Westmont College since 2004. She is currently a psychology Ph.D. student at TBA University with interests in the psychology of religion and spirituality.

About the Advisory Board

Scott Atran, Ph.D., conducts research and is centered in the following areas: cognitive and linguistic anthropology, ethnobiology, environmental decision making, categorization and reasoning, evolutionary psychology, anthropology of science (history and philosophy of natural history and natural philosophy), Middle East ethnography and political economy, natural history of Lowland Maya, cognitive and commitment theories of religion, terrorism, and foreign affairs.

The evolution of religion is a topic he explores in his book *In Gods We Trust* (2002). He is based both at the National Center for Scientific Research in Paris and at the University of Michigan. His recent work has focused on suicide terrorism. He has marshaled evidence that indicates that suicide bombers are not poor and crazed as depicted in the press but well-educated and often economically stable individuals with no significant psychological pathology.

Donald Capps, Ph.D., is Princeton's William Harte Felmeth Professor of Pastoral Psychology. He draws on his training as a psychologist of religion in both his teaching and his writing. In 1989, he was awarded an honorary doctorate in sacred theology from the University of Uppsala, Sweden, in recognition of his publications in the psychology of religion and pastoral care and of his leadership role in the Society for the Scientific Study of Religion, for which he served as editor of its professional journal from 1983 to 1988 and as president from 1990 to 1992.

J. Harold Ellens, Ph.D., is series editor for Praeger's Psychology, Religion and Spirituality series. He is a research scholar at the University of Michigan, Department of Near Eastern Studies. He is a retired Presbyterian theologian and ordained minister, a retired U.S. Army colonel, and a retired professor of philosophy, theology, and psychology. He has authored, coauthored, and/or edited 111 books and 165 professional journal articles. He served 15 years as executive director of the Christian Association for Psychological Studies and as founding editor and editor in chief of the *Journal of Psychology and Christianity.* He holds a Ph.D. from Wayne State University in the psychology of human communication, a Ph.D. from the University of Michigan in biblical and Near Eastern studies, and master degrees from Calvin Theological Seminary, Princeton Theological Seminary, and the University of Michigan. He was born in Michigan, grew up in a Dutch-German immigrant community, and determined at age seven to enter the Christian ministry as a means to help his people with the great amount of suffering he perceived all around him. His life's work has focused on the interface of psychology and religion.

Harold Koenig, M.D., M.H.Sc, is an associate professor of psychiatry and medicine at Duke University. He is director and founder of the Center for the Study of Religion/Spirituality and Health at Duke University; editor of the *International Journal of Psychiatry in Medicine,* and founder and editor in chief of *Research News in Science and Theology,* the monthly international newspaper of the John Templeton Foundation. His latest books include the *Handbook of Religion and Mental Health, The Healing Power of Faith: Science Explores Medicine's Last Great Frontier,* and *Religion and Health: A Century of Research Reviewed.*

Koenig completed his undergraduate education at Stanford University, his medical school training at the University of California at San Francisco, and his geriatric medicine, psychiatry, and biostatistics training at Duke University Medical Center. He is board certified in general psychiatry, geriatric psychiatry, and geriatric medicine and is on the faculty at Duke as professor of psychiatry and behavioral sciences and associate professor of medicine. He is also a registered nurse.

Koenig has published extensively in the fields of mental health, geriatrics, and religion, with nearly 250 scientific peer-reviewed articles and book chapters and 26 books in print or in preparation. His research on religion, health, and ethical issues in medicine has been featured on approximately 50 national and international television news programs (including all major U.S. news networks), 80 national or international radio programs (including multiple NPR, BBC, and CBC interviews), and close to 200 national or international newspapers or magazines (including cover stories for *Reader's*

Digest, Parade magazine, and *Newsweek*). Koenig has been nominated twice for the Templeton Prize for Progress in Religion. His latest books include *The Healing Power of Faith* (2001), *The Handbook of Religion and Health* (2001), *Spirituality in Patient Care* (2002), and his autobiography *The Healing Connection* (2004).

Andrew B. Newberg, M.D., is director of clinical nuclear medicine, director of neuroPET research, and assistant professor in the Department of Radiology at the Hospital of the University of Pennsylvania. On graduating from the University of Pennsylvania School of Medicine in 1993, Newberg trained in internal medicine at the Graduate Hospital in Philadelphia—serving as chief resident in his final year—and subsequently completed a fellowship in nuclear medicine in the Division of Nuclear Medicine, Department of Radiology, at the University of Pennsylvania. He is board certified in internal medicine, nuclear medicine, and nuclear cardiology.

In collaboration with the Departments of Neurology and Psychiatry, Newberg has actively pursued neuroimaging research projects, including the study of aging and dementia, epilepsy, and other neurological and psychiatric disorders. Additionally, he has researched the neurophysiological correlates of acupuncture, meditation, and other types of complementary therapies.

Newberg has presented his research at national and international scientific and religious meetings; his numerous published articles and chapters cover the topics of brain function, brain imaging, and the study of religious and mystical experiences. In addition to the extensive press he has received, he has appeared on ABC's *World News Tonight* and is coauthor, with Eugene G. d'Aquili, M.D., of *The Mystical Mind: Probing the Biology of Belief.*

Recently, Newberg received a Science and Religion Course Award from the Center for Theology and the Natural Sciences to teach the course titled "The Biology of Spirituality" in the Department of Religious Studies, University of Pennsylvania (spring 2000).

Raymond F. Paloutzian, Ph.D., is a national and international expert in the psychology of religion and spirituality. He received his doctoral degree in 1972 from Claremont Graduate School and has been a professor of experimental and social psychology at Westmont College, Santa Barbara, California, since 1981. He has been a visiting professor teaching psychology of religion at Stanford University and guest professor at Katholieke Universiteit Leuven, Belgium. He is a fellow of the American Psychological Association (divisions of general, teaching, social issues, psychology of religion, and international), the American Psychological Society, and the Western Psychological Association and has served as president of the American Psychological Association's Division 36 (Psychology of Religion and Spirituality). The division honored him with the 2005 Virginia Sexton Mentoring Award for contributing to the development of other scholars in the field. He wrote *Invitation to the Psychology of Religion* (2nd ed.1996; 3rd ed. forthcoming) and, with Crystal Park, edited the *Handbook of the Psychology of Religion and Spirituality* (2005). He is currently writing chapters on religion and spirituality for handbooks by Oxford University Press and Blackwell Publishers. His current research focuses on religiously motivated child abuse and medical neglect and on a systematic review of the literature on spiritual well-being. Paloutzian is editor of the *International Journal for the Psychology of Religion*.

Kenneth Pargament, Ph.D., has conducted nationally and internationally known research that addresses religion as a resource for coping with major life stressors. His research has also examined how religion can be a source of struggle for people facing major medical illnesses. He has studied the process by which people create perceptions about the sanctity of aspects of their life activities and the various effects of "sanctification" for individual and interpersonal well-being. Most recently, he has been developing and evaluating spiritually integrated approaches to psychotherapy. Pargament won the William James Award for Excellence in Research from Division 36 of the American Psychological Association. He also won the 2000 Virginia Staudt Sexton Mentoring Award from the American Psychological Association for his generous work in encouraging both faculty, undergraduate, and graduate research in the psychology of religion. He has published extensively and his work has received national and international media attention.